INDECENT PLEASURES

INDECENT

PLEASURES

The life and colorful times

of WILLIAM TARG

Macmillan Publishing Co., Inc.

NEW YORK

Macmillan Publishing Co., Inc.
866 Third Avenue, New York, N.Y. 10022
Collier Macmillan Canada, Ltd.

Library of Congress Cataloging in Publication Data

Targ, William, 1907–
    Indecent pleasures.

    Bibliography: p.
    Includes index.
    1. Publishers and publishing. I. Title.
Z278.T27   070.5   75-15991
ISBN 0-02-619700-6

FIRST PRINTING 1975

Designed by Jack Meserole
Portrait illustration on title page by Susan Silverstone Sage

Printed in the United States of America

For my cosa nostra
ROSLYN *and* RUSSELL
and JOAN *and* ELISABETH *and* ALEXANDER
and NICHOLAS
with all my love

I cannot imagine a more self-centered affair.

—F. N. DOUBLEDAY

But even the most trivial happenings may carry a certain weight.

—WILLIAM CARLOS WILLIAMS

Contents

1 / 1　*First Person Not So Singular*

The Rhythm · My Friend Aldus · Vanity, Etc. · My Family · Free
Association · Interlude 1 · H. Miller · Listen, Writer! · Type It! ·
Curriculum Vitae, a Few Preliminaries . . . · What's in a Name? ·
Nobody Believes Me! · Interlude 2—Breaking the Habit · Disaster in
Chicago · What I Learned at School · Japan's Superagent · Call Me
Leamhsi · Precocity · Bookshop Remembrances Past · Payment De-
ferred · Give the Man the Three Dollars · Chicago Booksellers ·
Chicagoana · From the Album · Anne · A Child Shall Lead Them ·
Bloody Sunday, Chicago–Style · Crazies and Crooks · Sandburg
· Confessional · Magic–Black and White · World Publishing Co. ·
Theodore Dreiser · Dorothy Parker: A Footnote · Papa and the
Baron · Juvenilia · Making It with the Children · Up in Smoke

2 / 87　*Journals: Nights and Days in the Life of . . .*

The Gorgeous Gemini · The Sins of the Fathers · The Irish Can
Be Thankful · Dublin Memoir · Lesbos in Soho · A Table for One,
S'il Vous Plaît · From the Journal: London/Frankfurt/Paris, Sep-
tember–October 1974 · The Luncheon Circuit: Paris · Ditto: Lon-
don · Cocktail–Party Time · Getting Ethnic; or, *Neshuma* (Soul)
Food in Berwick Street · Dialogue in Frankfurt, and Other Notes ·
October 12, 1972: New York · Woolworth's · Allen G. · From the
Journal: March 4 · A Day in the Life of . . . : A View of Beckett ·
From the Journal: de Beauvoir · A Spree in Gomorrah: September
20, 1971 · A Day in the Life of . . . : July 24, 1974 · Domestic
Stuff · The Golden West: August 1974 · The Negresco Bar and a
Birthday: May 27, 1972 · London: May 1972 · From the Journal:
Paris, May 1971 · Mind over (Fecal) Matter · Diary Extract: A

Week in the Life of . . . . · Only in Brazil: Christmas—New Year's Eve, 1971–1972 · Bahia: New Year's Eve

3 / 138 *"A Profession for Gentlemen," Did You Say?*

Total Recall · Les Girls and the Top-Banana Syndrome · You Can't Take Id with You · Sexism and the Sea Lion · Ego-Tripping · Book Contraception Now! A Few Truths · Up the Union! · Continuity vs. the One-Night Stand · Who Is Sylvia? · Negro · Send No Money · Jacket Jive · The Hot Center · The Paperback Pie in the Sky · Advances: Hardback Department · High Schlock · Statistics Are *Out* · Quality · The Pebble in the Shoe; or, What to Do about the Returns Problem · Over the Transom · More about Advertising · The "Power" of Advertising · A Sad and Familiar Story · Committees · TV-Persuasion · Movie Tie-Ins · The Bookseller · Osmosis · Huneker and Schma' Ysroel! · Sic Transit Michaux · Lagniappe and Negotiation · Censorship Is Not Beautiful · Where Do Publishers Come From? · A Publisher Named Jim · Instant Immortality · Of Mice and Men: A Pride of Publishers · Some Real Bookmen · Of Women and Books · On Agents and Agents · David Higham · Drugola/Payola: Dire Prediction · Vanity, Vanity · Publishers on Publishing · Penguins Are for Reading · Spacemanship

4 / 230 *Lo! The Editor*

The Editor: Is It a Bird, a Plane . . .? · Advice · The Education of an Editor, Part 1 · The Education of an Editor, Part 2 · The Education of an Editor, Part 3

5 / 274 *Special People—And a Few Others*

Brigid Brophy · Corwin · *Sui Generis* · Harry Golden · Marianne (Craig) Moore · Footnote to Intellectual History · Abel · Morley · A Touch of Gallic · H. D. · Chester Himes, Native Genius · Sir George · L. C. Powell, Librarian and Man · Palinurus (1903–1974) · Pat Covici · Another Incomparable Max · J. C. F.: RIP · Portrait of a Publisher as a Shit · Bennett

6 / 307 *Prejudices/Personals/Proposals/Predilections*

Song of Myself (No Apologies to Whitman) · Why Women Should Be Imperious Chauvinists · Snapshots · Retreat · Cosmology: Rumblings in the Solar Plexus and Elsewhere · More Rumblings and Non Sequiturs · Scraps from the Journal: More Cosmology · Husbands: Beware of Poets · More Snapshots—and Some Memorable Moments · Me and William James · About Money · Wino · Longevity · Modest Proposal No. 16847 · Liberation Statistic, Pioneer circa 1960 · Gallant Ladies of Letters · The Public Conscience · P. E. N. Forever! · From the Journal: Remembering a Great Lady · Mad about Mozart · Something Happened? · La Vie Intellectual · A Few Favorites That Didn't Make It · Getting Away with Murder · My Favorite Story · So Who Needs the Moon? · Speaking of Sex · The Last of the Libertarians · My Favorite Recipe · Reincarnation Department · Prejudices and Very Private Adores/Abhors

7 / 335 *Lo! The Writer*

Verbosity · To Be a Writer · Originality, Wherefore Art Thou? · Adjectivitis · Etiquette for Authors · How to Write a Bestselling Novel · Telling It Straight · The Expletive and I · The Novel Is Dead: Death-Wish Department · Are Authors Human? · A Book Is Born · More Book Ideas · Trollope and the Writer · Talking · Honesty in Journalism · The Writer-Teacher · Teacher vs. Popularizer · How to Write a Novel in One Easy Lesson · Superstar · The H – – k Writer · So Where's *Moby Dick?* · The Big Payoff · Descent of the Man · Saroyan · When an Author Gets Mad— · Cummings · Simenon

8 / 365 *The Collector*

The Virus · First Principles: Collect What You Like · Closeup of a Collector · The World's Greatest Book Collector · Book Collecting for the Smart Money; or, What the Disillusioned and Bewildered Stock Market Speculator Can Turn to for Solace, Culture, and Some Profit · Death of a Bookshop · From the Journal: "A Thing of Beauty" · John Carter · Lawyers and Literature

9 / 385 *The Bookish Thing*

Quality Will Out · C–S (1840–1922), Binder–Printer · Typography: A Dialogue · I Do Not Love Thee, Doctor Fell . . . · Mr. Typophile (1897–1966) · Give the Eye a Break! · "Perfect," Did You Say? · B. R. (1870–1957) · Beatrice Warde · Bookmanship

10 / 407 *Egress*

Book Reviews: The Agony and the Ecstasy · Finally . . . · Envoi

414 *Recommended Reading*

417 *Index*

Acknowledgments

My thanks to the following for generous assistance in the preparation of this work: Andreas Brown, Chuck Finberg, Raymond C. Hagel, Abe Lerner, Mario Puzo, Lorraine Steurer, Roslyn Targ, Clyde Taylor, Jody Ward, and Toby Wherry.

INDECENT PLEASURES

1 First Person Not So Singular

"Who's going to ghost it for you?" asked Walter Minton, president of Putnam's, when I announced my intention to write this book. He scrutinized me with the eye of an entomologist examining an insect that had proclaimed its intention to compose a symphony.

I should have answered immediately, as did Harriet Beecher Stowe when asked if she was indeed the lady who wrote *Uncle Tom's Cabin*. You'll remember that she said, "I held the pen; God dictated."

Editors who write books are properly objects of suspicion. How can one dare to write a book while holding down an editor's job, which is a full seven-days-a-week commitment? How can one be objective as an editor *and* a writer? How can one find the time?

Well, it can be done.

For the newcomer to writing, here are the facts:

I wrote this book on a one-day-a-week basis. I holed in, away from home and office, and spent eight hours each week for ten months—writing. I spent another hundred hours cutting, editing, polishing, adding. And then another hundred hours doing it all over again.

The womb into which I escaped from the world was a small (12-by 12-foot) office across from the New York Public Library on Fifth Avenue. I set myself a schedule of twelve rough-draft pages per day, and in ten months I had my complete first draft finished—some five-hundred double-spaced pages.

And, oh yes, I surrounded my office walls with shelves and some fifteen hundred books from my home library. I had a small refrigerator installed, and a lounge chair. The details may be of interest to would-be writers. You will decide whether the effort was worthwhile.

This book is an unorthodox synthesis. While it tries to achieve an organic form (orderliness is one of my compulsions), I don't stick to chronological sequence; no need for that. I'm on a reconnaissance. My purpose is to show you one man's life (skipping the gummy juvenilia) within the framework of my book-publishing and bookselling history:

Ray Hagel, my publisher (who proposed this book), told me that I could write anything I pleased, and that he'd publish anything I wrote.

Short of libel, of course.

Fair enough. And to prove that the Book is still the last stronghold of free expression, I've taken him at his word. So if you're interested in writing, reading, the process of bookmaking, book design, book collecting, publishing, one publisher's way of living, the gossip of the trade and some of the curious or bizarre fauna, then I have a few things to disclose.

Aside from bookmanship, there are some short sermons here, lectures, gripes, guideposts, travel recollections, practical hints—some never before offered in a book on the general subject of publishing. There are observations on a few scummy characters I've met, as well as on angelic, noble persons, giants—and pygmies. There's a bit of bloodletting; some therapeutic thrusts. At times I've made my point with a hammer; other times, as gently as I could. When I ran dry, my bookshelves rehydrated me—with memories.

Who's my ghost? Actually there are many ghosts working here —not forgetting the ones shacked up in my genes, the genes donated to me by my parents, two sturdy refugees from Ukrainian pogroms who died in their late eighties. (My mother, a noble woman, tended bar in Russia–Poland as a girl; her mother weighed two hundred and twenty pounds and smoked cigars. My father was a tailor, a thoroughgoing peasant right out of Central Casting for *Fiddler on the Roof*.)

I'm being helped by friendly ghosts, ghostly echoes from certain great days and white nights in Chicago and elsewhere; and I draw heavily from my bookshelves; from notebooks, diaries, journals, and calendar notes; and from many travels recalled. The multicolored spines and jackets of books on my walls are "ghosts," all reminding me of exhilarating (or grim) hours, marvelous en-counters.

My wife Roslyn helped me beyond measure. Mario Puzo, who read much of this work, helped and flattered me by expressing astonishment that an editor could write at all, let alone read. (The dog walking on its hind legs. . . .) Friends and associates, numerous authors, editors, publishers, film people, booksellers, agents, books, music, *places*—they are all my ghostly helpers in one way or another.

The promise I've made to myself is to avoid the practice of many autobiographers, namely, using baloney-talk. (Jean Rosenthal of Laffont calls certain kinds of books "baloney-books." Vonnegut would call them horseshit books, I think.)

I'm beholden to no one except you, my reader. You, who put down cash in the hope that you'll learn something and also be entertained, are my creditor, my conscience. If I fail, may you per-suade my publisher to return your money.

I promise not to dilate on the precious or to use words such as *angst* or *Zeitgeist*.

The Rhythm

Okay, so what does an editor really do? Well, here's one composite, characteristic day that may answer the question:

By 9:00 A.M. (I get to work at eight-thirty) I've finished with the morning's mail—opened it, noted brief replies on some letters for my secretary; typed a few informal answers without carbons; begun reading two book proposals sent by agents. Neither is of interest; one deals with cancer, the other with some insurance scandal. An invitation from Nina Broad to a Columbia film screen-ing; two authors seeking contracts on the basis of brief (three-and four-page) outlines, both first books. My secretary will know how to handle these, based on a few sentences I scrawl on the accompanying letters.

The upcoming Sunday *New York Times Book Review* reaches my desk; I check it for reviews of our books and find one, about a column and a half in length. Of no use to anyone since it doesn't review the book but rather tells us what the reviewer knows about the subject. The front page offers a familiar "kiss of death" essay-review, elegant literary formaldehyde.

Now to make some notes preparatory to a meeting in my office with a first novelist. The manuscript has been read by me; a contract has been signed ($4,000 advance) and a bit more work is called for by its author. She is skittish, reluctant to make further changes or additions—or so it seemed on the telephone. I don't want to ruffle her feathers, make a fuss, but . . .

I decide to be persuasive. The first eight pages of her novel introduce nine characters, mostly by name. They're faceless. Hard to assimilate. They must be established. If one of them were called, say, Popeye, well *that one* would stand out. But Allen, Mary, Alexander, Harriet, Lawrence, Fred, et al.—they simply must be visible, sketched in somehow.

Chapter three must be cut; it drags. There's too much school minutiae, not enough interesting dialogue. Something spiky needed here. The secondary lesbian character is shadowy—all we know is that she has a letch for the heroine. But what is she *like?* The psychological damage the author is concerned with in the motivating of a strange young boy is not clear at all; calls for something less oblique. Clear the air!

And so on. I make my notes, and at nine-forty-five in comes the author. A lovely young woman. She is surprisingly amenable, amiable, willing to do more work—in full agreement. No contest! She promises to return the manuscript in four days. I promise her lunch if she keeps her word.

A rush call from the production department for jacket flap copy. A book of mine on primates, on which I've worked for six months, is coming off press in a few days. I pull out my file on the book and make notes, then proceed to dictate the blurb, biography, and so on. I rather dislike this part of the job, but we have no system that accommodates blurb-writing. It's the editor's responsibility. It gets done in a half hour. I really don't mind—I have a special warmth for the book and its author, and I'm hoping for some decent sales, a paperback deal.

At 11:00 A.M. two manuscripts reach my desk, sent by messenger from two agents. Both look promising, but after sampling the opening pages of each, I decide to take only one home for reading. A Western novel, not quite an "oater," apparently well written. The author gives us two opening pages of sheer Western poetry: a magnificent sunset scene, with a giant oak silhouetted against a blood-red sky, ragged rocks—the works!—bringing echoes of Walter van Tilburg Clark's *The Ox-Bow Incident.* (That novel and its film were first-rate; set in Nevada in the late 1800s, the 35-year-old story of the lynching of three innocent men accused of cattle rustling is now enshrined as a Western classic.) I fantasy finding something of that quality—or perhaps a Western Faulkner.

At noon I head for a luncheon meeting with a literary agent. He's one of the old Establishment, a horse thief at heart, but venerable. His list of authors is formidable, mouth-watering. We've been negotiating for a week on the terms for a first novel by a southern woman of considerable talent. My plea for a modest advance cuts no ice with this pirate in navy blue flannels. He finally makes a miniscule concession, a compromise; and it's a deal. A bottle of wine is called for, to celebrate—but whose victory? As we leave the restaurant he hands me a manila envelope, an outline for a biographical-cum-legal work by a well-known jurist. I promise him an answer in a few days. I never keep this particular agent waiting.

Back at my office—a pleasant ten blocks' walk—and some phone messages await me, one from my wife. I call her back and learn that we will be entertaining a Brazilian publisher for dinner that evening. (There goes my manuscript reading.)

An author phones to inquire: "How come my book can't be found in the Eighth Street Bookshop?" Another author wants to know if we can persuade Scribner's to give his new book a full window display if he "pays the *rental charge?*"! (Now there's a notion.) Another call from a friendly publisher whose ploy is usually to pass on a bit of juicy gossip and then cadge a book—this time he wanted Edward Gorey's *Amphigorey.*

The next call is a messy one: how come his royalty statement shows 20 percent fewer sales than I reported a year ago, on publication date? I point out that the figure I quoted was for "copies shipped"; that a returns-policy exists and a vast number of books were returned by the booksellers and wholesalers. He's outraged, calls the net figure a lie, and threatens to get his lawyer and accountant to look into the matter. I beg him to think twice; the expense will be great and the result, zero. Our figures are accurate.

A call asking if I will appear on a panel to discuss censorship. I decline.

An author rings to ask when an ad will be run on his new book. I point out that we ran one two weeks ago. "Yeah, but for chrissakes, that was a chintzy one. I mean a man-sized ad." I ask him for patience; let's wait a bit until we see if there are reorders in the next ten days or so. He mutters something and hangs up.

Am called into an emergency meeting to discuss an offer made to us through one of our editors—a multiple submission (auction) —a six-page proposal by a VIP from Washington. The agent asks for a $50,000 "basement" and a ten-day deadline. We spend over an hour on this discussion, then decide not to participate.

Four-thirty; mopping up, last-minute paperwork, signing some letters. Gossiping with the rights director, hoping for a piece of good news. (A first novel of ours is being "auctioned" and the figure stands at $7,000—nothing dramatic but, considering everything, acceptable. It's a tough season for reprints.) The author will be told of the deal when we speak to the agent. I decide to take him to lunch to pass on the news—after the sale is officially closed. (It closes at $15,000.)

Homeward-bound at five-thirty. A taxi to the village. Our friend from Rio will meet us at seven for a drink, and I phone Casey's for a table at eight.

We part company at around eleven. I manage to read some of the manuscript, after all—some fifty pages. I find it less than enchanting. The opening pages deceived me; a few pages had been gussied up to catch the eye. The story was pretty banal (big-mortgage-foreclosing yarn) and the author had imposed some literary icing on a cliché story. His limitations will confine him to the old level of horse operas, despite his try for effects. Too bad. Well, at least the agent will get a prompt report (alas, negative) in the morning.

And so to bed. Lying there and reviewing the day before slipping off to sleep. My mind shifts to the editorial meeting we'll be holding the following morning. I begin to analyze the several projects I will present to my associates—and I fall into a dream: a ballet of sandpipers on a sugar-white beach in Antigua.

My Friend Aldus

All my adult life I've revered the name and memory of the supreme Venetian, Aldus Manutius, the first publisher-scholar. He was the fountainhead of our profession. All editors should be familiar with some of the facts of his life. (Among his staff, as an editor, was Erasmus.) Aldus was the first publisher of many of our classics, including the works of Homer and Aristotle. He was a totally committed man. I once owned some of his books, but they are now resting in the University Library at Austin, Texas.

Aldus once wrote to a friend (A.D. 1514):

> I am hampered in my work by a thousand interruptions. Nearly every hour comes a letter from some scholar, and if I undertook to reply to them all I should be obliged to devote night and day to scribbling. Then through the day come calls from all kinds of visitors. Some desire merely to give a word of greeting, others want to know what there is new, while the greater number come to my office because they have nothing else to do. "Let us look in on Aldus," they say to each other. Then they loaf in and sit and chatter to no purpose. Even these people with no business are not so bad as those who have a poem to offer or something in prose (usually very prosy indeed) which they wish to see printed with the name of Aldus. These interruptions are now becoming too serious for me, and I must take steps to lessen them. Many letters I simply leave unanswered, while to others I send brief replies and as I do this not from pride or discourtesy, but simply in order to be able to go on with my task of printing good books, it must not be taken hardly. As a warning to the heedless visitors who use up my office hours to no purpose, I have now put up a big notice on the door of my office to the following effect:
>
> > Whoever thou art, thou art earnestly requested by
> > Aldus, to state thy business briefly and take thy
> > departure promptly. In this way thou mayst be of
> > service even as was Hercules to the weary Atlas,
> > for this is a place of work for all who may enter.

Emerson once alienated a number of his friends by posting a similar message on his study door. I commend it to writers and editors.

Vanity, Etc.

Anyone familiar with the Book of Ecclesiastes is conscious of the evanescent quality of fame. Today's raging best seller is a challenge to one's memory a few years hence. The Broadway or film star of the day is often the job-hunter a few years later. The home-run hitter of this season is benched a few seasons later. "Vanity of vanities; all is vanity," said the son of David.

An unremembered Hibernian once said, "And what has posterity done for me?" The kind of comment one might expect from I. B. Singer. He once said to me at breakfast (a memorable morning in Nice), when I asked whether his vegetarianism precluded the eating of smoked fish, "Why should I eat fish? What did a fish ever do to me?" So when someone asked me why I was writing this book, and was it for posterity, I replied, "Not at all." It was being written, first, for money; secondly, for the edification of my family and friends. If an outsider wants to look into its pages and pay for the privilege, well and good. He will do it at his own risk, of course. But to return to the subject before me, it is not intended for posterity—that's far too abstract for me to handle. But, as in a good book on plumbing or house wiring, there may be some practical hints here, maybe a few laughs, too.

It's hard not to quote Saul Bellow's opening words from his novel, *The Adventures of Augie March* (possibly his best book): "I am an American, Chicago-born—Chicago, that somber city—and go at things as I have taught myself, free-style, and will make the record in my own way; first to knock, first admitted, sometimes an innocent knock, sometimes a not so innocent." The quotation, with its Sandburgian echo, is pertinent, if overfamiliar.

Putting it another way, in cruder form, you can take a Chicagoan away from Chicago but you can't take Chicawgo out of a Chicagoan—another context of course. The Chicago accent and *aura* are not easily shaken off.

My Chicago "spiritual" heritage, something not easily articulated—unless one is an Algren, a Terkel, or a Bellow—will keep emerging somehow. My ashes are bequeathed to that city's beautiful lake since I've altered my will; the New York East River is now sickeningly impure. By the way, Clarence Darrow's ashes are in Chicago's Jackson Park lagoon.

I have two things in common with the late Saul Alinsky: he and I both came from Chicago's slums. I'm a product of Stanley Kowalski country—Chicago's northwest side. Don't look for the site of my birth; it was razed by fire. It's probably a parking lot now; fantasying, I'd like to think that a decent pizza parlor inhabits the space.

I agree with Alinsky's dictum that "there can be no darker or more devastating tragedy than the death of man's faith in himself or in his power to direct his future."

My roots are in Chicago; that's why I don't eat red meat, French sauces, oysters, octopus, snails, eels. But pot roast and potato pancakes (*latkes*), yes. I would wish my last meal on earth to be a hot pastrami sandwich on Jewish sour rye bread. Now you know all. (Some might say, "the worst.")

To paraphrase James Joyce, "I'm a man of small virtue," inclined toward bibliomania and good writing. I'd be honored with the one-word epitaph, *Bookman*. My livelihood has been from making and selling books and serving as an obstetrician to authors. My private life has been, in large part, devoted to the acquisitive, namely, rare books and autograph material. I thank my stars for this hobby, this safety valve. It is, I believe, a much safer pursuit in the long run than, say, transient blondes, cards, booze, or horses. From childhood (when the gift of a few blocks of white notepaper would bring me pure joy), I had the bookman's passion. My destiny was obvious—to be a bookman.

My Family

There are probably fifty persons on this planet named Targ. (I can't speak for China—there may be a million Targs or T'angs in that part of the world—so I'm speaking only of the Western part of our planet.) Three of them are my grandchildren.

I have a brother, a pharmacist, in Chicago; an older sister lives in California with her ophthalmologist husband. I also have dozens of cousins, nephews, and nieces, many of whom I have never met. Among my favorite relatives is Louis Goldblatt, Chicago department store "tycoon." (We had a dinner reunion in New York recently with Louis' wife, the former Roberta Pernecky. They are virtually Mr. and Mrs. Chicago, I'm told.) More about Louis later —he's one of a kind.

I rarely see my relatives. To cultivate them would take more time and energy than I can muster. I recall once, as Roslyn and I were watching a morning TV show, a woman was speaking on a social issue. When the program ended, I said to Roslyn: "That's one of my cousins. I'm very fond of her, but I haven't talked to her in ten years. I remember the morning she was born, in Chicago—her father phoned our house and I happened to pick up the phone and he gave me the news." I couldn't explain why it was that we were not in touch.

What does one do about a large body of relatives? Having a job that involves communication with hundreds of individuals (authors, editors, publishers, agents, and the like), there's barely time for a private life, private pursuits, and leisure. So I've chosen, in my middle years, to eschew most relatives, excepting of course my son, daughter-in-law, and my grandchildren.

The above answers the queries about my relatives. I've been called callous and lacking in family feeling. But I can only reply, "It's my life and I expect no rewards in heaven." Roslyn is still waiting to meet some of my Chicago relatives. I'm sorry she never met my mother, who was a saint.

──────────

Free Association

There are several types of memoirs: the "David Copperfield shit," as someone called it, and the books by Henry Miller and Simone de Beauvoir. These two authors are gloriously candid and human all the way, with no concern for self-hurt. There are some publishing memoirs that are useless and boring, having little relevancy in the life of today's publisher or writer.

Before getting down to further autobiographical details I must speak of a publisher's memoir I read not too long ago. It was written in a kind of embalming fluid, one of the worst I've ever read. (I've collected and read a few hundred publishers' biographies and histories over the years.) The book I'm referring to is Victor Weybright's *The Making of a Publisher*. It was unquestionably the deadliest example of a personal statement. (A private judgment, of course; perhaps others may think it a noble classic.) He appears to me pompous, self-consumed with his own importance, and seems to believe that he lifted American literacy to its present level single-handedly. He's preoccupied with name-dropping and fancy horses and elegant motorcars and great associations. On only one point in his book do I agree with the author—his "spider" characterization of his ex-partner Kurt Enoch.

Later on I will speak of some first-rate publishers' memoirs by some of the men who built the American and British publishing industry as we know it.

In the late fall of 1974 Roslyn and I were having dinner in Paris with our friend Eugene Braun-Munk, editor at Stock. It was in one of Eugene's favorite restaurants; the name escapes me and he'll never forgive *that*. At any rate, he came through with one of his characteristic bon mots, to wit: "In the end, your best friend could be a suppository." Which brings to mind:

Editors, being human, should be warned about two hazards fairly common in their profession: alcoholism and hemorrhoids. Neither is a laughing matter. I'll deal with the latter first.

Hemorrhoids are caused *in part* by excessive application of one's bottom to a chair. Bodily activity is essential to decent health, and may I urge that, whenever possible, you get up from your desk, move about, deliver that memo yourself, go to the mailroom instead of sending your secretary. Take walks frequently and fewer taxis. (Taxis have increased their fares by more than 17 percent in New York in three years, which is another reason for walking.) The editor's life is too sedentary for good health. So get up and move it.

The following "Interlude" may seem an unlikely subject for a book of this sort, but I think it will not be without interest to many readers. There will be other "naturalistic" segments throughout the book, so be forewarned.

———————

Interlude 1

Proctosigmoidoscopy: a medical examination that costs one's entire composure. Two years ago I experienced for the first time the indignity known by the above unpronounceable word. Consider the scene, dear reader: all clothes off except the socks. "Up, up!" urges the doctor—onto the black plastic-covered examination table (why is the surface always so cold to the skin?); on elbows, knees, and with nose pressed *into* the table, ass thrust upward. "Higher!" commands the *gnadige* herr doctor. He then inserts a sixteen-inch, wrist-thick, plastic tube (proctoscope) that is illuminated within and which expands upon pressure of an air pump. The insertion is, of course, straight up the rectum to the sigmoid flexure. (Sixteen inches!) Loss of composure! Embarrassment and shock are heightened when the doctor blithely summons his pretty young nurse into the room to aid in the little drama. Scene 2: I rest on my elbows, nose flattened on the black plastic covering— rectum aloft, stuffed, and with several inches of as-yet-uninserted plastic tubing protruding from it. Disconcerted, outraged, yes; but I am determined at all costs to retain my cool. I begin counting to myself, to one hundred, then backwards. I shut my eyes and concentrate on the publisher's autobiography I just read; I next wonder how a homosexual would respond to this treatment. (Sixteen inches!) Suddenly it is all over, the tube slowly withdrawn. As I climb down, shakily, wobbling from the table, I sigh, and note happily that the young nurse has vanished. I leave the office with a feeble good-bye to the nurse, who is now in the reception room; I'm hoping fervently that I will never, never in this life encounter her socially, this young woman who witnessed my intubation. Shame must enter into such a situation regardless of one's *savoir faire,* one's determination to be mature (mature!) about it all. Loss of dignity beyond imagining. But I am, in the end, proud of my ability to keep my equilibrium throughout. I smiled, vastly relieved, on the way home, although twenty-four hours later I still feel an ache in the colon, and start thinking of a diet of blancmange and soft custards. Ych. But, to the point, the results are termed satisfactory by the doctor. Another cancer fantasy dispelled. If you think you're not easily fazed, arrange for a proctosigmoidoscopy.

Afterthoughts: the blessing of Preparation H; vow to ride in as few taxis as possible, and walk as often as able.

H. Miller

Before going any farther—that is, into the personal disclosures—I want to speak of my mentor-hero, Henry Miller. I've kept him in mind from the start. I feel him behind me, peering down at my typewriter, searching for slipups. "No bullshit," I keep hearing him say, as a reminder. As I dredge in memory's valleys and write and prepare to move forward, I see him and his endearing crooked smile, and I hear his Brooklyn-tough-guy voice. And I think, there's a man, a *mensch,* with an eye on the truth, a man with the life juices flowing still, despite his arteriosclerotic legs, his arthritic hips and back; indestructible. I hope when this book is published, he will see and read it. I hope he'll be around for a while longer.

Henry Miller is one of our giants. I wish someone with clout would so name him, officially, and give him the Nobel Prize, and thank him for having liberated us. (Erica Jong and Sandra Hochman can thank him too, for in their novels, one finds a kinship between Miller and these liberated and gifted young women; there's some of his spirit in their writing, in their view of life, in their determination to face up to life and live it fully.)

In 1935 I was lucky enough to get and read the very-much-forbidden *Tropic of Cancer.* I have the book now, a first edition copy, signed by both Miller and Anaïs Nin, an early intimate, who wrote the Foreword. What a volcanic, explosively comic, and ribald novel; and I remember my laughing out loud—as I did when I first read Rabelais. And the shock of seeing the sex words spelled out boldly! Whenever I visit Paris, this book comes to mind. I wonder why Grove Press or the Limited Editions Club don't issue an illustrated edition of this novel, with photographs or drawings.

To recognize the genius of Henry Miller one doesn't have to read his novels; just read his essay, "The Staff of Life," from his book, *Remember to Remember* (New Directions, 1947). There too you'll find a model of good, clear writing; wholesome declarative sentences, and some fresh ideas. His subject is bread, of course. But you will be enchanted by even his latest book, *Insomnia, or The Devil at Large*, written in his eighty-second year! He still wants to fuck every woman in the world.

Listen, Writer!

From a lifetime of involvement with words and writing, and from my own attempts at writing here, I've learned one fact: There Is No Such Thing as a Publishable First Draft. A strong back is the answer to good writing.

Type It!

E. M. Forster once said, "How do I know what I think until I see what I say?" That's precisely my position. I can think on the machine and I can type far better than I can write by hand. Conditioned from my teens to think on the typewriter, seeing the words come alive on the sheet of paper in the machine's roller, I'm able to evaluate what would be indecipherable and incomprehensible in holograph.

In the end, I suppose, all writers are defeated if there is any sort of sensibility left in their hearts and fingers.

However, one must make a start. And a finish.

Curriculum Vitae, a Few Preliminaries . . .

(Usually, this is where the lying starts.)

The above is a flossy way of saying it. Here's the nitty-gritty of my life:

The birth certificate says Chicago, Cook County, Illinois, U.S.A., March 4, 1907. (Yes, I'm a Piscean; I love water for bathing and viewing.) My name was originally Torgownik, from the Russian, meaning "merchant." (I often fantasied that I was related to Turgenev and that Torgownik was a corruption of that writer's name.)

My name was changed to Targ when, at eighteen, I entered the employ of Macmillan—as an office boy. The manager, a marvelous character in his late fifties named Tankersley, took me aside one day shortly after I had started to work. He said that no one could spell or pronounce my name, and did I mind truncating it. I didn't mind; that job meant more to me than my name or *anything* in the world. About thirty years later, I made it legal, in New York. Philip Wittenberg took charge of the legal details.

There are memories, much ground to cover, and I'll do my best not to be tiresome. I'll spare you childhood diseases, diarrhea attacks, childhood parties, picnics, visits with relatives, classroom traumas, acts of cowardice and indecencies, pets, adolescent sexual fumblings, summer-camp stuff, parental tensions, spilt milk, and so forth.

The outstanding event of my late teens was having a half dozen poems of mine accepted by *Poetry* magazine. On publication I swore I'd never write another poem (I was Rimbaud from Chicago!). I was a terrible poet and I've never understood why Harriet Monroe published the stuff. I got to know her and even represented her once at an Alfred Kreymborg reading (with mandolin). Kreymborg was fairly disgusted to learn that I, a nobody, was there in her stead. I remember his disdain and disappointment.

Very early in my life I was conscious of the political corruption and the crime in Chicago, of such names as Capone and Torrio and the blustering mayor Big Bill Thompson. I was aware of the gangsters and crooked cops who dominated the city, the vile men who ran the town, the payoffs that took place in the courtrooms and elsewhere. Even the Black Hand was a memory of my Chicago childhood. The Black Hand was real; I knew firsthand of its existence.

Also, while still a youngster I became aware of the lawyer-hero, Clarence Darrow; his name in Chicago was an awesome one, especially after he saved the lives of Loeb and Leopold—saved them from hanging, that is. (We had dinner with Leopold in New York on August 5, 1971, three weeks before he died.)

Today, living in New York City, I'm conscious of the similarity between Chicago and Manhattan. For some reason, very often when I put thirty-five cents in the bus coin box, I'm reminded of what Darrow said in one of his speeches, in Chicago in 1902: "When I ride on the streetcars I am held up—I pay five cents for a ride that is worth two and a half cents, simply because a body of men have bribed the city council and legislature, so that all the rest of us have to pay tribute to them." I remember hating the Chicago Public Library because I had a sense of the political corruption of the city seeping into that institution; I never borrowed its books. Probably my loss. I gather from Ralph Newman that the library today is transformed, that it is in every way serving the public well. Perhaps Mr. Daley has looked into the matter.

Otherwise, very little has changed in Chicago. Crime and corruption and crooked politicians abound and flourish as much as ever. Is there no solution? Al Capone died in 1947 but his influence lingers on. The Syndicate continues to rule, the evil order prevaileth. But at least the city is solvent, unlike Manhattan.

By the way, Bob Cromie, book doyen of the Midwest and the *Chicago Tribune,* not to mention ace TV interviewer, is also one of the town's leading authorities on Chicago's criminal history. Some day I'd like to persuade him to write *the book*. He has done a few things in the field, but not nearly what he's capable of doing. (Meanwhile, George Murray, ex-Chicago newspaper crime reporter wrote an excellent and withering study, *The Legacy of Al Capone,* which I edited for Putnam's in 1975).

Cromie wrote *the* biography of Dillinger and, also, with another old Chicago newspaperman, his friend Herman Kogan, a fine Chicago book entitled *The Great Fire—Chicago, 1871,* a Putnam book. The results were very agreeable. Cromie was the recipient of the George Foster Peabody Award for his TV interview series "Book Beat," the best thing on the air relating to books and authors. He relaxes and actually humanizes the authors he interviews, and unlike most newspaper reviewers, he lets us know what the book and its author are all about. He also invariably shows that he has actually read the author's book, or books. No Johnny Carson, he. Kogan, prolific in various writing areas, is the author of *Big Bill of Chicago*, the biography of Chicago's notorious mayor. He also wrote *Lords of the Levee*. The town bubbles with talent. Irv Kupcinet, whose autobiography, *Kup's Chicago*, I edited while at World, also continues to thrive and remind the rest of America that there's a cultural beat in the Midwest.

In 1937, Twentieth Century-Fox made a picture called *In Old Chicago*. It reproduced the Chicago Fire magnificently. Watching the windy city ablaze, with Alice Faye and Alice Brady and Tyrone Power in the foreground in a wagon at the city's lake shore, is something to witness if you're a disaster freak. The picture is due on the late late show soon.

What's in a Name?

About thirty years ago, when I had to locate my birth certificate in order to get my first passport, I had to visit Chicago to search the Chicago archives; no one seemed able to locate it. I discovered that I was not properly named: the document said "male baby Turgonik." I was unnamed and misspelled. I explored the mystery and learned from my mother that it was planned that I be named *Velvel*, a kind of Yiddish version of Willie or William—possibly Wolf. I had been born at home, and someone forgot to notify the authorities promptly.

I was called Velvel until I entered kindergarten. There I became William, officially. I've been called "Willie" by a few relatives; only one "outsider" has called me "Willie"—Storer Lunt, ex-head of Norton's. Why he chose to call me that I will never know. He did it with a happy perversity, I think—and with affection, I hope. And he always preceded it with a "Well, HELL-oo," followed by a high pitched *"Willie."* Usually across a room or some crowded place. I really didn't mind; Storer is, or was, entitled to the privilege, being, as most publishers who knew him will attest, his own man and delightfully eccentric, imbued with Elizabethan bombast.

The foregoing is probably one of the more pointless stories in this book; I record it for the edification of my grandchildren.

Nobody Believes Me!

When I was five years old, my Aunt Carrie took me to see Anna Pavlova dance. We sat in the topmost row of the gallery of Orchestra Hall. Only through Carrie's tiny pearl-covered opera glasses was I able to see the performance. I remember the doll-like figure in white, a snowflake of a figure, dancing *The Dying Swan,* which (I later learned) was arranged for her by Michel Fokine. The scene is vivid in my mind now, and I can see her on that immense stage on her delicate toes, a miraculously exquisite, fragile, and unearthly dancer, circling backwards rapidly, ever so daintily, with such perfection. (Backwards!) No dancer I've seen has matched the wonder of that performance, although I'm sure it's my romantic imagination favoring the divine Pavlova's legend. One day when I mentioned to that balletomane without peer, Edward Gorey, that I had seen Pavlova dance, he gave me a searching look as if to say, "Look man, you weren't alive then." But I was, I was. Pavlova died in 1931. Her *performance* took place in 1912. I was born in 1907.

Aunt Carrie was also responsible for cutting short my musical career—inadvertently, of course. I was taking violin lessons at a tender age, for my mother had fantasies of my becoming a concert violinist. So Carrie took me to hear the great Heifetz. We went to the concert hall, climbed the gallery stairs, and I saw and heard the man. What I heard was fantastic, magical, inimitable. I knew at once that if I lived to be a hundred I could never approach Heifetz; his skill and style were matchless. When I returned home that night I announced that I would never take another violin lesson. My mother was heartbroken—for at least a week. My brother and sister cheered. They were no admirers of my so-called music-making on the grubby ten-dollar fiddle I was using at the time.

I was also around when World War I was declared. I saw Woodrow Wilson *plain* one day, in an open carriage on Michigan Avenue. What I recall most about that period was that, in grammar school, our teacher was a passionate devotee of Wilson, the man who promised to keep us out of war. His photograph was on our classroom wall. One day I was depressed when two of my favorite uncles were drafted: I took a pencil and drew a Kaiser Wilhelm moustache on Wilson's photo. I was expelled from class for a day. (Fifty-six years later I edited Ishbel Ross's biography of Mrs. Woodrow Wilson. I also learned what a horny man he was.)

What else do I remember? (I forget what I had for dinner last night.) The headlines shouted by the newsboys in our neighborhood in Chicago, announcing the Russian Revolution. The whole idea was incomprehensible to me. Also, I recall the mysterious killing of Bobby Franks by two "nice boys" from the South Side, the now-famous Loeb and Leopold kidnappers. As mentioned earlier, we had dinner with Leopold in New York shortly before he died. We took him to dinner in Greenwich Village—a Neapolitan bistro—and we listened to Leopold speak Italian and Spanish to several people there. He seemed to feel that he wasn't getting sufficient recognition as the "greatest criminal celebrity" of the century. He was involved in some do-good activity in Puerto Rico.

Interlude 2—Breaking the Habit

Unlike Langston Hughes who says somewhere that "I was saved from sin when I was going on thirteen," I began my sinful career as I approached "manhood"—age thirteen. I started to smoke. Surreptitiously, of course. My reason for smoking was, in part, opposition—defiance if you will—to my father. I detested Hebrew school; I attended it until I was confirmed because my hateful father *willed* that I go. My father also thought smoking was immoral. (He forgot that my grandmother smoked cigars.) I also took to cigars, starting with White Owls at fourteen.

At the age of fifty-nine, I was consuming about sixty cigarettes a day; also five or six cigars. And at night, before going to bed, I'd smoke a few pipes while reading. I would smoke in the morning as soon as my toes touched the floor, and I stopped only when I returned to bed at night. I smoked all through meals. My clothes reeked from cigar smoke, as did the house, the draperies. My habit cost me about six dollars a day, and therefore I was spending over two thousand dollars a year on tobacco. An expensive "monkey."

In 1965, in London, on a business trip for Putnam's, I contracted a bronchial infection, I was told by the hotel doctor to stop smoking for a week or two. I followed his instructions. Actually, I had no choice, since I was coughing heavily. When I returned to New York, I told Roslyn that I hadn't smoked for two weeks and that I wasn't going to start again. I don't think she believed me. But I stopped—cold.

How did I do it? First, I informed everyone I knew that I had quit. I let my associates at Putnam's know that I had "quit for good." To resume would have been embarrassing. Publicizing my nonsmoking decision helped me keep my vow. Then I decided to give away some of the money I was saving by not smoking—a fake philanthropy, but a prop. It helped. I gave shoeshine boys, washroom attendants, barbers, hatcheck girls, cab drivers, waiters, and others extravagant tips. I must have handed out, in *extra* tips, over five dollars a week. It felt good. By not smoking I was "spreading joy." It made me feel noble. I kept up this hypocrisy for almost a year. (How long can one keep up *that* role?)

To close this boastful saga of my Great Character, I have now gone without tobacco for ten years; not one cigarette has reached my lips during that time. I admit it isn't easy. I often long to smoke, especially when I smell the aroma of a fine cigar. After a cup of coffee, the desire for a cigarette is almost overpowering. Formerly, it wasn't possible for me to work at the typewriter unless I had a cigarette going; nor was it possible to sit in on a meeting without a cigarette or cigar. But I gave them all up. It can be done, and the point I want to make is: it can be done without systems or hypnosis or yoga or group efforts or prayer. Sheer bull-headedness will do it.

I feel it is essential to record my personal smoking history here. But if it inspires a single person to quit smoking, I'll not feel rewarded; I really don't care if you do or don't smoke. The truth is, while I'm now a total abstainer, I miss tobacco very much; the other night I dreamed I was lighting up a Monte Cristo. In my dreams, as I find myself lighting up, I do so with a great sense of guilt. A fine case history for interested psychiatrists—but really, the subject can be boring; the subject can be talked down to a nullity.

Disaster in Chicago

The rash of disaster films of late reminds me of an event I witnessed as a boy in Chicago.

My cousins, the Goldblatts, had a four-story department store on West Chicago Avenue. They lived across the street from the store. While visiting the family one day, we heard and saw the street begin filling up with siren-screaming fire trucks, ambulances, and police cars. The Goldblatt store across the street was *collapsing*. Actually crumbling before our eyes. An excavation taking place next to the Goldblatt building caused a breach in the foundation and Goldblatt's store began to turn to rubble—just as buildings appear to do in those Hollywood disaster films.

We were glued to the window, gasping with wonder and fear. We saw people running out of the doors. I can't begin to describe the scene: hundreds of people running back and forth; firemen, policemen, everyone trying to take hold of an extraordinary situation.

Suddenly, we saw Louis Goldblatt (he was then twenty-four) coming out of the store, carrying a young woman in his arms. Later we learned that Louis went heroically from floor to floor when the news of the disaster became known, and kept shouting "Fire!" urging everyone to leave. The floors were caving in, ceilings were collapsing. He picked up one young woman who had fainted and carried her out of the store. (The papers printed the photo the following day, together with the story.) This took place in May of 1927.

While the Goldblatt store disaster didn't compare to the California earthquake or the Chicago Fire, it was a scene to remember. Recently, when Louis and I were doing some reminiscing during one of his visits to New York, he filled me in on the details. He denied being a hero, although the Carnegie Institute cited him for bravery. Interestingly, while the event occurred fifty years ago, Louis remembered the name of the young woman he rescued— Mae McGinnis. Memory banks.

━━━━━━

". . . I never graduated at all. I didn't even have my degree. That's why I'm so informed!"

—ROBERT DUNCAN, poet, in dialogue with
ALLEN GINSBERG (*Allen Verbatim*)

What I Learned at School

After about a year and a half of high school, I dropped out. I was not exactly a rebellious student; perhaps merely imperious. I made the decisions regarding which classes I would attend, and when. The so-called regimentation went against my grain, and I knew I was not long for Marshall High School, which was located on Chicago's northwest side.

Only two courses were of interest to me: Printshop and English. At the printshop I learned to set type by hand and print small broadsides, booklets, cards, and such. I even printed an erotic poem for a girlfriend—an edition of one copy. I had the unhappy experience of watching her tear it up into tiny bits. It contained several four-letter words, I recall.

The smell of ink, the feel of type on paper (I liked letterpress because of the bite of metal on paper), and the mechanism of the press fascinated me. I printed a few of my own poems, which fortunately no longer exist. The notion of a small, private press was impressed on my mind and has stayed there. I wonder why more young men and women don't look into printing and book design as a way of life. Some of the greatest private presses were operated by amateurs.

My printing teacher, a handsome Scotsman, became my friend and taught me much about the "philosophy of printing." I often visited him and his wife after I quit school. I regret that I can't remember his name now; I owe him a great deal. Once I recall telling him about a novel I had just read, by Virginia Woolf, and he smiled. "Didn't you know," he said, "she was a printer, too? She and her husband Leonard operated a handpress. They used the imprint *Hogarth Press.*" I recall this piece of news being more exciting than the novel I had just read, *The Voyage Out.*

The other course, English, held my interest because Shakespeare was made to come alive for me in that class. (I had a private theory that Hamlet was Jewish.) I was fortunate in the teacher, and here again my memory fails me as to her name. But I remember her face and elegant manner. She was a tall, lean spinster with auburn hair and a beautiful face with deep-set brown eyes. She quickly realized that I was not long for academe; I often played hooky and when she would ask me where I had been, I would say I'd been home, *writing poetry.* She would only smile. She spoke privately with me one day and suggested that I go to the library and look into the works of someone named Lafcadio Hearn. My interest in the exotic must have prompted this.

She was an *intuitive.* I followed her suggestion and a new world opened up for me. The gifted half Greek-half Irish Hearn galvanized me at once. I read everything by and about him that I could lay my hands on. Among the first of his books that I read were *Chinese Ghosts, Kokoro, Chita, Two Years in the French West Indies,* and *Out of the East.* His *Japan* had an especially strong appeal. I also loved his early New Orleans journalistic work—his pieces published in the *Times Picayune.*

Later, when I became a bookseller, I collected Hearn's first editions; I also published a small, badly written but well-printed book on Hearn in 1935, which I dedicated to my son Russell. I remember how immersed I was at that time in all things Japanese. I had a good library dealing with Japanese history and culture; also Japanese dolls and many original Japanese prints, including works by Hiroshige, Hokusai, Moronubu, Utamaro, Toyokuni. (Utamaro's were the hardest to procure.) A retired banker and print collector named Judson Metzger befriended me and helped me in my *ukiyo-e* print collecting. I bought about twenty-five prints from him. He was my print-*guru,* and was tireless in teaching me secrets of the masters, the subtle differences between one print and another. No two prints of the same subject (like fingerprints) are alike. This is discernible with careful study.

When my son was born I was strongly tempted to give him a middle name—Hiroshige; but my wife Anne protested, pointing out that it could be a handicap, so I dropped the matter. I think it was

Metzger's suggestion to begin with. Russell *Hiroshige* Targ might have been a burden for the scientist he became. (If he feels deprived, he's certainly at liberty to adopt it now.) By the way, one of the best introductory books I can remember reading on Japanese prints is by James A. Michener—*The Floating World*.

Japan's Superagent

Tom Mori, officer of the Charles E. Tuttle organization of Tokyo, is one of our favorite foreign literary agents and we always enjoy a drink or meal with him when he's in New York. He's ebullient, travels in the proverbial seven-league boots, and negotiates for, and represents, hundreds of books each year for the Japanese market. His instincts and eye are unerring, and he manages to make more important deals than almost any other foreign agent.

One day I mentioned to Tom that I once had a great collection of Lafcadio Hearn but that the books were gone; all I had left was a first edition of *Some Chinese Ghosts*. Two weeks later a box arrived at our house—fifteen Hearn paperbacks. Better than a pound of caviar!

I've never really regretted being a high school dropout. The rigors and regimentation of school interfered with my indiscriminate reading; I was simply incapable of taking direction from teachers, unable to follow a circumscribed course of study or reading. No harm. I learned to lie glibly about my lack of education. Later, when anyone asked me where I was educated I would reply, "Chicago." Almost always, it was taken to mean *the* University of Chicago.

The city of Chicago was my school: its writers and artists and newspapermen, the booksellers, the Art Institute (where I first saw and handled a *Kelmscott Chaucer*), the Museum of Science and Industry, the Shedd Aquarium, the Adler Planetarium; the great parks, the Civic Opera, Grant Park, and the Gold Coast—the Gothic beauty of the University of Chicago's buildings along the

Midway (I lived near it for several years), and the great lake front. The public library did not appeal to me at all. I had to *own* any book I wanted to read; to borrow a book was distasteful to me.

I was fortunate in knowing in the early Chicago days Richard Wright, August Derleth, James T. Farrell, Saul Bellow, Stuart Engstrand, Nelson Algren, Lloyd Lewis, Carl Sandburg, Meyer Levin, Lawrence Lipton, Studs Terkel, Louis Zara, Vincent Starrett (another *guru* of mine, but in the field of rare books), and many other gifted men and women.

The Art Institute was my home at least once a week on Saturdays, and I never ceased to marvel at Michelangelo's *Pietà* (a perfect, actual-size copy is housed there), and the richness of the Impressionist collection (oh, the Monets!), and other treasures. Many years later, at World, I had the pleasure of helping in the publication of a catalog of the Art Institute's paintings.

I worked on this catalog with Allan McNab, one of the museum's directors. It was he who introduced me to the great art collector, Chester Dale. I'll never forget the days we spent in his Plaza Hotel floor-sized apartment in which he housed Van Goghs, Lautrecs, Picassos, and others. Mrs. Dale did much of the "explaining," while Chester made us extraordinary martinis which, by the way, he announced were forbidden him by his physician. He died six months later and his paintings went, not to Chicago, but to the National Gallery.

With the great renaissance of architecture that Chicago has enjoyed in the past several decades, the city may be surpassing New York in *many* respects.

I was commenting on the richness and variety of Chicago today to a native New Yorker, and he replied, "Yeah, but deep down, it's a pretty shallow city."

Call Me Leamhsi

At age eighteen I was born (as Jack MacGowran said when he first met Samuel Beckett). It was when I first entered the book publishing world.

I got an office boy's job that called for doubling at the sales desk and the typewriter (I also relieved the elevator man at noon). It was with the Chicago branch of The Macmillan Company. It was heaven, paradise, Nirvana! Macmillan's stockrooms were the Elysian fields, the gardens of Hesperides. There in the book-filled happy hunting grounds I discovered Nietzsche, Dostoevsky, Turgenev, Neihardt, Teasdale, Yeats, Chekhov, Schweitzer, Tagore, Lindsay, James Stephens.

My salary was eighteen dollars a week, but I would have paid *them* if necessary. I was surrounded by books, and my job gave me access to every crevice and corner of the company's six floors, which were jammed and piled high with books, many of them out of print, uncataloged—small-quantity importations long-forgotten and written off, by authors I had never heard of. Pure opium.

I brushed up against *live*, famous visiting authors, and being slightly pushy and author-struck, I got to meet some, including Vachel Lindsay. (I remember his visit to our office and his booming voice as he read one of his poems in the manager's office, a voice that carried over the chatter of the office typewriters.)

The experience of reading galleys was mine—reading books in *advance* of publication! That was thrilling; then I'd wait to compare my views of the books with the reviews that appeared later. I read hungrily and widely, including some dimly remembered Macmillan novelists such as E. Marion Crawford and Eden Philpotts, whose works I devoured but remember hardly at all today.

I moved as though on roller skates. I was Mr. Eager Beaver around the clock. I made it known at once that while I ran errands, handled city orders, and typed bills, I could also read manuscripts and would probably be chief editor shortly. I let it be known that I was a whiz in the poetry section and that *I had had some poems published.*

After numerous reminders to various executives, I was handed a sheaf of poems one day and told to read and report on them at once. I was in heaven: my very first manuscript to read and judge.

I took the parcel home, read the poetry carefully—some sixty pages of the stuff—and brought it back the following morning. I was an editor, a professional reader for one of the world's greatest publishing houses. I wondered how long it would take me to replace Harold Latham, the company's then editor-in-chief. (He later brought *Gone with the Wind* to Macmillan.)

The executive who had given me the manuscript took a look through my report and the manuscript, then turned to me. "I ought to fire you on the spot!" he said. I saw a homicidal frenzy in his eyes.

Astounded, I asked, "What is wrong, sir?"

"Everything!" he replied. "No one but a jackass would be so dumb as to make editorial remarks *on* someone's manuscript—and *in ink!* And your comments are too goddamn smart-ass for your own good. Now get some ink eradicator and remove every one of your stupid comments—and don't ever ask to see another manuscript. By the way, the author is Mrs. ———, the wife of a vice-president of this firm."

I had used my beautiful (bar mitzvah) fountain pen to write in purple ink, like Virginia Woolf, on the manuscript; my indoctrination in the mystic art of literary criticism.

About a year or so after I began working at Macmillan, I had my introduction to sex, in a total sense. Despite all earlier encounters with girls—dates, dances, parties—I had never actually achieved, as the *manuals* put it, penetration. But in the stockroom of Macmillan, on Prairie Avenue in Chicago's South Side, on the streets where teenage prostitutes were available at a dollar "a toss," I met my young true seducer, a thundering blond, blue-eyed girl named Bertha. On a stack of Charles Beard's *Rise of the American Civilization,* the company's big best seller that year, we made ardent love. (Sex and books have been interrelated for me ever since.) She was older than I—about twenty—and totally sophisticated in the sexual arts. Later, I took her home one afternoon when my family was away. We made love in my sister's great double bed, the Number One bedroom of the house. I recall (with gooseflesh and rising of hackles) opening a new bottle of Shalimar perfume which one of my sister's beaux had given her; it dropped on the floor. The mystery of how that bottle got opened and spilled on the floor was never solved, although my sister, a fairly perceptive young woman, must have made a pretty shrewd guess. She was about ten years older than her age, a worldly and beautiful redhead. I was shameless. Callow.

Eventually, Bertha was fired. It happened suddenly. I learned to my sorrow that she had been "putting out" to about a dozen other employees, including an assistant office manager. I think his feelings were hurt when he learned that his inamorata was an

indiscriminate *alley-catter* (his phrase). I was stunned. She was
fired without a day's "notice." She was a lively, laughter-eyed girl;
a lovely, spirited female; fellatio was one of her specialities. I met
more than her equal later, a Russian brunette, whose talents were
almost as great; but the details will remain private; the subject is
not germane anyway.

Publishing proved educational in every possible way. Working
at Macmillan gave me the big chance to read widely and learn
the book business on the side, as it were. I learned how to get along
with fellow workers, how to cope with anti-Semites in the office
and shipping room, and how to use my fists. Also, I learned how
to wrap packages; open packing crates; type orders, letters, and
publicity releases. I also sold to certain local booksellers and later
to teachers and librarians.

But my involvement with masses of books reminded me (many
years later) of Thomas Wolfe's experience with books in his Ashe-
ville local library. I gorged myself insanely on books as he did,
although I doubt that I had nearly his Pantagruelian capacity.
Where Wolfe claimed to have read thousands, I probably read
hundreds. It was a prolonged orgy with virtually no letup, at least
none that I can recall. No vacation or holiday interfered with reading. I was the boy in the candy store—and it was all mine.

Dictionaries were among my earliest favorites, and with the
first serious money I ever acquired, I bought a large Funk and
Wagnalls College Edition. I would often take it to bed. My "game"
each night was to learn five new words before going to sleep.

At Macmillan there were countless books into which I would
dip, usually at lunchtime, sitting on a "riser" of books with my sandwich in hand. Some were books most readers seldom encounter,
books which were supposed to "broaden my horizons" beyond
imagining. One of those really did—Eric Partridge's great 1,200-
page *Dictionary of Slang and Unconventional Language*. In it re-
posed some eye-popping words and phrases, including words relating to the female pudenda, not to mention words dealing with
"sexual connexion." This book became my bedside reader, my
"fun house," for many months, and I enjoyed discovering Middle
English vulgarity and subtle, literary usages of obscenities. This
book led to some of Partridge's other books, which showed how
frequently the Bard employed wholesome but bawdy words in his
various plays; they were later euphemized or bowdlerized. I also

enjoyed Partridge's *Dictionary of Clichés,* especially those from the sixteenth century, wherein I found some pretty gamey phrases to enliven my speech and amaze my friends.

Partridge, devoted to words all his life, considered himself an "adventurer" and preferred the excitement of words to the stock exchange. Lucky man to have found a lifelong career-hobby in the ocean of words.

Macmillan's stockroom introduced me to many other scholars of equal interest and value, but the big *Dictionary of Slang* still remains with me as a reminder of those exhilarating days. Partridge is still alive as of this writing, living in England, in his eightieth year, and playing with words. A book is due from him soon, I suspect.

Speaking of dictionaries, and digressing a bit, I want to record that my favorite lexicographer in all the world—a man of incredible competence—is David A. Guralnik, editor-in-chief and top man on the totem pole of *Webster's New World Dictionary.* This book, first published by World in 1953, is, in my judgment, the best, most civilized college dictionary extant. I *read* it regularly as some breakfast-eaters devour their cornflakes each morning. It is rich in crystal-clear, cameo-pure definitions. But I must tell this story on Mr. Guralnik, just to confirm the fact that even lexicographers are human.

One day while browsing through the book, I encountered *Coryate, Thomas,* 1576?–1617. I confronted David with the question: "How can you justify including Coryate's name in your dictionary when he is surely unknown to most of the human race? There must be a thousand other names better known that are not included."

"How in hell did you happen to come upon that entry?" asked David.

"Well, I once owned a first edition copy of Coryate's book— *Coryate's Crudities.* But if you want my opinion, it hardly merits inclusion in an American college dictionary."

David studied me for a moment, then said, "This secret is between us, right? Well, I wrote a thesis on Coryate in college; I have an affection for the old boy. And that's my justification. Now for God's sake, keep it to yourself."

I promised to keep it a secret; I'm sharing the secret with just you and a few other friends. It seemed to me, though, that you just might be interested in knowing how certain names get into dictionaries.

During my employment at Macmillan I had a major chance encounter that precipitated the opening of the bibliophilic doors of my life. (The details will come along later.) I had been possessive about books long before age eighteen, but I was beginning to seek out books in a special, fastidiously acquisitive sense. Book *ownership* became a *drive*. I spent six months' savings to buy a first edition of Beardsley's *Le Morte d'Arthur* in the original twelve parts (1893–1894) with the original wrappers, one of three hundred copies on Dutch handmade paper. It is a visually exciting book. My mother understood the extravagant purchase and forgave me, although the money I'd been saving had been earmarked for a new winter coat.

Precocity

As you may have gathered, I was a precocious (indiscriminate) book-reader; buzz-saw fashion, I went through many feet or yards of books each month. Some of the books were real oddities.

For example: Krafft-Ebing's *Psychopathia Sexualis*. I was in my late teens, visiting our family doctor. I noticed the book with the strange title on his shelf and pulled it down for a quick examination. Instantly I knew I had to read it. It smelled of evil and sexual brimstone. Catnip. The doctor let me borrow the book. Later on, I bought a used copy from a bookseller.

No book I've ever read gave me such a sense of fright, such a view of the sexual underworld—or lower depths—of life. I was agitated. No book I've read since, including the works of the Marquis de Sade, had the impact on me of Krafft-Ebing's book. The sexual aberrations he described kept me eye-popping and dizzy, shaken. I doubt that any book of pornography or criminal or pathological behavior covers so much detailed ground. It gave me a monumental psychic hangover. The one frustration I had was in the large number of Latin words and phrases used in the book. The Latin was there to prevent the innocent from getting the nitty-gritty facts to which so many of the case histories led; the Latin was maddening; many a sexual account was for me left pointless —the erotic punchline missing—because Herr Krafft-Ebing chose to diagnose or characterize an act or situation in Latin. Of course, in each case, my imagination ran wild. I got a Latin dictionary but that didn't help much. Krafft-Ebing's vocabulary was too rarified and exotic to be included in the ordinary Latin lexicons.

I let a girlfriend borrow my copy, fantasying all sorts of interesting results. (She was decorous and easily bored.) She returned the book to me with the comment, "Very amusing." Girls obviously know something boys don't know.

Many years later, in 1964, at Putnam's, when I was searching my card file of Book Ideas, I noted a suggestion I had made earlier, that is, to publish an unexpurgated, fully translated edition of *Psychopathia Sexualis*, with every Latin word Englished. Minton agreed to my proposal and I secured the services of a Latinist, Dr. Harry E. Wedick, for the translation; and I persuaded Dr. Ernest Van Den Haag to write an introduction. The book was published in 1965 in a handsome cloth edition; later we put it into a paperback edition.

The book is a gold mine for novelists looking for "motivation" and insights into the more weird areas of human behavior; there are hundreds of dramatic (if sick, sick) elements in this "momentous" book. A bit of sexual abnormality never hurt any novel.

It was first published in 1886, in Stuttgart. Freud, then in his thirties, found it of great interest and obviously made use of it.

Believe it or not, I also borrowed, from the same doctor, the seven-volume set of *Studies in the Psychology of Sex* by Havelock Ellis, and read it with unrelieved astonishment. To my mind it is still the most important single work on sex *ever* published. Ellis died in 1939. His biography by Isaac Goldberg, now out of print, is worth tracking down.

———

Other adventures awaited me at Macmillan. One day, out of the blue, the office manager asked me to prepare for a month's trip to and through the state of Iowa. The purpose: a "goodwill mission" to give away samples of books, mostly textbooks, and to entertain librarians, teachers, educators. No orders needed to be written. I was to cover the entire state and bring *the word* of Macmillan to the land of corn and casaba.

I visited every county seat in the state, learned a great deal about public relations, travel, checking in and out of hotels, restaurant behavior, tipping—and more about sex. Iowa's back roads were not all bucolic, I discovered. Certain hotels turned out to be more than met the eye; young women of irresistible allure seemed available at every turn, available as fresh corn. When I think about the escapades, encounters, checking into small hotels with a female companion without a thought of propriety or safety, I marvel at my nonchalance—or stupidity. I was totally fearless. I would not have that kind of courage today. Indeed not.

Two episodes come to mind at once, and at the risk of seeming to trespass on Frank Harris' terrain, I must note them briefly: a young woman with ash-blond hair, wearing a tight beige sweater, sitting beside me on a dusty train in Iowa, calmly turned to me and asked where I was stopping. I told her the name of the town. "What hotel?" she asked. I told her I had phoned ahead for a room at the ——— hotel. She said, "How odd. That's where I'm going." When the train stopped, we got off; the hotel was a five-block walk. She came along with me. She had no baggage. I registered in my name alone; she stood by, smiling. Then she followed me up to my room. No sooner were my bags on the floor than she began to attack my belt buckle; attack *me* is more like it. Sexual ferocity— my first experience in the Big Arena.

The second "episode" was with a pretty young schoolteacher. I met her in the county superintendent's office. When I left, she walked along and asked if I would like to have tea with her; also, she wanted to show me her hand-painted china: she was an artist. I accompanied her to a small bungalow. She seemed to be living there alone. We did have tea; she did show me her china painting. And then she invited me upstairs to her bedroom. I entered the door; she closed and locked it. I did not leave until the following morning. I was totally depleted.

The hazards and dramatic encounters are "enough to make a book." But most educational of all were some insights I got into publishing.

The politics of getting textbooks adopted was an eye-opener to me. I soon learned that the merits of a book did not necessarily determine its adoptions, and that adoptions were big business. I learned how grand campaigns and strategies were prepared months in advance in order to land a contract. Many thousands of dollars were spent, in many ways. The details cannot be gone into here, but Machiavelli and Don Corleone must have been the patron saints of the textbook traveller.

After four years at Macmillan, I decided I would enjoy having my own bookshop. My personal library consisted of around eighteen hundred books, many of them sets. The latter were bought by filling out mail-order coupons to Scribner's, Houghton, and other firms who then specialized in such sets. (Too bad the subscription-set business is now obsolete—what a great way to get to read and own collected writings of the major authors.) I also had many used books which I bought from most of the antiquarian shops in Chicago (Powner's and Nedwick's come to mind), and of course hundreds of books published by Macmillan, bought, in the main, at 60 percent discount—"damaged" books.

These books, plus eight hundred dollars borrowed from my mother, represented my capital. I was greener than grass; knew nothing about running a bookshop, accounting, the economics of a one-man business. I had observed other shops, in particular Ben Silberman's bookshop on East Chicago Avenue—I think he called it the Borzoi Bookshop until Knopf told him to lay off their trade name. At Silberman's I discovered the wonderland of Borzoi books (with their Dwiggins binding dies) and first bought there the books of Thomas Mann, Knut Hamsun (I read *everything* I could find of Hamsun's), Sigrid Undset, the exciting titles in their several series, including the *Blue Jade Library*: books by Barbey d'Aurevilly, Baron Corvo, Villiers de L'Isle Adam, Andreyev, Istrati, Haldane MacFall, and many other "door-opening" works. And, of course, there were the books by H. L. Mencken and George Jean Nathan.

Nathan and I became good friends when I moved to New York; we often ate and drank—mostly the latter—at his favorite "watering places," the Algonquin, the Colony, and 21. He produced two anthologies of plays for us at World. While a cruel snob, he was kind to me, always warm and courteous. One subject he preferred never to discuss was the theatre. I learned to respect his wishes in this matter, and from this also learned never to argue with a specialist in his field. I visited the theatre on opening nights with him, once with the handsome Wolcott Gibbs, and it was, of course, embarrassing when Nathan would turn to me during the first intermission and ask, "Had enough?" which meant we were leaving. I felt every eye in the house on us as we left. I think he is the patron saint of our John Simon. Nathan was totally uncompromising, fantastically erudite.

Nathan died in 1958, having left behind a large body of fine critical work. He also left a tradition that no one on the New York scene has yet equalled. His wit and genius for interpretation of the drama has never been surpassed by any active New York dramatic *journalist*, certainly. While for many years he professed a kind of misogyny, his romantic inclinations and affairs were fairly legendary. His great loves were Lillian Gish and in his final years, Julie Hayden. His home for many years was the Royalton Hotel, directly across the street from the Algonquin. That street, between Fifth and Sixth avenues, was the hot center of New York's literary life, certainly in the Nathan period.

Anyone curious about the man should read his *World of George Jean Nathan* and *The Theatre in the Fifties.* The first book of his that I read, *The American Credo,* prepared me for a lifetime of adulation of the man. His *Smart Set* and *American Mercury* material was always catnip for me; he made sparks fly. I found his style and chutzpah pure exhilaration. We all loved him for his writings on O'Casey.

One vivid recollection: Early in our relationship, in 1945, we were having a few Scotches at 21—it was late in the afternoon—when a waiter came over and said, "I'm sorry to disturb you gentlemen, but I have some sad news; Mr. Roosevelt has just died." Nathan stiffened, stood up, turned to me, and said only two words: "Let's leave." We left, and I walked him down Fifth Avenue to Forty-fourth Street; he barely said a word. As we shook hands to part, he had tears in his eyes, I saw, and he said, "This is one hell of a bad day for all of us, Bill."

———

Backtracking for a moment: I must record an extraordinary literary encounter I had at the age of fourteen. I ran into a three-foot stack of magazines, back numbers of the magazine, *The Smart Set*. Discovering these magazines was comparable to walking into an Oriental harem, an Arabian Nights' dream. I can't begin to convince my reader what a giant leap forward that was for an impressionable young bookworm. Let me digress briefly:

The Smart Set was founded in 1900 and ran for thirty years. A complete set would be not only a fine collector's prize, but a "desert island library." Carl R. Dolmetsch compiled an anthology of pieces from the magazine in 1966 (Dial Press), and anyone interested in seeing how sophisticated our forebears were should take a look at some of its contents. (*The Smart Set*'s founding and publishing history are narrated in that anthology.) Of course, in my youthful encounter, most of the authors' names were new to me, not to mention much of their vocabulary. I was sent to the dictionary every half hour, checking out exotic and highly flammable words.

In the pages of *The Smart Set* was the first American appearance of James Joyce's two stories, "A Little Cloud" and "The Boarding House," stories which Ben Huebsch was to publish shortly and which Ezra Pound had touted to *The Smart Set* editors, Mencken and Nathan. Other writers published by *The Smart Set* were Robinson Jeffers, Ezra Pound, D. H. Lawrence, Edna St. Vincent Millay, Dorothy Parker, S. N. Behrman, Damon Runyan (he used Alfred as his first name in those days), O. Henry, Lord Dunsany, Howard Mumford Jones, Eugene O'Neill, F. Scott Fitzgerald, and many others. In the pages of these magazines, a cache of some twenty-five issues, my eyes were opened to many aspects of literature and life; I read the newly discovered authors ravenously.

In those days, H. L. Mencken was the writer I worshipped the most, and I read and adored his *Treatise on the Gods* and all his volumes of *Prejudices*. And I'll never forget my shock and outrage when I discovered the late Walter Lippmann taking potshots at Mencken. (Attacking *my* god was unthinkable, sacrilegious!) I think Lippmann was writing for *The New Republic* at the time. His talents in the field of satire and literary criticism were outstanding, but that he dared to take on my Mencken struck me as an act of impiety. By the way, parenthetically, it was Lippmann who showed tremendous courage years later in being among the very first to attack the Pentagon and the U.S. government on the issue of Vietnam. When he was making his attacks on our Vietnam position (Art

Buchwald was also showing his satiric muscles early on the same subject), it was an act of both vision and courage.

Bookshop Remembrances Past

I opened my first shop at 808 North Clark Street, not too far from the warehouse where the St. Valentine's Day massacre took place, and not more than a few doors from Chicago's famous little theatre, The Playhouse. I was also a block away from the great Newberry Library (where I first saw the first four Shakespeare folios and the first edition [1644] of Milton's *Areopagitica*), and the famous Bughouse Square, where the town's radicals spoke each night—a variant of London's Hyde Park and New York's Washington Square.

Naturally, in this environment I got to know a wide variety of men and women—poets, newspapermen, actors, artists, vagrants. The poet Maxwell Bodenheim often visited my shop, but he was, in the end, so great a problem with alcohol and womanizing that I had to order him to stay away. (He literally attempted raping my female assistant and I had to separate him from her traumatized body.)

In my bookshop I learned a few basic facts about life. While I managed to stay in business over twelve years, I was undercapitalized every step of the way. I hardly knew a day's respite from the pressures of bills. The Great Depression took my meager capital in one overnight *scoop*: the savings bank where my few dollars were deposited never reopened. It's hard to believe today, but there were many banks that did not reopen, did not recover from the "bank holiday." There was no federal insurance then.

While life was grim and money scarce, I was not lacking in "dumb courage." Shortly after the crash and the loss of my savings, I set up The Black Archer Press, where I issued an occasional limited edition and also some of my own compilations dealing with rare books. I was always broke, but somehow there was always a printer and binder around who had confidence in me. Those were glorious days. I designed books, fantasied about fame and fortune as a publisher, and remained insolvent, oddly, for years on end. I wasn't sufficiently in debt to anyone to prove a burden and a receivership case. I was just a broke but happy bookseller-publisher. I didn't know any better.

Somehow I managed to trade in my car every fifteen months or so for a new model; I got married and maintained a modest flat and even had a live-in maid when our son was born. I think we paid her eight dollars a week plus room and board. I also published, for a few years, a monthly tabloid called *The Book Collector's Journal,* which was great fun—but it lost money with deadly regularity.

Life as a small bookseller in Chicago in the thirties was no bed of roses; it was scratch, scrounge, and scratch each day. Nevertheless, there were many great moments, roller-coaster fun. The constant money squeeze wasn't as painful in retrospect as one might think.

I sometimes sold erotica (as did most booksellers) in order to help pay the rent. One of the chief sources of these books was a man, whose name escapes me, who worked from home and supplied books on call. He would get a telephonic message relayed to him at some secret hideaway. Within an hour or two, the book would materialize. We got twenty-five dollars for a copy of *The Memoirs of Fanny Hill, My Life and Loves* by Frank Harris, *Lady Chatterley's Lover, Josephine Mutzenbacher's Memoirs,* and other high-octane examples of hard-core pornography. Today, of course, these books are pretty tame stuff and available in low-priced paperbacks. I remember that our supplier was something of an artist and binder and would also make these books available with photos, hand-colored prints, and deluxe leather bindings. Handling some of these books was quite educational, and I'm referring to the customers as well as the books. The buyers were often distinguished members of the community, although I must admit I can't recall any clergymen among my clients. Speaking in terms of literature, there are very few pornographers today who can match the quality of the pornographic classics of the nineteenth century and early twentieth century. In short, there's nothing new, or better, and, excepting Henry Miller, we haven't progressed in this category of literature. Of course, *The Story of O* is an outstanding exception.

One late evening a Eurasian girl came into the shop. I recall her wearing a pink blouse and a slightly frayed pale green skirt. She stayed late, browsing, saying nothing—ignoring me, in fact. I finally saw that she wasn't going to buy anything, so I started to turn out the lights. At which point she asked, "Wouldn't you like to make love to me?" I won't try to describe my astonishment. She was a beautiful girl, right out of a Gauguin painting; she wore beautiful, large gold earrings.

"I don't have any facilities here," I answered.

"That's okay," she said. "Turn out the lights and we'll do it on the floor."

When it was over—and I must report that I found it an extraordinary experience—we got up. She looked glum. I felt the need to say something complimentary, so I said, "Those are beautiful earrings." Whereupon she slapped my face, her eyes blazing. She turned and left. I never saw her again. Gallantry, expertise—obviously something was lacking in my deportment that night. I was twenty-two years old at the time, learning slowly.

When I opened my bookshop I printed a "souvenir" booklet for my customers, a copy of Hearn's *Tale of a Fan,* on Japanese vellum. I no longer have a copy. I also published a deluxe edition of Hearn's translation of Gautier's *One of Cleopatra's Nights,* set by hand and, oddly, with the Ingres *Seraglio* as a frontispiece.

A friend and mentor was Ben Abramson, the town's leading personal bookseller. Ben helped me in many ways and was generous with credit. I knew his stock quite well and often sold to my customers books that I had seen on his shelves. "I'll have the book for you in an hour," I'd tell my customer. And Ben would have it delivered to me. He gave me tips and advice about British books, and I learned a good deal from him about fine printing and first editions. Short and stocky, with curly red hair, he was a nonstop raconteur, a master salesman. He would memorize pages from books he was espousing, and his sales performances might have justified admission tickets. I owed so very much to him in my beginning, bookselling days. I'm sorry that I wasn't able to reciprocate when he came on troubled times. Ben's daughter, Deborah Benson, is still carrying on his tradition in West Cornwall, Connecticut. She's a bright, avid bookworm. In a burst of generosity she gave me a morocco-bound copy of Ben's famous *North Wall Catalogue.*

One more note on Ben Abramson. His shop was a long, narrow one; it ran the full length of a short street and had a door at both

ends. Ben often worked late, and one evening I dropped in for a
short visit. I'll not forget that experience. He had two secretaries
working for him. Each sat on a chair at each end of the shop. Each
was taking dictation from him. Ben had a fifth of gin in his hand,
and as he sipped from it, he paced up and down the shop's length.
He kept up a steady stream of dictation. As he reached the middle of
the floor, he would start dictating to the girl ahead of him. He kept
this up without appearing to notice me, and I left. This was a
virtuoso performance worth recording on film. I was mesmerized.
Ben was one of the best and most prolific letter writers I ever knew.
In fact, he would threaten customers that he would cut them from
his correspondence list if they would not buy more books. Ben
often wrote a three-page letter to sell a five-dollar book. Each letter
was an original, wildly entertaining and full of chutzpah. He was
one of a kind.

Booksellers should not be collectors, but, as indicated, I couldn't
resist collecting Hearn. I had most of his books at home and cher-
ished them. One hot summer day, with business at a low ebb, a
limousine drove up to my shop and a sprightly little woman stepped
out and entered.

"I understand you have some first editions of Lafcadio Hearn,"
she said. "I have a granddaughter who should start collecting, and
I'd like her to start with Hearn; I lived in Japan for some years and
like his books."

A serious problem was posed. Business was lousy. I had unpaid
bills, and I had a fine collection of Hearn at home, some four blocks
away.

"If you come back in an hour," I said, "I'll show you the best
collection of Hearn in town." She returned later and bought the
entire collection, for some five hundred dollars, I recall. The sale
of these books caused me real anguish; but then, booksellers have
no business collecting. Bills have to be paid.

When the bombing of Pearl Harbor occurred, I was advised by
friends to dispose of my Japanese collection—prints, dolls, books—
which I did, stupidly.

Every small bookseller should be blessed, as I was, with a customer who can be classified as Lady Bountiful. Mine was a wealthy
widow who lived alone in the Seneca Hotel on Chicago's Near

North Side. Her passion was for fine bindings. Her purchases from me averaged about $7,500 to $10,000 a year. Her collection was visually dramatic; her hotel living room walls were shelf-lined and filled with leather bindings of every imaginable color and style of tooling. I scoured catalogs and New York sources for books with which to provide her. Ben Abramson supplied me with many. I had one problem: she was lonely, and liked me to visit with her on an evening now and then. These visits were difficult on several counts—they kept me away from home and my family; we did not have much in common except the books I was selling to her; and, alas, her knowledge was limited. There's a threshold . . . We had one quarrel, when she asked me to catalog her library. I simply was not up to it and she became angry at my refusal. She offered me a handsome fee and I still refused. Our relationship drifted and I sold her fewer books. In many ways I was relieved, though the loss of income was not easily accommodated. So after about four years of "pushing leather," I lost a valued client. I think that this experience is in part responsible for my indifference (intolerance?) to modern "fancy leather bindings"; I prefer the original publishers' bindings. To a collector, the original binding is of course essential.

Books solely as objects of interior decoration are intolerable. A yard of green, six feet of red, and four yards of brown—that kind of fine-binding collecting is no collecting at all. But I am not putting down the real collecting of bindings. And for the novice, I call attention to the fact that some bindings are works of art; and interestingly, some of the finest of the nineteenth and twentieth centuries were executed by women. I've been lucky enough to have owned or handled over the years some exquisite examples of the binder's art, many by women, including the great Englishwoman, Sarah T. Prideaux, as well as Alice Pattison, Charlotte Ullman, Katherine Adams (one of the masters), May Morris, Edith Diehl, Louise James, Florence Walter, and others. These women are of course the "Rembrandts" of this profession. Their works are incomparably beautiful.

It comes to my mind that before I found a job with a publisher I tried to get an apprentice's job with a bookbinder in Chicago but was unsuccessful; perhaps it was just as well, since I am not terribly skilled in handwork of any kind. Changing a typewriter ribbon is my speed—which reminds me of the most ignominious job turndown I ever experienced. When I was about seventeen, I applied for an usher's job at the B & K movie theatre in Chicago. About fifteen young men were lined up for consideration by the head usher. I flunked out. For weeks I brooded over the rejection, little realizing how lucky I was not to have gotten the job. Because a few months later, along came my rendezvous with destiny—Macmillan. But I must say, getting turned down as a movie usher bruised my ego painfully.

Payment Deferred

During my years as a bookseller, one of my steady customers was a shy, quiet, but intensely cultivated young man named Saul Bellow. He bought many used books from me, and one day he took along with him a twelve-volume set, *The Works of Tolstoy.*

A number of my steady customers bought on the installment plan: so much down, so much a week. Bellow paid for the Tolstoy set on that basis. (Oddly, I had originally bought that set the same way, through a mail-order subscription house.)

Years passed. One night I ran into Bellow in New York; I think it was at the opening of his play, *The Last Analysis.* As he saw me approaching, he took out his wallet, extracted a bill, and handed it to me.

"What's that for?" I asked.

"I remembered that I owed you for one final payment on the Tolstoy set—five dollars. Sorry it took me so long; here it is."

I was speechless.

"I can't take it, Saul," I said. "Statute of limitations. Besides, please don't embarrass me."

"Embarrass, hell! I owe it to you. It's about twenty-five years overdue, and you could really add a hell of a lot of interest to the debt."

I refused to take it. "I'd rather be able to tell my friends you owe me five dollars," I said.

A few more years passed. Then one evening, in New York, I met Saul's new wife. On being introduced she said, "Oh, Bill Targ! We owe you five dollars." Whereupon she opened her purse and pulled out a five-dollar bill. The ensuing conversation was a repetition of my previous one with Saul. I refused to take the money.

Let it be known to the world that Saul Bellow owes me five dollars. His children will be involved in this matter in years to come —probably with my grandchildren. I will continue to hold out. However, if he would care to inscribe a copy of *War and Peace* for my collection, that would settle the debt.

Give the Man the Three Dollars

On August 28, 1940, I sent a letter to H. Jack Lang of Cleveland. He was a well-known collector of literary and historical letters. Just the other day—about thirty-five years later!—he returned a Xerox copy of that letter to me. He had learned that I was writing a book and thought it would be amusing to remind me of the "good old days."

I reprint the letter in full; it will indicate how I worked at my trade when things were tough:

August 28th, '40.

Mr. H. Jack Lang,
1010 Euclid Ave.,
Cleveland, Ohio.

My dear Mr. Lang:
Every so often a bookseller runs his horrified eyes over his crowded shelves, tables and floor to encounter the ever-growing accumulation of literary debris which seems to be his sole heritage. . . . So, in browsing thru my stock today I encountered a 3 volume set which no one could possibly want today except as a door stop . . . a set which, without special and zealous effort would remain to moulder into eternity.

Then I thought of you, my one and only fancier of Letters. Ergo, the set is promptly dusted off and packed up ready for shipment. I take the unforgivable liberty of burdening you with the set in the hope that you might be charitable enough to give it shelter. The set is: LETTERS OF GEORGE SAND. Published in London, 1886. Aside from a few vandalously ink-stained pages, the set is in reasonably good shape. As to price, I note several previous owners' prices which seem at the moment almost astronomical in view of my anxiety to dispose of the set. So, after careful deliberation, I am asking $3.00.

Now the question remains: if you don't give two hoots for Miss Sand and her letters, the set isn't worth the paper on which it's printed. But, if you feel it might fill the well known "gap" in your library, it's a colossal bargain.

At any rate, don't hesitate to return it if you find it incompatible with your requirements.

Cordially yours,
William Targ

Quite frankly, I can't remember whether Mr. Lang ever sent me the three dollars.

Chicago Booksellers

There are two dynamic booksellers in Chicago. First and foremost is Carl Kroch, the prototype of the big, modern, well-organized executive bookseller. His stock of books is unequalled anywhere for variety, and includes one of the largest assemblages of paperbacks in America. He may very well be the largest single outlet for books (at retail) in America. (He sells over seventeen million dollars' worth of books a year!) His internal systems should serve as a model for booksellers who want to survive.

Also in Chicago is Stuart Brent. He's equally dynamic, but his philosophy of bookselling is "effusive personal." He will probably outsell anyone when he likes a particular book; he is evangelical when one appeals to him. If he dislikes a book, forget it—it's not for sale in his North Michigan Avenue shop. Stuart has a marvelous gift of gab—he's nonstoppable—but he usually makes sense. He's one nonconformist in the book business who has succeeded. And the odds are tremendous. One of his customers once said to me, "Stuart talks too much, but when I want a book, I buy it from him; I trust his wild enthusiasms and he's never let me down." What a testimonial.

Chicago is probably America's second city—for books.

Chicagoana

The Lincoln Park Zoo was one of my favorite Sunday-outing spots, as well as the University of Chicago's Midway, where lush grass was plentiful and muggings were not yet part of the ambience. On hot sultry nights the lake front was where we would cool off, swimming, broiling hot dogs, larking. Parties in small hotel rooms until dawn. Before I was married there was a long period when bottle parties were the thing; you phoned your favorite bootlegger and he delivered "white" or "brown" in pint-sized bottles which were concealed on his body. The price was, I think, two dollars a bottle. Once in a while, we would learn of someone going blind or mad as a result of drinking the stuff. I was one of the lucky ones. And there were the famous Chicago speakeasies. We'd take a date, sit down. A teacup was placed before us. The "Scotch" was poured into the cups and we'd sip it like tea. Hot jazz combos would play and we would dance until early morning. I feel nostalgic as I look back on that boozy period in Chicago. Authentic gangsters would be sitting elbow-to-elbow with college kids and couples out for the night. During that period, I fancied a cane and carried it (subconsciously as a protective weapon) and even began collecting canes. Finally I got rid of the lot and the foppish practice. I had Vaseline-slick Valentino hair in those days, and a long black mustache. I weighed around 135 pounds, was usually in debt, and had not a care in the world. My tiny bookshop on North Clark Street was almost a club; friends, including Bughouse speakers, wobblies, winos, convened there. We'd hold debates, hot arguments. Once in a while, someone would buy a book. We'd often head for the B & G coffee shops for post-midnight hamburgers. Or to one of our favorite chili parlors where chili-mac and coke could be had on Chicago Avenue for fifty cents. Some evenings I'd go off alone, prowling in the second-hand shops, searching for "finds," first editions, or "sleepers" unrecognized by the dealers. I earned a bit of money at this.

For years I longed to go to Japan; I wanted to visit Hearn's grave and see the places he described in his books. I planned and saved for the trip. But as of this writing I've not been there yet. Perhaps I will go someday. (Art Buchwald, who has been there, told me that he would recommend that I make the trip but *not* to take my wife. He didn't elaborate.) I did finally visit the French West

Indies, and Hearn's spirit was upon me as I walked the streets lined with pink stucco shacks; and the back roads of Martinique. (We stayed at a rather primitive hotel where the food was superb but the accommodations were—to employ Roslyn's characterization—"pissoir.")

The musty air in an antiquarian bookshop is both romantic and asphyxiating. From Ben Abramson I learned that a cup of cologne in the water bucket used for washing the shop's floor could give the place a pleasing odor and counteract the mustiness. Luckily, one of my customers was a manufacturer of cheap perfumes. I made a deal with him: he would bring me a few quarts of cologne each month and swap them for books. My porter thought I was a bit queer, but the customers commented on the pleasant smell—in fact, complimented me on achieving the ambience of a whorehouse.

One of the strangest customers I ever had was a dwarf-sized sword swallower. He was tattooed from head to foot, wore high boots, an embroidered jacket, and an Australian Bushman's hat. He claimed to be an Australian, but I detected a Bronx accent. He carried a three-foot sword and, without warning, he would draw it from its scabbard, tilt back his head, and swallow it. (Linda Lovelace had nothing on him.) It was an unnerving piece of behavior that he'd sometimes perform in the presence of several customers. When he withdrew the sword from his gullet, he would give us all a contemptuous look and walk out. He had a mad look in his eye at all times. He once claimed to be a descendant of Rasputin, which, in view of his Australian "credentials," was a bit much. But he did have that Rasputin look—very intense and rather threatening—and he even made veiled comments on fantastic physical injuries he had inflicted on certain enemies. One day, he and I were sharing a pint of gin toward closing, and in a moment of recklessness I said that I thought he was really Jewish. He stopped coming to my shop from that moment. I was relieved.

Another customer was a notorious bootlegger. This was during the Prohibition period. He, like my widow-client, had a passion for fine bindings. There were many cases of alleged brandy and Scotch that I exchanged for Whitman Bennett's "deluxe bindings." He would deliver the booze in a Cadillac. Alas, the brandy and Scotch were used up quickly, but I'm sure, somewhere in Chicago, several hundred books in elegantly tooled bindings remain "unconsumed" on some bibliophile's shelves.

From the Album

In 1933 (about the time I was first married), Chicago became a highly visible spot on the map: the World's Fair took place there, and notable among the exhibits (zoological and otherwise) was the fan-dancing performance of Sally Rand. What stands out most clearly is that Anne Jesselson (my first wife) served as Sally's press agent. As a result, Sally became a factor in our lives for a while. Anne was an imaginative and courageous p.r. woman. When there was no story, she invented one. I doubt that Sally Rand remembers the background of some of the "items" that appeared in the press, local and national, but Anne was the inventor of many of the "news" stories. Anne also arranged for Sally to ride naked on a white horse at a local art ball as Lady Godiva. The purpose, of course, was to get Sally arrested and on the front pages. It worked. Getting a horse to ride up Michigan Avenue is not an easily arranged feat, but Anne worked it out and even arranged for the bail.

I hope Sally (now in her seventies) is still dancing and entertaining around America as this is written. She is/was unique in show business. She's done just about everything in the name of entertainment, and her collection of blue stories is a match for any comedian's, including Red Buttons and Milton Berle. I recall one she told me one snowy day as I was escorting her from her theatre dressing room to a dinner affair at World Publishing. Sally, in sequins, was the key speaker. Her subject was "Sex and the Bible." She was an authority on both, and she rocked our staff.

There's one story she told me, privately, about an Englishman who is told, on his first visit to America, to be sure to see New Orleans. Some of its features were explained to him and he was eager to experience them firsthand. On entering one of the best restaurants on Bourbon Street, he asked for roasted cat. The waiter was nonplussed and said that the restaurant did not serve such a dish. "Call the manager, please," said the exasperated Englishman. When the manager came, the Englishman repeated his order for roasted cat. "Sorry, sir, it is not on our menu." The British gentleman looked the maitre d' up and down and said, "And I was told that some of the best-eating pussy in America could be found in New Orleans—another burst illusion."

Sally was a fine raconteur. One evening, in New York, she was visiting us at home after a late show. As she sat on our sofa sipping Scotch and telling stories, our son, aged about fourteen at the time, sat on the floor goggle-eyed at this exotic beauty. She told a story about working with a ten-foot cobra in a nightclub in a southern tank town (maybe it was Key West). As she spoke, she raised her arms, put her hands into her hair, and lifted it off her head. It was a wig, the first Russell had ever seen. Underneath, Sally had a very short crewcut. I think my son was startled, but he appeared calm. Without appearing to notice, he asked, "And then what happened with the cobra?"

Among Anne's many and diversified clients, including evangelists, food faddists, and college professors who hankered after a bit of limelight in their academic lives, was a musician, a refugee from Hitler's Germany. His name: Max Rudolf. In 1940 he came to Chicago, where he conducted and also taught music at the YMCA College and elsewhere. Anne managed to get him some newspaper publicity that helped, I think, to bring him to the attention of the New York musical world. He joined the Metropolitan Opera Company staff, where he did auditioning and conducted operas from time to time.

One day (I think it was in the late forties) Max's wife phoned and invited us to hear a performance of *Don Giovanni* which Rudolf was conducting. We were to be the Rudolfs' guests, occupying Rudolf Bing's box, no less.

This was, of course, a Big Event for Anne, in view of her earlier efforts on Rudolf's behalf in Chicago. Our emotions ran high as we watched the maestro conduct the glorious Mozart. After the performance we went backstage to greet our friend Max. I'll never forget his kindness when he greeted us and said to the stage manager, "I'm sure Russell, Anne, and Bill would like to take a walk across the stage."

This was an inspired notion. The three of us walked slowly across and back the old Metropolitan's stage. We felt and sensed the presence of the cast of *Don Giovanni* who had performed there just minutes before. I swear we felt and heard reverberations of the music as we strolled across the ancient boards of the great opera house. The dust had literally not yet cleared. We were all touched with emotion.

Russell, still in his early teens, was especially moved by the experience. Every time I hear a performance of *Don Giovanni* (my favorite opera), I think of that walk across the Met's stage. Every music lover should have that experience—at least once.

Anne

Anne and I were married in May 1933. She died of renal failure in February 1965. Thirty-two years of marriage to one of the most extraordinary women I've ever known. Her outstanding characteristics were forthrightness and generosity. She was loving. She was incapable of deceit, and her truth-telling was the cause of extreme pain, not only to the victim but to herself. She once had occasion to tell off Bobby Fischer, the chess master, who had spent an evening at our home (his sister Joan is married to my son) and he left angrily. It was like telling off Maria Callas. But when Anne died, Bobby sent me a handwritten condolence letter, signed. Joan expressed surprise, since Bobby never writes letters or signs anything. Obviously, Anne's forthrightness had moved Bobby.

As for her generosity, Anne repaid kindness threefold. Gifts of flowers, books, jewelry, records, were an almost daily habit of hers. But she was also unforgiving of rudeness, and liars were not allowed in her presence; nor were boasters.

She was a witty letter writer, one of the best punsters I've known. She was a creative publicist and performed professionally until her health deteriorated. She was an indefatigable reader. Everything from Horney to Kierkegaard to Nathanael West and John Updike and Salinger; especially, she devoured the Freudian analysts. She adored Dixieland, and her real gods were Miles Davis, Charlie Parker, Thelonious Monk, Dizzy Gillespie, and also Billie Holliday. She surprised me one day with a lengthy analysis of Gil Evans' arrangements and spoke of his genius in terms I had never suspected. She not only loved music, but knew who was responsible for what. Miles' trumpet spoke to her as Mozart spoke to me. She loved Monk and Miles, the men, for their cool indifference to the public. "They know who they are," she said.

As a mother she was without peer, totally committed to Russell. When we moved to New York she spent the first weeks—morning, noon, and night—teaching him the transportation systems, bringing him to each of the museums, including those in Brooklyn. She took him to lunch in the Plaza, 21, Luchow's, Chinatown. He attended matinees, concerts, ballets, and the opera with her. She read endlessly to him and gave totally of herself.

She was an *alpha* person, but flawed. She did not drink wine or spirits, but believed that when there was champagne on the table it should be kept coming. When we first saw Elvis Presley perform, on an Ed Sullivan broadcast, and I found him distasteful, she quietly pointed out that while some would greet his performance with revulsion, he was a one-man revolution, and probably a new epoch in music was at hand—that he was an original who would be imitated widely and soon. She saw *that* long ago. She also called the score on Marlon Brando when we saw his first performance in *A Streetcar Named Desire*. "Always remember who the originals are," she said. (I consider him America's greatest actor, hands down.)

Anne's enemy was schizophrenia—a lifelong adversary that fragmented her life, her personality, her mind. Her perceptions were clear, her judgments sound, except as they related to her own being. A sense of inadequacy, a lack of self-esteem defeated her. Living with peas under the mattress . . . When she died I learned how deeply she was loved by many people, some of whom I barely knew. Hundreds of letters arrived to tell me who and what Anne was. But I already knew.

A Child Shall Lead Them

A father is educable, and the child is often best qualified to act as his teacher. The child can give the parent faith in him and in all youth, which means the youth of the future. The truth which most parents won't face is that a teenager is often wiser than his parents. I know this for a fact. My son taught me, when he was in his early teens, that adults worry too much, have too little confidence in their children's judgment; that most parents are indeed fear-ridden, uptight, square.

If a father is lucky, he avoids making some of the dumb speeches, the well-meaning speeches, we're all familiar with: "I'm telling this to you for your own good," and all that. (Obviously we're not trying to do him harm!) I learned quickly how pointless and inane it is, "giving advice." My son once stopped me cold by pointing out that what I was telling him was *trite.* "I already know all that, Dad," was his reply. "Most kids do."

I can't recall my son ever making a judgmental error.

My son is now an adult, but he still has the "Joe college" look of a twenty-year-old. He's six feet four, has brown curly hair, wears glasses, and is addicted to tweeds. He's thin and clearly not an Establishment type. Since his vision is somewhat far from 20-20, he holds reading matter close to his eyes. Consequently he's developed a remarkable memory; when he delivers a lecture it is always without notes.

As a child, he took apart every mechanical gift he got: watches, trains, radios, and such. He always managed to put them back together again. His interest in mechanics certainly wasn't inherited from his father, nor was his precocity in mathematics. I play no games, but my son excelled in chess, bridge, and other table games in his early teens.

He would sometimes startle us with his free use of language, but he never took advantage of his inalienable liberties, as he understood them to be: free speech and free opinions, freely expressed.

When Russell went to camp, we felt, as did most parents, that there were real hazards to think about. Since Russell's vision was limited, we kept our fingers crossed with respect to such matters as climbing and, in particular, water. We hoped he would learn to swim and be careful. Two weeks after he left for camp (a Boy Scout camp) we had a letter from him. He had *learned to swim,* he said, and was now teaching smaller children to swim, and he was also a *lifeguard.*

The following summer, at the same camp, he sent us a letter asking us to grant written approval for him to smoke. "The kids are all smoking and I might as well join them; I need parental approval."

We wrote and granted approval, if that was his wish.

Russell never smoked a cigarette in his life. He simply was curious about our attitude—testing, one might call it.

I recall debating heatedly with him about Cuba when Castro came into power. He felt Kennedy and the government should have recognized and supported him, and that Kennedy and all of us would live to regret our negligence and poor judgment. He also called the folly of the Vietnam affair from the beginning, when we first sent in our small groups of "expert advisers." He seems to have had some special political foresight which we lacked. He's never been wrong, politically. We keep checking him out after the fact.

Russell was not a joiner: he belonged to only two organizations —the Boy Scouts of America and the Manhattan Chess Club.

I think he would make a fine president.

It seems to me that countless thousands of young men and women around us have Russell's qualities. Not seeing and understanding them is *our* problem. Recognizing a special kind of maturity in our youth takes a special kind of maturity in adults; many of us lack it. I hope I did well by my son, that I didn't disappoint him in my own life, didn't embarrass him through false posturing and pontification.

We gave Russell a few breaks; for example, when he was in his early teens we managed to get front row seats to many of Toscanini's NBC concerts, when the maestro was in his prime. Russell enjoyed watching and hearing the maestro cursing out one musician or another in Italian, spittle flying. Russell was fascinated to see this amazing perfectionist at work. He loved the music, too. But what interested him most, I think, was watching this master musician control a large body of musicians, many of whom were prima donnas, and making them work in miraculous harmony. His taste for music developed, and from Beethoven and Mozart he gradually moved to baroque—and then to Joan Baez and Bob Dylan.

Russell got to see good plays. We attended the opening night's performance of Beckett's *Waiting for Godot;* we saw Bert Lahr in his greatest performance. I remember spending the rest of the night lying in front of our fireplace, discussing the play and its meaning. And it was Russell who concluded first that we had witnessed something marvelous. He was in his teens then.

We experienced together many other great plays; also ballet and opera, and much chamber music. Wagnerian opera was one of his early passions.

We took him to good restaurants and urged him not to look at the price column of the menu. So he developed a taste for lobster. But he also liked pizza and chili con carne. Alcohol and tobacco did not interest him at all, although in recent years he drinks California wine in moderation, as do his wife and three children. They live in Palo Alto.

Russell was aware of the lack of censorship in our house. We had some ten thousand books at one time, and he knew that any book in the house was available to him. It was okay to read Jack London, Harold Robbins, Tolstoy, Proust, Kierkegaard, Plato, Ouspensky, James T. Farrell, Camus, Freud, Krafft-Ebing—and yes, "sex books." He was often surprised to learn that we had a book in the house that one of his "intellectual" friends had urged him to read. He once asked me if I had ever heard of Kafka, and when I pointed to a small row of volumes, all by and about Kafka, he smiled.

The entire spectrum of literature was his to enjoy, including books on stage magic, an early mutual interest. Finally, he moved into works on mathematics and physics, philosophy and drama. He spent one whole year (in his spare time) reading the Greeks. Paranormal literature also interested him at an early age, and today he continues to pursue that area professionally as a dedicated *scientist*.

As a boy Russell always had his own room, with absolute privacy. We never turned him down on any reasonable request, and he was rarely unreasonable. He went to Europe alone at age eighteen, with a round-trip ticket and $300 (all from his own allowance savings). He returned a month later with over $150 in his pocket. He made lifelong European friends on his trip to England and France.

Russell had more courage than I; higher standards, too. I learned about civic responsibility from him. He could and would take a stand. He was not afraid to be vocal. In an understated fashion. He signed petitions and demonstrated. Russell also had a better sense of money than I. He knew when it was important to be extravagant, but mostly he was intelligently frugal.

He taught me that there was a time when only a punch in the nose was the proper response to a given situation, or when pacificism was in order.

When he left college he took a job at a Long Island laser laboratory—his specialty was research. He helped build one of the first lasers in America. His salary was "man-sized," but when he went to work, his clothes were quasi-hippie. In summer he'd go to his laboratory in Bermuda shorts, open sandals without socks, a sport shirt, and a beret. I pointed out to him that this kind of dress was unsuited to anyone holding down the kind of responsible job he had. He reminded me that he was hired and being paid for his research capacity, his *work*, and not his dress, and that if he was not producing, the most elegant and proper clothes would not help him hold down the job. He wasn't afraid to give up his job later (for lower pay, by the way) when he learned of a job at a college where he could work and learn something that concerned his future, something in a special area of nuclear physics.

Russell never used taxis, except in grave emergencies. He was always careful with money. But he would buy the best champagne for our anniversaries and birthdays. He dated girls, bought them Mexican silver jewelry if his interest was great enough. He never minded paying a stiff price for a good book.

His house in Palo Alto is full of books, records, pictures. His family entertains countless visitors from all over the world; he has close friends even in Iceland. He owns two houses in Palo Alto, four bicycles for his family, and a large station wagon. His family adores him, even though he can be tough on occasion. He will go to any lengths to make his children happy, and most of his leisure time is devoted to them.

What I'm trying to underscore here is that my son, at an early age (in his early teens) had me needlessly worried because of his informal, hippie lifestyle. Once he brought a girlfriend home, introduced us to her briefly, then took her to his room and closed the door. She wore no shoes. At about three in the morning I got up and saw a light under his door. I knocked and entered. He and the girl were huddled over a bridge table, deeply involved in a game of chess. I never opened his bedroom door again, uninvited.

Russell did laser research for Sylvania for some years; then he was offered a job at the Stanford Research Institute to experiment in paranormal areas, with emphasis on ESP. He took the job gladly. He's conducted many experiments in ESP and has written articles on the subject, one of which he wrote with his associate, Dr. Puthoff. It was published recently in the British magazine, *Nature*, the first of its kind ever allowed in its sacrosanct pages.

Extrasensory perception is his chief personal and professional preoccupation these days. Whether my personal interest in psychic matters and magic, and his own personal interest in stage magic as a boy, helped to bring him to his present preoccupation, I can't say. As a physicist he has pointed out to me that one must keep an open mind; besides, he believes that there will be a breakthrough eventually, a telepathic communication breakthrough. I can only admire and support his determination to explore this fascinating possibility. We may yet tune in on the brain waves of others.

I've watched my son (now in his forties) develop as boy, man, and father. My contribution toward his development was really minimal; he gave me more than he received. I learned early, by observing his *cool*, his assured approach to all problems and situations, that youth is underestimated today. That parents and educators are unnecessarily fearful of their children's future because of their so-called permissive and liberated behavior and attitudes.

I feared, from time to time, for Russell's future and his welfare, as do most parents, I suppose. Why? I discovered that such matters as job and money were minor concerns in the end; jobs and money were not *that* important, not *that* hard to achieve. What was important, I learned, by observing my son, was being oneself, one's own man; doing what one felt was right for oneself.

What my son chose, when still a boy, was his own destiny. He repudiated Hardy's "life's little ironies," fate. He chose to guide his own life. He repudiated cynicism *as a boy*. Free will, "objectivism," seemed to make up his philosophy—in his teens. And what is remarkable to me about his success as a human being is that he has never been manic about success, about "making it." In fact, I know few persons who take so much time out of their lives for play, for the pure enjoyment of life.

Bloody Sunday, Chicago-Style

When Anne and I were first married in Chicago in 1933, we took a flat on North Dearborn Street. It was the Bohemian part of town, called the Near North Side. We had little money, but we had weekly "parties." Every Sunday was open house, with red wine, black bread, and salami unending. I recall watching Maxwell Bodenheim in our living room one Sunday night, swallowing a pint of gin without removing the bottle from his lips: there was a five-dollar bet involved. Larry Lipton, Marxist guru and literary Olympian, was making it with a pretty young University of Chicago student and I recall his punch line, "But honey, I have a douche bag in my apartment. What's to worry?" It was that same night that we heard about a shooting up the street. Later we saw John Dillinger's bloodstains on the sidewalk in front of the Biograph Theatre; it was just a few blocks from our house.

Dillinger, the betrayed bank robber, was shot on Sunday, July 22, 1934, after leaving the movie house where he had seen a Clark Gable film. David Wagoner, a fine poet, wrote a poem covering the event; it's in his book, *Staying Alive*. (Why don't poets write about such events anymore?) I had followed Dillinger's career with care—it had lasted for about a year, I recall. It was pretty historic stuff learning that Public Enemy Number One had been shot down a few blocks away. Right out of the wild Western movies. Despite the many Chicago gang-war shootings, I had never seen an actual shooting in Chicago.

Why did I feel so responsive to Dillinger's death? He had robbed banks; killed, I think, some sixteen people; terrorized the Midwest; made fools of the police. I had an empathy for the man, an involvement with him in his plight, and some pity, I suppose, because he had been fingered by a girlfriend ("lady in red"). As I read Wagoner's poem I relived that unbearably hot bloody night in Chicago, one of the hottest, as Wagoner tells us:

> Chicago ran a fever of a hundred and one that groggy Sunday.
> A reporter fried an egg on a sidewalk; the air looked shaky.

We don't make gangsters like Dillinger anymore. When they have that kind of talent, they wind up in Washington.

Crazies and Crooks

I love eccentrics and scoundrels, so long as I'm not obliged to live or work with them—at least not too closely nor too often.

Eccentric books are something else, and they are among my

favorite reading. By eccentric, I mean bypath subjects not usually encountered. For example, I enjoyed reading a book entitled *The Most Remarkable Echo in the World*. It was written by H. M. and D. C. Partridge, and privately printed in New York in 1933.

The book attempts to prove that Mark Twain (Samuel L. Clemens) was the author of *Alice's Adventures in Wonderland* and other works attributed to one Lewis Carroll or Charles Lutwidge Dodgson. It also proves conclusively that Mark Twain wrote the works of Edgar A. Poe. Twain wrote the works signed by several other authors, but I won't go into that because it will be too much for the reader to assimilate. What is important in this book is not only the scrupulous logic employed by the authors to prove their contentions, but also the illustrations which help support their claims.

If you can find a copy of *The Most Remarkable Echo in the World*, treat yourself to some heady reading.

Another toothsome book to be read for fun and fiendish fascination is *Forging Ahead*, by Wilfred Partington (Putnam's, 1939). It is "the true story of the upward progress of Thomas James Wise, Prince of Book Collectors, Bibliographer Extraordinary, and Otherwise." It is also the account of the greatest book forger in history, one of the scholarly crooks who "got away with it." Wise amassed a great library which he sold to the British Museum. Librarians, collectors, and booksellers will find the book "educational" as well as entertaining.

A book I enjoyed hugely and recommend to all publishers with a bent in the direction of crazies, eccentrics, and particularly the outrageous in our profession, is Ralph Straus' book, *The Unspeakable Curll* (London, 1927). Curll, a villainous eighteenth-century English bookseller-publisher, died in 1748. He was a publisher of pornography, and a pirate-inventor of memoirs and letters. Very often, on the announced death of a famous man, he would prepare and advertise the *Life and Letters of . . .* , usually based on the fevered imagination of one of his hacks. I love this description of him in Amory's *John Buncle*: "Curll was in person very tall and thin —an ungainly, awkward, white-faced man. His eyes were a light grey—large, projecting, goggle, and purblind. He was splay-footed and baker-kneed. He was a debauchee to the last degree and so injurious to society, that by filling his translations with wretched notes, forged letters, and bad pictures, he raised the price of a four-shilling book to ten . . . he likewise printed the lewdest things. . . ."

If you can locate a copy of this book, buy it at any price; you have a great treat awaiting you—if there's a bit of black villainy in your heart, you may even pick up a few ideas that may not seem as outrageous today as they were in Mr. Curll's time. (I know a few paperback executives who could give Curll a run for his money.) No novelist could have invented this man, not even Dickens.

Any of the above books will provide more fun than the TV show you planned to watch tonight, including the gloppy Edwardian soap operas imported from our British cousins.

Sandburg

Not too far from Chicago, in the town of Galesburg, Illinois, Carl Sandburg was born in 1878. His parents were Swedish immigrants and his father, a blacksmith, couldn't write his name. Carl dropped out of school at age thirteen and hoboed his way across the country. In 1908 he married Edward Steichen's sister, Lillian, and they had three children. In his latter years he made his home in Flat Rock, North Carolina. The Sandburgs raised goats.

Carl emancipated Abraham Lincoln—he took him out of the hands of the politicians and phony patriots and gave him back to the people. I think his biography of Lincoln, especially the one-volume edition, is the best American biography ever written. I think his poetry is underrated beyond belief. He was a force, an original (though a Whitmanian), and his death in 1967 cost America plenty. There's no one around like him. I'd love to read *his* comments on Watergate.

I knew Carl in Chicago and was even guilty of pirating a small work of his: I once took a book review of his, of a book of poems by a girlfriend of mine, and used it as an introduction to her second book of poems, which I published. I "neglected" to get his permission. He phoned me one day and said, "Targ, you owe me a dinner." "A pleasure," I replied, "but how come?" "Well, son," he said, "you stole a piece of property from me and a dinner is the price." I got the message. We gathered at the home of the poetess, who lived on South Shore Drive. Carl brought his guitar, and while we ate "meat and potatoes," his standard meal, he told stories, and later played the guitar for us. A private concert with our shoes off.

In later years, he and I would meet occasionally in New York. He would phone at odd hours. I once took him to 21 for dinner. When we arrived and the maitre d' saw who was with me, he got all heated up, and asked, bowing to the floor, "Where would you like to sit, Mr. Sandburg?" Carl replied in his slow drawl, "I wanna sit where I can see the *ceelebreeties*." So we got a fine table against the wall, downstairs. (Louis Goldblatt and his wife, and Roslyn and I had dinner at 21 on January 4, 1975, and by coincidence, we were seated at the same table. It was spooky, in a way, and I note this bit of information for collectors of spooky trivia.) Eating with Carl always offered a bit of drama. He wouldn't allow the waiters to remove the rolls or bread: "That's my dessert, son," he'd say, putting his hand over the plate. When I would give him a fine Havana cigar, he'd break it in half and "save the other half for later." If you ever savored a good cigar and saw someone break it in half, you know how I felt. Shaken.

The only time I ever met Tallulah Bankhead was when I was invited, together with Harry Golden and a few others, to speak at a Memorial Service in New York City shortly after Sandburg died. We all spoke briefly; I told a few personal anecdotes, including the one about Carl's elephant memory regarding reviews of his books—the bad ones, that is. When it came time for Tallulah to speak, she rose, looked around and said, "I can't compete with these men and their memories. I'm going to sing." And she sang a sweet, touching song for Sandburg. And while Bankhead was never known for her dulcet tones, it was a moving tribute. It was a young girl expressing her love in a very personal and special way, and she was *the* showman in the crowd. We had a few drinks before and after the services, and I cherish my brief encounter with this rare woman. She was as special in her way as Sandburg was in his. Both are treasures forever lost and irreplaceable.

Harry Golden, who was a friend and neighbor of Sandburg, had written an authorized biography of Sandburg in 1961 which was published at World. It was one of the editorial experiences I relished with special feeling, since I was involved with two friends on a mutually pleasurable enterprise. I had expected all sorts of temperamental situations to arise during the writing and publishing of the book. Not a harsh word, not a problem, ever. When it was published, I went to Chicago with Golden and Sandburg, where Carl Kroch gave the book a magnificent sendoff in his great store, and Kroch threw a fine old-fashioned Chicago party at his club. Sandburg and Golden signed books by the hundreds. They both looked like a couple of old-time hoofers, telling jokes, shaking hands, laughing, and surreptitiously sipping Old Grand-Dad as they worked over the stacks of books.

Confessional

In 1941 I wrote a number of poems which appeared in a *Chicago Tribune* column. They were signed Charles Yu—my Chinese (T'ang) period. My Black Archer Press (talk about vanity publishing!) published the stuff in a volume entitled *Poems of a Chinese Student*. (Norman Forgue's Black Cat Press printed the book.) It was great fun. Once, a woman's literary club called "my publisher" to invite me to speak to them. I appeared, and as I sat on the platform I could see all the eyes surveying the floor, looking for *Charles Yu*. "He doesn't look Chinese," I could imagine them saying. I got up, discovered that my speech was in another suit, stammered, confessed my shameful intrigue, recited two wretched poems, and left. Here's one of the poems from the book—a collection purporting to be written by a Chinese student attending the University of Chicago:

ART EXHIBIT

My co-education friend
Miss Jones
Has kindly taken me to visit
The great annual display
Of paintings by the artists
Of this great City.

As we walk through the yellow dusk
Of the exhibition rooms
Miss Jones explains
The Significance of each work . . .

In the air
There is a great twittering
Of artistic admiration . . .

And I ask my humble eyes
Why among these hundreds of pictures
There is not one to compare
With a horse-painting
By Han Kan . . .

Considering everything, it is not surprising that I never became a poet. In fact, I stopped writing poetry when the above-mentioned book was published.

Magic—Black and White

My interest in stage magic began when I first saw Houdini perform in a Chicago theatre—from the first row! I built a good library on stage magic and I could saw a woman in half (theoretically); then my interest switched to the occult: demonology and witchcraft, and the like. The collection took on a somber tone. I had the Montague Summers books published by John Rodker, and many others. I collected out-of-print books on sorcery, possession, the black mass, etc. And then I moved into other realms: Ouspensky, Gurdjieff, Krishnamurti, Besant, Blavatsky. The latter fascinated me and I tried hard to read and understand her *Isis Unveiled* and *The Secret Doctrine*. Her name delighted me—Helena Petrovna Blavatsky—what a mouthful! And what a personality. She was Russian-born (1831–1891); she influenced William Butler Yeats, Thomas Edison, General Abner Doubleday, Piet Mondrian, and thousands of others. She maintained that she was a virgin despite having a husband and numerous male friends. She founded the Theosophical Society in 1875. After having read a dozen or more books on the subject, by Colonel Henry S. Olcott and others, I still am not sure what "theosophy" means—and therein lies its enchantment for me. Jacob Boehme invented the word, but I doubt that I'll ever get time to pursue *his* works.

When I "founded" my Black Archer Press in Chicago, I published a handsome English-language edition of Huysman's *La Bas*, with a frontispiece etching by John Groth. It was John's first book illustration for *any* book—and it's the one illustration he regrets. (He's illustrated many books, including Hemingway's *Men Without Women, War and Peace,* O. Henry's stories, and several works for the Limited Editions Club.) I don't own a copy of my *La Bas,* and if any reader of this happens to own one that he wants to sell me, please write. The frontispiece shows a baby being disembowelled by Gilles de Rais. Groth, who likes to do bullfight and prizefight pictures, was squeamish about this assignment.

I can't account for my interest in occult matters, since I've belonged to no group and attended only a few lectures. (I detest occult meetings.) One vivid recollection is seeing and hearing Manley Hall, a lecturer who must have been inspired stylistically, as a speaker, by Ouspensky. At any rate, as a carry-over of this early interest, I bought and later published (for Putnam's) a number of works dealing with occult and related subjects. Some, such as the von Daniken books, Eileen Garrett's autobiography, a book by Sybil Leek, several by Susy Smith, Carroll Righter, and others, brought us good-to-substantial profits. (I even published Dunninger's *What's on Your Mind?* while at World. He was one of the most skillful performers I've ever known.)

In February of 1975 I had lunch with Sybil Leek, England's most famous witch. We celebrated the publication of her book, *Driving Out the Devils,* and had some glorious devil-talk. She actually read my mind. I told her I had an idea for a book and a certain word would identify it. She stared at me for a second, then called out the word. God's truth! Then she inscribed my copy of the book in purple ink; a treasure. Why do I get a charge (the jollies) out of this sort of magic? Perhaps there is a warlock lurking in our family background, named *Torgownik the Great?*

One of the hazards of dealing in books on magic is the clientele. Most collectors of such books are honest, friendly, amusing, garrulous—some are suspect. One afternoon a well-dressed—almost too well-dressed—man came into my bookshop and asked to see my books on stage magic, sleight of hand, etc. I opened one of my glass cases where some forty books and pamphlets (a few were pretty rare) were housed. He proceeded to examine them. The phone rang in the back of the shop, and during the time it took me to answer the phone, make a brief reply, and return to my customer, he had left. Yes, you guessed it. He had taken with him about a dozen books and pamphlets. His pace must have been equal to lightning; there was no sign of him in the street.

Obviously my would-be customer was a master of legerdemain on several levels: sleight of hand and invisibility.

World Publishing Co.

In 1942, after several moves of my bookshop—the latest to Chicago's "Loop"—I got out of the retail book business. The struggle to meet expenses became a drag. I was offered a job by Ben D. Zevin of the World Publishing Company in Cleveland. We had met on several occasions. I was to become editor of World's Tower and Forum books (low-priced reprint editions bound in hard covers). I left Chicago for good. The prospects intrigued me and, indeed, I found the job an exhilarating one. I was now relieved of the problem of the overhead of a small business; I could expect a paycheck regularly, and I'd be doing what seemed pretty natural to me. Also, I'd be going to New York City each month to secure reprint rights. A heady prospect.

I was exhausted and the change seemed to me providential. I recently checked some old records and discovered that I had been earning about sixty dollars net a week out of my business. This was in 1942. How we managed to exist I'll never understand. And that income covered the cost of rent, food, clothing, medical bills, and the maintenance of an automobile!

When I left Chicago to join World in Cleveland, I managed to pay up most of my bills; only a few personal debts (loans from two relatives) followed me, and I paid those off within two years. I was never again in debt, except for certain long-term obligations incurred through buying rare books. (Most rare-book dealers were obliging about giving me payment-plan arrangements when I was moving into the deep end of the bibliophilic pond.)

Most young editors today are not familiar with the Tower Books we published at World in the forties. Yet many millions of them were sold. They were cloth-bound, jacketed books, library size, and retailed at forty-nine cents. Later, the price went up to fifty-nine cents. I dare say that *most* of the titles we published are to be found today in paperback editions and still going strong. Some of the authors I secured for Tower Books were Carter Dickson, James M. Cain, Dashiell Hammett, Ellery Queen, Eric Ambler, Raymond Chandler, Agatha Christie, Erle Stanley Gardner, Edna Ferber, John O'Hara, James T. Farrell, Mignon Eberhart, Leslie Charteris, Dorothy Sayers, W. Somerset Maugham, Georges Simenon, and Frances Parkinson Keyes. I would make monthly trips to New York to negotiate for reprint rights. We issued some fifteen titles each month.

One of my favorite sources for books was Knopf, where Joseph Lesser proved an enduring and valuable friend and guide—he taught me much about the "arithmetic" of book publishing. We often lunched together until his retirement to Florida in 1973. Joe Lesser was a man totally without guile; he either answered a blunt question in an open, straight fashion, or he'd ignore it as being confidential information. I believe Alfred Knopf and his wife Blanche depended heavily on his counseling and friendship.

Included among my early activities as reprint editor for World in Cleveland was the preparation of anthologies. As an ex-antiquarian bookseller, my knowledge of books was fairly broad. I could assemble the contents of an anthology easily, from anywhere on any subject, between one weekend to two or three weeks. And that included the writing of the Introduction and Notes. I produced about a dozen of them; some were published under distinguished names. I also put together collections of works by such writers as James M. Cain, John O'Hara, and William McFee. In these, the authors wrote their own Introductions; of course. I also did a great deal of work in the American West category, an area that occupied me for quite some time. This interest stemmed from a gift to me, when I was in grammar school, of a stack of old (some quite rare) Western magazines and a set of Zane Grey's novels. I fell in love with the West and read widely in that field for some years. Later, while at World, I compiled several anthologies, one of which was published by Penguin.

Crime fiction was also a special enthusiasm of mine in that period at World. I read and contracted for reprint rights to hundreds of books by virtually all the leading police novel writers. I also worked in related fields, which included suspense, terror, ghosts, and of course the hard-boiled school of crime writers as well as

the British school. I secured for reprint many newcomers from
Lee Wright's *Inner Sanctum* list (Simon & Schuster) and I enjoyed
these in particular. I always called her—and I still think of Lee as
—our *"crime queen,"* although she works in other categories as well
today—at Random House. One of the most popular books from
S & S at that period was from a nonbook writer, Gypsy Rose Lee.
Her novel *The G-String Murders* sold many hundreds of thousands
of copies for us at World. Gypsy was a lovable woman in every
way.

I persuaded Frederic Dannay (half of the Ellery Queen team)
to prepare a special work for our Living Library on the subject of
crime fiction, which he did with great success. It was called *20th-
Century Detective Stories* and contained not only fourteen stories
never before published in book form in America, but also a reader's
guide to the 101 most important books of detective-crime short
stories. It is a valuable book for all crime-fiction students. Haycraft's *Murder for Pleasure* was my bible, of course.

During that period I had had an extensive private correspondence with Anthony Boucher, with whom I planned to collaborate
and publish a book listing and describing the hundred greatest
books of crime fiction of all time. We had mountains of notes and
recommendations; we had heated battles (calipers and scales were
employed!) to determine which books stayed and which went. In
the end, our book did not get published. Both of us were afraid to
lay our "reputations" on the line. The correspondence and lists are
somewhere in our "archives." Tragically, Boucher is no longer here
to continue the project.

At that time I set out to form a personal rare-book collection of
the "great crime fiction of all time." I saw Fred Dannay's collection
(now in Texas) and thought I might make a try at assembling
something along those lines. What a wild delusion! I was well into
the program when I saw that it was far too big an ocean to swim;
the prospect was formidable, not to mention expensive, and I gave
up after acquiring about 250 volumes. I swapped them off to a
bookseller for credit in another category—fine printing. What I
regretted most was parting with first editions that were inscribed—
books by Eric Ambler, Chandler, Hammett, Cain, "William Irish,"
Lillian de la Torre, Queen, and many others. They're now scattered
to the four winds.

If you're interested in knowing why I was defeated in my plans, here are some of the "unobtainables": *Poe's Tales,* 1845; Morrison's *Martin Hewitt, Investigator,* 1894; Grant Allen's *An African Millionaire,* 1897; Wilkie Collins' *The Queen of Hearts,* 1859; George R. Sims' *Dorcas Dane, Detective,* 1897; Robert Barr's *The Triumphs of Eugene Valmont,* 1906. And there were numerous others. I did manage to get a dozen important Conan Doyle items, including *The Adventures* and the *Memoirs,* etc., of Sherlock Holmes.

Apropos of Dashiell Hammett, master of the hard-boiled detective novel and a powerful force not only in American crime fiction but in American *fiction,* I find it odd that *The New York Times Book Review,* a few weeks before Christmas 1974, devoted its front page and three additional columns to Hammett's *The Continental Op,* published by Knopf at $7.95. The irony is that a comparable collection with the same title was first published in book form, in paper covers, in 1945, with an Introduction by Ellery Queen. In a season when hundreds of fine new books were not being reviewed "because of shortage of space," the *TBR* indulged itself in extravagant treatment of *a reprint* of Hammett's archival pieces. (Don't misunderstand; I'm a Hammett card-carrier).

In 1945, when the paperbacks were beginning to prove too competitive, World Publishing gave up the Tower and Forum books and I was sent to New York permanently, to start a trade-book division for World. *From scratch*—one book at a time. Ben Zevin felt the time had come.

Coming to New York to live was a turning point in my life. I thought about this move long and hard. The Big Apple. I considered the "format" of my future, weighed my innermost thoughts and desires, and came to the decision that I wanted, most of all, to have an involved, committed life, not a meaningless adventure. That it would be a mistake to try for power, bigness, status. (I've seen too many men with power-hunger develop psychic hernias.) I wanted none of New York's chic and the games played by the so-called in groups.

I wanted a decent life for my family; a chance to thrive and savor some of the great city's delights. But it was important that we adhere to basic principles. My son's education was a major consideration.

My work was, of course, the sustaining force, and my need was to transmit and share the excitement of my work with my family. My ambitions were defined. I wanted to be part of the world that produced books. My secret desire was to be associated, somehow, with the making of a few *important,* lasting books. I wanted to help authors realize their goals. I wanted to share in a few literary triumphs. And the leisure to enjoy life with my family. Also, I knew that my private passion—the collecting of books—would be fed amply by the rich sources available in Manhattan.

I also wanted the goodwill of my colleagues. I needed to succeed and knew that the task before me was more than a challenge: it was a ten-to-one-odds gamble against me. And this added zest to the move. Ben Zevin was putting into my hands the chance to build a living organism from the ground up. I knew—in the quiet dark nights when sleep wasn't possible—that I was on the proverbial spot. I decided that I was good enough, strong enough, equipped enough to make it. And I also decided that if I failed, it would be a glorious failure. Which is to say, not a stupid dud. The details, or a few of them, follow.

But what mattered most to me was *how* I was going to live, and I myself would decide that. My so-called destiny was going to be, at least partially, in my own hands. The interior explosion, the awakening, came suddenly. Krishnamurti somewhere speaks of "psychic explosion."

We found an apartment on Eighth Street, between Fifth and Sixth avenues, directly across from the old Whitney Museum. We were smack in the heart of the Village! We had *four* marble fireplaces, a sloping living-room floor—and mice. We had fun, and many wonderful parties were held there. A woman with an extravagant mink coat lived above us; she was a dipsomaniac with a longshoreman's vocabulary that penetrated walls. One morning, I found a partially nude young woman lying in front of our door. I stepped over her and went to work, mentioning the matter to a policeman on the beat.

We lived around the corner from the Richard Wrights and baby-sat for their little Julie several times. Dick Wright, whom I knew in Chicago, was unhappy, felt persecuted, discriminated against—with ample reason—and was making plans to leave America for Paris. I had the pleasure of publishing two original books of his at World, although earlier, when we were in reprint publishing in

Cleveland, I had published his *Uncle Tom's Children* and *Black Boy*, both of which brought him a wider audience since they became available in the Woolworth, Kresge, and other chain stores around the country. The two books we issued at World, as originals of course, after Wright went to Paris to live, were *Eight Men*—a collection of stories that I edited—and *The Black Curtain*. Everyone who met Dick loved him on sight. We often had him to our house for parties or meals, and of course his charming wife Ellen. I remember at one evening's gathering, Calder Willingham was visiting with us; we had just reissued his first book, *End as a Man*. This young, flaming-haired southern "genius" was wildly comic. He turned to Wright at one point and said, "Tell me, Mr. Wright, is it true that all Nigras have a tibia that is two inches longer than a white man's?" Wright exploded angrily after a double-take, then saw that Calder was exercising a bit of his "southern" diabolic humor and he proceeded to laugh. I was never sure how Dick really felt about that question. He may even have done some research on the matter later.

I saw Wright in Paris, for lunch at the Mediterranée, about four months before he died. He seemed ill at ease and took a variety of pills from little bottles all during the meal. Then suddenly he burst out into a heavy sweat, stood up, and said he had to go home. I asked him if he was all right and could I do anything for him. He said no, and left. I watched him hurry home. He obviously had serious medical problems. I never saw him again. A great artist, a man with the juices of life always flowing, he has not been replaced in American literature.

———

Getting back to World Publishing and our trade department: I believe the first book I bought for our list was Basler's edition of *Abraham Lincoln's Writings and Speeches*, with an Introduction by Carl Sandburg. Ralph Newman, an old friend from Chicago, acted as the agent. I went to Chicago, carried the manuscript back to New York, and we had a very handsome volume designed; we got Joe Blumenthal for the job. Abe Lerner, our production head, felt that the book was too important to trust to a lesser typographer. The end result was a joy, and I'm proud to have initiated our trade program with that fine book.

I was asked to come to Chicago on publication date to join the

Civil War Round Table group there for some Lincoln and Civil War talk and to toast Roy Basler. This I was glad to do, although I was not a true member, having had less than casual interest in the minutiae of the War Between the States. When I got up to speak, I made one of my more notable public faux pas: I pronounced the historic place where Lee surrendered to Grant in 1865 as Ap*POM*attox (accenting the second syllable). All my life I had *seen* but never pronounced the name; now that I was called upon to speak it I realized how goofy my pronunciation was; I heard some chuckles among the audience. I repronounced the name correctly, but too late; I was found out.

Ralph Newman, by the way, is the man who appraised President Nixon's private papers and got himself a bit of newspaper space as a result. Years later, in 1974, Ralph brought me the hitherto unpublished, generally unknown autobiography of Mrs. Ulysses S. Grant, which we recently published (1975) at Putnam's, with Bruce Catton's Introduction and John Y. Simon's Notes. In her autobiography Julia Dent Grant denies that Grant ever drank.

We employed Carl Van Doren's services at World as general editor of a new reprint series initiated by Ben Zevin, The Living Library. Bennett Cerf had some hot words with Zevin, protesting that we were competing unfairly with his Modern Library, which was, of course, nonsense. Van Doren was a lovable man: a scholar; a wit; a fine, disciplined writer and teacher. There was a nobility in both the man's face and character—and no affectation. I recall one party we held on Eighth Street. There was a large assortment of well-known writers present, including, among others, Fred Dannay, Anthony Boucher, Richard Wright, James T. Farrell, and some mystery and S-F writers from England. We had a woman helping out and she was in the kitchen, working away. I saw Van Doren leave the party, go into the kitchen, sit on a stool, and start a lively conversation with the maid. He was with her for a good half hour, asking about her life, her views, and so forth. He cared about people. His biography of Benjamin Franklin is still the best.

Which brings to mind the fact that in 1952 we published at World a well-edited, 608-page, one-volume edition of *Grant's Memoirs*. Of historic interest: the retail price was six dollars—and that allowed for a wholesome profit! The binding was "library buckram"; there were headbands and the top was stained. It was a loving and scholarly job for which we were all grateful to E. B. (Pete) Long, of Lombard, Illinois. Exactly one year following publication, we were astonished to find a sixteen-page review of the book in *The New Yorker,* by no less a critic than Edmund Wilson. We were out of stock at the moment. Luckily, the author was not around to question us. I don't have Wilson's review at hand but I remember, with some dismay, that it opened with the announcement that our book had some typographical errors. (He might have reserved that information for the end of his review, wouldn't you say?)

Another book I sponsored and put through (with Abe Lerner's skilled guidance) was an edition of *The Illustrations from the Works of Andreas Vesalius,* which we published in 1950. I was very lucky in getting two top-notch scholars for the translation—Drs. J. B. de C. M. Saunders and Charles D. O'Malley. This great Renaissance landmark in science and art, with the excellent text and annotations, is one of my proudest accomplishments as an editor. And it was beautifully designed and printed. The book was successful in every way and was reprinted numerous times.

Perhaps the boldest attempt I ever made at World, to produce a monumental typographical work, was the facsimile reproduction of the *Kelmscott Chaucer.* This book, which I had first examined at the Chicago Art Institute library as a boy, haunted me for years; I was determined to own a copy one day. I hardly expected to be involved in *publishing* a facsimile of it, but that's exactly what I eventually did.

Here's the story in brief. One day, in one of the most difficult personal periods of my life, when I was witnessing my first wife's most desperate hours of depression, a rare-book catalog reached my desk at World. It was from Philip C. Duschnes. I leafed through it, found an offering of a *Kelmscott Chaucer* in the white pigskin Doves Binding, one of the most beautiful books in the world. Its price was $1,650. It struck me as hopelessly expensive (I was drowning in medical bills at the time) but an instinct drove me. I left my office, took a cab to the Duschnes' shop and asked to see the book. After two minutes, I said to Philip: "I can't tell you when I'll pay for this, but I *want* it." He replied, "Take it, Bill; pay when you can." I put the folio volume under my arm, unwrapped, and left. Back at my office I fondled the pages, caressed the lovely white blind-stamped binding. The book brought me both joy and peace. A needed comfort.

The *Kelmscott Chaucer* was printed at William Morris' Press by Emery ·Walker in 1896. There were eighty-seven woodcuts by Edward Burne-Jones throughout. Cobden-Sanderson's Doves Press bound my copy of the book.

Later, when I proposed the facsimile edition to Ben Zevin, he agreed enthusiastically. We even reproduced the Doves' embossed design on our covers. John T. Winterich wrote an Introduction for our edition. World published the book in 1958. It went through four printings and was a most profitable venture.

I recently saw a copy of the original book in a dealer's catalog. It was in the blind-stamped Doves' white pigskin binding. The price was $16,000. My copy, of course, was in Texas, with the rest of my collection of press books and books about books.

When Philip Duschnes died, I felt his loss deeply. We had been friends for over twenty years. His wife Fanny asked me to speak at the funeral services, and I did. I related the foregoing story of buying the *Chaucer* and how the details of payment were of no interest to him. Philip Duschnes provided me with many of my book treasures, but the manner in which I acquired the *Chaucer* from him—just a bare few words were exchanged—was a deeply felt and remembered experience.

As for having allowed myself to part with the book, and its great appreciation in value—that's another matter, with an obvious moral attached.

As a result of a long and heavy preoccupation with scissors-and-paste books, I developed an allergy: I couldn't stand the sight of anthologies. I looked on them as almost nonbooks. I guess I felt that anyone could assemble their contents with little effort, on short notice. Anthologies belong to the cookbook category. I would decline any anthology that came my way.

But one day, some time after Maxwell Perkins spoke to me about an imminent revival of F. Scott Fitzgerald, I approached Alfred Kazin about putting together a Fitzgerald anthology, a book of critical appreciations. Kazin liked the idea and produced a fine book for us, *F. Scott Fitzgerald: The Man and His Work*. We published it in 1951 and it was well received. This is an anthology I'm proud to have initiated.

Another first-rate anthology that we published at World was

the late John Crowe Ransom's *The Kenyon Critics*. I was long a fan of Ransom and had a number of first editions of his early books, including his rare first work, *Poems About God*. When Ben Zevin called me one day to ask how I felt about publishing a collection of material from the *Kenyon Review*, I jumped at the chance. Although I never got to meet Ransom, we had a lively correspondence. Interestingly, the last editor of the *Kenyon Review* was George Lanning, my secretary-assistant at World for several years in New York. (I later published his first novel, *This Happy Rural Seat*.) It gave me great pride when he was appointed editor of the *Kenyon Review*, and conversely, when George phoned one day several years later to tell me the magazine was being discontinued, I was furious that so excellent a publication had to die. It was one of the best "little magazines" in the country. Ransom founded it in 1939 and edited it for thirty years. After almost twenty-five years, the Kazin and Ransom books still look good, and I cherish my personally inscribed copies of both.

We published other serious critical collections at World. In most cases they were modest projects but they lost us no money and brought our name to the attention of writers, the serious book buyers, and the libraries. Harvey Breit comes to mind at the moment and I must record what pleasure it was in the mid-fifties to publish his book, *The Writer Observed*. His essays on Eliot, Faulkner, Hemingway, Dylan Thomas, and others were light but perceptive— far above the journalism standard of a newspaper. I believe that book went into a few printings. In that same period I got Louis Kronenberger to compile a book of critical essays on G. B. Shaw. I remember nothing about that book's sale, but I know that Kronenberger was unconscionably late getting the manuscript together.

Another anthology we published at World was *The Antioch Review Anthology*, edited by Paul Bixler; he had been head librarian at Antioch College. The book, published in 1953, is out of print, and that's a pity. It contains poetry, fiction, essays, and reviews from the *Antioch Review*, one of America's best quarterlies— 470 pages of material worth anyone's time. Stanley Edgar Hyman, Ralph Ellison, and James T. Farrell were among its many contributors.

Speaking of Stanley Edgar Hyman, in 1963 we published at World a first-class book of his entitled *The Promised End*. We found the author and his book irresistible. He wrote a fine book on

Nathanael West; also a murderous attack on Alfred Kazin with which I disagreed completely.

In his book which we published were excellent studies of Thoreau, Melville, and Steinbeck, and a particularly perceptive piece, "Negro Literature and Folk Tradition." It is books such as Hyman's that give a publisher cause for the "inner smile" of content.

William (Bill) Cole is probably the foremost poetry anthologist in the world and he became a World "property" very early in our trade publishing history. We published several of his many collections of poetry for children, including the handsome *The Birds and Beasts Were There*. I believe they're still in print. Bill's taste in poetry is catholic and impeccable. He's an institution in the book industry and has written countless thousands of words about the mores of the industry. One day I suspect he'll produce the ultimate, Boswellian history of American book publishing; there are few mysteries left for him in our world. Bill Cole is among the best-liked members of the fraternity, and I've considered his friendship one of the bonuses of being a part of the New York scene.

Theodore Dreiser

I spoke with him twice—long distance from New York to his California home. We were working on a new edition of his *An American Tragedy* for World's Living Library. He was polite and cooperative on the phone, and very pleased that we were getting his novel back into print. At that time almost all of his books were out of print.

Later, in 1950, I met his widow Helen—he had died shortly after we published our edition of his novel in 1945—and we gave her a contract for her own book, *My Life with Dreiser*. Helen Dreiser was a charming, totally feminine woman, radiating sexuality. We had many meetings, visits, walks, and luncheons during the processing of her book. Alas, many of the stories she told me about Dreiser she would not allow me to include in her biography of her husband. Some were horrendous, especially those about his women. Helen indicated that he seemed to need three or four women a day, and that his sex life was a revolving door. He was also a man addicted to violent rages. None of this was disclosed in her loving tribute to the man, although much of her published story can be called intimate.

A year or so after we published her book, she had a stroke and went to live with her sister, who had a farm in Oregon. Helen had another stroke and was finally totally incapacitated.

One day I flew out to Oregon to see Helen and her sister; I was making an effort to bring back into print all of Dreiser's out-of-print books, and I brought with me a blanket contract covering some dozen titles which World wanted to reprint. I was shocked to find Helen lying in a giant-sized crib; she was unable to speak except to utter a peculiar cackle, or laugh, from the side of her mouth. It was unnerving. She had put on a great amount of weight and looked like a giant kewpie doll in her crib. (And I had stupidly brought her a giant-size box of chocolates from New York.)

I spent the day at her sister's farmhouse with the family lawyer. When I left, I had with me a signed contract that would restore to print, under World's aegis, Dreiser's major works. My sense of pride in this achievement was great, since I was an admirer of the man's work and believed that millions of readers were being deprived of important literature. The contract produced many thousands of dollars for the heirs of Dreiser. It was, needless to say, a coup for World.

As I look back on those days when I was seeing Dreiser's widow and reading her warm, loving tribute, I realize that I had been remiss as an editor in failing to get from her more details of their life together. The intimate elements that she did not want made public I left out, of course. There was much that she didn't want to disclose; nor should I—except I can't resist relating one incident of how Dreiser came at her with a straight razor one morning in a towering rage. They had just made love, after which he jumped out of bed and proceeded to get dressed. While he was shaving, Helen began to accuse him of going off to see another woman. It was then that he tried—but fortunately failed—to slash her with the razor. She indicated his total animalistic behavior in bed, his insatiable hunger for *woman.*

I'm told that Dreiser was a difficult man socially. I know that Saxe Commins, his editor, found him immovable in the matter of grammar or syntax. I still regret not having met him, not being able to shake his hand and tell him how much his books had meant to me in my young manhood, books such as *The Genius, Sister Carrie, An American Tragedy,* the *Cowperwood* series.

―――――――――

Dorothy Parker: A Footnote

I pursued her for a year; she was a bit of mercury that I was unable to pick up. We had drinks frequently, one very nice lunch, and a private dinner in my Warwick Hotel suite with her French poodle in attendance.

Her stories and poems I considered pure gold, and told her so in person and in a book review I wrote of her *Viking Portable Reader* (1944). I made it clear to her that I thought her short story "Big Blonde" put her in the Short Story Hall of Fame. She smiled. She was witty, gentle, brooding (her beloved husband was at war), self-deprecating, and honest. Once when she was asked why she wrote, she replied, "Need of money, dear." And on the subject of her childhood she said, "All those writers who write about their childhood! Gentle God, if I wrote about mine you wouldn't sit in the same room with me." (Please read Marion Capron's interview in *Writers at Work.*)

One afternoon when we met, I exclaimed, "Did you see that marvelous full-page piece X wrote about you?" Her eyes filled with tears. "Yes, I saw it. And X is a shit." Dorothy Parker cried easily in the final year that I knew her.

She was cynical about Hollywood. The Utrillo on her wall was an unboasted-about "trophy" exemplifying the loot one got out of Hollywood, which she hated.

One brief, characteristic exchange comes to mind. We were talking about women poets, and I asked her what she thought of Millay. "Edna Saint Vincent Millay writes, not from here," she said, pointing to her head, "not from here," pointing to her heart, "but from here," pointing to her crotch.

Dorothy Parker was a big-hearted, small-sized woman with some wonderful attributes, lovable qualities—and courage. But she was also, as I said, mercurial. The book she promised to write for me (a project I had proposed) never materialized. She would often point to her typewriter and say, "See that sheet of paper in the machine? That's for your book." But I wasn't permitted to see a word. I don't believe she intended writing the book, but she would have been embarrassed to tell me so bluntly. She was capable of that sort of kindness.

There isn't anyone writing today with Dorothy Parker's character, personality, talent. The last time I saw her was when I took her to the door of the lobby of the Warwick after she'd been visiting me. Dorothy and her poodle. It was cold and pouring heavily. She had no coat or umbrella, and I begged her to let me take her home in a cab. She said no, she wanted, needed, to walk. I saw her and her dog walk off into the night in the cold rain, and I found myself getting wet around the eyes. I should have insisted on seeing her home, but I know when I've been ordered to lay off.

Papa and the Baron

I never met Ernest Hemingway, although I've read almost everything he published and many of his letters. (And Roslyn, Ben Zevin, and I toasted him in absentia at Sloppy Joe's Bar in Key West.) But I did get to know him, once removed, through his brother, Leicester, whom Ernest called "Baron" for some reason known only to himself; Leicester didn't.

Shortly before Ernest died (he shot himself in 1961, making every newspaper headline in the world), I met Leicester at a party in John Groth's studio in New York. John had known the Hemingways for many years; he had illustrated (for World) *Men Without Women,* and Ernest Hemingway had written an introduction to John's book, *Studio Europe.* Leicester and I took to each other and we had lunch the following day. We discussed his plan to write his brother's biography. It was fairly certain that Ernest would not have approved the publication of such a book in his lifetime, although Leicester reports a conversation with his brother in which Ernest said, "Jeezus, Baron, someday I'd like to have somebody who really knew me write a book about me. Maybe you'll be the one."

Leicester certainly knew the many sides of his brother; it was only in the latter years—the Mary years—that they saw very little of each other. While it was Leicester who introduced Mary to Ernest (they had worked together on a Chicago newspaper and she had expressed great interest in meeting his famous brother), once she married Ernest, Leicester appeared to be persona non grata at the Hemingway *finca* in Cuba or Key West—at least so Leicester told me. But there was still some brotherly contact over the years. Leicester had enough contact and enough recollections of their childhood in Michigan and Illinois, of the young-manhood years together, of Ernest's life abroad and at war, of Ernest's life within his family in Illinois, of time spent together fishing, to help him in the writing of the biography. And Leicester's memory seemed faultless.

Leicester was a trencherman; I've never met a more hearty eater, a more table-happy man. He was friendly, noisily rich with goodwill. His style was not even remotely that of his brother's, but they had a few basic traits in common, one being a zest for adventure and "new worlds to conquer." They were physically similar: both were husky, thick-chested men addicted to giving friends bear hugs and bone-crushing handshakes. They were rugged, burly men, never too serious about themselves. My impressions of Ernest come chiefly from Leicester, although Harvey Breit, a close friend of Hemingway, told me much about the writer, confirming my impression of the man.

Leicester once possessed a large collection of letters from his brother; I read them with hypnotic interest. They were intimate, often wildly funny, autobiographical, sometimes angry (he was furious at his mother for her negative attitude toward his book *The Sun Also Rises*). But because of the strictures in Ernest's will, the letters could not be published. They will probably never be put into print, which is a pity. (I own a number of his letters, bought from collectors and dealers. One is to a writer who was planning to go to Spain to fight in the Lincoln Brigade. Ernest wrote him cheerfully to say that fighting the Fascists would prove to be a good experience and would provide him with rich material for stories or a novel; but that if he were killed [!] it was for a worthy cause.)

The book Leicester wrote, *My Brother, Ernest Hemingway*, was published in 1962. Leicester's wife Doris worked with him, as did many friends—as did I. The book was a success; it proved financially worthwhile for Leicester, what with a good trade sale, a full serialization in *Playboy* (Spectorsky bought it from me [for

$25,000], sight unseen, over the long-distance phone), and we got a good paperback reprint contract. Unfortunately, Leicester invested most of his earnings in "establishing a pacifist republic" on a minute piece of land near the West Indies. It was an "island" in name only, a tiny protuberance out of the waves which he had discovered but which was not sufficiently visible above the water level to achieve his dreamed-of reality—Hemingway's Island Republic. Leicester even had postage stamps engraved for his dream island; but the whole enterprise was a bust, costing Leicester months of labor, agony, a boat, and his savings. I must say I admired his courage and vision, but I was dubious from the start and told him so. He gave me one of his searching, but pitying, looks: I was an unimaginative square.

The book has proved, and should continue to be, useful to Hemingway's biographers. Ernest's portrait by his brother is candid, affectionate, fascinating. *The New York Times* reviewer called the book "kind and well written." I think it was more than that: it is a repository of valuable family data which no one else could have provided.

Hemingway's reputation, too much maligned in recent years, is due for a turnabout soon; he is still one of our national treasures and his influence on writers and writing is felt constantly. Fitzgerald, also his friend, went into a long slump, but recovered eventually as one can quickly tell by checking the number of his books that are in print today. Hemingway's short stories are among the greatest this country has ever produced, and several of his novels are landmark works, as is his *Death in the Afternoon*, the supreme work on bullfighting.

Getting back to Leicester, an unkind if witty reviewer once said of his first book, a novel, "This proves the importance of being Earnest." A cruel comment, but true. Leicester learned very early in life what it meant to be brother to "Papa" Hemingway.

Juvenilia

During my early years at World in New York, trying to build up a good children's book department (as well as an adult list), I doubled in brass and served as children's book editor. After a few years it was necessary to get a good, full-time editor, and Ben Zevin hired the late Velma Varner. I learned a good deal about what children read, what the librarians like and don't like, and I worked with a number of authors of children's books or "young adult books." At the same time, my interest developed in another way, and I started to collect rare and first editions of juvenile literature. In time, I had a fairly good collection.

The by-product of this interest was my book, *Bibliophile in the Nursery*, which was published in 1957. It is still in print in a library edition, I believe. I think it is still the only book of its kind. If you're interested in collecting in that area, you might take a look at the book.

Meanwhile, I can't resist quoting an excerpt from the book's Introduction, since I feel as strongly about the matter now as I did in 1957:

It has often occurred to me that too few children are seen in bookshops. Why is it that Mama seldom allows junior to accompany her when she goes a-hunting books? The child should be invited to visit bookshops, be allowed to browse among the shelves, and be given a real sense of welcome and freedom. It is in the atmosphere of the bookshop that the child can best sharpen its young bookish wits, pick up the language and unique vocabulary of bookmen. Being given a chance to rove fresh eyes over the endless, tantalizing juxtaposition of titles, getting the opportunity to handle books and make one's own purchases—these are important elements in one's education. If a child is allowed to visit museums and theatres, then why not bookshops? And among these I certainly underscore the antiquarian variety. Let the languid and detached bookseller who scorns the small fry's modest means beware. A child's pennies can foreshadow serious interests and significant purchases. The child develops hobbies with rapidity and fanaticism, and the hunger for books will best be fed in the atmosphere of the bookshop and through the ministrations of a sympathetic dealer. From comics, stamps, and TV an interest can become inflected bookward, overnight. The lineage of many a bibliophile begins with a child at a bookshop bargain bin, making *the* first, exciting purchase. (My first purchase, I recall, was a ten-cent copy of *Under Two Flags* by Ouida, at Powner's Antiquarian Bookshop in Chicago, at the age of twelve. As heady and unforgettable a romantic experience as any boy is likely to experience! Cigarette is still one of my favorite heroines.)

The children's classics of world literature remain popular (certainly in terms of sales) despite "popularization" by rewriting and, more perniciously, by abridgment. You know the process; it carves away reason, insight, and thought to leave the bare bones of action and plot. Abridgment turns each work it touches into a "chase." *Huckleberry Finn* becomes a kind of dragnet for a runaway slave; *Moby Dick*, the headlong pursuit of a whale; *Crime and Punishment*, the chase after a killer. If the abridger's shears close on Shakespeare, we are left with what one of Thurber's fey ladies once described as "the Macbeth murder mystery." The only abridgment we favor, frankly, is that of the abridger. Permit the child to do its own abridging by skipping any part found dull, but give the reader the chance to make the decision. The chances are the cetological passages in *Moby Dick* will prove fascinating; the chances are every word of Dickens and Scott and *Little Women* will be devoured. Book abridging is not new; and even Newbery practiced the ugly art; but the practice is on the increase and remains reprehensible. Art should not be capsulized for the sake of commerce or in the mistaken notion of easing the child's entry into the world of books.

I recall a letter to *The New York Times*, by Joseph H. Lederer, in which he speaks of Fielding's *Tom Jones* and "Maugham's heartless emasculation" of this novel. "He called it one of the world's ten greatest novels," said Lederer, "but you would never guess it from the insipid Fieldingless product: a sort of Classic Comics version, which amputated the author's style, leaving a convenient commonplace narrative." Ironically, Maugham also deleted the following passage from Fielding, in which the great English novelist said, "I intend to digress through the whole history as often as I see occasion, of which I am myself a better judge than any pitiful critic whatever; and here I must desire all those critics to mind their own business and not to intermeddle with affairs or works which no ways concern them."

Dr. Johnson commented to Boswell: "Sir, I would put a child into a library (where no unfit books are), and let him read at his choice. A child should not be discouraged from reading anything that he takes a liking to, from a notion that it is above his reach. If that be the case, the child will soon find it out and desist; if not, he of course gains the instruction which is so much the more likely to come from the inclination with which he takes up his study."

What the youngster misses in a popularization of a classic is precisely the qualities that made the work classic, those universal insights into human nature, the passages of thought and description that have moved generations of readers. It is these qualities that the world at large treasures. We must not deny the child the desires it needs to gratify by substituting TV and abridgments for the original works. TV on rare occasions will send the young viewer to the book, but it happens too infrequently. Let's not kid ourselves. We may ask, with A. B. Guthrie, Jr., "Does our developing generation have to hear sounds and see pictures in order to entertain illusions, with the consequence it loses out on the greatest illusions of all?" Extending Dr. Johnson's comments, let's fan the natural inquisitiveness of the young reader by exposing it to *all kinds* of books. Not the homogenized, sanitized, pretested, and seal-approved books. I become impatient with the "progressive educators" and scientific-reading dragomen with slide rules and calipers who want to protect the young reader. If a youngster finds escape, pleasure, adventure in certain teenage fiction—in mystery, science fiction, and adventure stories—don't try to shield him. Let's allow the child to do his own choosing, because in the end it will be proved that all reading is good. Be sure there are plenty of good books around the house, and the child will find them in good time, provided that the pleasure of reading isn't watered down by well-meaning, carefully counseling, and censorial parents. Let's keep the book intact. And let's forget about the "sin" of being a slow reader. I fail to see any virtue in the ability to zip through a printed page, unless it be the editorial columns of a newspaper.

Reading aloud to children in the home is one of the most important ways of reaching the child with books.

Let the child have his books, his own books, and plenty of them. The possessive spirit can be enkindled, and one of the first steps is to see that the child has its own bookcase or shelves. In the formative, impressionable years, expose the youngster to book gifts with frequency. The child is a natural collector. It will collect stamps, marbles, butterflies, and other things with a zeal which, if properly directed, will turn it into a book collector. Teach it to catalogue the books it acquires, and the merits of a clean copy as against a soiled one. The sense of possessiveness that develops will make a lifelong reader.

It's apparent that, numerically, women dominate the children's book departments in publishing houses today. I feel strongly about the need for more men in this area of publishing.

This is not to put down women's competence. By and large, I think women are sensitive and responsive to certain "junior" manuscripts, but there are books which perhaps only a man will be able to evaluate objectively and with a special market sense. As previously mentioned, I worked as a children's editor and developed certain types of books to which I believe I was more suited, more intensely attracted to, than a woman. This is, of course, arguable, but I must say that in this connection one author in particular comes to mind, and I wonder whether I wasn't more responsive than a woman might have been. I'm thinking of the late Edwin Tunis.

Tunis was among my favorite "junior book" authors at World. In 1952 I published his *Oars, Sail and Steam*—now a classic—and I look back with special feeling to the many hours Tunis and I, and sometimes his wife Lib, spent together. I think World published a total of seven of his books. They dealt with crafts and history and such matters, and he wrote and illustrated each. Ed Tunis had a million dollars' worth of talent—and human kindness to match. I hope his books are all still in print.

Making It with the Children

Some years ago I was invited to give a talk on children's books to a group of teachers and librarians. I had just published my *Bibliophile in the Nursery* and was getting a bit of attention as a *maven* in juvenile literature. I accepted the invitation.

When I arrived at the assembly hall, I discovered that two other speakers were also going to be on the program: Fred Melcher, then editor of *Publishers Weekly*, and Eleanor Roosevelt.

If I had had the courage I would have walked away from the scene. Competing with these two people was getting into the big time too quickly for my taste. However—

I was on first. My talk about the history and development of children's books must have been pretty dull. The applause was polite. Mrs. Roosevelt followed, and she enchanted everyone in the hall, including me. She simply *talked* to the audience about her children and grandchildren, telling how, by giving them books as earned presents and reading to them, she had instilled a love of books in her family. She was memorable; I could have kissed her for her warmth and wisdom.

Fred Melcher got up, and I must say he was smart. He realized there was nothing he could say. So he admitted as much and then proposed that they join him in a few songs! And believe it or not, he started to sing children's songs, and the audience, and we on the platform, joined in. Melcher was a rare bird, a fanatic about reading and children's books and bookselling and free speech and everything that made sense in our profession. But he was also a shrewd showman. The memory of that morning, with all those librarians and teachers watching us and responding, taught me something about the life force of Fred Melcher.

Up in Smoke

We published hundreds of good trade and children's books at World; some of our trade books reached the best-seller lists—there were three of our books on one TBR Best Seller List in one season. Many of them earned substantial profits. Some of the writers on our list were Ludwig Bemelmans, Brigid Brophy, Marchette Chute, Norman Corwin, Thomas Craven, Simone de Beauvoir, Theodore Dreiser, Ilya Ehrenburg, Clifton Fadiman, Howard Fast, Gerold Frank, Lucy Freeman, Michael Grant, Peter Green, Friedrich Heer, E. J. Hobsbawm, Stanley Edgar Hyman, MacKinlay Kantor, Charlton Laird, Lin Yutang, Arthur S. Link, Margaret Mead, Art Buchwald, Harry Golden, Peter S. Feibleman, Richard Mason, Ashley Montagu, Field Marshal Montgomery, George Jean Nathan, Frank O'Connor, Peter Quennell, Lawrence Clark Powell, Howard M. Sachar, Bruce Rogers, John Carter, Kate Simon, Sacheverell Sitwell, C. M. Bowra, Frank G. Slaughter, Christopher Sykes, Robert Traver, Edwin Tunis, Ninette de Valois, Victor W. von Hagen, Frances Winwar, Richard Wright, and many others.

The children's book division flourished, as did our fine paperback series, Meridian Books, which was founded by Arthur A. Cohen. (The graphics direction was handled by Elaine Lustig.)

World was over fifty years old; it was showing a healthy growth, with steady profits and an effervescence that indicated great things to come. Our trade and children's lists were respected; agents wooed us. We ran a tight ship, gave our editors their heads, and enjoyed building a publishing imprint. (Bruce Rogers designed our colophon.) I was proud of my informally run office; all doors were open most of the time and meetings were always informal. We were publishers!

What delighted me most was Ben Zevin's disregard for excessive paperwork. We were never restricted in acquisition. We published whatever we found suitable and convenient. We were not obliged to forecast profit and sales. (Try that on your conglomerate brain trust.)

Came *der tag*. The *Los Angeles Times* took over. Before the contracts were dry, New American Library influence began to affect the business and our morale. NAL wanted control of World's trade department. Their attempts at running a trade book business were elephantine, as were their appetites for personal power. "Executives" were hired who were ignorant about trade publishing. Their religion was "Market Survey." God-given bookman's *sechal* was missing. Charts and statistics guided them; forecasts extending five years into the future were prepared. (Though none of them knew what we would be publishing in the upcoming season.) None of their thinking had to do with bookmanship. They were market analysts with slide rules up their arses and a power glint in their eyes. Each had a big executive smile on his face. Life could be beautiful.

Their eagerness was for instant expansion, quick profits.

Result: outrageous decisions, preposterous foreign deals, behavior that defied all understanding. They began hiring and firing, and with a few exceptions the new regime didn't know—as the saying goes—which end of a book was up.

World was suddenly in the hands of megalomaniacs, financial katzenjammers, packagers, and wheeler-dealers. There was hardly a bookman in the crowd. One of the new top executives once boasted to me that he was having great success in terminating about half of the company's staff, and he considered this a singular and praiseworthy accomplishment. "It cuts the overhead," he explained.

With the *Times-Mirror* takeover the World trade department began to undergo immediate changes, thanks to the Olympians who were put in charge, none of whom knew anything about hardbound trade publishing. Flashy packaging and *co-publishing* became the name of this game.

One said to me, "Hard, soft—what's the difference; they're all books." When I pointed out that a "hard" book had an editor working with an author over a manuscript and that there were many complex elements in the making of an original book—as against buying reprint rights to an already published book—he scoffed and said I was inventing a mystique; that "books were books." The situation became sick; they hired and fired; they twisted and turned, trying to make a great showing.

The behavior of the heads of New American Library would provide a fascinating study. The principals walked out of the firm with millions of dollars, while veterans, faithful employees, were fired ignominiously. Eventually, after incredible losses involving millions of dollars, came the disposition of the company's fine printing and binding plants and other properties—and the company went up in smoke. The lists were peddled off, the Bibles and dictionaries were sold to Billy Collins of London. (I think it was one of his most triumphant business achievements, and no one was more suited to take over these works than Sir William.)

Soon World will become a pale footnote in publishing history. For me, and some fifteen hundred ex-employees of that fine old firm, it is a melancholy story suited to treatment by a novelist. I earnestly hope that Ben Zevin decides to tell the whole unvarnished story—as only he is qualified to do.

I had worked for World for over twenty-one years, and when the company was sold to the *Times-Mirror* complex (for reasons dealing with personal conflict and "power play" within the Zevin family), I resigned. I declined the contract offered me; it was, I felt, an ignominious one in many ways, although every other executive chose to sign up for "practical reasons." My reasons for leaving World are fairly well known in the trade. (Certain agents knew that I'd be leaving *before* I'd made the decision.)

When I handed my resignation to Ben Zevin, then chairman of the board, he reminded me that by quitting I would forfeit severance pay which, I recall, amounted to around $25,000. I could only get it if I stayed on, he said—until I was fired. The whole prospect of working with the new management and deferring to the new management was too loathsome to consider, so I left, relinquishing the severance money due me. I told Zevin, who urged me to reconsider, that I'd only be giving that money to a psychiatrist anyway if I stayed on at World, and that I was already losing sleep and getting uncomfortable.

When I left, the staff gave me a farewell party. Perhaps I had one Scotch too many because I was reported as saying, in my "fare-well address," that all my friends at World were urged to be careful, that they would be swimming among barracuda and their under-bellies were in hazard—something along those lines. I was proved bull's-eye right within a few years.

Walter Minton of Putnam's heard of my disenchantment and offered me a job. (I had resigned officially one day before I met with Minton.) Minton gave me the precise job I asked for—senior editor—and the salary I wanted. This was in the spring of 1964. He was fair all the way.

When I took over my new job I began to phone my World authors. Happily, some thirty authors chose to come along with me to Putnam's. I recall that I signed some twenty-five contracts within a two-months' period. Minton approved each and every contract. Art Buchwald, Simone de Beauvoir, Harry Golden, Ashley Montagu, and Lin Yutang were among those authors. New personal contracts for me and salary increases followed quickly at Putnam's and in recent years my income (including bonuses) has been among the highest in the industry among editors. In 1974 my income was over $76,000. (In 1942, when I started at World, my income was around $5,000.)

How often have I thanked my stars that Putnam's is not part of a conglomerate and that Walter Minton, head of the firm, believes in individuality and informality—and believes in people, rather than computers. Putnam's has prospered under the leadership of Minton. I've often been asked what it is like to work for him, and my answer is simple: He's a tough, brilliant publisher, a shrewd and able businessman. We often disagree, but while he has shown doubt or displeasure over some of the books I've brought in, not once in eleven years has he vetoed a book I wanted to publish. I don't want to boast, but during my tenure (twelve years) at Put-nam's, in no year did I lose money for the firm. That goes far toward a good relationship.

Until recently, I acted as editor-in-chief; but in February of 1974 I decided I would prefer to work exclusively on my own books. I wished to be less involved in company (corporate) busi-ness unrelated to my particular books and authors, and to spend less time in the office. (I love to read manuscripts at home.) It seems to be working out well. Having returned to my former title of senior editor, I find that while I'm working as hard as ever, there is a bit more equanimity in my professional life.

There's always that next book I'm eager to read and publish, and my "stable" is still a good-sized one.

2 *Journals: Nights and Days*
in the Life of . . .

NOTE: *Most of the following is drawn from diaries, notebooks, and a sort of journal I've kept irregularly. It's presented in no particular order. Forget chronology; inherent in each piece will be the time and place of the event, although the time is usually of no importance. All of it reflects some of the life and activity —private, public, and professional—of an editor-publisher-bibliophile. Some of it is highly personal and is eminently skippable, especially if you're interested only in the secrets of scaling the heights of literature. Some of it may even depress you. Hang in there anyhow, please.*

The Gorgeous Gemini

I had never known a genuine Gemini intimately. When I married one I had no notion of what I was getting into. A few days after my marriage I had lunch with Carroll Righter, the astrologer, whose books I was editing. When I told him that I had just gotten married he didn't ask who, but *"What sign?"* When I told him, he shuddered. "Bill, don't you know that Pisceans should never marry Geminis?" I stared at him in shock. "But Carroll, it's done. We're married; it can't be undone." He finally agreed that there were some exceptions whereby the two signs could live in harmony—but watch it! Later, as a Christmas present to my wife, I had Righter prepare her personal horoscope, and when it came, it proved to be an extraordinary, bull's-eye report, covering some confidential and intimate details known only to the two of us.

Anyway, when he finally met her (he gave us a gala 21 lunch as a wedding present) he fell hook, line, and sinker for her, and it was he who began referring to her as the Gorgeous Gemini (or sometimes, Gregarious Gemini).

I'm talking about Roslyn, of course, the woman (the twins) in my life; the irrepressible literary agent and my loving "bosom companion." When in action, she has the energies of three, and though her number of languages is limited, she seems to have the gift of many tongues. Hers is "method" language; she does it with a smile, a flash of her eyes, a wave of her hands, a nose-to-nose brush, and contact! I'm sure that in Outer Mongolia or Bulgaria she could communicate with the natives after thirty minutes on their terrain.

She'll take most dares, go anywhere at a moment's notice, do all the outrageous things which Geminians are famous for, such as returning purchases, knowing in advance that something *has to go back,* even though acceptable. She'll pick up a T-bone and gnaw it boldly, even in Lutèce; steal cookies while having tea with Paul Getty in his English mansion; hold and conclude a telephonic book auction while watching, through her office window, a luxury liner come sailing up the Hudson at sunset; outconnoisseur the vintners and call the vintage year for most wines; outcouture the couturiere; sit fixated at midnight before the telly as that oldie, *Wuthering Heights,* unrolls; read and appraise a 400-page manuscript in one afternoon; and find time for a long Bal à Versailles-bubble-bath soak with the latest *Cosmo* in her hands. Henry the Eighth would have liked her.

Roslyn and I met a few months after the death of my wife. We had never met before, strange though it seems, since I did know most of the literary agents. She was an associate of Horch Associates at the time. (She now owns the firm, called the Roslyn Targ Literary Agency.)

At that time, in early 1965, I was making the rounds of the agencies, beating the bushes in search of a "big, new novel." I had cooked up an International Fiction Award contest at Putnam's and was devoting a lot of my time to the project. Horch's was an office I had never visited and I felt obliged to make a call. The visit changed my life.

I found Roslyn warm, honey-blond, charming, intelligent. And more. She radiated a force, an electricity—exactly what I was in need of at that particular time (Sam Marx calls her "electrifying").

We talked books and publishing, and I quickly made a dinner date with her.

Our "trysting" place was the famous (now defunct) Jumble Shop in the Village, hangout for authors and publishers (Thomas Wolfe often ate there in his Village period). She asked me not to bother picking her up; she'd meet me there. She arrived in a cab and as I stood at the curb, opening the cab door, I realized she was in trouble—a zipper on her dress was not fully closed. I helped her out, fumblingly but gallantly, and escorted her into the restaurant.

The conversation and rapport precluded going to the theater— I had tickets for two one-act Pinter plays—and we found no need for "outside entertainment." She was enchanting, beautiful, radiant. We met often thereafter, rendezvoused at the Plaza Oak Room (my then-favorite dining room) and also at the Grand Ticino in the Village for pasta and scampi. (We are in love with its owner, Mary Adams.) Shortly after our paths crossed in London, Florence, Paris, Rome. Life was renewed for me. We were married a few months later. Russell, my son, came in from California to be my best man. It all happened about ten years ago.

Roslyn has given me back my youth, and I like to think my statistical age is belied by my energies and joy in living. We have a rather remarkable home life, and I've made, through her, new friends throughout the world. I was pleased to find that she had the friendship of publishers and authors everywhere, and that she was on a first-name basis with them. In Barcelona, in Milan, Lisbon, Rio, Istanbul, Athens, Paris, London, and Madrid there was a cordial welcome for her, and that happily now included me. Our travels together, visiting publishers (and there were some fairly wild adventures in these encounters), would make up a small volume. Roslyn opened up a large part of the world for me, and in particular, made me feel, know, and understand Paris—the city we both love with special ardor. I came to *know* Paris—through and with her—in the biblical sense!

The foregoing is a brief answer to those who ask, "How did you two meet, anyway?" And I record it out of immense pride. More "Roslyniana" later.

The Sins of the Fathers

Several years ago while in Rome, we visited with Erich Maria Remarque. It was in his penthouse apartment at the Hotel de la Ville, at the head of the Spanish Steps. A beautiful sunset was in the making and we were examining one of his latest acquisitions, a baroque end table. (He had been collecting these antiques compulsively for some years.) But I was interested in his new, about-to-be-completed novel. End tables bore me.

"If it isn't committed to a publisher," I said, "could I read your new manuscript for Putnam's? We'd be proud to consider your book if it's free."

He studied me for a moment, then replied, *"Never to Putnam's."*

The reply cooled me for a moment, puzzled me. "May I ask why not Putnam's?"

Long pause. Then, sitting back and looking at the ceiling, he answered: "Because your firm turned down my novel, *All Quiet on the Western Front.*"

"Is that really possible?" I asked, almost speechless.

"Not *possible*—true! In 1929, when *All Quiet* was already a great hit in Europe, it was offered to someone at Putnam's. They needed a best seller at that moment, as it so happened. But some idiot said he would not publish a book by a 'Hun.' "

Silence. Finally, I asked, "Are you going to visit the sins of the fathers on the sons? After all, none of us at Putnam's were around the firm in 1929."

"Sins of the fathers," he laughed. "Yes, I am." Then he added, "I'll never forget or forgive that affront, that particular rejection."

At which point, his wife entered the room and I began sipping my Campari and soda. The liqueur had suddenly turned more bitter.

I reported this to Walter Minton, and he confirmed the truth of the matter. Some day he may want to tell the whole story himself.

The Irish Can Be Thankful

Nobody really knows why the Irish produce so many first-rate writers. Dorothy Parker once said, "The English write much better than we do, and the Irish write better than anybody."

When you stop to think about that starry roster of names—which includes Swift, Sheridan, Dunsany, Oliver St. John Gogarty, Oscar Wilde, Synge, O'Casey, Beckett, Stephens, Frank O'Connor, Joyce, Lavin, George Moore, Elizabeth Bowen, Sean O'Faolain, Lady Gregory, Yeats, Shaw, Liam O'Flaherty, Brendan Behan, and so many others, one must, to coin a phrase, take pause.

Why are there so many Irish writers in the top-drawer, or genius level, of literature? What other bit of land on this earth so tiny (it's about the size of Maine) has contributed such literary riches to the world?

Why do the Irish seem the most blessed in the gift of gab area? And why are their pubs so inviting? I remember visiting The Bailey in Duke Street when I was in Dublin, a hangout for writers, drunks, and wits; it was Brendan Behan's favorite watering place as well as Gogarty's. It was in this pub that Gogarty uttered his famous improvisation on seeing a friend enter with a patch over one eye, "Drink to me with thine only eye." The Irish also produce some fine singers, due possibly to their well-lubricated larynxes!

The truth is, no one has a reasonable explanation; meanwhile, let's be thankful—and let the Irish be grateful. Take away their beautiful women and manly men, their capacity for boozing, their wit, their actors and singers and writers—take that all away and what have you got? Their image in world history would be a sorry one. Sons and daughters of Erin, be thankful.

One of the best American novels, written by a Minnesota Irishman, F. Scott Fitzgerald, is *The Great Gatsby*. Another American Irishman, James T. Farrell, wrote some of the best naturalistic fiction of the century, the *Studs Lonigan* trilogy. And then there's Eugene O'Neill.

Dublin Memoir

Frank O'Connor (pen name of Michael O'Donovan) was born in Cork in 1903. He was one of my favorite writers and my favorite Irishman. Handsome, charismatic, a fine raconteur, and man of goodwill, he was recognized universally as one of the modern masters of the short story. He revered the English sentence. His prose was limpid; his characters visual and out of life; his themes, the bitter-sweet realities. His sense of humor imbued his stories (as did Sean O'Casey's).

Each of O'Connor's works was honed and polished to a state of perfection. Even after a story was published, his instinct to continue editing and polishing persisted, and he would often pick up a pencil as he began to read one of his stories appearing in *The New Yorker*. He was also a splendid teacher. Tolstoy was his master.

I went to Ireland in the fall of 1965 to discuss a book project, his history of Irish literature, on which he had been working. It was to be based on his lectures at Trinity College in Dublin, and he had promised it to me for Putnam's. When I got to Dublin I found the city bleak, gray. The River Liffey looked leaden. But once I entered the O'Connor household and met his wife Harriet and their adorable daughter, the city brightened up for me quickly. Their home was filled with sunshine, jokes, laughter. I was given a capsule tour of the city, which included all the obvious Joyce and Yeats landmarks.

O'Connor had invited me, saying, "You bring along some Irish whiskey and I'll produce some fine young writers for you to meet."

A fair deal it was. I never expected the kind of welcome I got. We held a "press party" at the airport restaurant that evening. Mary Lavin also came (the two greatest living Irish storytellers at my table!). It was an effervescent group, among whom were a number of young poets and newspapermen. More than a few quarts of Irish whiskey were polished off. Wit and songs and good talk aplenty. Pictures were taken but, alas, I can't locate them now.

Frank died a few months later, on March 10, 1966. The book, *A Short History of Irish Literature—A Backward Look*, which we published in 1967, is already a classic. I've not been back to Dublin; but I remember—on the mini-tour they gave me—Mrs. O'Connor pointing to the plaque on the floor in St. Patrick's Cathedral marking Jonathan Swift's burial spot. I knelt down and placed my hand on the brass plate; it was a very special moment for me. Swift has been a lifelong hero of mine (among my nonconformist collection); there has never been his equal in literature or in public life. While some declared Swift a misanthrope, he was always concerned with man's welfare. His *A Modest Proposal* has inspired many a "proposal." As for his masterpiece, *Gulliver's Travels,* can you name a book to match it?

We had published at World O'Connor's book-length essay on Shakespeare, as well as his book on the short story, *The Lonely Voice.* I don't agree with him on Katherine Mansfield—he said that she lacked heart; I really can't accept that verdict on a writer whose every story is so dear to me. One bit of proof that O'Connor was one of the sharpest and most aware of students (as well as of practitioners) of the short story is his tribute to Sherwood Anderson's *Winesburg, Ohio.* O'Connor says, "It is from this remarkable little book that the modern American short story develops and the Americans have handled the short story so wonderfully that one can say it is a national art form." Read O'Connor's Introduction to his book *The Lonely Voice,* and get yourself an education in the art of writing a short story. Please.

Lesbos in Soho

Big pub-date orgy in New York's Soho: a publication party (June 24, 1974) for Kate Millett's second book, *Flying.* Kate inscribed a copy for Roslyn. It was a mob scene: writers, painters, actresses, TV performers, transvestites, the press, and continuous rock music. Immediately after the party, we got to see the first review. A horror. During the next few weeks other reviews began to appear; *they were coming at Kate with cleavers.* The reviews were murderous—Guignol. Anger, contempt, fury: a lynch-mob atmosphere seemed to be driving the book reviewers to the limits of their vituperative powers.

So when I sat down to read the book I was prepared to dislike it. Surprise. *Flying* is an important book; an honest, profoundly moving, illuminating, autobiographical document. It gives us the sense of what it is like to be a lesbian in the seventies, and the lines (I can't remember whose they are) "You must live through the time when everything hurts" kept coming to mind. Kate Millett is a thinking, passionate, compassionate, and totally honest woman. Her book will be recognized properly for what it is, though it may take another decade.

I now know what it must feel like when one is being stoned to death. I watched the fury and felt for Kate; I watched this gifted and worthy author suffer.

What a painful, public act the writing of an honest book can prove to be.

A Table for One, S'il Vous Plaît

Confession: I was telling a colleague in Paris that I must have some sort of perverse or selfish streak in me, not visible to friends. I admitted to taking a posh lunch all by myself—at Maxim's—and enjoying it hugely. I had heard that one of my books had just hit the center of the *Times* best-seller list. I was going to enjoy the "triumph" quietly, privately, yet extravagantly, with a bottle of champagne. Sans company or conversation. Alone at Maxim's.

My friend frowned and said, "There's nothing more *infra dig* than lunching alone *in such a place.*"

Of course he missed the point completely.

I *wanted* to be *alone,* to relish something very special in the life of an editor. I didn't want to share that "high" with anyone. Of course, if Roslyn or the author of the book were in Paris at the time, that would have been different. They would have joined me. But under the circumstances, I preferred a solo luncheon, unsullied by shop or other talk. There was no one in Paris at that time with whom I wanted to share my delight.

Oh yes, I wrote to the author and sent him the original Maxim's bill—as a "souvenir." I thought he might insist on picking up the check, but he didn't.

From the Journal: London/Frankfurt/Paris, September–October 1974

A visit with old publishing colleagues in London—Matthew Evans and Peter du Sautoy of Faber & Faber. Result: a contract for a biography of Nureyev for Putnam's. The book is by the London *Times* ballet editor, John Percival. A biography by a dance journalist–critic who knew the man, Nureyev; and his career appeals to me. This is the kind of project an editor enjoys taking on: a universally interesting subject by a top-notch professional.

And there was a bonus. A VIP invitation to Westminster Abbey for the unveiling/dedication of a memorial to W. H. Auden. Evans had a spare ticket for a stall in the Abbey for a ceremony I wouldn't have missed for the world. (I cancelled two dates to make it.)

It took place on the second of October 1974. I entered by the Great West Door in a downpour. The cathedral air was filled with what I can only think of as a *glut* of organ sounds. (I'm allergic to organ music.) The ceremony took place at four in the afternoon, and as I looked at my salmon-colored admission card, the "4 pm" kept reminding me of another poet who died not so serenely: Federico García Lorca, who was murdered by Falangists during the Spanish civil war—the Spanish poet whose *Lament for the Matador* ("At five in the afternoon . . .") is one of the treasures of poetic literature. Four in the afternoon—and Wystan was being paid the greatest tribute England can offer a poet.

Sitting in the stalls among some of the superstars of British literary aristocracy and listening to the graceful and moving tribute by Auden's friend, Stephen Spender, and hearing and watching Sir John Gielgud read ever so precisely, so effectively, the poems "New Year Letter" and "In Memory of W. B. Yeats," I realized anew how well the British deal with ceremonial affairs. The poet laureate, Sir John Betjeman, unveiled the Memorial Stone and placed a laurel wreath upon it.

The organ sounded and the great choir sang lustily, filling the Gothic air with Mozart and Bach. Pomp and ceremony; gold and red everywhere, and granite pillars soaring above us in the choir and transepts, while outdoors, sodden and gray, a soaking London. (Some seats were vacant because of the heavy rain.)

As the archdeacon of Westminster read from Ecclesiastes, I kept thinking of Auden, an unpretentious man (addicted to wine and stiff vodka martinis), a neighbor in Greenwich Village for many years. We often saw him shopping for vegetables and bread and cheese in our favorite Village markets. He was a big hulk of a man who once said of himself, in introducing Marianne Moore at a lecture, that he had "two big clumsy left feet . . ." My mind drifts back.

I'm reminded of a brief evening with Auden in New York some years back, with Harvey Breit, who also departed this life at too young an age. (I worked with Harvey on his first and only novel.) It was in a cozy bar in the Village and we were having a few drinks. I was trying to persuade Auden to write a small book of poetry—"Only sixty-four pages, Mr. Auden"—and how he howled at my presumption. It was to be about Abraham Lincoln. I had in mind a portrait-poem of the brooding, melancholy man viewing the world around him *today*. Auden declined the offer, but admitted that the idea had merit and suggested a few candidates for the job, one being his friend Stephen Spender. (Spender did succumb to my proposal and I drew up a contract which he signed. But, alas, later in London, having tea with him at the Savoy, he admitted defeat, saying he simply found the assignment beyond him. He said he had written some lines, but I never saw a word; so we cancelled the agreement.) I was perhaps too pushy with Auden, but I must say that Harvey Breit supported me in the matter.

I remember talking with Auden about Leonard Bernstein's "symphony," *The Age of Anxiety*, which the composer admitted had been inspired by Auden's poem. I asked Auden if he had a royalty share in the sale of the recording. He snorted and said, "Not one penny did I get out of it, nothing but a few *words* of credit on the record album." He seemed unhappy about the matter and the subject was dropped. Then, somehow, we got into the game of U and non-U (Nancy Mitford's book, *Noblesse Oblige*), which was then popular. I seem to remember that he found the use of the word "ill," instead of "sick," inoffensive, and he joked about it. I'm sorry to admit I rather broke up the mood of the visit when, as a book collector, I asked him if he would inscribe my copy of a small poetic pamphlet entitled *The Platonic Blow* (it was his raunchy valentine to the homosexual act of love), which bore his name as author. He delivered a one-word negative and the subject changed abruptly. He had already signed my first-edition copy of his first book, *Poems* (1930). Somehow, I managed to brush aside my gaffe; we had another beer. As you may now have gathered, book collectors are brazen. Likewise editors.

Auden's craggy face, his warmth, his aura of courtesy and humanity came back to me as I sat in the historic cathedral, a witness to the homage in words and music paid to this great poet. And I wondered how he would have responded to the solemnity, the Bach *Fantasia in G* performed in his honor, and the frequent references to the Holy Ghost.

And who will inherit Auden's mantle? That's a guessing game no one seems able to play with enthusiasm or conviction. The great ones are going fast. Old Sir John Betjeman, florid and heavy, moving slowly to the exit as the mighty organ soared, seemed to me not the man; surely Spender is the heir.

As I was leaving I commented to one of the scarlet-attired "ushers" on the elegance and comfort and strategic view of my particular seat. He chuckled and said, "Sir, you were sitting in the Queen's stall."

———

London. The old refrain. The familiar tramping grounds. And always the rain: twelve out of fourteen days it rained.

Nevertheless, the walking is good. Mayfair, Curzon Street, the Strand, Bedford Square. City of Rolls Royces and stately monuments, Georgian homes, Kensington Palace, and the British Museum with its Elgin marbles and Shakespeare's only known autographs; the queues; Chelsea; Big Ben; the rich Covent Garden smells; Soho, St. Paul's Cathedral, the mighty Thames, Westminster Abbey with its echoes of great coronations; the blood-reeking Tower; the Savoy Grill . . .

My twenty-fifth visit to London.

To the young editors who envy the seniors making this annual book-search—your time will come. When it does, make the most of it. But remember, in order to mine this terrain properly, conscientiously, you must give it *everything:* stamina and nerve and a controlled temper. Nimble footwork, and at the same time, good public relations and manners. There's little time for larking, for diversion, the Tate, the theatres, the National Gallery. In the two weeks I spent in London this trip, I had forty-one appointments, including several dinner evenings with friends in the trade. I received and screened thirty books, galleys, and manuscripts, and a dozen outline proposals. I found only two books for Putnam's from the lot!

To visit forty-one agents, publishers, editors, and authors within a two-week period in London calls for a regimen of disciplined energy. Granted, there's some elegant dining and wining along the way (followed by Alka-Seltzer). But it's muscle every step. And there's the matter of reading. Too little sleep. The hotel apartment is stuffed with galleys, proofs, manuscripts, books. They've got to be read, sorted out, carefully screened. Catalogs and lists must be checked; local newspapers watched for reviews. And there's the homework: correspondence, record-keeping, packing and shipping of materials to the home office or back to the senders.

Reading *on the spot* is the big job. Certain immediate commitments are required. One mines for gold, for the shock of recognition. One reads and reads until the eyes blear and the head swims. Reading for pleasure? Forget it. One reads against time, trying to judge for market and quality, for the force of language that rewards the reader, for talent that makes a special claim to distinction.

So, when the eyes glaze and the brain dozes, it's time for a stroll —providing London isn't excessively "dewy." Sundays are best. An hour or so in St. James's Park in West End, with its rich emerald pile carpet of grass; the swans, ducks, pelicans, and geese in and around its lake; the pigeons underfoot; the larger-than-life flowers blooming robustly in the rich black soil—and the welcoming benches. (Joyous reminder of other London walks in other times, including the tulip-rich embankment behind the Savoy.) A perfect interlude, especially if the great blue English sky is offering those golden bursts of bone-warming sun from time to time. I plan to sit a while and thaw out, but suddenly a noisy family descends on my bench. I find the children immensely unlikable and move off. I go to the gates of Buckingham Palace to check out the two picture-postcard soldiers guarding the premises. No change. Then I turn and nod to Her Majesty Queen Victoria, perched high before the gates. (Joke: "How was your bridal night, your Majesty?" Answer: "We were not amused.")

Then a slow walk back to Mayfair, to the Connaught, hoping to "do" another manuscript or two before bedtime. But an invitation to have supper with Michael Meller punctuates the day pleasantly, with wine and good slivovitz and lots of gossip about both sides of the Atlantic—and no one is a greater repository than Michael the Gee.

Monday: The British male has changed not at all in dress or manner. As I walk to my early-morning appointment, I start to count the number of proper Englishmen I pass, that is, those men, that breed of Englishman, still dressed in somber dark suits and starched collars, carrying toothpick-thin umbrellas, reminding me of the late Cyril Connolly's remark (in his *The Rock Pool*) made in another context: "The chill wind that blows from English publishers, with their dark suits and dark umbrellas, and their habit of beginning every sentence with "We are afraid . . ." As for the English *birds*—yes, they're still called birds despite the efforts of Germaine Greer—they are as sunny as ever in the miniest of miniskirts or their pre-Raphaelite maxis; a thousand light-years ahead of the men. Many are also wearing slacks and cowboy denims to work. Although one night, while standing in front of the Curzon movie house waiting to see Fellini's latest (the real show was on the street), I saw a procession of everything in the style lexicon from freak-out to cowpoke-chic to Burne-Jones and Klimt. I think the English women are far ahead of the Americans.

Of course it's not all sweat. Not all of it. Certain of the European publishing fraternity are rare birds, foxes, skilled hunters and traders; and it's often fun dealing and duelling with them in their offices, in the dining rooms and bars, or in their clubrooms and homes. (One of the great ones, the shrewdest, is Billy Collins.) Some of them are delightful raconteurs. One agent displays outrageously gorgeous waistcoats. And then there's another who never cleans his fingernails and seldom changes his shirt. Some are lovable, endearing. Some grubby. Some are peacocks and pretentious bores, or worse. And there's one particular British agent who will never win gold stars for truth-telling. One ends up drinking too much to deaden the ordeal and more Alka-Seltzer. It must be very rough on the American women editors coming over. The lone woman making the scene should be prepared to endure the solitary discomforts of the traveller, unless she can plan ahead for some good evenings with publishers, agents, and editors for social as well as business sessions. Although I believe there's no evil in going to the theatre alone if the alternative is being with someone who is tiresome.

We must face the fact that almost no one tells the total truth. I'm tipped off on a certain very "hot property." I'm slipped a set of proofs in confidence; the publisher has sworn me to secrecy for the present. Classified goods. I take the proofs back to the hotel. A visiting American publisher drops into my room for a drink and he spots the proofs on my desk. He says, "Want to take my advice, Bill? Don't waste your time on *that* one. I read it a week ago and it's for the birds—a loser." I blush, embarrassed to have been taken in.

But no harm. This is a business, essentially. The rug-peddling game. Show biz with Byzantine aspects to it.

I'm dined by a publisher at Claridge's; the place oozes haute cuisine, and my host is subtly probing for our "big upcoming book." He's trying to wheedle the essential information out of me. I tell him about it, of course.

Another publisher takes me to La Bussola for lasagna, my favorite pasta. We go through the same old waltz and I find myself not enjoying the good wine and food. Then I entertain an agent at Mirabelle's (a £20-affair, including the brandies) and I end up with a so-so first novel that will eventually sell 3,800 copies.

My favorite London hotel, year after year, is the Connaught on Carlos Place. It is small and personal. The ambience and service are perfection. (And that king-sized bathtub!) I use its dining room often, and every one of my guests feels complimented to be invited there for a meal. George Rainbird tells me it is his favorite, and "the best dining room in London." (Try the Scotch beef.) On sober second thought, I think New York's La Grenouille surpasses it. And no one makes better chicken potpie or scrod than New York's Algonquin. (But no one knows how to cook tripe properly.)

Everyone seems apprehensive in London (late September 1974) over the political and economic situations; everyone eagerly awaits the evening news. Considering our recent Watergate escapades, the Nixon debacle, etc., the British political drama seems tame, lacking in color. I'm bored with the talk. Perhaps I'm callous or ignorant, but I've got a *deja vu* feeling about these English crises. What really seems to matter is the grim high cost of everything. And Arabian oil vs. the world—and the fate of Israel. And the deterioration of New York City's morale and economy under Mayor Beame.

Sometimes a trip is simply for seeding purposes, for looking but not buying. Possibilities are noted. One hears of a book not yet completed; a year later it comes along, providing the agent remembers that you asked for it, and providing you remembered to remind him that you asked for it. Some agents forget. On occasion I've turned down a book in Europe in its gleam-in-the-eye stage, and bought it on the subsequent trip. One can't generalize about buying manuscripts. One must at times use sheer gut reaction rather than logic.

Never buy under pressure or in desperation. Better to return empty-handed than with a dozen cats and dogs. Remember, one major book is all you need to bring back to justify your trip. Rule of thumb: If you've spent around two thousand dollars on your trip and brought back one book that justifies a first printing of 25,000 copies, you have no problem. Chances are you'll bail out from subsidiary rights alone. But buying books that merit 4,000- to 6,000-copy first printings is very often, in America, the amateur's way. Don't get caught up in the numbers game.

Looking over the books I've contracted for over the years, I find that the percentage of foreign books in my personal stable is very small, less than 5 percent. So why do we bother about these expensive, time-consuming trips? Well, one also *sells* books abroad; there's the matter of placing rights on books where one has control. Sometimes a good book can be placed in the right hands, at the right time, on a quid pro quo basis. Scratch my back and I'll scratch yours.

The trips are worthwhile in another sense: one picks up information, gossip, sometimes vital news about authors who are unhappy and shifting, are becoming available, etc. And also, it is good simply to get away from one's desk and observe the customs and lifestyle in other parts of the world, watching the booksellers' and publishers' activities in London, Paris, elsewhere.

The Frankfurt Book Fair, which is part social, part business, part *drag*, will pay off. Charles Dwoskin, Putnam's editor-specialist in co-publications, always manages to secure the choicest art and gift books on each Frankfurt trip; as for the general run of trade books, the Fair is not the likeliest pond to fish in.

Meeting men and women, old friends, such as Ledig and Jane Rowohlt, Rudi Scherz, Fritz Molden, Albrecht Knaus, Willy Droemer, Robert Laffont, Jean Rosenthal, Rainer Heumann, Erich Linder, Nurcihan Kesim, Christian de Bartillat, Marie-Pierre and André Bay, Yves Berger, Alain Oulman, Pierre Combescot, Michael Meller, Lex and Mary Gans, Gerd Fleischer, Juan Grijalbo, Mary Kling, Nicolas Costa, Per Gedin, and many more European and American friends and those we entertain in America—these encounters add pleasure to the Frankfurt experience. One must not forget the *wurst* and lager orgies at the outdoor stands in the sun (when the sun appears), and the chanting of the Maoists.

A few good friends and behold! the sun is shining regardless of the natural elements. For instance, Frankfurt without Hazel Guild (correspondent for *Variety*) and her husband Rolf Stroth would be unthinkable. Whatever delight is to be found in that city, these two friends brought to us. Even walking the cobblestoned byways of the town under their guidance turned the "dewy" weather into something magical. They knew the precise beer *stub* where we could find a bit of nontourist pleasure; they knew the curious shops, the odd buildings to view. But friends aside, there is little to admire about the city—and this applies to most of its hotels. And the amenities. I think the rudest waitresses in the world are to be found in Frankfurt; but it may be that they simply detest Americans.

Paris—well, Paris is always Paris. Roslyn and I had the good luck to get the penthouse (Room 812) at the Pont Royale and its fifty-foot terrace gave us an unmatched panoramic view of the city that included *everything*, including Paris' Taj Mahal (Sacre Coeur), the Eiffel Tower, and the rooftops which should drive any painter mad. Even from the bathroom we got the view, and for giving you this tip (Room 812) I expect a bottle of Mirabelle from each reader having this experience on my recommendation. As for the Pont Royale service, there is a saint working there, a young Frenchman named Philippe Lamson; ask for him—he's back of the reception desk. Yes, he speaks English.

Was my 1974 trip a success? Staying away one month is not always advisable for a busy editor, and the pileup awaiting me back home is part of the price. But I think back on certain books I acquired for Putnam's and about others that are promised me, and I feel a few will prove out.

A memorable visit with John Collier (over a broiled turbot) at the Connaught dining room; recalling the quiet charm of the man, his reticence, his total honesty and warmth, his lively eyes, and I'm grateful that my work brings me in contact with some of the literary wunderkind of our time. (He sent me an inscribed copy of his *Paradise Lost,* which I found masterful.) I also had dinner with Joyce Elbert, who knows and tells more about women than anyone except Freud, and who is a most forthright interpreter—in fiction— of the sexual life of women.

Personal indulgence: I also bought fourteen first editions in London and Paris, eight of which are on Connolly's *Modern Movement* list. Also some Jean Genet titles that have eluded me for several years, and not forgetting a mint copy of the first edition of *Madame Bovary* in original wrappers.

Footnote: First-timers on a trip to the European market need some help, so here's one piece of advice you shouldn't overlook: get yourself a good, all-utility pocketknife, one of those nice Swiss jobs with corkscrew, bottle-cap opener, etc. You can't imagine how often a knife is essential in an editor's life: opening packages, cutting pages of books; opening envelopes, and the like. This may seem like a piece of banal advice, but think about it. And of course, don't forget the paper clips, rubber bands, and adhesive tape. The hotels aren't too generous with stationery, so take along a supply.

Joke: A publisher says, "I hear you're writing a book; what is it about?" Answer: "It's about a hundred thousand words."

―――――――

The Luncheon Circuit: Paris

Lunch with Ellen Wright, old friend and Simone de Beauvoir's agent, at our favorite restaurant, La Coupole. And who should walk in but Simone de Beauvoir and Jean-Paul Sartre. Simone has had a shoulder accident (hit-and-run thieves in Rome) but looks well in her turquoise blue turban. Sartre having serious eye problems. They are warm, and are seated two tables from us. Very pleasant encounter. Dinner same place the following night with Roslyn and Alfredo Machado in town from Rio. Alfredo, who must always travel deluxe, checked into a superchic apartment at L'Hotel, the decor and ambience of which I'm unable to describe. Parisian baroque? Perhaps. It's one of a kind.

Chez Auguste: This charming restaurant on rue de Tocqueville is a one-star rendezvous for Eugene Braun-Monk, with whom we had a great four-hour dinner. Paté, seafood, and pink champagne, horse-play and spirited book talk. A few interesting manuscript tips.

Lunch with Alex Grall, who heads up the publishing house of Fayard (old friend of Françoise Giroud, the French Minister of Women's Affairs) at Les Anges, another bestarred restaurant. (Roslyn had pheasant.) After lunch we cross the street to visit Grall's huge art-filled apartment (fifth-floor walkup), and he insists on giving me three French books, all first editions, by Cendrars, St. John Perse, and Genet. What a great dessert! Then off to Vuitton, where Roslyn wishes to buy a few Vuitton bijoux, "carry-ing objects" such as key rings, jewelry containers, etc. I loathe the place and the snobbish clerks and the initialled goods they sell at what I consider outrageous prices. I argue that Woolworth can match most of the merchandise at one-tenth the price. Roslyn puts me down as a dumb peasant. Which I may very well be. After all, Vuitton's stuff "wears like iron, lasts for years."

The Charles de Gaulle airport in Paris is one of the most excit-ing engineering achievements I've ever seen; American airport architects should fly over and study it. Right out of the Fantasy/ Sci-Fi world.

———————

Ditto: London

Lunch with Ben Glazebrook, elegant, witty director of Constable. He loves and understands food and wine and is flat-tered at my choice of a red Burgundy (at the Connaught). What I especially like about Glazebrook is that he is a *bookman*. He is mindful of the great tradition of Constable and carries the responsibility of the directorship with humility and authority. We had a fine if inconclusive discussion on today's publishing problems. We also talked of Trollope, always a mutual favorite subject.

Cocktail-Party Time

No visit to London is complete without at least one publisher's party (there are sometimes three a week), and no one does them better than Mark Goulden and Jeffrey Simmons, at W. H. Allen's posh quarters on Hill Street in Mayfair. In this case the guest of honor was Gene Kelly, whose biography, by Clive Hirshorn, Allen was publishing. Kelly wasn't there; the flu kept him away. But the party was gay, with ample food and drink and good company, including some friends from New York's publishing fraternity, among them Elaine Geiger and Jerry Gross. Heather Jeeves (can you think of a name *more* English?) of Pan is there and is heated up over the prospect of buying a new "big one" being auctioned that very day; by coincidence, it's a Putnam novel. And there's a big buzz around at the sound of high-six figures in the offing. (In the end, Bantam got the book, a thriller, for $365,000.) Heather is also eager to learn the latest on Mario Puzo's new novel— her firm published *The Godfather* in paperback—and I assured her that the author was diligently at work, chained to his typewriter and eating vitamins.

W. H. Allen have offices that compare to some of those in Milan —there's nothing like a fine winding staircase to impress visitors. Goulden and Simmons seem to have discovered the rhythm of publishing for fun and profit.

Getting Ethnic; or, *Neshuma* (Soul) Food in Berwick Street

On each trip to London I manage to sneak off one night, alone, for a dinner at Goody's, the one totally Jewish restaurant in London. It's in Berwick Street in Soho. I mentioned this to our old friend, Jane Goulden, while she was in New York on a visit (she's Mark's wife, of course), and she smiled. "Bill, there isn't a dish they make there that I can't duplicate. Better!"

She really stopped me. I had no idea that Jane cooked *at all*. I won't try to describe her home and lifestyle, the Rolls, the parties, etc. So I said, "Can you duplicate their super lokschen kugel?"

"And what's so special about their kugel?" she asked.

"Well," I replied, "it has about nine ingredients."

"Let me tell you," she said. "Almonds, raisins, apples, vanilla extract, cinnamon, orange rind, lemon, hair-thin noodles, sugar— that's nine, isn't it?" Pause. "Well, mine will have *one more* ingredient—a surprise."

"Terrific," I said, "When will you be serving it?"

"Any time you wish. Just give me twenty-four-hours' notice and you're invited."

So one day soon I expect to be eating Jane Goulden's lokschen kugel, à la Goody's, in the Goulden's Mayfair mansion in London. I must remember to bring along some orchids and emeralds in reciprocation—and a gallon jug of Manischewitz' best. I suspect that Goody's will be eclipsed by Jane and I can't wait.

If you're of that persuasion, come along.

I know there's an undue preoccupation with food in this book. I quit smoking ten years ago (as mentioned earlier) and I'm sublimating.

Dialogue in Frankfurt, and Other Notes

"Excuse me, sir, aren't you Ladislas Farago?"
"Yes. And who are you?"
"My name is Martin Bormann."
"Impossible," replies Farago. "*I* am Martin Bormann."

There are surprises in store when the conversation relaxes and one gets away from shoptalk. For example: superexecutive Jeremiah Kaplan, Macmillan's man with a "hierarchical difference," and I were having a quiet drink in his suite at the Intercontinental in

Frankfurt. (He runs Cassell's in London.) I admitted my passion for reading and collecting modern poetry. Lo and behold, he began *quoting* from some of my favorite poets. He, too, likes Sexton, Kizer, Jong, Rich, Rukeyser, and others of this school; he has *read* them.

After a long day and evening, arches aching from working the publishing vineyards, here's a recipe for relaxing: get an eight-ounce container of Aramis Muscle Soothing Soak. Spill a dash of this powder into a very hot tub, and soak for fifteen minutes. (A Scotch and water at the tub-side can't hurt.) The Aramis powder contains granules of seaweed and minerals, and it will turn the bath water a bright sea-green. For a few moments you are literally the jolly green giant. This noncommercial plug is presented in the interest of weary editors. A hot tub, in any event, never hurt anyone. Paco Rabanne deodorant after the tub is also recommended, just in case. The label says *pour homme*, but I'd call it a unisex product.

The best book England has produced in this century is, in my opinion, *The Concise Oxford Dictionary*. It's my favorite travel companion and I urge every editor to carry it with him on trips. When short of reading matter, say, at 4:00 A.M., try the *C.O.D.*—fifteen hundred pages to nibble at, profitably. An educative and civilizing book for all seasons. It will also help to improve your spelling.

October 12, 1972: New York

Simhat Torah, a day for dancing the hora, giving sweets to the children, singing Hebrew songs, celebrating the giving of the Ten Commandments. A rare New York sky: clean, a vibrant cobalt blue.

On the morning's televison a young black lady with an Afro hairdo proclaims herself a Hebrew and expounds on black Jewishness and the meaning of today's holiday. (Black Ethiopian Jews in New York are not uncommon.) What she failed to convey to her audience was the importance of the Decalogue in the ethical systems of Judaism. In today's world, and in New York in particular, commandments relating to killing, stealing, lusting for one's neighbor's wife, bearing false witness, honoring one's parents, etc., seem archaic, obsolete, ironic, and perhaps downright funny. The Divine Law today is summed up in one word: survive. (Melvin van Peebles said, "Winning is everything.")

I wonder why Jim Bishop hasn't thought of writing a book entitled *The Day Moses Was Handed the Ten Commandments.* Bishop was present on other important occasions, such as the assassinations of Lincoln and Christ.

Spent the day fussing and fretting over the galley proofs of Paul Bowles' autobiography, *Without Stopping.* No cause for jubilation. A compendium of names. I commissioned the project with high expectations in March of 1969, and received the revised proofs in late 1971. Hundreds of figures—names—from the world of the arts are mentioned in his chronicle, but precious little that sheds light on their lives and psyches. I fear the book will be clobbered, called a classic of understatement, and that a lot of Bowles' devotees will be disappointed. (My fears were realized.) However, there was no way to budge the author from his position of caution. Unbudgeable Bowles, an author fearful of laying bare his real view of life and certain friends. ("I'm more interested in landscapes than people.") I know that reviewers will think or say, "Too bad Bowles didn't have a decent editor." Gore Vidal asked for a set of proofs to read, but failed to make comment.

Nevertheless, I admire Bowles; he's an artist and a master storyteller—and a gentle man.

To bed with Cass Canfield's book of memoirs, *Up and Down and Around,* 50 percent of which is good publishing history and gossip, and 50 percent boring; for who really cares, today, about pampered childhoods set in elegant high society surroundings and wealth? Canfield was a "working stiff" with style; he was shrewd, nimble-footed and nervy, able to make a quick decision or deal. He worked with duchesses as well as longshoremen, not too worried about ethics or fine points of negotiation. A bookman. A collector of William Blake. A cool man, gifted with humor, taste, and especially a zest for good living. Does the new, young breed of editor really know what a Cass Canfield is all about? Does he care? We have few publishers today with Cass Canfield's talents, alas.

Woolworth's

Rare day in June: a bubblegum-pink leather wrist-watch band in Woolworth's window on Fifth Avenue catches my eye. I remove my scruffy black alligator band, enter the store, locate the counter, and attach the pink band to my watch. Reactions: my secretary says, "You must be kidding." The advertising director spots it and mutters, "What the well-dressed editor-in-chief is wearing these days." From the publicity department comes, "You've come a long way, baby." But I have never been happier with a $1.50 purchase or with a decision. Roslyn smiles, is tolerant. Hopes perhaps that it will go away. I can never resist browsing in Woolworth stores, both in New York and in London. Counters always offer bright new gadgets, colorful notebooks, gaily colored ballpoint pens, amusing gifts. Woolworth brings joy to millions each day.

Allen G.

Reading Allen Ginsberg's *Indian Journals,* I concluded that Walt Whitman would have liked the book and the poet.

Much of the book I hate, fail to understand or care about. I realize that I'm not qualified to accept the work or be objective about it. I've felt for some time a strange cool toward most Asiatic Indians: their dress, food, mores, cultural pretensions, and dubious mysticism. (I almost choked to death on Indian curry while flying Air India.) Perhaps Mrs. Indira Gandhi and her phony slogan *Garibi Hatao* (Banish Poverty) offend me. The tensions between castes, the hunger, superstition, inflation, the dying at every turn, the corruption everywhere in India—these don't help me to appreciate the beauties found by Ginsberg in that country. I am a

Gandhian, a pacifist revolutionary in spirit. I am not a Communist nor a follower of that philosophy, but I confess often wondering how much better off India would be under another form of government. India's present political situation, despite Narayan, seems to me hopeless, and the irony is that Prime Minister Indira Gandhi continues to hold immense power . . . and the people starve. (Perhaps when this book is published, she will be out—on her imperious derriere.)

But Allen is a saint, no doubt about it; likewise he's a deadly sober citizen, a "Christian Jewish gentlemen," when one gets down to the main issues of life. Ginsberg understands the art of keeping the cosmic cool: he says, "Bless you," where someone else might say, "Piss off." I recall a dinner with Ginsberg and Timothy Leary (at Casey's in New York). Allen ordered lobster and champagne (as did Leary) and I wondered how one could equate the spirit of his poetry and his lifestyle with his sybaritic tastes. I am especially fond of Ginsberg ever since G. wrote a lengthy inscription in my copy of his book, *Siesta in Xbalba* (shameless admission), which Ginsberg mimeographed on board a ship heading for Cape Alaska in 1956—his very first book "publication." I conclude that Ginsberg is more generous than most poets I know, always deeply loyal. I tried unsuccessfully to publish the collected poems of G., but he's faithful to his first publisher, City Lights in San Francisco, where his *Howl* was launched.

In 1974, on April 18, I listened to Peter Orlovsky deliver Allen's acceptance speech for the National Book Award in Poetry given to him for his *Fall of America*. I've seldom heard a more moving or pertinent statement. The reading by Orlovsky was thundering and also to use a simple and familiar word, *thrilling*. My impulse was to stand up and cheer; but I didn't. (Apologies, Peter.) Later, Andreas Brown published the acceptance speech, a document well worth reading; and if you're a collector, worth owning.

Alas, Allen's "om ah hum" intoning didn't help much when the mugger's arm embraced his throat on East Tenth Street in New York, resulting in the loss of his wallet. But he did keep his cool. His poem "Mugging" commemorates the shameful event.

The year 1974 saw the publication of an annotated Allen Ginsberg volume, long needed by his fans. It includes his tapings and comments around the country in early 1971, when he made the rounds of campuses and schoolrooms, talking to students. Gordon Ball, of the University of North Carolina, did the annotating, supplying all the background stuff Ginsberg's devotees, not to mention future historians, would need. This is *the* intellectual life, circa 1970s, and we get a fine view of the poet's thoughts on just about everything cosmic and terrestrial: Blake and Pound and drugs and the CIA and publishing. (He favors the private or modest press but publishes *this* volume through McGraw-Hill, one of the largest publishing houses in the world. The book, by the way, presented a tough typographical challenge, and Elaine Gongora handled the design well. But the binding! It's got a "sleaze" material on the cover, and it's *perfect-bound,* which is okay for hardware catalogs but not, I'd say, for Allen's book.) It's not a major book, but it certainly will give the newcomer to Ginsberg an introduction to the man and what he's all about. And that's plenty.

Why am I giving this space to a secondary Ginsberg book? I'd do the same for Whitman were I writing my book in the late 1850s.

From the Journal: March 4

Another birthday. Roslyn prepared a party, a birthday celebration. I'm admitting to only thirty-nine—Jack Benny's poor joke, but a magical number, smile-producing. Roslyn invited thirty-nine guests, some of them pretty girl editors, agents, some of my favorite authors, friends from the writing and publishing world, including Art Buchwald, Mario Puzo, Abel Green, Eric Segal, the John Koblers, Ralph Daigh, the Leslie Wallers, the Herman Rauchers.

Mario's birthday present was a giant crystal ball from Tiffany's; Buchwald's, wooden block letters of various shapes and sizes that spelled out my name ("So that you can play with yourself" said Art). Two cases of wine, Scotch, vodka, etc., were consumed, and mountains of shrimp, salad, ham, cheese, turkey, sausages, cakes, nuts, fruit. Some fifty guests showed up and the house was jumping. Puzo and Segal went off to the bedroom to compare royalty notes; they both had big best sellers at the time. It was the best party ever.

Parenthetically, Mario recalled our luncheon at the Algonquin in late 1968, the day I invited him to lunch in order to bring him some "special news." Mario was heavily in debt at the time, "piss-poor." I carefully spelled out the details of the paperback sale of *The Godfather* for $410,000. Clyde Taylor, rights director at Put-nam's, had closed the deal that morning. I explained to Mario that we now owed him not less than $205,000 in American dollars. He turned to me, paused, then said, "I don't believe a fucking word you've told me." And then he added, "This must be some kind of Madison Avenue put-on."

When we left, he walked up Fifth Avenue with Roslyn—she'd been to lunch with us—and he asked her, "Is Bill putting me on?" She reassured him. It was a great day in the life of an editor as well as an author.

I had contracted for Mario's novel from a verbal run-through; there was no outline, no synopsis or sample chapter to read, as has been reported by one or two motion picture executives. Of course I had read Mario's two previous novels. They were first-rate books, though commercial failures. He had been introduced to me by a friend of his who told me that Mario was broke, was being turned down by his previous and other publishers around town. Puzo and I met; I liked him. We talked; I wanted him for Putnam's and we gave him a contract for $5,000, with a $1,250 down payment. The agreement was drawn through his agent, William Morris. It turned out to be the most profitable single novel ever published by Put-nam's and by Fawcett, the paperback reprinter. At this writing, it has sold around fifteen million copies in various editions in the United States alone. What it sold throughout the world I can't say, but it was definitely a best seller *everywhere*. It has outsold all of the major bestselling novels of our time.

The film, too, was a record-breaker. If my memory serves me, until the paperback rights were sold, *The Godfather* had few sup-porters at Putnam's. Clyde Taylor was my strongest ally.

When we attended the New York premier of the *Godfather* film, Mario stole the show. Among the guests were Henry Kissinger and Raquel Welch and most of the *Godfather* cast, but Mario was the only man in the room with charisma. (And he wore a rented tuxedo; he refused to buy one. He also refused to wear socks.) When asked to make a speech, he first removed his tie.

To bed at 2:30 A.M. A happy birthday indeed, ending in elation and total exhaustion. Lying in bed, checking off facts: of now moving toward the "sunset years," my future, health, sex, finance. I lay there pondering the meaning of it all, and what the "career" thus far added up to. Achievement and delusion. Vanity, Ecclesiastes, the sun also rises . . . ran through my head and finally brought on blessed sleep, relieving me of further confrontation with the insoluble questions of life. Roslyn had given me another golden day.

Footnote: On Tuesday, December 10, 1974, Mario invited the Mintons, Clyde Taylor, Page Cuddy, and the Targs to Pearl's Restaurant for a Chinese banquet. We joined him there with his family and Francis Ford Coppola, the director of *Godfather I* and *II*. We spent two hours gourmandizing and three and a half hours film-viewing *Godfather II;* we left exhausted. Some of us felt that the film was as good as the first, but could stand a bit of editing. My feeling is that the two parts, properly edited, with some flashback scenes juxtaposed, would turn the two *Godfather* films into one of the most powerful films ever made, a five-hour epic of American crime. (Later, Pauline Kael seemed to agree with me, in her *New Yorker* review.)

Mario had written some highly inventive and dramatic new sequences for the second part, adding dimension to the epic. Much of the original novel was utilized beautifully—material not used in Part I, such as the young manhood of Don Corleone in Sicily and in New York's Italian section. Meanwhile, Mario is devoting his energies to his new novel, *Fools Die*, which I feel will surpass *The Godfather* as a novel in many ways. I've already read large segments and await the completed work, as do millions of readers everywhere.

———————

A Day in the Life of . . . : A View of Beckett

A bleak and cold Saturday morning in February 1973 in Paris. Sitting in the lobby of the Hotel Montalembert, I was awaiting the arrival of the Most Important Living Writer in the World. (My characterization.) The prospect was dizzying, almost beyond my endurance.

It struck me with the force of a sexual spasm that now, today, here—a week before I was to turn sixty-six years old—I ought to start keeping a journal with regularity. I had some travel diaries from past years, but nothing that recorded real conversations, unique encounters, *memorable* experiences. I could start with the auspicious meeting before me; a good opening.

I grabbed a sheaf of the hotel's stationery that was at hand—small, thin, blue sheets of paper—and began to make preliminary notes and to prepare a few conversational gambits to help me along in case the meeting lagged. I had a handsome new Parker pen (with real ink and a gold tip) and as I wrote, it occurred to me that this was what writing was all about: sitting with pen and paper, feverishly clawing at one's brain and innards for ideas.

Newcomers to the craft of writing often ask about the precise technical details for *starting a book*, becoming an author. The above tells it all. The answer in a nutshell is: always have pen and paper handy. Take the bull by the horns.

At this precise moment I looked up and saw my visitor entering the lobby. He was, of course, Samuel Beckett. (I was Bill Targ, from Chicago and New York, waiting for *Godot*.) Beckett's arrival was punctual—at 11:00 A.M., as agreed. At the stroke of eleven he came through the doors and brought fresh air into the lobby and into my life. He stayed with me until eleven-fifty.

(*I recall having dinner with Jack MacGowran one night, just as he was to leave for Berlin to perform in a Beckett play. I asked him why he didn't think about writing a book, recording his recollections of Joyce, O'Casey, Beckett, Yeats, and others. Such a book would make marvelous reading. He replied, "Bill, I don't know how to write a book, or how to begin it." I said, "What was it like when you first met Beckett?" And he replied with a burst, "I was born when I met Beckett." My answer was obvious: "There's the opening line of your book." Unfortunately, Jack died six months later.*)

I had fifty minutes of cosmic contact with Beckett. Let me tell you about this man. He had a bright-red woolen scarf around his neck; his cheeks were ruddy from having walked from his flat on a windy and cold morning. His eyes were alive, shining and piercing, and they held laughter too. There was infinite courtesy in his manner. His hair—well, you've seen pictures of Beckett and his rooster's comb—and the marvellous lines around his eyes and in his cheeks that give him the look of a prophet. I quickly discovered that he could smile, laugh readily. I handed him a bottle of Jameson's Irish Whiskey on behalf of our mutual friend, John Kobler, and he was delighted with the gift; he cradled and embraced the bottle.

I studied him for a moment, then began by saying that I felt I was sitting with a Martian. This made him smile, and he didn't try to deny it. He just looked at me, waiting. Then we got to talking: about our mutual friend Jack MacGowran and his premature death, his last performance in *The Plough and the Stars* in New York, and the tiny role Jack had had in the film *The Exorcist*.

We talked about the recent performance of Beckett's miniplay, *Not I*, in which Jessica Tandy performed the solo role in New York. Beckett compared it to the British performance and observed that the American performance was reported as being somewhat lacking, that the actress had been reading the text from a concealed tele-prompter, which was apparently not the case with her British counterpart. I asked him to inscribe my copy of *Not I*, which I had cadged from Matthew Evans of Faber & Faber, in London, the day before.

I also asked him to inscribe my two copies of the first French edition of *Godot* (Paris, 1952). (One of them was "one of 35" copies.) He showed surprise at my "one of 35" copy which he pointed out was very scarce. (I had recently paid a fortune for it!) After he'd inscribed my books, he asked me if there were any I still wanted, since he was unencumbering himself of possessions, and I was welcome. (He sent me an inscribed copy of *Echo's Bones*, which I did not own. It awaited me on my return from Europe; Roslyn met me at the door with the book in hand, saying, "Here's your birthday present!")

Beckett and I talked about Simone de Beauvoir, whose agent I was meeting at noon, and out of the blue he asked me if I recalled the closing lines of *La Force des Choses*, the third volume of her autobiographical series. I remembered it well, not only because I was her American editor, but also because I had questioned the translator about that very sentence, which ended, ". . . and yet, turning an incredulous gaze toward that young and credulous girl, I realize with stupor how much I was gypped." I had challenged the word "gypped." Beckett observed that the translation should have read, "I've been *had* by life." I asked him what he thought de Beauvoir still wanted from life, since she apparently had everything except a child and a wedding ring. Beckett leaned forward, almost nose to nose, and said, "Mr. Targ, no woman knows what she wants." I believed him, and pass his comment on to my reader— surely one of the most cogent observations ever recorded. (Of course, Freud had made the same comment.)

Beckett asked me if I had any desires—a curious question from a relative stranger, a question out of context. I said I had two desires: one, to be always ambulatory; and second, to be as wise as Sam Beckett. This brought a lusty laugh but no comment. Then I asked him about his desires. He replied, "I have no desires." He looked searchingly at me as though awaiting a question. I thought of death.

I asked him if he'd like a lift to his home, since I was going to La Coupole, but he declined, preferring to walk. "I walk whenever possible," he said. I put away my book treasures and then we parted at the hotel door.

In passing, I must record a belief I've held for some years: that the two most "seminal" plays of our century are Beckett's *Waiting for Godot* and Michael McClure's *The Beard*.

Later in New York I found in my library the perfect word-portrait sketch of Beckett, by Kenneth Tynan, in his review of Beckett's *Happy Days*. He says, "Study the author's photograph that stares out of the programme. Note the wrinkles between his eyebrows, converging in a crossroads of anxiety; and the look on his face, at once accusing and aghast, as of a man about to be struck by lightning, or a child who has been spat on without warning. This head, one feels, has been cropped for execution, and in its eyes the guillotine looms. This is our author, a prophet who cannot help seeing beyond creature comforts to the engulfing grave." The perfect portrait. Everything Tynan recorded was true, but there was also the laughter in the eyes. It was this special element that gave me a sense of heightened gladness in meeting Beckett. We have corresponded ever since.

Why was I in Paris? I came there for a day-and-a-half visit (from London) to secure for Putnam's, by preemptive offer, a French novel—Pierre Rey's *Le Grec*—which was about to be put up for auction in New York. Walter Minton and I had several reports and synopses, and we felt it might be a good commercial bet, a story in the "Harold Robbins tradition." I got it. Following my business meetings and the visit with Beckett, Ellen Wright and I went to my second favorite restaurant for an orgy of smoked salmon, white wine—and ice cream. Then she came with me to the Gare du Nord to see me off on a train to Brussels. (Another French airline strike.) I flew from Brussels to London. Nightmare all the way. And when I finally got to London, at around ten o'clock, I thought I'd find a quick meal on the way to the Connaught. I saw a pizza sign, had the driver stop, and went in. Dear reader: *Never order a pizza in London,* especially if you are an American pizza aficionado, which I am. It was dreadful. Luckily I had a supply of Rolaids at hand.

From the Journal: de Beauvoir

Terrifying and sobering—these two words come thrusting into my consciousness as I complete the reading of the manuscript of the English translation of Simone de Beauvoir's book, La Viellesse, *which Putnam's will publish under the title* The Coming of Age. *This book, the eleventh work by de Beauvoir with which I've been involved as editor and publisher in America, seems to me monumental, the summa: perhaps even more important than any of her earlier books, including* The Second Sex. *I ponder over what she terms "the secret shame"; I linger over her sentence, "Old age is not a necessary end to human life."*

I remember a particular visit with de Beauvoir in Paris one June afternoon, two years before, in her sun-drenched duplex apartment facing the Montparnasse cemetery. She was about sixty then, but bubbling with girlish vitality, laughing, urging "more whiskey" on me. She showed me amusing faked snapshots (LBJ, with vampire fangs, attempting to seduce a young girl, etc.) talking about our mutual friend, Nelson Algren. ("Why is he angry with me? I'm his friend," she says. I try to explain.) At that time I was publishing Algren's *Notes from a Sea Diary*. Algren loomed most visibly in the third volume of her autobiography, *Force of Circumstance*. (She dedicated *The Mandarins* to Algren; we published it in 1956.)

De Beauvoir spoke of how nature played her cruellest tricks on women and that a woman's mirror was her enemy after fifty. I knew how subjectively she was involved in old-age matters; it had been her preoccupation for some years; I had been ordering certain American books on gerontology for her.

Who doesn't worry about life after sixty? I insisted that I would enjoy every possible hour of my life while on this "collision course," as living after sixty must be viewed. I consider myself capable of at least another decade of good living; both my parents died in their late eighties. My mother began to show signs of senility at eighty-five; she couldn't remember my name. "I know your face, but your name escapes me," she said to me one day when I visited her in her "retirement home" in Florida. The shock of that moment has not left me and I often wonder when I will forget so totally. I've read too much about the brain and know how fast the brain cells are dying.

I intend to work as long as I am ambulatory and mentally competent, and sex will assuredly be a good part of my living program. As for *The Coming of Age,* when I secured a contract for the book from Ellen Wright, de Beauvoir's agent (and Gallimard's, the French publisher) at an advance of $7,500, Walter Minton said to me, "But who will buy such a book? Such a depressing work, with all those grim facts about old age." I argued its merits, its market, and also referred Minton to the best-seller history of de Beauvoir's book in France. When we secured $150,000 for the paperback rights, Minton smiled, although he may have been temporarily speechless. The book was chosen as one of the five most distinguished books of the year by *The New York Times Book Review,* and its sale, at ten dollars a copy, was excellent. Talk about exaltation, of a publishing triumph, of being proved right "in thunder."

A Spree in Gomorrah: September 20, 1971

Rosh Hashanah: What does a Jewish book editor do on the morning of this holy day? He sits up in bed, stares out through the grimy and rain-streaked bedroom windows, recognizes the day, and falls back on his pillow.

My awakening. A view from our tiny penthouse in Greenwich Village. The sky is soggy, clouded yellow, warm and wet—another filthy day. But it is still morning and who knows? The Empire State

Building is fogged out completely, a granite shadow. Later, as the Con Ed clock shows nine, the clouds begin to spume and travel westward toward the Hudson and the Jersey shore. The sun can't quite make it through the polluted sky.

I get up to take a look at our "garden." The pink petunias on our terrace are valiant and erect in their blue-green boxes. The marigolds are going great. All else seems bleak. An ambulance is screaming up Sixth Avenue: a fire siren is heard out of the East Village. I look down Sixth Avenue from twenty-one stories above the street and I note that the traffic is thin: the taxi drivers are in their beds or in the synagogues. Or at Nathan's at Eighth Street and Sixth, having coffee.

No laboring for me in the Putnam's vineyard this day. Not this son, whose lineage (I sometimes brag) is of the Hebrew priesthood, the *cahens.*

Roslyn is off to her office, to a VIP appointment: a film contract to wrap up.

Scanning the *Times:* (more bombings, rapings, stabbings; more lies out of Washington and Gracie Mansion and Attica prison.) Then a poached-egg-and-bacon breakfast with a large cup of mint tea with Greek honey. A hot, cologne-drenched tub; the fragrant steam is pure indecent pleasure.

While dressing I put on a Mozart quartet; I choose a light sports jacket and slacks. I have a desire, undefined—and a premonition. The desire and premonition build. I yield easily, happily.

Anyone who collects autograph letters doesn't need to check the Yellow Pages to find a dealer; he goes to Mary Benjamin on upper Madison Avenue just before noon. That's what I did. A taxi trip uptown for a leisurely visit, a gossipy visit, with the perdurable Mary Benjamin, the town's leading dealer in autographs. My destiny for the day. I hadn't seen her in ages; I had a yen for some exciting new acquisition. As always, Mary was warm, cordial.

It was a lucky trip. I bought a holograph letter from the pen of Gerard Manley Hopkins, written eight years before his death. This was an especially exciting acquisition—my first Hopkins letter. Inspired and inventive, this sprung-rhythm-mad genius of a Jesuit died at forty-five. "He died in 1889 and rose again as a living poet in 1918," says W. H. Gardner. What a legacy he gave us. What a debt the post-Victorian poets owe him, as does almost everyone else worthy of the name "poet."

Getting this letter, on this particular day, is one of the coincidences that boggle certain minds, those with extrasensory attributes. Of course, only a crazy—yes, cracked—autograph collector would carry on as I do here, or understand what this is all about. (My collection of letters totalled 2,635 at that time.) What was so unique about this purchase? And why would anyone be so interested in this story?

Well, I neglected to mention that I had been browsing through a copy of Hopkins' poems just that morning before leaving the house, and the thought struck me that a Jewish editor reading a Jesuit poet on this holy day was some kind of oddity. And then came the desire—to find a Hopkins letter to put into my first-edition copy of the book. Today I must track down that letter. I had never seen a Hopkins letter offered for sale in any dealer's catalog. Mary Benjamin's aura floated into the room, surrounded me. I hadn't seen her in several years. The decision to see her on this particular day, Rosh Hashanah, would be meaningless to her or most readers of this account. Why wasn't I at my office, working, instead of building up a case for a fantasy letter by a Catholic poet. But why belabor it?

The real point is that when I met with Mary and asked her, in the most casual tone, whether she had run into any Hopkins autograph "material" of late, she replied, "Not for years" (pause) "but I did get one, oddly enough, just yesterday."

Yesterday.

Certain forces were conspiring, moving to favor me.

I left Mary Benjamin's office and took a slow walk down Madison, then Fifth Avenue, feeling free as the birds wheeling overhead. The Hopkins letter was wrapped securely and in my hand. The sun was now clearly, blazingly, out; the yellow sky had turned robin's-egg blue. I was exhilarated by my Hopkins "experience" and the emergence of the sun. I walked as far as the Plaza Hotel. I stood there for a few moments watching the postnoon traffic, the kids with their balloons, a few girls eating lunch by the fountain. Then I took a taxi to the Algonquin; it was almost deserted. I had a martini and their famous chicken potpie. I murmured to myself, "Happy Rosh Hashanah, world."

Back in my pajamas and robe. I spent the afternoon reading Hopkins and pleasuring my ear with Bach, Mozart (*The Requiem*), Corelli, and Julian Bream playing Villa-Lobos. All this sound while reading more of Hopkins: "The Windhover," "Pied Beauty," "The Wreck of the Deutschland." I was reading from the first edition of course, edited by Robert Bridges, a fine copy in dust jacket acquired from Dawson's in London a few months earlier. This was my latest and still-futile attempt to memorize Hopkins—a rough task for any-one, impossible for me. I turned to a few other poets: the early Rilke poems of 1906–07—"Oh, so much heaven . . ."; then to Diane Wakoski—the heartbreaking but still quite funny jealousy poems from *Greed*, Parts 5–7—really letters to her beloved and wandering Tony. And I laughed out loud when I came to her dedication in *The Motorcycle Betrayal Poems:* "This book is dedicated to all those men who betrayed me at one time or another, in hopes they will fall off their motorcycles and break their necks."

A delicious, goofing-off day.

Roslyn came home early. Dinner: a *boeuf bourguignon* prepared laboriously and most lovingly by her the day before; eaten with the aid of a glowing Burgundy; then pears, strawberries, and Brie. Then Williams Pear Brandy.

Later, to bed, reading a just-received catalog from a Parisian book and autograph dealer. And lo, a Hopkins letter is offered! The first I've ever seen in a catalog. The price is outrageous but I study the entry and description carefully. Then the decision to buy it is negative. I have my letter. But the coincidence is shattering. Should I order it anyway, and thus own *two*? No. I'm destined to have one. A good one. Greed must not enter into this complex (cosmic?) matter. Enough.

Concluding a good day, the first of the Ten Days of Penitence. "Peace to all Jews everywhere," I found myself murmuring into Roslyn's ear as I slipped off to sleep around midnight, remembering that prayers are in order this day, even for confirmed athiests—and I'm a card-carrying one.

In my dream (a genuine Chagall sequence) I am holding a giant shofar. I am again a boy in Chicago, in a synagogue, blowing ear-piercing cries through the horn. My chest aches. My father, bearded, in white and gold vestments, is at my side, reading from his *Mahzor*, pinching me—my arm and neck are green and blue—out of some Byzantine pique. (I was always misbehaving "like a goy," whistling through my teeth, reading goyish books.) I awakened briefly; the

Empire State tower, which usually fills the bedroom window, is blacked out now, but there are intermittent cloud-and-light (Walkyrian) effects.

Back to sleep, shaping my body to Roslyn's for warmth and comfort. Thus ending a day for special rituals, benedictions. A rare day, in my mid-sixties, a day in which I shunned all toil and dedicated myself to pleasure. A Jewish editor on a holy day—on a spree in Gomorrah.

A Day in the Life of . . . : July 24, 1974

A visit from Mario Puzo this morning; he's taken off over forty pounds since his heart attack five months ago; looks great in his new beige "bush suit," promises delivery of his new novel "by the end of this year"; he puts it in writing for me. Says Mario: "There's only one way to lose a lot of weight—have a heart attack!"

While gossiping with Puzo, a call comes through from Malibu. Jerome Lawrence phoning to invite Roslyn and me for a weekend at his Malibu house. He also wants to throw a "reception" for us. His house is one of the showplaces of Malibu. I feel like a character out of *Women's Wear Daily*, a jet setter.

Lawrence published his play, *The Gang's All Here* (with his partner, Robert E. Lee) at World; they also produced the play, *Only in America*, on Broadway. He and Lee and I got to know each other through these projects and kept in touch thereafter. They are both hardworking, talented men.

I'm again working with Lawrence, this time on his biography of Paul Muni entitled *Actor*, a project I love. I promise Lawrence I will bring along the final proofs of his book (the "blues") when I come to Malibu—they'll be ready just then—and he's ecstatic. By coincidence, Puzo is taking a house in Malibu shortly, so he and his wife Erika will come to the Lawrence party. What's so great about all this is that Roslyn and I have been discussing the fact that we've had no vacation this year. The vacation matter becomes a special "problem" because my son Russell and his family threaten to disown me if we don't visit them in their new Palo Alto home "damned soon." The Lawrence party would be convenient, since we'd be able to go up to San Francisco from Malibu and see some of the beauties of the California coast. It simplifies everything.

As I talk with Lawrence, saying yes (yes!), I can see, hear, and smell those whitecapped blue-green waves rolling in on those sugar-white beaches, and I'm already mainlining the pungent ichthyoidal air over the telephone wires!

Lunch with Ashley Montagu, whose new book, *Frontiers of Anthropology*, I brought along—the first copy to reach me from the binder, and the twelfth book we have published together. He seems "content" with the book, a two-year project and one of three back-breakers on my 1974 calendar. A lively visit as always (at the Algonquin, of course) and we talk about writing and his getting to work on his autobiography in particular. He finally laughs it off. "Too much work." But I think I left him with a feeling that he should be writing it now. I must prod him. He once produced two books at my instigation: *Human Heredity* and *The Cultured Man*. I recall that he acknowledged my share of responsibility in his Introduction.

This proves to be a landmark day; the headlines declare a unanimous vote by the Supreme Court, putting Nixon in his place at long last: he must turn over his last tapes to the impeachment committee. For a while, it looked as though Caesar Nixon could defy the Constitution and the Supreme Court. "Only in America" could this happen.

Domestic Stuff

Roslyn and I have a quiet dinner at home: chicken breasts sautéed in butter with those lovely small onions—shallots—white wine, and garlic; salad; wine; Brie; apples. Then off to hear the Spanish pianist Alicia de Larrocha playing Mozart at Avery Fisher Hall. What a marvel she is—Mozartian to the core. And how good to see the Hall completely sold out, and on a filthy rainy night at that.

Then home to catch the TV late-news roundup, the impeachment proceedings, local rape, arson, and mugging reports; and so to bed.

The Golden West: August 1974

San Francisco is now my favorite city after New York and Paris. In the summer of 1974, Roslyn and I visited the California coast and rediscovered San Francisco in all its new and ancient glories. It's an architect's dream city: all students of architecture should spend a year there. It is unsurpassed anywhere in the world and I say this mindful of the wonders of Chicago and New York. The Hyatt-Regency Hotel, with its silent, swift-moving spaceship elevators and its wonderland lobby, is something one should pay to see. I hated to leave that hotel, kept wandering about its lobby, caressing the waters of its black pool, ogling the terraced walls.

We sipped Portuguese Mateus Rosé wine and ate a local cheese for breakfast in our room; we sunned ourselves on the terrace of the pyramided side of the building, and gazed at the golden bay. The whole Embarcadero Center area is magical, and I think I'd rather take a child to see it than Disneyland. We took my two young grandsons with us and they behaved with respect and happiness.

An evening with San Francisco's leading author, Herbert Gold, an old friend and one-time author of World. We chatted with his beautiful wife Melissa and their "love-drop" children. Their enchanting bay-view house on Francisco Street is a writer's dream retreat, although Gold does most of his writing elsewhere. We watched the sunset from his windows and then went off for dinner to Modesto Lanzone's: we found its pasta equal to the best of Rome or Sicily. We talked about his latest novel, *Swiftie the Magician,* and the current New York literary "situation." Then came a bit of "nightlife" and an ice-cream orgy (Gold is an ice-cream freak, as am I) and a visit to our table by a young blond woman who, Gold said, spent her days and nights "writing my book" in the *Deux Magots*-imitation bistros on Pierce Street and Broadway. (She wore a large button on her breast with Artaud's portrait on it.) The partial manuscript she showed me was a pathetic confessional of drug-taking, soliciting, bustings, and lesbian encounters in local jails. I had published Herbert's second novel, *The Prospect before Us,* one of his best books, I think; but the subsequent one, *The Man Who Was Not with It,* was declined. When he asked me (eight or ten years later) why I had rejected it, I asked him, "Did you ever make a mistake?" He accepted that answer gracefully.

Herbert gave us as a parting gift a framed primitive Haitian painting; Gold and we share a great love for Haiti.

Next morning we had a lively visit with bright, attractive Alan Rinzler at his Rolling Stone office, where we discovered that New York was not necessarily the sole publishing arena of America. Alan showed us some of his recent books, imaginative graphic designs, and book layouts; and he gave me an inscribed copy of the Straight Arrow *Underground Comics,* which only a comics addict–dirty old man would appreciate. (Subsequently Alan left the job for greater challenges.)

At Malibu, in the house of Jerome Lawrence—a "pleasure dome" and a museum of Lawrence and Lee theatrical memorabilia. The guest room in which we stayed contained a piano and over a thousand books on shelves rising up to a 35-foot-high ceiling. There was a luxury bath and a great bed which, said Lawrence, Tennessee Williams had last slept in. Lawrence and I spent part of the day going over the final proofs of his biography, *Actor,* and then he gave us a great bash with some seventy-five guests, among whom were Christopher Isherwood, Albert Maltz, Robert Nathan, Mario Puzo, Norman Corwin, Viva and Michel Auder. Also some movie people and story editors (Ruth Nathan, Pat Kelly, the Sidney Skolskys, Ross Hunter, Marcia Nasatir). The following night Lawrence and the Targs had dinner with Erika and Mario Puzo in their beach house down the road, a great spaghetti and meatballs bacchanalia with uncounted bottles of chilled Dom Perignon to wash it down. Mario was in his best form that night: barefoot, barechested to his navel, an eight-inch Havana cigar in his mouth—the supreme host. Everyone loves Mario on sight.

We hated leaving Lawrence's house, his pool, his beautiful garden, and art and food. Every hour with Lawrence was enriching.

A high spot of our trip was a visit with Henry Miller. Bedridden with arthritis of the hips, this indestructible eighty-two-year-old wunderkind entertained us, while lying in bed, with recollections and anecdotes and wistful observations on women: "Give me a black-haired, slanteyed Japanese woman anytime; someone pliant and submissive. They're the greatest!" Whereupon, Roslyn hopped into his bed as a challenge (fully clothed, of course) and we took some snapshots of that scene. Jerry Lawrence also got into Miller's bed and the threesome was photographed by me; the photos are prizes. I said, "Forgive her, Henry. Roslyn is a shameless hussy making passes at a defenseless eighty-two-year-old man." He replied, "I'm not too old yet, Bill."

He inscribed my *Tropic of Capricorn* and the rare little pamphlet, *Money and How It Gets That Way*, published in 1936. It was dedicated to Ezra Pound, who had also written on the subject of money. In the recent period of money anxiety and inflation I found Miller's closing sentence worth reading aloud in the bedroom: "For when all the theories of economists are exploded, those who had the good sense to keep a 'mobile quantum of cash' on hand will be the least cruelly deceived."

Henry asked, "Who said that, Confucius? Some Chinese sage?" I showed him the page, proving that the words were Miller's. In taking a hard look at Miller's face, it crossed my mind that he might in fact be part Chinese; the eyes and expression were Oriental.

Henry Miller continues to be among my favorite living writers. We spoke about Beckett, and he said that he had seen the opening night performance of *Godot* in Paris, and while his understanding of French was limited, he had predicted the play's success.

In the midst of our two-hour visit with Miller, he suddenly said, "I need a synonym for the word 'horny.'" He elaborated: "The Op-Ed page of *The New York Times* is publishing an article of mine on Erica Jong's *Fear of Flying*. In the piece I use a few words which the *Times* considers not suited to a family newspaper. The word 'horny' bothers them in particular and I'm damned if I can think of a synonym for the word."

We discussed the problem and came up with a few good suggestions, including a ladylike "amative." Then I remembered "love tickle" from Brecht's *Threepenny Opera*. It seemed to arouse some serious interest. Miller didn't recall the phrase, but finally he decided that no word could substitute for "horny," a time-honored and universally understood word. (I like it better than lustful.) I'm not sure that "horny" should be considered an X-rated word, and I pointed out to Miller that the word "asshole" had appeared in the *Times'* hallowed pages, which news astonished him. "I can't believe it," he said, shaking his head.

I checked out the Wentworth-Flexner *Dictionary of American Slang* when I got back to my New York office and found the following synonyms for "horny" (in case you are curious): carnal-minded, lusty, sexually obsessed. None of these does the job, and I think "love tickle" may be the nearest thing to it. Correspondence on this subject is invited.

My "visitor's gift" to Miller was a little book, *The Characters of Theophrastus,* published in 1836. The book is full of whimsical physiognomical sketches. It reminded Miller of an incident in his youth. He was sitting on a park bench in Brooklyn, he said, desolate, jobless, broke, with no prospects before him. He had fifty cents in his pocket. He looked up, and across the street saw a phrenologist's sign, offering to read head bumps for fifty cents. He walked over to the storefront office of the "headologist" and had his skull protuberances examined, paying his total capital of fifty cents in advance. The phrenologist concluded that Miller would be a great architect!

Miller no longer lives in Big Sur; he's chosen the more traditional atmosphere of the Pacific Palisades, not very far from Malibu and near other writers, including Christopher Isherwood. As we visited the Big Sur country we thought of Miller constantly; his writings have caught the spirit of this beautiful, rugged coast. His spirit is everywhere in the Carmel-Big Sur-Monterey country; this part of America is an eye-opener for me.

Note: One of the best books I read in 1974 was Digby Diehl's, entitled *Super-Talk.* Aside from being a delightful and talented man, he is a great listener. (We met him in Frankfurt and know, firsthand, what a *mensch* he is.) In his book, especially the opening chapter devoted to Henry Miller, you will find insights that I'm not able to give you. Miller reveals himself openly, beautifully, underscoring everything I have tried to say here. I urge my readers not to miss Diehl's wonderfully recorded conversations. He closes his interview by quoting Henry Miller: "What is the most important thing in life? It is Spirit, with a capital S. Without it you are nobody, nothing, or to put it another way—pure shit."

The visit to Robinson Jeffers' Tor house, in Carmel, built by him of sea-coast boulders, was another momentous experience for me. I had discovered his poems in the twenties, and "Tamar," "Roan Stallion," and "The Woman at Point Sur" were shattering, poetry-awakening experiences. I had, until then, encountered very little in poetry on the theme of primitive sexuality and lust, certainly not in such stormy terms. Jeffers' negativism, his depressed attitude toward the world around him and modern civilization are reflected in his medieval stone house by the sea. I found it hard to leave, and plucked a few flowers from the roadside nearby as souvenirs of the visit. And I remembered the line from his poem, "Divinely Superfluous Beauty," "The storm-dances of gulls, the barking game of seals, Over and under the ocean," as we drove away from his handwrought stone house on this beautiful tree-and-boulder-rich shore.

My son Russell, his wife Joan, and my two grandsons Nicky and Sandy chauffered us on our Carmel safari and to the Jeffers house, and elsewhere. Altogether, it was a sun-drenched joyous holiday. I hadn't seen my two grandsons in several years and they had, as I've said, threatened to disown their grandfather if I didn't visit them. I think we made up for lost time, playing ball and throwing frisbees with them on the dunes, lunching in Sausalito, taking a great Chinese meal with them in Palo Alto. I hope to return there again, and soon. We missed my thirteen-year-old granddaughter Elisabeth, who was in France, near Nice, studying French. She had already "mastered" German the year before.

The Negresco Bar and a Birthday:
May 27, 1972

The Negresco Bar, Nice, France: It is Roslyn's birthday and I decided in the late afternoon to arrange a birthday party in the bar around midnight. The word was spread along the *plage,* "Tell all friends to come," and some fifty guests showed up, including Stephen Spender, Mary McCarthy, James Baldwin, and publishers and editors who were attending the Nice Book Fair. After the party, at 4:30 A.M., Roslyn, Baldwin, Alain Oulman (of Calmann-Levy), and I went up to our apartment for a nightcap, finishing a bottle of J & B while sitting on the floor looking out at the inky sea. "Poor Martin," moaned Baldwin, sitting lotus-fashion on the floor, pounding the carpet with his fist, tears rolling down his cheeks. Martin being, of course, Martin Luther King. Finally, as we prepared to part, Baldwin grabbed me in a bear hug and kissed me on the lips, the first male kiss on the lips I had ever received. Said Jimmy in parting, "You're one motherfucker I can trust." An unexpected compliment, a reward for being honest with him.

He promised me a novel, not delivered as of this writing.

It had been a full day, which had included a drive from Nice to Cannes (at about a hundred miles per hour) to see *Death in Venice*, which Roslyn and I enjoyed, particularly the photography and the Mahler score. Many in the audience didn't share our response; a homosexual novelist sitting near us called it grotesque. But Stephen Spender, sitting in front of us, rose majestically to his full height and proclaimed it magnificent. The Cannes film preview was followed by a champagne party at the villa of a woman descended from Jay Gould; she wore black sunglasses all evening; hers was an overfurnished house with a large collection of paintings signed by famous names such as Van Gogh, Degas, etc. When the wine was exhausted, we returned to the Negresco for dinner. After which, the birthday party took place.

I think that if I had a choice of my deathbed location it would be in an ocean-view top-floor suite at the Negresco in mid-May, with the windows open, the curtains flowing inward, and the lovely Dufy seascape before me. I'm told my taste in this hotel and place is deplorable: baroque-decadent; but my choice stands.

The above is recorded and included here to indicate to newcomers to book publishing that one of the dividends of being an editor is the chance to experience some of the beauties of other lands. Most of France, Italy, Spain, England. Make what you can of them, as often as you can. To justify your travels, there are authors in all of these places, not to mention good inns and restaurants. And hotels in which to shack up with your beautiful wife.

London: May 1972

At the Savoy. My twenty-third visit to the city—the annual search for publishable manuscripts in the creaky highways, warrens, and byways of publishers'/agents' offices. Result: only one contract offered for a quasi-scientific book on archaeology (*Chariots of the Gods,* by Erich von Daniken) from Ernest Hecht, head of Souvenir Press ("discoverer" of Arthur Hailey and the super ice-cream concoction, "Fujiyama," featured at *Le Drugstore* in Paris).

The British fiction this season is worse than ever: tolerably written British flummery with no content, mawkish themes, and pretensions.

Viva visits the city to help launch the British edition of her novel *Superstar,* through the auspices of Anthony Blond. A "psychedelic" cave party for her, and some amusing publicity. Liza Williams (*Up the City of Angels*) from Los Angeles attends. Joined Viva and her husband Michel at a late-night BBC broadcast in which she talked about how the "British hate babies." She had been evicted from her hotel restaurant because she chose to breastfeed her five-month-old baby Alexandria in public. "While the English adults gorge themselves on beef and beer, the babies are expected to starve," said Viva on the British airwaves.

Viva photographs beautifully—a cross between Carole Lombard and a Botticelli maiden. Front-page stories everywhere. Viva, despite her "underground style," is a model mother and can hardly keep her hands off the child—dressing, diapering, feeding, caressing, cooing. Michel stands by, slightly embarrassed. Viva characterizes the British formality as "a lot of shit." (*Serving as Viva's editor on her novel was no lark for me. We often nearly came to blows since she refused virtually all editorial guidance. I once said, "But let's be reasonable, Viva, you're simply not a writer." She answered with "That's the filthiest thing anyone ever said to me." Roslyn, Viva's agent on the book, adjudicated the quarrel by insisting that I kiss Viva and make up—and take everyone to dinner. Which I did.*) Then off to Paris where Roslyn awaited me with engagements galore, including a dinner with the Curtis Cates.

It is about three years since I served as Viva's editor; I recently reread some of the book and found myself enjoying it as much as ever; and I relived, with something of a glow, certain of the dramatic hours when Viva and I were locked in "mortal combat." She is indeed a *writer!*

I was intrigued by a comment made by Viva in *Women's Wear Daily* in June of 1975: "Sometimes I take a Zen attitude—being a woman is one step above being a dog." I wonder whether her decision to stop eating meat, smoking, drinking, and taking Excedrin had anything to do with this point of view.

From the Journal: Paris, May 1971

Food, wine, publisher and writer friends, and books in glorious abundance, especially the latter. On the rue de Seine, a tiny bookshop barely visible to the hurrying transient, owned by M. Bernard Loliée, is the equivalent of an opium den for me. Here I buy French books—first editions of Camus, mostly inscribed. Here I bought the first books of Rimbaud, Verlaine, St. John Perse, Genet, Céline, St. Exupéry, and others. All first editions in original wrappers. Here is where I acquired my beloved first edition of *Fleurs du Mal,* the unexpurgated first issue with the lesbian poems intact. No trip to Paris is thinkable without one or two visits to Loliée's.

Roslyn, who discovered and introduced me to the shop, bought me a few autograph letters there, including a wicked one by Verlaine. I secured manuscripts by Genet and Ionesco and Sartre there, and a short story in Colette's hand. Also, two holograph letters from Rilke and an inscribed copy of his *Die Sonette an Orpheus.*

(In October of '75 we visited Loliée's and Roslyn bought me a first edition of Valéry's *La Jeune Parque* (1917) as a "valentine present.")

Of course, I was in Paris on business, visiting Laffont, Stock, Fayard, Gallimard, Flammarion, and many other publishing firms. Roslyn is my interpreter and also my "advance *person*"; as I said earlier, I owe to her my acquaintance with the whole European publishing world. She made Paris in particular the "second home" for me. What a gift!

Mind over (Fecal) Matter

Watching dogs romping in the fields, in the country, in great open spaces, is always a joyous thing; their presence and their bark and their happiness, especially with children, add to life's simple satisfactions. Their pure, expressive eyes, their panting and pawing, their welcoming and friendship-assuring manner are beyond my powers to describe. Walking a dog along a river bank. But—

Dogs in the city are criminally out of their environment. Restricted to small rooms and crowded sidewalks, with heavy traffic at every turn, the dog's life becomes unnatural. As would any animal's.

Obviously the interest in dogs is enormous. There are, as of this writing, around 450 books in print dealing with all matters relating to dogs: feeding them, breeding them, training them, etc. Dog food commercials must produce hundreds of millions of dollars in revenue.

The dog-story writers, the dog photographers, and the writers of books about dogs convince me that dogs take precedence over children in millions of families. I doubt that a mother would take her little child for a walk in a heavy rain or snowfall as she would her dog. The human escort of the dog is one of the wonders in our city life. Many lives seem bound up to the rhythm of the dog's life.

In the high-rise building where I live, there are probably no fewer than fifty dogs. Some tenants have as many as three dogs, all living in a four-room apartment. No matter. What does concern me, and what genuinely interests me as an observer of the oddities of human behavior, is the manner in which dog owners rearrange their lives to accommodate the shitting habits of their pets.

I've witnessed men and women walking their dogs at six-thirty in the morning and after midnight, in rain and storm and in blizzard weather. I've listened to dog owners holding serious conversations with their dogs. I've seen little women walking dogs almost their own size. Some dogs are miniscule, some virtually horse- or pony-size.

My concern is not with the lifestyle of dog owners, but rather with the hazards of *walking* without stepping into dog shit. It is everywhere, not only off the curb, but on the sidewalk. Getting out of a taxi calls for the utmost vigilance.

One day, in reading a piece by Kenneth Tynan, something caught my special interest. He referred to "the neat pyramids of dog excrement on the sidewalks outside the grander apartments. 'How do you know it's dogs?' Charles Addams once said to me, and the hair rose on my scalp." Of course only Charles Addams would ask such a question; perhaps we're being needlessly hard on the *dogs*.

Perhaps I'm being needlessly dogmatic, but those "ca-ca" signatures left on the sidewalks, curbs, and streets by "man's best friend" (and God help man if *that's* true) keep me in a perpetual state of distress. (But I am keeping this to myself; think of the outraged mail I'd get from dog lovers; a confession of wife-beating would bring less response.)

Diary Extract: A Week in the Life of . . .

November: Six cocktail and dinner parties in nine successive days, plus a premiere screening of a film and an opening night of an off-Broadway play. We walked out of both film and play midway in the performances. As for the parties (for celebrity hunters and collectors), here are some of the guests we met, several for the first time: Charles Addams, Saul Steinberg, Bel Kaufman, Isaac Bashevis Singer, Penelope Gilliatt, Gerold Frank, Gay Talese, Mario Puzo, Elizabeth Janeway, John Hawkes, Diane Wakoski, Alfred Kazin, Anne Birstein, Anthony West, Sue Kaufman and her husband Dr. Barondess, Evelyn and John Kobler, Jack and Gloria MacGowran, Edward Gorey, Pauline Kael, Betty Comden, Bosley and Florence Crowther, Fritz Molden. Too little sleep, too many manuscripts to read. I found myself hard put to cope, for the intake of booze and wine was at a record high. The consumption of Rolaids and aspirin began to alarm me. The foregoing was followed by two boring weeks on "jury duty"—sitting, endlessly waiting, a dull procedure that resulted in no hits, runs, or errors for anyone. Except that I found time to discover a writer introduced to me by Alfredo Machado.

Jorge Amado was the author, and I read three of his novels while awaiting my jury service. I loved *Gabriella: Clove and Cinnamon,* a delicious concoction of history, sex, and characterization in abundance. More about Amado immediately; we met him in Bahia in Brazil at Christmas.

Only in Brazil: Christmas–New Year's Eve, 1971–1972

'Rio: first impressions. Heat is constant and penetrating; rain excessive. Rio streets are clean, built for walking, especially the Copacabana area, where we stayed. Contrary to the travel brochures, very little English is spoken. Luckily, our hosts, Gloria and Alfredo Machado, the publishers, served us well as interpreters.

The money (the *cruzeiro* is about five and a half to the dollar) is often a bit of shabby paper, hardly a token of money as it is known in the United States. I can't understand why the banks don't recall and destroy this filthy, worn-out paper money; certainly it is unhygienic to handle.

Taxis are the cheapest in the world, and perhaps the most efficient. Architecture, scenic views, beaches, and food—all are notable and pleasing. Brazilian pop music is wretched, boring. Hospitality is warm, and the eight or nine homes we visited were charming, civilized, filled with good Brazilian art, books, records.

Many bookshops in Rio; plenty of reading matter on every level. Many good bistros and most alcohol is inexpensive; but Scotch is prohibitive, costing about three dollars per drink, or about twenty dollars per fifth. Yet, Scotch seems to be the most popular of all drinks.

Meat and fish always good; great steaks and filet mignons and crisp french fries. We learned about the joys of the Brazilian dish, *feijoada*, rich with meats and black beans but not readily duplicated by American chefs. Ice cream is excellent; pineapples and oranges always at hand, not forgetting the delicious minibananas. (Why are there no large-sized bananas such as we get in the States?) Flowers are abundant and cheap; a dozen long-stemmed roses cost only $3.50 to $4.00.

Could locate only one rare bookdealer in Rio, named Kosmos—

but could find nothing to buy; mostly historical, Latin American stuff and a few incunables. (Not a book by Neruda!)

———————

Bahia: New Year's Eve

At the tropical tree-and-flower-paradise home of Jorge Amado. He lives like an emperor. He is a loved-on-sight person; he speaks no English but manages to perceive everything, and he communicates somehow. He is the warmest of hosts, and entertains some thirty-five guests, including the artist-muralist, Carybe. Mrs. Amado is hospitable in the extreme (she wore a hippie tee shirt), as are Jorge's eighty-five-year-old mother, his brother the doctor, and the other members of the family. Amado's house is virtually a museum, with a rich collection of paintings, sculpture, interesting objects, and found artifacts of nature. Two days later we visited the house again for Sunday brunch; more of the same warmth. Gaiety reigns, singing (mostly bawdy songs), and gentle horseplay. One of the musicians, a delightful, bearded young man, a journalist, sang a song about Marie: "Poor Marie, she's always tired. Why? Because Marie fucks in the morning, Marie fucks at noon, Marie fucks at night. Poor, tired Marie." Those are the lyrics, and the household breaks up with laughter, including the teenagers and the old folks. How captivating it is. Noted that Amado drinks hardly at all, and moves about his house nervously, spending very little time with any individual. He fondles his four bulldogs with a special tender affection.

The artist Carybe draws humorous and erotic sketches for the guests as souvenirs; he gave us a caricature of Amado with an enormous penis, and Jorge, after examining the drawing carefully, inscribed it, "certifying" it for accuracy! The guests burst into laughter. He also inscribed two of his books for us, *The Violent Land* and *The Two Deaths of Quincus Wateryell.* (The latter is an especially handsome example of Knopf's bookmaking.) I also acquired a few other inscribed books, one from the poet-publisher, Alvaro Pacheco, a delightful, hospitable man.

A series of scenic trips with the Machados, including a visit to the top of Corcovado, with a view of the Bay of Rio; took snapshots at the foot of the giant Christ figure in granite, the statue that dominates the city; also luncheon atop the new 36-floor hotel, Nacionale, as guests of its p.r. director, Oscar Ornstein. The hotel astonishes one for beauty and imaginative design, and its fantastic views of the ocean and mountains at every turn. Cost twenty million dollars, I am told. There is nothing quite like it in the States. It was designed by the Brazilian architect Oscar Niemeyr. Some thirty beautiful bikini-clad girls—part of the hotel staff—are hired to sit around the swimming pool to entertain lonely visitors.

A midnight visit to witness voodoo dances proved disappointing; Roslyn and I seemed unable to get on the wavelength of the white-clad bebustled dancers who swayed and revolved and rotated and occasionally prostrated themselves before the huge black priestess. Something by way of magic or stagecraft was missing. It may have been psychic impotence on my part. Also, I had just recently finished editing a book on voodoo (by Robert Pelton) and the subject did not entrance me as it might have a novice. Truthfully, it was boring.

Daily swimming in the Copacabana Hotel pool, with sunbathing on the beach directly across from the hotel. Result: a very dark suntan and deep lethargy. In three days I looked like a native. The hotel rates are certainly lower than in the States, about fifteen dollars for a large single room with bath.

In Bahia the annual Fisherman's Festival takes place, with perhaps a hundred fishing boats out in the water in a colorful procession. Music, wild drinking, and general hijinks in a 95-degree temperature. Lots of *batidas* (sugar cane distilled, pure, in assorted flavors) consumed ashore, and shortly we were all smashed.

Dinner at the Machados' elegant home, with a spectacular view of Rio, proved the most delightful of all our meals. They were the most devoted, thoughtful, and generous hosts; Alfredo even provided the press with daily "stories" about the activities of the New York Targs; even my *batida* "expertise" was noted!

Other impressions: the picture-postcard sunset on Botafogo Beach; Bloody Marys and lunch in the elegant Museum of Modern Art dining room; the aerial view of the Maracana Stadium, "biggest in the world"; midnight walks on La Plage de Copacabana; listening to live vibrant performances on the guitar by Rosinha de Valencia at Monsieur Pujol; and especially to Chico Buraque in a "deluxe production" of his *Construcao*. Souvenirs of Rio include purchase of Heitor Villa-Lobos recordings, a rope hammock, boar's-teeth necklaces, and voodoo jewelry. Memories that will be around: the filet mignon steaks at three dollars per serving, and the handsome native nightclub entertainers.

What I missed in Rio was book talk; shoptalk, that is. The bookshops were, to all appearances, drug or stationery shops. The ambience of the New York, London, and Paris stores was missing—the bookish chic and deep-down literary ambience of the big-city bookshop. Publishers and editors with whom I spoke talked only of advances and sales, nothing else. One publisher did talk to me of a Portuguese edition of Joyce's *Ulysses*, published in 1966. (About two thousand copies were sold. I hesitate to think of the publisher's loss on that enterprise.) American paperbacks are available at outrageous prices. But plenty of newspaper kiosks are visible, and a large variety of newspapers and magazines.

The absence of neckties and jackets in restaurants and the posh nightclubs interests me; during three weeks in Rio and Bahia I did not wear either. That is being civilized, *liberated*.

Rendering the quality, the felt lifestyle of the Brazilians, is not easy; it merits study. There is much here, above and below the surface, to admire, to love. Amidst the profusion of green and the natural wonders, there is the vitality of a lively people, their zest for life; a Whitmanesque fellowship (among men) is visible at every hand. The beautiful manliness of their embrace.

I hope to return to Brazil one day soon. If the Machados aren't there to greet us, we will be devastated. Alfredo is the "man for all seasons," a good publisher, a man who laughs easily, and loves life. One of the best hosts we have ever known.

Ernest Hecht, the British publisher, had sent Roslyn a long, handwritten personal guide to Rio, with restaurant and other recommendations—a miniature, personalized guide that proved absolutely foolproof. Hecht knows Brazil, since he finances most of the soccer matches there, I'm told.

3   *"A Profession for Gentlemen,"*

Did You Say?

Total Recall

In his *Diary: 1935–1950,* Cesare Pavese says, "The richness of life lies in the memories we have forgotten." This is demonstrable. I keep confirming this as I assemble this potpourri.

To produce a book such as this is a matter of pressing buttons, employing memory acupuncture techniques (perhaps the word is "acupressure.") Psychophysiological buttons to be pushed, probing the no-man's-land of neurophysiology. Triggering memories buried in the most recessed areas—you'll be astonished at the autobiographer's potential, the "stockpile"!

The cybernetician's view of life becomes suddenly clear to me as I summon up "memories forgotten." Each memory segment speaks of a particular moment. What a marvelous machine is the brain, that it can retain and spell back so much. (I'm beginning to sound like old Arthur Brisbane.) I suspect I could produce a *Remembrance of Things Past,* not with Proust's talent, but certainly in terms of sheer *volume.*

If I had another lifetime I'd devote it to the understanding and exploration of the animal muscles, the communicating organs, the information processing systems we all possess. What a kick, recalling the fifty- and sixty-year-old episodes in one's private history! Possibly, we might look further back—into previous incarnations. (Which I believe is possible, by the way.)

But how to recall some of the events of a fortnight ago! I must find some spare time for a reading of Norbert Wiener.

One of the most important, though commercially modest books I've brought to Putnam's was *The Brain* by C. U. M. Smith, an

English biophysicist, which was published in 1970. I secured it from Faber & Faber. It was a source of satisfaction to me, an enduring book, first-rate in style and content. It was well reviewed, but sold poorly, even in the subsequent paperback edition. (Something may have gone wrong in our promotion procedures.) That book should be in the hands or libraries of intelligent college students concerned with Mind and related matters.

I often think of one paragraph in that book in which the author gives us some grim facts: *The average adult brain consists of thirty billion nerve cells; the cells die at the rate of a thousand a day throughout adult life. They don't reproduce themselves, so the number of cells diminish with a deadly regularity.*

If you have a pencil handy figure out how many brain cells you have left, then act accordingly.

I recently published (at Putnam's) a book called *The Intelligent Universe* by an Englishman, David Foster. It is quasi-philosophy, based on cybernetics, and has a long introduction by Colin Wilson. I find the subject hypnotic but admit that some of it is beyond my understanding. We are all computers, Foster claims, all part of a gigantic, cosmic Computer.

Imagine praying to a colossal computer in the sky—and why not?

Extending the conjecture, consider the sexual potential of a computer—and would you want your sister to marry one? The purpose of life, says Foster, is to be more intelligent, to maximize our mental potential.

Les Girls and the Top-Banana Syndrome

NOTE: *A brief excerpt from the following piece appeared as a "Letter to the Editor" in* Publishers Weekly, *November 30, 1974. It flushed out a lot of letters and verbal comments: some of them thorny, some complimentary, some vague, such as, "You've got your nerve!" The national president of the Women's National Book Association, Mary V. Gaver, sent me an intelligent and most respectful two-page, single-spaced letter. I won't quote her out of context, but in essence her argument is that some women are lucky when they get to work with supportive men, but such men are in the minority. She agrees with many of my views, not with all of them. I hope the following complete "letter" doesn't provoke heated correspondence nor the burning of me in effigy.*

There's a lot of verbiage published and voiced on sexism, women's rights, equal pay, opportunity.

The coalition of sex, brains, indignation is a powerhouse with which to contend. Some of the recent utterances, in print and vocally, are sensible; some merely well intended; much of it, pure propaganda. Some of it is downright nonsense. Also boring.

Let's take a look at Les Girls and the top-banana syndrome. The first and foremost point to make is that an attractive, charming, or feminine woman will often be a sex object to a man—and to some women. This is "what every man knows." Intelligence, wit, competence, and muscle are the plus factors, the elements that *can* get her where she wants to go. In business, that is.

The November 11, 1974 issue of *Publishers Weekly* stopped me cold. Beginning on page 22, and running for six full pages, was an article/symposium, edited by Ann Geracimos. It was entitled "Women in Publishing: Where Do They Feel They're Going?"

Why so much space to that old chestnut about women being held back? With the paper and space shortage, six pages of rapping about such subjects as the ignominy of being a secretary! Elizabeth Gordon of Harper & Row said in the article, "If I were giving young women advice now, I'd say, don't take a secretarial job." The whole symposium struck me as an exercise in desperation, with speeches signifying a desire for some sort of power (abstract?) fulfillment, rebellion.

Okay. *But what's wrong with being a secretary?*

Someone from outer space reading the article might construe the secretary's job as something demeaning, subhuman, on a level, say, with tending a washroom, demonstrating cold cream in a department store, hairdressing, waiting on tables, charring, posing for advertisements in *Screw* or *Cosmopolitan*, or blowing strange men in massage parlors.

Well, it isn't.

There's no better springboard to a top job, to fame and fortune, or, if you will, to marriage and a home in Palm Springs, than the secretary's chair. But getting to the point (with Scout's-honor sincerity), if you want to be a member of the book publishing community, if you really want to learn the business of books, there's no better way than via the office of an editor or any other publishing executive. Which includes the advertising, production, sales, publicity, or promotion departments.

A hundred and one matters relating to publishing cross the desk of an editor. Most of what goes on is shared with the secretary at hand. The intelligent secretary becomes privy to all of the arcane stuff taking place, and participates in the action. And learns. An editorial secretary can learn about the temperament of authors, about manuscripts and proofs, advertising copy, publicity releases, review media, manufacturing details, jacket art, and other phases of book publishing. All one has to do is keep the eyes and ears open— and the pores. And being well-read doesn't hurt. (I once interviewed a young job applicant and when I asked her about her favorite authors she replied, "William Shakespeare." I waited, then asked, "Anyone else?" She paused, searched the ceiling for a moment, then said, "I can't remember for sure, right off." She was a Manhattan high school graduate.

Perhaps I had unnerved her. Except she wasn't very bright. Facing her during the interview was a wall of books published by Putnam's and other firms. There were lots of authors she could have cited. But she wasn't nimble.

Young women: If you want to learn the book business (and that's really what I'm concerned about here), if you want to get ahead in any area of the business, take a secretarial job unless you have a specialty or qualifications that should take you into an executive or administrative job. Qualifying for a secretary's job isn't duck soup. And good jobs are scarce—for men as well as women.

You must know how to spell; can you really?

You must type well, punctuate, take some form of dictation, use the English language with some decent grace, speak clearly, be aware of the basic amenities required in a business office. You must bathe regularly (*PW* deleted *that* from my letter) and you must wear shoes or a reasonable facsimile. (Some sneakers are charming.)

Baby Doll dresses won't help nor too much visible skin.

And please, try to be a self-starter. Which means, don't wait to be told that the letters written at closing time must be stamped and mailed at once; that a phone message should be written down, especially if it is from an author; that a smile on occasion helps relieve the tension in an office. And don't be an ear-bender.

If you're on your toes and are not too disagreeable a personality, it's hard not to move ahead. The advancements that occur in your office are usually not handed out—they're earned—unless you are related to the boss.

Performance, some animal heat, personality, and persuasion will get you up on the escalator. Be modest in your ascension. (But don't be afraid to assert yourself.) Performance counts most. You must make your presence and work contribution felt, but not your desperation. Your ambitions must be registered, but not with pile-driver impact. Some workers fail to get that better job simply because the employer wasn't aware of their needs. Find *your* "happy medium."

I recall an incident at World during the time I was children's book editor. When I felt it was no longer possible for me to handle the work, we searched outside and found a first-class editor, Velma Varner, and hired her as head of the Children's Book Division. The moment the news was out, two of the junior editors in our office came to me with tears and hysteria: Why weren't they hired? Why did I choose to slight them? The simple truth was: I hadn't the faintest notion that they were interested. Their qualifications aside, at no time had either of these young women indicated that she would like to move into the chair of children's editor-in-chief.

It's essential to speak up, sound off; not abrasively or threateningly, but speak up you must if you think you're ready for the next step up the Big Apple ladder. If you're good, that is, if you have a real track record of production, of moneymaking, of having brought a touch or more of glory to the firm, then you're ready. Put it to the Mr. Big of your company, straightforwardly. Harry Golden would say, "You're entitled." There are still a few knuckle-headed VIP heads of firms who "don't want the girls peeing with the boys." In such a case, you have a choice; perhaps you should take a walk.

But are you sure, absolutely sure, that you want to be top banana in your department or in post Numero Uno? I ask because I suspect it isn't anything like your fantasy indicates. Some of the people occupying the top plateau have ulcers, tough mortgage payments, stultified private lives, and deflated stocks in their portfolios, not to mention sticky extramarital situations, bad livers, and insomnia problems. Also—and this is important to remember—Up There, the terrain is beset with land mines, and there are sharp knife-wielders hankering to slip it to you. Freud would call the female yearning for power *ulcer envy.*

The aforementioned *PW* article went on to say: "Companies prefer married men and unmarried women." If it means what I think it means (and I think it's a put-on), then only male heterosexuals need apply for publishing jobs. Do you really need statistics?

I believe that any women who has the *ardor* to succeed at the top-level job in any profession, including politics, can do so if she's able to show the drive. Admittedly, it has been tough for women in recent years, and it is still tough. I've known some first-rate women editors in past years, and while they were well paid and honored, they never made editor-in-chief. Today, in the seventies, conditions are improving; women are making it, in status and money.

There are top jobs for women in most business and cultural areas. I don't think there's a real systematic conspiracy at work in America, keeping women from getting their share, their place. Habit rather than discrimination by design is more like it. Women must lean harder, show them, learn how to *make demands,* as do the men.

Deforcement by the male is diminishing each year as more women assert themselves and management becomes more realistic and more humane.

Getting the title: Women are gradually getting everything they've been after. Betty Prashker is editorial director at Doubleday; Patricia Soliman is editor-in-chief of Coward, McCann & Geoghegan; Regina Ryan heads up Macmillan's trade department. It's a simple formula: these women produced, delivered the goods, earned their keep, plus. These women also have charm, plus chutzpah. The combination endears them to everyone not made of stone.

The real discrimination exists not so much between the sexes as between the *powerful* and the *powerless.* A woman has a built-in force, an innate power, and if she fails to use it, she must not blame sexual prejudice. The bearer of the pudendum will often be made to "suffer," by virtue of her physical distinction. And some women will never get the jobs they're after. Neither will certain types of men. Men with long hair are still suffering discrimination; so are men whose wives are vulgarians, alcoholics, or nympho-maniacs. The gays, on the other hand, are definitely in.

When a giant publishing corporation lays down edicts, decree-ing that its writers must avoid "sexism" in their books, one can only sit back and howl. Imagine telling a serious writer not to refer to a woman as "a fragile flower," "a goddess on a pedestal," "a sweet young thing," nor for that matter, "a henpecking shrew." It's the male's inalienable right that McGraw-Hill is trying to usurp. Yes, that's what they tried to pull recently, in an eleven-page "guidelines for equal treatment of the sexes." The woman's enemy is apparently language. McGraw-Hill's party line is: There's no Difference Between Man and Woman.

In short, they've gone bananas.

What about woman's rights, the right to call her husband a "slob" or a "crummy bastard"? No one is trying to boycott *that* right.

There are, I suspect, more lame-brain male editors than female. The women in the juvenile book departments are no longer stereo-typed drudges and spinsters. They know the "words," and use them when needed. Recently I heard a lively young woman editor call an author, "you mother," and believe me, he knew what she meant. Yes, there are a few witches around, but the charmers outnumber them. And there are some marvelously attractive newcomers, all fresh as the proverbial daisies. They may not be demon gram-marians or perfectionists as spellers, but—

As for equal pay: to the best of my knowledge women in pub-lishing are getting paid on a par with men—the house scale may be low, which is another matter. I know that the turnover in female employees among publishing houses is great, and the reason is usually money. *Thinking* heads of houses are coming to the realization that you can't play the old game anymore. Only the primitive, fossilized holdouts fail to realize that a woman can take top-level responsibility and can be creative and loyal as well. Even when she has beautiful legs.

Les Girls will resolve their problems. But let's keep the issue of sexism out of the struggle. Like racism, it will be wiped out, when and wherever intelligence prevails. Like cockroaches, no matter how hard one fights to exterminate the old prejudices, they are still around us. We must just keep at the exterminating.

The book industry is singular, I believe, in the profusion of women now employed in it. Women are functioning in almost all areas of the business. The book clubs and reprint houses are also significantly represented by women. The rights-permissions departments are dominated by them; some of them are superstars. A *pride* of notables comes to mind: Page Cuddy, Milly Marmur, Beverly Loo, Barbara Neilson, Patricia Breinin, Paula Diamond, Jean Rosenthal, Kathy Robbins, Sabina Iardella, Lila Karpf, Joni Evans, Barbara Adams, Irma Heldman, Connie Sayre. There are a number of others, and they're all producers. They belong!

Of course there are some able men in the subsidiary-rights areas as well; but the women, somehow, seem to be in the majority. It's true that a few top male editors and publishing heads handle the rights on their own major books. By and large, though, this has become a woman's game. I'm not sure why, except that I've seen some in action. For example, I've watched and heard Page Cuddy charming some publisher into a deal on the phone—expertise and charm at work. No male I know could have outdone her in her selling performance. Feminine and effective. No con, but a virtuoso, who might even do well running General Motors. (Their stock could recover under her guidance.) Some of these women could sell the Brooklyn Bridge at least once a week, and before breakfast at that. Are they more percipient judges of character, better poker players? Perhaps. But some of them, tigers though they be under their Estée Lauder facades, are still "fragile flowers," "goddesses on pedestals"—and also "shrews." Why deny it? Without their innate femininity, their *difference,* how dull they would be. A subsidiary-rights director can do her job while flaunting a miniskirt, a flash of thigh, a skin-tight sweater. And a breath of Halston's fragrance. No order issued by High Authority (nothing personal, Harold McGraw) can stop a woman from being a woman and being so characterized in a book or article. Talk about intellectual confusion, society gone barmy!

As the lyric goes, "There is nothing like a dame," and if your employer orders you to follow the so-called nonsexist "guidelines," I'd suggest defenestration.

My wife owns and runs—and very successfully—her own literary agency. She started there as a secretary, fresh out of Hunter College. (She never felt demeaned as a secretary, by the way.) Eventually, after many years, she bought the business from her savings. When I feel like introducing her as "the Missus," she has the grace and aplomb to smile it off. She is a woman of the world and understands that the gentle "battle of the sexes" adds to the pleasures of a male-female relationship.

I can name other women who have "made the big time" in the publishing world: Leona Nevler, Helen Meyer, Patricia Day, Eleanor Rawson, Eleanor Friede, Ursula Nordstrom, Helen Wolff, Elaine Geiger—these are a few who come to mind. They are women of real achievement in publishing. I'm sure you'll find that the percentage of female executive personnel is growing.

Any bright, well-intentioned, and hardworking woman (with minimal neurosis) can make a big splash in the book scene if she has real talent, if she's willing to take the roughing up, the compromises, and the rest of it—as do the men. They've been doing it in the magazine field for years.

Whether women will agree that *anything* is possible for a woman in publishing is something I can't nail down here. Many will not agree with me, of course. Don't ask me why. Ask Bella Abzug.

There are also many women in top jobs (and in ownership) in the literary agency field. Some of their offices are virtually harems; members of the male sex are almost invisible. Many male authors seem to prefer women agents. I can't tell you why. I can guess, of course; so could Freud. From years of experience with literary agents, and with one in particular, I can assure you that the woman agent on the whole has high competence and is totally dependable. A few alcoholic exceptions notwithstanding.

The publicity and promotion departments are also prominently female-managed; women have the skill, tact, and charm to handle that most difficult creature—the author—and a publisher would be pretty foolhardy to practice sexism in his publicity department. I think women are also imaginative publicists; they are able to evaluate literary material and present it in an intelligent, palatable, and publishable form. There is no reason on earth why a woman should not hold down that job unless she is underqualified.

I think Harold Robbins summed it up in his fashion when he said, "Women are the only thing around that I can see that's worth making love to . . . from the standpoint of equal pay, equal treatment, I'm all for it. I would much rather have a woman light my cigarette than I would like to light hers. There's something luxurious about having a girl light your cigarette. In fact, I got married once on account of that." There's a moral in that statement, somewhere.

You Can't Take Id with You

Summing up the foregoing sermon on women making it in book publishing, and replying to a second thoughtful letter from Mary V. Gaver, my "position" is simply this: sexism is a miniscule element in the "top-echelon power game" and no effort, no means, no manifestation of the *id* should be overlooked in the realization of one's aspirations, namely, getting the job you want in publishing. Being a woman won't hold you back if you're good. Use all your powers in the getting-ahead stratagem. Life is short, the jobs are there—and you really can't *take* the id with you. Use it or it will get rusty.

Sexism and the Sea Lion

Fact The male sea lion will swim three thousand miles in icy black water in order to meet up with, and fuck, for twenty seconds, a particular slippery (comely to him) sea lioness sunning herself on a particular rock. Biological destiny picked her out for him. Inherent in this honeymoon sequence lies the sweet tyranny of sex. And I've got it on the highest authority (a distinguished anthropologist of the female gender who doesn't mind calling a female sea lion, "lionness") that the creature *likes* to be thought of as a *sex object*. Also, she doesn't mind if you fail to address her as "Ms."

Fact   Man is the Eternal Schmuck, literally.

Women are what they are and always have been. And will be. No authority, no ukase, will alter the basic interraction of men and women. No magazine article, no street demonstration, edict, talk show, no raised fist, will alter the male attitude toward the female—the heterosexual male, that is.

No one can really call Amaury de Reincourt a male chauvinist. In his book, *Sex and Power*, he says, "The scientific and historical records show that all the way from unicellular organisms to human beings, progress in evolution has been stimulated by an increase in sexual differentiation."

Let's keep the sexes clearly defined.

Ego-Tripping

One of the hazards of personal bigness in publishing —as elsewhere, including politics—is the loss of perspective and humility. I've seen heads of giant corporations and newly realized conglomerates morally derailed by virtue of big-time headiness. It occurs on the heights; it's a kind of vertigo. It brings on a confused, disoriented condition which, in turn, causes the victim to behave in manic fashion.

"I'm the boss and let everyone realize it," is one manifestation of this ego disease. But the smart superstar executive reverses himself, understates, plays humble, and above all, manages to keep his mouth shut publicly.

Nixon is a fine example of the man in power who got carried away with the führer notion. Such men usually get cut off at the knees before their careers are ended.

A publisher of books should be a businessman and leader, but he must not sound off publicly on his personal power; he must not be a blowhard, a "boss." Grace and modesty will serve his ends better than public ego-tripping.

Editors should walk softly, carry no big stick, and speak in firm but subdued tones about their triumphs, actual and potential. The deeds will speak for them, and there is no better way to proclaim one's talents than through the publication of a splendid book or the achievement of a best seller. I doubt that Maxwell Perkins ever said "I'm the boss." Nor his boss, Charles Scribner.

Top executives need not necessarily take a course in *method* humbleness, but they might make an effort toward an appearance of humility in public—especially when they've got it made. Gloating over the failure or disaster of another publisher—e.g., a Clifford Irving situation—is certainly bad manners. Disasters and mistakes can occur in any house, large or small.

I've seen an editor's voice and posture change overnight as the result of being appointed to a top-echelon post. A flossy title, together with a bit more authority, can distort or destroy a man or woman. Next time you find yourself being carried away by your title, reread the Book of Ecclesiastes. Sending Third Reich-type memos to subordinates is out of fashion. Informality is a wonder-worker. Try it.

An editor's public display of status power is one of his most offensive characteristics. His posture (as though he were in fact the author) is a display of pure vulgarity and it will do him harm in the end—harm to his image and to his professional position.

As for editor's imprints: I feel strongly that there is room for only one publisher's name on a book. Why demand special public recognition by virtue of being a book's editor? I have yet to discover why a "Joseph Zilch Book" makes a book more attractive to the general public than a book simply announced over the publisher's imprint. The loneliness of the editor, the fear of anonymity, the need for celebrity status—these are sad and sometimes sick manifestations. First-class editors who have high professional recognition don't really need imprint recognition. Every time I see a book announced as a "blank-blank" book, I wonder why. I've yet to hear a satisfactory explanation.

Book Contraception Now! A Few Truths

Everything below is elementary. I make no startling disclosures. What I do here is to simply remind you of facts. I cite these facts for the benefit of the newcomers, the young editors, for the record—the Doomsday Book, if you will.

Everyone knows that too many books are being published. Most of the new ones are expendable, marginal, trashy, or duplications of those previously published and readily available.

In 1973, almost 40,000 new titles and reprints were published in America. Early 1974 figures indicated an increase. Like a moving glacier, like pollution or political corruption, there seems no way to contain the evil. The production flow increases, and now there are some 435,000 titles in print in this country.

The international paper swindle (my personal characterization), which accounts for the higher costs of books (paper in 1974 was double the price of 1973) drives the books to ridiculous price levels. Binding technology has not yet caught up with the high-speed presses, and sewn books are more expensive than ever. Eventually, only well-funded libraries and institutions and the remaining solvent members of the public will be able to afford the new books. "Inflation" is going to keep most of the books out of the hands of the general public. Which includes the hands of students and children.

In one sense, the paper shortage may prove a blessing; it will help to contain the growing production figures. Publishers may finally become selective.

The numbers game is being played by the old-line publishers and the new hotshot entrepreneurs. And the paperback publishers, too. In the end there will be a lot of tears shed. Some real blood, too. A study of six months' *Publishers Weekly* announcements will disclose to any interested reader that we're really in the soup. That fewer and better books are needed, but nothing is being done about it. Crap of every description continues to be announced for sale: the word "crap" is used here advisedly. Books as bad as the worst motion pictures are being published. And *that's* bad. (I have a theory that the low standards of motion pictures have corrupted the writers' standards, in that the writers believe the public *wants* the inferior quality inherent in most films and TV shows.)

Eliot Fremont-Smith wisely points out that the glut of mediocre books is hurting the good ones: "Before publishing problems get sorted out, a lot of publishers, particularly the big commercial houses, are going to have to cut way back on their lists."

One of the reasons for the excess of output (the new executive breed refers to books as "product") is the myth (in American free enterprise) that one must do *more* of everything each successive year. If you published fifty books last year, then you should increase the output by not less than 10 percent this year, and so on.

Rubbish, of course. It's possible to publish fewer books and enjoy more dollar-volume. Selectivity. I call your attention to John P. Dessauer's comments (*Publishers Weekly*, October 7, 1974) which makes the statement far better than I can:

> When we think of the virtues of publishers there is one we are likely to place high on the list: discrimination. Obviously not every book published will or need be a masterpiece; there is ample room for light, even frivolous entertainment, and for the indulgence of the strangest tastes, in a pluralistic society. But whatever is published can, should, and it now seems may have to be, good *in its own genre.* Surfeit and mediocrity are luxuries we can no longer afford. Unless we are prepared to suffer internal strangulation, to suffocate under the weight of millions of unwanted and unsalable books ground out yearly, we shall have to find ways to curtail the industry's overproduction.

Bravo, John Dessauer!

Selectivity. That's the answer. It's possible to maintain a healthy business on an even keel, with fewer books. Fewer and better, that is. And WHO is to decide? Ask any child of twelve what he/she thinks about your last year's list, and you'll get your answer in basic English.

Ask any intelligent bookseller or librarian.

The problems of book distribution and the delivery of books are still with us. And booksellers can't possibly accommodate more than a mere fraction of the books coming off the presses. Certainly the public can't.

Overproduction will eventually give the industry a giant-sized case of impacted constipation, so that it will take bankruptcy, liquidation, and a high colonic to achieve catharsis, not to mention years of convalescence. (In 1974 one major publisher saw the light and took drastic action by cutting his list and staff drastically. The industry was aghast at the "bloodbath" but in the end, as a practical business measure, it made sense.)

So who is the true villain? There must be *one place* where the blame may be assigned.

The answer is clearly The Business Office. The acting head of the firm, the chief executive officer or whatever he chooses to be called—he's to blame.

Not the editors; not the sales, advertising, or publicity personnel. The acting head of the firm insists on "beating last year's figures," no matter how. The business-managerial mind is concerned with one thing: making the stockholders happy, kidding them with figures. Bigness, "growth." Growth is the magic word: keep growing, until you burst! So, more titles, more product, bigger lists. The numbers game.

So who's responsible?

The business manager.

And the coffee-table books keep coming and getting more expensive.

And the stock market listings continue to shrink.

And the retail prices keep escalating.

And the shredding machines are sharpening their teeth.

(The above bit of graffiti is offered to the industry with the full knowledge that the reader has already turned the page with a yawn.)

Up the Union!

A young woman who is active in labor unions recently asked me for my views on unions in the book publishing industry. She also solicited my comments on sex discrimination in jobs, equal pay, etc. I was asked, I think, because it came to her attention that I was writing a book about publishing.

My reflex response would have been something to the effect that a liberalizing movement already exists *outside* of unions. One has only to compare the modern publisher's office to the offices of the twenties. Today, a chief editor can be found sitting in a Yoga position on the floor of his office or standing on his head in the presence of an author, with no one perturbed or surprised. Tennis shoes, sports clothes, and denims are commonplace in publishers' offices. Secretaries earn salaries that were paid to top editors a decade ago. Expense accounts are virtually unlimited.

I promised the young woman that I'd think about the subject and try to determine where I stood. It's been a long time since my nascent radicalism, when I was preoccupied with Gompers and Debs and the Wobblies, with civil rights and the worker. For a long time I was conscious of labor and unions, especially during my early bookshop days when many of my customers were union organizers and heavily radicalized, when the talk was of the Industrial Revolution, the eight-hour day, the New Deal wage-and-hour legislation (in the thirties, I believe), the National Labor Relations Act, the Taft-Hartley Act. I once edited a biography of David Dubinsky and got to meet him and some of his top brass. But little of that experience rubbed off on me. In later years I read a number of books on labor; I also found some rather interesting and germane comments on the subject in Kate Millett's *Sexual Politics* and in Simone Weil's writings. Of late, I've become somewhat disoriented because of other interests. I find no heroic father figures among today's labor leaders, no civilized figure I can respect or trust. I'm cynical about most unions. So what I have to say on the subject is less than negligible; it's highly simplistic and personal. It will have no consequence other than to get myself labelled reactionary.

I've never been in a top-management position. I've hired a secretary or assistant from time to time, and made salary recommendations. And there my authority ceased. (I could propose the expenditure of a quarter of a million dollars for a manuscript, but that's not a matter for discussion here.)

Certain principles of Christianity might be welcome in the matter of employer-employee relations, and I'd gladly accept them. Some publishers do indeed practice Christianity under the guise of benevolent despotism or vice versa. However, I feel that palpable discrimination, exploitation, bigotry, racism, parsimony, and all sorts of neurotic behavior patterns exist (and will continue to exist) in business—and in book publishing. Businesses are people, not merely offices and arithmetic and "product."

I'd fire any racist in my employ. But I'm not sure I'd behave in a flammable manner over the issue of sexism. I see beautiful women as sex objects even when I admire their brains and skills. I feel that women are capable of holding down almost any job. But sexuality is real and can't be ignored under certain working conditions. It is already a very tired subject.

I'm for incentive-compensation for everyone. Any head of a house who refuses to pay out bonuses for exceptional performance and for occasional home-run hits is not being fair or realistic. He doesn't understand the power of spreading joy or that bonuses are good business all around.

Aptitude and talent must be paid for, without regard to sex or race or social status. One piece of relevance must be given consideration by the publisher-employer: a first-rate editor, which is to say, a self-starting and creative editor, can't be overpaid. Neither can a first-rate advertising person or sales director or copyreader; they are hard to find. Being penny-wise is folly in the literary labor market. Generosity, so-called cossetting, in the case of creative, *gifted*, employees, is sensible. And while humanness is frowned upon in business, try it some time—it feels good.

As for unions and labor laws: I think miners, police, firefighters, machine workers, and most blue-collar workers need special security and guarantees. Nurses and hospital attendants are terribly underpaid, as are teachers, and they should, I feel, be protected by unions. I'm not convinced that office workers, junior clerks, and assistants in publishing offices need unionization. A lot of clerks and junior editors have hierarchical fantasies and want highfalutin titles for status purposes; some would-be executives are hopelessly unqualified.

I think most factory workers are underpaid. Working at a machine can be dehumanizing, and to be underpaid while being dehumanized is, in my view, the worst possible fate.

If an editor or sales executive is any good, management will usually recognize his/her worth. Often (from close-up observations over many years) they get from management more than they would through union pressure. And without paying dues.

My view of unions is dimmed when I learn of the salaries paid to their leaders. There's nothing very Christian about these men, nothing Spartan about their lifestyle. I have a simplistic philosophy when it comes to labor. I am for better salaries and working conditions for the *laborer*. The only cause I would really become agitated over is the cause of Food. Not enough people get enough to eat. Until every living soul is able to go to bed at night decently fed, every other cause is so much bullshit. The Pentagon, which spends billions of dollars for arms, is my idea of obscenity in action. When a politician speaks up for more arms, I find myself retching.

I don't see how I, an editorial worker, can justify unionization. If I felt that I was being exploited or financially disadvantaged, I'd look for another job. My job, my salary, my future—these are personal matters to me and I'd be reluctant to have them arranged for me by a union. Besides, most union organizers I've met are distinctly unpleasant people; I don't like their personalities, their manners, their fanaticism. Most of them also have bad breath. As solid men and women of character, they are no match for the worker.

When I've had a problem, I went straight to my employer or his designated representative, on a one-to-one basis, and usually secured a resolution. This view, I suspect, is considered Neanderthal and reactionary. But I'm an admitted reactionary—an individualist.

Presumably, none of the above remarks will be of service to anyone interested in organizing an office or warehouse. Ask me something else, something simple, dealing with, say, how to acquire a manuscript, how to placate an irate author, how to wheedle an extra ad out of the advertising manager, and I'll find you answers. I can also handle such questions as reincarnation, arms reduction, conservation, the Middle East, and certain cosmic matters. In these areas I'm an expert.

———

Continuity vs. the One-Night Stand

There's nothing healthier in publishing than an intimate, long-range relationship with an author. Some writers erupt periodically and hopscotch the whole publishing terrain. There are authors who behave promiscuously as alley cats and publish with a variety of houses in the course of a career. Many are eyeing the green pastures of *original* paperback publication, responding to the strip-teasing of certain paperback editors. Some seem to be constantly suffering from "a change of life" syndrome. I know one famous author who has published seven books with seven different houses and is paranoid about all of them. His problem now is that no one publisher cares about his overall welfare. Which is unfortunate for him as well as for his publishers. No one really wants to make a serious investment or commitment in a one-project situation; no editor wants to endure the attrition and distrust of a prima donna on a one-book basis.

A wise author would rather fight than switch.

Continuity and constancy count in publishing. In my personal publishing history I've given endlessly of my time and energy to authors who "repeat," and I've been fortunate in the number of authors with whom I've enjoyed a continuous relationship. Among my most treasured writers is Simone de Beauvoir, with whom I've been involved as editor/publisher on no less than twelve books, starting with her *She Came to Stay*.

Another old friend and member in good standing of the "tried and true" brigade is Art Buchwald. He signed a two-book contract with me in 1960 (the first title was *Don't Forget to Write*) and he's published fourteen books with me thus far. Buchwald is unique (a man-bites-dog kind of man); he buys my lunch whenever we meet in Washington—at the Sans Souci, of course. Each of his books outsells the previous one. I don't recall ever having a quarrel with him, never a harsh word, but he will stand for no nonsense, ever, insofar as business procedure is concerned; fair behavior is the rule on both sides and no artful games are played. We first met in his Paris *Herald-Tribune* office in 1960, and within twenty-four hours, after reading a few hundred columns in one long afternoon and evening's gulp, we made a deal over a glass of Dubonnet (the strongest drink he'll take) at the California Bar across from his office. His popularity was international at that point; when he moved to Washington, it became greater than ever, despite the fact that his preoccupation was chiefly American politics and the foibles of Washingtonians.

Harry Golden, about whom I speak again elsewhere, is another of my longtime authors, with some sixteen books between us since *Only in America*. Ashley Montagu and Lin Yutang are others who come to mind, and Erich von Daniken and a number of others with multiple publishing scores under my custodianship.

But I'm belaboring my point; my purpose here is not to give a recital of personal achievements. There are sometimes excellent reasons for authors and publishers parting company. Sometimes an author has a close relationship with an editor, and when that editor shifts to another publishing firm, the author may go along. This is an understandable and fairly common practice. When the author of *Catch-22* found his editor moving from Simon and Schuster to Knopf, he followed him; the relationship was extremely close. One of the most common reasons is a familiar impasse, where author and publisher disagree as to the merits of a given manuscript. When the publisher considers the work lacking in merit, unpublishable, he usually tells the author to find another publisher—providing, of course, the author is determined to get it published. If a book must be rejected, then of course the relationship is severed, usually forever. Publishers can be wrong as well as authors. Editorial mistakes are frequently made in the best of houses. Sometimes very bad manuscripts will be published in order to preserve continuity and keep the author happy. Perhaps it's best in the long run to publish an author's inferior work; but it must be pointed out there's potential folly in mixing bad apples with good. Some authors have enough confidence in their editors to shelve a manuscript when it seems there is going to be no support, enthusiasm, or sales for the work if published.

An option clause ("on terms to be arranged") isn't very important, nor is it the answer; the relationship between publisher and author should be like a good marriage, going beyond a formal agreement. A deep sense of mutual respect and trust must prevail. When a quarrel or difference of opinion occurs, the two parties should be mature enough to work out the solution amicably and intelligently, remembering that an easy divorce isn't always the best resolution of a problem.

When one looks at the backlists of major publishing houses, such as Knopf, Putnam's, Macmillan, Random House, Scribner's, Harcourt, Pantheon, Simon and Schuster, Doubleday, Harpers, and sees the many authors whose *total* works are in print and under one roof, one can understand why the publishers are in a healthy condition. Knopf has titles in print today that they first published fifty years ago.

Advice to authors   When the vapors, the old weltschmertz, hits you, take a trip; but don't try to make a publishing decision. Don't be a one-night stand for a publisher if you are serious about your career. Your welfare and your future should be in the hands of someone who has a reason for caring about you.

Lelord Kordel, the nutritionist, with whom I've had a relationship since 1950 (*Health Through Nutrition*) and with whom I've published more than a dozen books, has made a profit for all concerned on every one of his books. He helped to alter some of my food habits; for example, I gave up sugar for honey in my morning tea. In twenty-five years Lelord and I have never had a heated word. Life can be beautiful with such authors. One of the secrets of his continuing good health is his even disposition. When a tough situation arises, I've noted that he smiles. He also takes frequent naps, he tells me.

The worst of offending authors is the newcomer who really thinks that his charm, his intelligence, and his genius are superior to his editor's or agent's. He will try to inveigle himself into the good graces of paperback and book-club editors, film story editors and others, believing that his personal charisma will work the miracles his publisher and agent failed to achieve. He is perhaps the most offensive of all authors. This author likes to switch agents and publishers, believing that they are not rendering him adequate professional service. In the end, everyone in the industry must avoid him. I wish such an author everything he deserves.

Who Is Sylvia?

Sylvia Beach was a young woman from Princeton who had a rendezvous with greatness. She went from Princeton to Paris and opened a modest bookshop. Her father was a Presbyterian minister and Sylvia "was in refuge of all that implied."

Paris became her paradise, and her bookshop on rue Dupuytren became the hangout of the international literary world, which included Hemingway, Fitzgerald, Cocteau, Pound, Stein, Gide, to name a few Names.

One of the most portentous opening sentences in any bookman's memoirs that I can recall is contained in her little book, *Ulysses in Paris.* She says there: "It was in the summer of 1920, when my bookshop, Shakespeare and Company, was in its first year, that I met Joyce."

Their meeting developed into friendship. The rest, as they say, is history.

What impresses me, as an editor-publisher and ex-bookseller, is the fact that this "mere slip of a girl," whose shop was severely undercapitalized, had the monumental chutzpah to ask for the publishing rights to Joyce's *Ulysses,* THE novel of the century. She was undertaking to bring in a whale. Energy and action in the disguise of a bookseller!

Every bookseller has a portion of printer's ink in his veins; obviously Miss Beach had more than a modicum. She was a passionate visionary, and she knew genius when she saw it. Her destiny was clear.

"Yet Joyce had no objection to putting *Ulysses* into the hands of ladies, or to ladies' publishing it," she says.

Margaret Anderson had been publishing *Ulysses* serially in her *Little Review;* Harriet Weaver, the angelic writers' patron in England (The Egoist Press) had been helping Joyce anonymously with money gifts and legal support. In New York, intrepid Frances Steloff was the American spiritual backer of Joyce and sold large quantities of *The Little Review,* including the suppressed issues. As for Joyce's wife Nora, I guess one could say she held it all together. Joyce, it appears, was surrounded and protected and abetted by women, and he was shrewd enough to know their value.

What I like especially about Miss Beach is inherent in the closing sentence of her book: "Undeterred by lack of capital, experience, and all the other requisites of a publisher, I went right ahead with *Ulysses.*"

Joyce's novel, *Ulysses,* took seven years to complete. (His *Finnegans Wake* required seventeen years.) The saga of Joyce's difficulties is not mine to tell, nor is this the place. But no better biography of any man has been written in our time than Richard Ellmann's *James Joyce,* and in its pages you'll find the full, rich, and very human details, and much about the "fragile and brave" Sylvia Beach. Some of the story, on a much different level, can be found in the book on John Quinn by B. L. Reid—*The Man from New York.* Quinn was a strange man, touched with a kind of genius, a prickly and acerbic man shrewd enough to manage to acquire the original manuscript of *Ulysses*. It is now in the Rosenbach Foundation Library in Philadelphia, and is presently being published in facsimile. The story of the *physical* manuscript and its peregrinations is worthy of a small monograph.

Anyone examining the 732 pages of *Ulysses* in its original 1922 Paris edition will quickly become aware of the colossal typesetting responsibilities involved, not to mention the proofreading job for everyone concerned. (Says Ellmann, "With Joyce the reading of proof was a creative act; he insisted on five sets, and made innumerable changes, almost always additions, in the text, complicating the interior monologue with more and more interconnecting details.")

As noted, Sylvia Beach was a brave woman. She was also generous, and gave Joyce a royalty of 66 *percent of the net profits*.

Most publishers today hold conferences, sales-projection meetings, and market analyses, as well as cost-estimate sessions (and some employ astrologers, I'm told) before undertaking far less demanding projects. In the end, in a case such as this, most publishers would throw up their hands and decline the book. I can just hear the arguments: "The author is difficult; certain disaster; too long and in need of drastic cutting; unreadable and unsalable; will offend the Irish. And that Molly Bloom monologue—wow!"

Imagination and courage on the part of *one* gritty and inspired person—that's more to the point in publishing than a committee decision. A cliché worth repeating in this context.

In America, *Ulysses* is now one of the crown jewels of Random House, a profitable backlist "item" and a living reminder of Bennett Cerf's acumen as a publisher.

Joyce's works are among the most favored of all modern authors collected, and a first edition copy of *Ulysses* (one of a hundred signed) brings around $8,500. Today the twenty-three issues of *The Little Review* containing the serialization would cost a collector around $1,000.

Marianne Moore said of Sylvia Beach: "How do justice to one with impact so great as hers, and unfailing delicacy? Who never allowed logic to persuade her to regret over-charity to a beneficiary; ardent, restive, forever exerting herself, to advantage and give pleasure to one who had, as she felt, benefitted her. During sixty years and more, this has been my impression of her."

And I find irresistible the following excerpt from Janet Flanner's essay on Miss Beach: "A part of her fame came from her being an amateur woman publisher with the courage to publish so daring a modern masculine classic as *Ulysses.* All of Joyce's gratitude, largely unexpressed, should have been addressed to her as a woman. For the patience she gave him was female, was even quasi-maternal in relation to his book."

Sylvia Beach, Harriet Shaw Weaver, Margaret Anderson, Frances Steloff, and Nora Joyce—all valiant women. Cheers to them.

Negro

Another bookwoman who showed courage and imagination was Nancy Cunard. It is not easy to characterize this woman, and the usual biographical reference books fail to disclose anything. But she had countless devotees—and an equal number of enemies—in her time. She published one of the greatest, if not *the* greatest, of all modern anthologies. In fact I know of no similar work of such quality, purpose, and importance. Its title is *Negro.*

Negro is an anthology assembled, ordered, arranged—willed— by Nancy Cunard. A folio volume containing 854 pages, it was published for her in London in 1934 by Wishart & Co., in an edition of 1,000 copies. The authors included in it, the editorial work involved, and the numerous illustrations add up to a staggering book. (The Daphne Fielding biography of the Cunards erroneously says *Negro* has 402 pages.)

Nancy Cunard worked on this book in England, France, and elsewhere—and in Harlem. In fact, she was the first white woman ever to check into, and live, at Harlem's Grampian Hotel with a male Negro. The press on both sides of the Atlantic was full of her "daring" and unorthodox behavior. Margot Asquith, lunching with Nancy's mother in London, said, "Well, Maud, what's Nancy up to now? Is it dope, drink, or niggers?" Nancy's mother, Emerald, was at a loss for words. Nancy could have replied—or smacked her— had she been there.

Nancy Cunard got writers such as Samuel Beckett, Norman Douglas, William Plomer, George Anthiel, Zora Neale Hurston, W. C. Handy, Arna Bontemps, Countee Cullen, Langston Hughes, Alfred Kreymborg, Louis Zukofsky, Arthur A. Schomburg, Ezra

Pound, and over a hundred others to contribute to her book. It is well printed on a high-quality calendered paper, and it is handsomely bound. Today it is a very uncommon book, seldom seen on sale or at auction. In 1969 a copy sold for £400 at auction.

The magnitude of this undertaking by Nancy Cunard must be recorded here as another example of *the intrepid woman.* She was not a professional publisher or editor, although she had produced some interesting slim, modest volumes when she operated her private Hours Press (including Samuel Beckett's first published poem). Her need to make a contribution toward an understanding of the universal Negro prompted her to throw all caution (and cost) to the winds. Like Sylvia Beach, untrained as a publisher, she produced a monument, a landmark book for the ages—and for a major cause.

Says Nancy Cunard in her Foreword: "It was necessary to make this book—and I think in this manner, an Anthology of some 150 voices of both races—for the recording of the struggles and achievements, the persecutions and the revolts against them, of the Negro peoples." *It was necessary,* and she did it. The book is as timely today as it was in 1934. It ends with the simple statement, "The White Man is killing Africa."

The book is a testament to truth, superbly, tastefully, and fearlessly presented. And it was done long before civil-rights activism.

Nancy Cunard was an original, an enthusiast, a "character." One of the personalities in Paris in the twenties, she was allegedly the model for Lady Brett in *The Sun Also Rises.* She was a journalist, speaking up against the Spanish pro-Franco forces. During World War II Adolf Hitler had her on his "enemies list" because of her French Resistance efforts. She scorned convention, and in compiling and publishing *Negro,* added her name to the honor rolls of publishing. A lone woman put it all together—and she did it the hard way. Nancy Cunard.

Send No Money

One of the greatest come-on ideas of our century is the slogan, Send No Money. You fill out the coupon (with a bit of larceny in your heart), the goods arrive, and you enjoy your purchase, thinking, "Let 'em wait." I refer to a minority of course; most coupon addicts pay up promptly. In the end, enough people do pay up; a small percentage gets written off. That's the American Way.

In utilizing this philosophy, the book clubs have developed, and are now giant conduits for, the publishing industry. One can build a gorgeous library by filling out book-club coupons. The initial purchase usually guarantees you real bargains: four books for a dollar. The clubs have backlists which include every manner of book, from fiction, art, and archaeology, to cookery and gardening books, classics, famous best sellers, books of information and entertainment.

No one need leave the house to be a book owner and reader. (But I pity the man or woman who doesn't know the pleasure of browsing in a bookshop. Second-hand bookshops are especially tantalizing. Spend one hour in a bookshop and your life and mind will be enriched; at least you will know what has been and is happening in the world.)

The clubs have developed highly persuasive systems for collecting money, and one must be endowed with a heart of rock not to respond to their collection letters. But remember, it is definitely a federal offense to use the mails to defraud, so why play games?

Book-club advertising is better than most publishing advertising, and publishers would do well to study club techniques, including their layouts and the typefaces used.

The essentials of a book-club ad are always easy to read, eye-catching. One is too often hooked, and quickly, by a photo and a headline. But of course the big book clubs have irresistible gimmicks which publishers can't employ.

By the way, Harry Abrams, the art book publisher, worked with Harry Scherman for many years, and learned many of his advertising techniques at the Book-of-the-Month Club.

Harry Scherman, who with Max Sackheim founded the Book-of-the-Month Club in 1924, was a mail-order Merlin. (He could also have been a great publisher.) I knew him for a number of years, and of all the men in the industry I have known, none matched him for his gentlemanly grace and courtesy. I once read the rough draft of a manuscript of his autobiography, *A Columbia Oral History*. I urged him to publish it but he always begged off:

"Not enough time to polish and revise it," he would say, "too much checking to do." I hope someone at the Book-of-the-Month Club arranges to have it edited and published. It is a mine of information for book people, and also a fascinating personal history. He lived a full and productive life, and millions of families have his cultural mark on their lives. Scherman's club was one of the major cultural forces in America, and someone ought to say so. Many authors enjoyed fame and fortune by virtue of this man, Scherman.

The book clubs have made it possible to buy a wide variety of books with ease, and in small towns where there are no shops, the club is a blessing. But one should visit one's local bookshop regularly, and one must never leave a shop without buying at least one book, even if it's a paperback. You might be surprised at the amount of knowledge the book clerk can make available to you. Not all, mind you, but some. It's no secret that book clerks are among the lowest paid workers in America, and if one of the book clerks occasionally doesn't respond with a big smile and eagerness, bear with him or her. Even cab drivers, who earn a great deal more money, are not always polite.

Jacket Jive

Too much fuss is made over book jackets. Why?

Authors and agents get hysterical when the subject comes up. They want to see the sketch, the proof; they are prepared to design it, if permitted, or to submit rough sketches. (One author I know submitted a jacket sketch for his book, giving as credentials the fact that he designed the family's annual Christmas card.) Some agents and authors detest certain colors and will beat their foreheads on the walls if the publisher doesn't listen. They don't know magenta from menstruation red, but they'll assert their ignorance.

Why?

The advertising world and the entrepreneurs whose concept of the Book is *Product* have something to do with it; likewise the detergent, deodorant, cornflakes packagers and their kin. TV and the films, the automobile advertisements and cosmetic promoters are influences, too—perhaps the worst.

Why is there so much trauma, so much trial and error and hot debate over jackets?

Well, to begin with, the design is an easy target for anyone with a dart up his sleeve, for anyone with a bit of familiarity with the language and mores of commercial art. Everyone is an expert, an art critic. Almost everyone in the publisher's office is "qualified," including the receptionist and mailroom clerk; they are always ready and willing to sound off on the merits or demerits of a jacket: "It stinks" or "How boring" or "How 1920" are some of the critical comments heard when a jacket sketch is shown.

And, of course, the simple truth is that there is more bullshit expended in this area of publishing than in almost any other.

To be intelligent about it, if a book's title and author's name and relevant copy can be read from a distance of twelve feet, it can't be all bad. Excessive use of color, illustration, complicated design don't add up to a successful jacket. Tarting up the jacket isn't enough.

A jacket is a poster; posters are made to be seen and read, and they must *inform* in some fashion. They should certainly arrest attention. Even through understatement. If one can't read the copy on a book jacket in a bookshop window, it isn't working for you. That's the basic criterion: instant legibility. Don't *defy* the browser. Give the reader a break.

Modest proposal: Why not consider dispensing with most of the pictorial, four-color jackets? Instead, why not use simple bold type, with a bit of tasteful type ornament? Many two-color jackets are effective, and I'd suggest testing two colors against four in specific cases.

A distinguished British publishing house has been doing just that for many years, and it is still thriving handsomely. I refer to the house of Victor Gollancz. Gollancz jackets were printed in black (or black and red) type on yellow paper; and they never hesitated to put on the face of the jacket a short, spirited blurb written by Gollancz himself, if he couldn't get a suitable quote from some recognizable name. (Alfred Knopf used to do this, too, on occasion, i.e., write his own blurbs and sign them.) Some of the Gollancz type jackets appeared on the original editions of great best sellers and modern classics. (George Orwell was one of his authors.)

Tell the prospective buyer what he wants to know about a book. And please, Trade Editor, don't try to imitate the paperback jackets. The mass paperback-market cover is not usually suited to the hardbound trade book. Very often, when a paperback cover is especially good, it turns out that it borrowed from the original trade-book jacket.

Probably no American publisher would dare or care to follow my above proposal, even if it meant saving many thousands of dollars a year.

The average four-color-process jacket engraving, plus original art, costs approximately a thousand dollars. What a waste of money in most cases.

Think about it. Experiment with a few jackets and see what you can achieve in effect and in dollar savings. Artists and engravers may hate you for it, but that's not the issue. If the book is salable, it will sell. If the book is a loser, four-color-process art won't save it.

Proof: In 1970, Putnam's published Erich von Daniken's first book, *Chariots of the Gods*. The jacket had red-and-black type on white-coated stock. No art whatsoever was used. And there was no author's photo on the back jacket panel. Bantam Books contracted for paperback rights, and over three and a half million copies have been sold; it is still selling. What is ironic is that our all-type jacket has been imitated numerous times by other publishers who have tried to rip off the von Daniken type of book.

No one knows why a book sells, and no one knows whether a jacket is a factor in the success or failure of a book. Taste does matter. A good jacket will please the eye and invite the viewer to look into the book. But only the stuff between the covers sells the book. Not "the sizzle."

A good jacket should reflect the character and contents of the book; it should reproduce clearly in advertisements. Beyond all this is theorizing bullshit. If you find yourself getting increasingly emotional over jackets, you may be sure that confusion will follow, not to mention booze and Gelusil addiction.

Megatons of fustian and adrenalin are expended in disputes over jacket design. Everyone seems to forget that the art director should be in charge, that art directors are hired to handle the jackets. Unfortunately, in many houses the art director's authority is chipped away, eroded by know-it-alls from the bleachers: editors, salesmen, and the head of the house. The latter is often Problem One.

An art director should hearken to criticism and suggestions, but the authority to say yes or no should rest solely with him. I've seen the sales-editorial-production-art staff of a publishing house on the verge of mass resignation because the head of the house arbitrarily decided to kill a jacket or alter it in some unjustifiable way at the last minute. Often after the engraver's proofs were at hand.

The expression "futzing around" would apply precisely to what goes on in jacket meetings: nitpicking, talmudic weighing and measuring of elements in the design, cudgeling the poor artist in absentia. An art director knows when he's got a bad jacket; he knows when the color is wrong, the type unreadable or unsuitable; he knows whether the composition works, whether the asymmetrical is better than the symmetrical. He knows how to handle the big as well as insignificant details. Presumably he also knows whether the jacket suits the particular book. To harass the art director with unreasonable criticism is a drag—and bad business.

Jacket design is not a haphazard thing; the graphic art sensibilities come from training and a special cultivation; amateurs think they know something about jacket art; but they are, in the end, still amateurs. Heads of publishing houses are usually amateurs in this area, too, even if they're geniuses in business matters. Usually, I've found, a finely honed business brain is not capable of making a judgment in jacket matters. Even when the boss is a collector of fine art, he's less than qualified to adjudicate book jackets.

The ideal jacket jury consists of the editor of the book, in conjunction with the sales and advertising managers *and* the art director. After discussion, the art director should call the decision. The head of the house should stay out of the jacket decision-making, unless he happens to be the editor of the book in question, in which case his authority should be equal to that of any other editor's, but not greater.

In my opinion the best jacket designs appear on German trade books. Every art director should spend a few weeks in German bookshops, or attend the Frankfurt Book Fair, to study the German jacket designs, not forgetting their brochures and catalogs, which excel.

For the aficionado: The first jacket recorded was used on Heath's *Keepsake*, 1833. See C. Rosner's *The Growth of the Book Jacket*, 1954.

A true story: I discussed the foregoing matters of jackets with the president of a large publishing house. He said he disagreed with me all the way. "Why?" I asked. "Because I'm the boss and I won't have a jacket that I don't like," he replied. (My private hope is that his art director tells him to go fuck himself next time he vetoes a jacket.)

The Hot Center

The action is where the rights director lives.

The hot center of a *Trade* publishing landscape is in the subsidiary department. What takes place there determines the publisher's state of health. This state of affairs is comparatively new, a by-product of the paperback revolution.

I have seen few publishers' balance sheets showing a profit from trade sales alone. Selling the physical hardbound adult novel is almost always a losing operation. Overhead and production costs are murderous. At this writing the costs are the highest in recorded history.

Only from the licensing and sale of *rights* can a publisher turn around from red to black. This situation may change some day, but at the present time this is the reality of trade publishing.

Rights money is an absolute essential; without it, publishing, despite certain joys attached to the profession, is a dreary, Sisyphean course. Clubs, paperbacks, serial, digest, excerpt, and film rights—these provide the profits. Even in the case of a genuine best seller (over twenty-five-thousand copies *sold*) there are seldom profits from book sales alone, merely ecstasy and intoxication—euphoria without monetary payoff. The costs of publishing are immense, by which I mean manufacturing, advertising, sales, and promotion; these are the persistent enemies of the balance sheet. Overspending is a fact of life in most best-seller experiences. If the publisher doesn't overspend on his own volition, the author, the editor, the agent, and the author's relatives will surely prod him into doing so.

Best sellers produce fevers and fervors: from every side there is pressure to promote, to advertise, to spend. Out of the dense complex of myths in publishing survives the notion that a big ad in the *Times* is the magical answer to sales. This idea should have been beaten to death by now—with a club!—but as yet it lives on, and each new author brings it to his publisher anew as an original idea with respect to his book. The author wants the publisher to follow the best seller recklessly, as it streaks through the sky like a comet. Throw parties, spend on more ads, lush it up, jet around the country first-class. When it is all over and the book disappears from the lists, the publisher's accountant searches his records, totes up the costs, and finds, too often, that the expenditures liquidated the profits. (A bottle of Dom Perignon now sells for around thirty-eight dollars at the Algonquin.) Woe unto the publisher if the rights director failed to come up with some major subsidiary loot, including a good six-figure paperback deal.

As a rule the subsidiary rights on best sellers are excellent. One would have to be pretty inept or unlucky not to cash in on a winner. Auctions for paperback and club money will have taken place. Foreign sales also are a factor unless, of course, the publisher has no share in this area.

While the publisher is checking out his expenses, the author, as a rule (and why not?), is relaxing in the south of France or in Malibu, enjoying the fruits of his and his publisher's labors.

Selling rights is not a profession for ladies or gentlemen, although I do know some lovely women and stalwart men who handle these matters. It's a blood-and-guts game, calling for a multiplicity of talents. One must be an oily auctioneer, a sweet-talking snake-oil salesman with a slide rule-cum-CPA mentality; and a bit of the fox's blood helps. The rights director, if truly qualified for the job, should be among the highest paid employees of the firm—possibly the second highest. The rights director's theme song is money, money, money, and the nub of his/her attack is the top dollar. The idiom or message is money. The results of the rights person's machinations and skill can affect the author's entire life—really substantially—not to mention the publisher's balance sheet. Where the rights potential of a trade list in a given season is on the weak side, then the acquisition editors need a goosing. The rights director must be tough and commercial.

Warning: If by chance in your philosophy is the abjuration of gold, kindly stay the hell out of the rights department!

Holding a telephonic auction is an art; don't underestimate it. Keeping one's cool and having a good memory is vital. Always keep a careful diary in front of you to recall conversations and figures quoted. An auction that runs into high-six figures calls for the control of a brain surgeon. One false move and disaster can result. No matter how high the tempers and tensions, it must be remembered that important sums of money are involved and the welfare of the author and the publisher is at stake. Don't ever lie about an underbidder's offer. It is dishonest and, in the end, injurious to your reputation. The respect of the entire industry must be kept intact at all costs.

Definition of a successful rights executive: a salesperson who is respected by the industry. Bob Banker of Doubleday is such a man. Milly Marmur of Random House is such a woman.

The Paperback Pie in the Sky

While I promised not to sound off with statistics, I'm sure the reader will be intrigued by the figure of around $300 million which represents the business the paperback publishers are enjoying currently. This figure is gradually catching up with the plateau of $375 million, where the hardback adult trade books are at present. It will surely pass it by a wide margin in another few years.

What does it mean in terms of the author?

Well, as a rule, the split on income from paperback rights is 50–50 between author and his publisher. Some contracts give the author 60 percent at a certain point; some go beyond that, giving the author 70 percent. There are some superstar authors who deprive their original publisher of ANY share of the paperback income. These authors expect the original publisher to make his profit from the sale of the hardback edition and from book clubs, where the split on club royalty is 50–50 between publisher and author.

Most of the publishers in trade books know that it is almost impossible to make a profit from the sale of hardback books alone. The exceptions are few. They look to the paperback and club income to bail them out. Elsewhere I've discussed the problem of advertising and promotion and how a best seller gets abnormal advertising budget money which, in the end, eats away the profit and the fun of publishing a so-called winner.

Modest proposal: Consider a 5 percent royalty on hardback trade-book sales up to 25,000 copies sold, 15 percent up to 50,000, and 17½ percent thereafter. To compensate for the drop in the author's hardback income on the first 25,000 copies, consider a flat across-the-board 60 percent share of paperback income to the author. This proposal, by the way, is personal, and does not reflect the views of my employer, publisher, or associates.

What's wrong with the foregoing?

The Authors League has been beating the drums for years for a greater share of paperback money for the authors. My proposal would and should satisfy the League and give the hardback publisher a chance to earn a profit from his trade sales.

The trade publisher operates the laboratory in which the author can function best. When paperback publishers reach out to seduce authors for original paperback publication they find their position weakened, even though they pay the author 100 percent of the royalty. They forego reviews by and large, also book club and library sales. Few serious writers want to give up the prestige and satisfaction of seeing their books in hardback, sewn, decently printed volumes that are permanent. Granted, an author must eat, and the money is more important than intangibles such as immortality and prestige. Everyone can be made happy by reevaluating the traditional income splits and royalty scale. It will cost the paperback publisher nothing, of course.

On a historic note: At lunch recently with Ralph Daigh, who was formerly Fawcett's generalissimo and is now a consultant (Leona Nevler is the very able new major domo), I was reminded of some paperback facts which I'll pass along to you.

It was Fawcett, in the early days of the "revolution," who held the torch of greenbacks (Ralph Daigh's language) that set off the conflagration which led to the currently enormous advance payments made for reprint rights. From 1955 to 1973, Fawcett set all records for high advances, topping their own previous high in each case. But going back a bit:

The first big advance that told the hardcover publishers that the paperback boys were growing up was in 1949, when $35,000 was paid for Norman Mailer's *The Naked and the Dead.* The record was subsequently broken by Signet, who paid $100,000 for James Jones' *From Here to Eternity.* Then along came Fawcett, who paid $101,505 for *By Love Possessed,* James Gould Cozzens' best seller. (I gather from Ralph Daigh that their determination at Fawcett was to beat all previous advances.) This was in 1955. Fawcett's next record-breaker was $400,000 for William Shirer's *Rise and Fall of the Third Reich*. At this time they also paid $100,000 for *Lolita*. But the purchase that really convinced everyone that Fawcett was here to stay was their $700,000 advance on James A. Michener's *The Source* in 1965.

Time marches on—and Fawcett paid a guarantee of $1,000,000 —the first million-dollar advance in paperback history—for Michener's *The Drifters* and six or seven of his older books.

Ralph told me that all of Fawcett's guarantees at more than $500,000 have paid out and earned the authors more than the advances.

The complete Fawcett story must be told by Ralph Daigh and Leona Nevler one day, of their early adventures with Penguin and New American Library. It's a story not mine to tell here.

Lest I forget, it was Leona Nevler and Ralph Daigh who read the first draft of *The Godfather* and paid Putnam's a $410,000 advance. The peak figure in paperback advances was reached in July 1975 when Bantam paid Random almost two million dollars for Doctorow's novel, *Ragtime*. Comment on this transaction would be an act of supererogation.

Because there's some misconception regarding the nature and role of the paperback editor, here's my definition of that individual: his/her role is to read, be aware of, and choose trade books as they are published, or from proofs, and to determine through divine, occult, or other means which will sell and which are worth reprinting. The potential power of the reprint editor is formidable.

The reprint editor tries to "buy" reprint rights at the right time and the right price, and provide the distributor with one or more best sellers each month. Without "lead books," a paperback editor will find his personal fortunes waning fast.

Reprint editors also *think up* original projects, usually dealing with explosive or topical matters, headline subjects, and publish them quickly. Oscar Dystel and Marc Jaffe of Bantam Books are two masters in this area of publishing.

There is the trend, of course, where the reprinter is trying to secure both hard- and soft-cover rights to books, with the hope of laying off the hardcover rights on a trade house. Most trade publishers will not consider acting in this secondary role, and therefore many manuscripts contracted for by reprinters are going begging.

The problem is obvious: trade publishers are reluctant to favor re-printers who are poaching on their domain, competing for original material. And the big question stands: Are the editors on the re-printer's staff qualified to work with original manuscripts, particu-larly new fiction? In the end, the author may find that his book will appear only in paperback; that the big trade publisher prefers not to be the tail wagging the dog. Time will tell whether the paperback publisher will succeed in preempting the trade publisher's his-toric role.

A reprint editor thrives on the output and sweat of the trade-book editor and publisher, and the trade-book publisher and editor live by the profits from reprint and other subsidiary revenue. A mutuality akin to marriage. The trade-book editor works with the author, sometimes as long as a year, over a single book. The reprint editor can buy the book in a five-minute conversation on the telephone.

The reprint publisher is, in one sense, the ultimate publisher, since he is involved in *mass distribution* which is the essence of the definition of publishing—to disseminate. No trade publisher can match the reprinter in disseminating books, and when the job is done on a saturation basis it is indeed a miraculous performance.

To each his own—but let's not confuse the identities or functions of these two editors.

Advances: Hardback Department

The dollar advance against royalties, paid to an author on the signing of a contract, is a wholesome arrangement, enabling an author to eat, work, and thrive. A publisher must be realistic about the money paid to an author, and if the author has no other source of income, then the publisher must take full account of this fact.

Suppose I've paid an author a $10,000 advance, and the net sales and earnings from his book don't recover the advance. Does the author refund the unearned portion of the advance? Don't be silly. It's the publisher's risk.

A great many advances never earn out, especially in the case of fiction. When an average novel reaches only a modest sale, say, 3,500 to 5,000 copies—and there is no subsidiary income from paperback, clubs, or serials—the publisher loses money. The author, too, may have lost money in terms of time expended on the book.

Too many marginal novels are published, but they keep coming.

The custom among literary agents—to put up some books for auction bidding—creates a serious problem for the publisher. If he feels that he can pay only X number of dollars as an advance, and the agent expects X plus—what to do?

My philosophy vis-à-vis the advance "problem" is not to pay one dollar beyond what I feel a book's potential may be. even if the factors involved are prestige (getting a famous name for your list) or getting the author's future books. The reasoning is obvious: if we overpay deliberately on one book, we'll be expected to do the same forever after. Being generous to an author is fine; but paying to the point of foolhardiness is another matter. To be absolutely fair, pay on the basis of the real quality and potential of the particular book. In no case in my personal history did an author resent the small advance that was followed by a great financial success. Authors forgive quickly when the gushers begin to spout.

Paying six-figure advances is a rough kind of ballgame. The big-name authors with great track records deserve six-figure advances —it's eminently logical. But I insist that such payments are decisions for the company's board of directors and sales directors, not for editors. No editor should take the responsibility for paying sums that will rock the boat and create possible havoc. In my opinion, no six-figure price should be paid out as an advance without some up-front assurance from a paperback or book club "partner." This is now the custom, and there is nothing unethical in seeking out such support up front.

Some editors like to practice and boast of high-advance chic; my advice is, you'll sleep better avoiding that kind of game.

Recently a famous old Boston publisher got into a bidding situation and paid an advance of $100,000 for a fair-to-middling book, hoping to get bailed out through a plump paperback deal. The top paperback bid for the book was $25,000. The book died on the vine despite heavy advertising. The moral of this little tale is that there was no logic, no justification, for paying $100,000 for the book. A fever developed and a publisher got carried away.

Getting a well-known author on one's list only to lose serious money is Cold Comfort Publishing.

High Schlock

If there's any significance to the above characterization—and I make no heavy claim for its historical or literary relevancy—it is simply to note, in these schlock-drenched times, that it has import by virtue of its being a billion-dollar commodity.

Ours is the Epoch of High Schlock.

HS is a quality that may be found in all areas of our culture. It's presence, like an odor or smog, is palpable. Its fragrant presence, like overripe bananas, is evident in our literary atmosphere. The odor is strong in the celebrity-oriented magazines, motion pictures, and talk shows.

Because of the HS dominance in our environment, I feel the need to anatomize and consider it here briefly, and my concern, naturally, is mainly with writers and their HS goods.

Before going further, I propose that the book-page editors officially designate a space each week for HS coverage. Like cookbooks, how-to books, how-to-get-the-last-ounce-of-joy-out-of-your-orgasm-books, HS should be given decent attention, as a public service.

HS is, in book terms, a genuine craft, and a *genre*. It is a category in our writing-publishing industry and must be considered a commodity. Few can imitate a genuine HS novel. As many writers have discovered to their pain and frustration, one can't just sit down and write a Jacqueline Susann or Harold Robbins novel. Disappointment must follow each such attempt. HS is a special art; it is a source of wealth for dozens of practitioners and the secret of this art is well guarded.

The HS genre is familiar to most editors. It is repugnant to some. Any editor with a Ph.D. (or employed by Scribner's) will frown upon it. It evolved in our time, putting an end to the age of pulp fiction. It rendered such novelists as Edith M. Hull, Temple Bailey, Anne Parish, Faith Baldwin, and Kathleen Norris obsolete. (Interestingly, William Rose Benét's *Reader's Encyclopedia* has an entry for Mrs. Norris, but none for Robbins or Michener.) With TV, porno films, and erotic photo magazines available everywhere; with the pudenda and pubic hair now common over-the-counter articles of commerce (in high-gloss living color), one should not quarrel with the HS novel.

Before we push our thesis further, I must point out that HS novels must not be confused with "pussybooks," a fiction category of the sixties and seventies that kept countless writers eating regularly. (It became a cottage industry in New York and Los Angeles.) They were the pornocrats, grinding out hard-core stuff for an audience that, for me, defies description. Most of the big paperback houses were producing the porn-product quietly, but with an assembly-line regularity. The big mystery is why the pillars of propriety did little or nothing to stop the flow of these sexual goodies. That these little "fuckbooks," these "cockcunt" books, were available to one and all on candy and news counters along with Hershey and Baby Ruth bars, is one of the wonders of democracy. All civil libertarians must be proud of the American right to publish these hard-core novels. We probably bred the horniest and most sophisticated crop of teenagers in all history. I once overheard one bright youngster ask: "Any new nookie novels?"

No, no, no. HS novels deal with more than sex. The patented mix includes skillful storytelling, high society, political rivalry, Hollywood, power, old and nouveau money, oil, gold, and such stuff. And losers, too. The reason for the sex is to grab you at the crotch while the HS Scheherazade spins the plot.

HS calls for a kind of genius. Harold Robbins didn't make it at first, but the genius was there all the time. His first efforts in fiction were literary. After a few attempts, however, he learned that good reviews were not enough; he found the Secret Upward Trail and proceeded to scale the heights of HS.

Susann made the grade with her very first novel, which had been preceded by a modest literary effort, a lovebook to her dog. Irving Wallace worked in nonfiction areas before he hit his big HS stride. His first two books were biographical. Then he made it, like a fresh oil gusher makes it, with a whoosh heard 'round the world.

When I used the word "genius," I was mindful of the reader's reaction, the reader's wince. But logic tells us that anyone who can write a story that appeals to a broad international audience, and hence sells millions of copies, is, ipso facto, a genius. The dictionary includes in its definition of genius, "a great natural ability for a particular activity." *Vide* Wallace, Hailey, Michener, Wouk, to name but a few.

Chicago bookseller, circa 1930. (The mustache had to go!)

May 1, 1933. Anne and I in my first bookshop at 808 North Clark Street, Chicago.

Chez Targ, in the Standard Club Building in Chicago's Loop, circa 1940.

LEFT: Richard Wright. New York, 1947.   RIGHT: Louis Goldblatt to the
rescue. Chicago, May, 1927.

Humphrey Bogart and W. T. discussing *The Treasure of the Sierra Madre.* This
edition of the B. Traven novel was one of our most successful World film
books. Bogart's performance in the movie version helped.

George Jessel listens while Carl Rose sketches. A book is born!

As W. T. looks on, Ellery Queen (Frederic Dannay) and Carl Van Doren confer on the "Sherlock Holmes" pipe that Targ presented to Queen. New York, 1948.

RIGHT TO LEFT: Bruce Rogers, Abe Colish, Fred Melcher, Abe Lerner, and W. T. at the Colish printing plant when the first proofs of the *Bruce Rogers World Bible* were being checked.

Celebrating the publication of the Fleming-Wolf biography of A. S. W. Rosenbach at Sessler's Book Shop in Philadelphia, November 4, 1960. LEFT TO RIGHT: W. T., John F. Fleming, Edwin Wolf II, and Justice Curtis Bok.

TOP: Two members of the stogie brigade: Art Buchwald and Harry Golden. (Photo/Jimmy Tafoya, *Detroit Free Press*)   CENTER: Ralph Daigh of Fawcett presents Mario Puzo with a bestseller award for *The Godfather*. BOTTOM: With the Alfredo Machados and Oscar Ornstein at the Hotel Nacional in Rio. (Photo/Kazmer Takacs)

Chester Himes and the Targs at the Algonquin.

LEFT: Herman Raucher (*Summer of '42*) studies his editor's see-through shirt from Brazil.   RIGHT: With John Kobler in Westport, Connecticut. John had just delivered his manuscript of *Capone*.

LEFT: Gene Shalit drops in to chat with Roslyn—on my birthday.
RIGHT: Superstar Viva on publication day, 1970. (Photo/Bill Yoscary)

LEFT: Rapping with Allen Ginsberg. (Is he listening?) (Photo/Bill Yoscary)
RIGHT: On the town in San Francisco with Herbert Gold. In background is framed picture of a Haitian friend—our souvenir of the evening.

Roslyn and Henry Miller in Pacific Palisades, California.

Tennessee Williams takes a few moments off to discuss the Putnam *World of Tennessee Williams* project. (Photo/Bill Yoscary)

The irrepressible agent, Tom Mori, of C. E. Tuttle, Tokyo.

TOP: Jerome Lawrence relaxes at his home bar between labors on *Actor,* his biography of Paul Muni. (Photo/Rusty Morris)   BOTTOM: *Cosa Nostra:* Joan, Roslyn, Nicholas, Russell, and Alexander Targ in Palo Alto, California. Missing is Elisabeth, who had left a few weeks earlier for a summer in France. (August, 1974).

Andreas Brown and Edward Gorey partying it up in New York's Soho.
(Photo/*Soho Weekly News*)

Ms. Frances Steloff and admirer.
(Photo/Bill Yoscary)

Roslyn—my favorite photo. Summer, 1975. (Photo/Bill Yoscary)

Simone de Beauvoir—sui generis. (Photo/*Saturday Review*)

The New York Times (by Ernest Sisto)

PERFECT PITCH: Marianne Moore, the Pulitzer Prize poet and baseball buff extraordinary, tossing out the first ball to open the season at Yankee Stadium yesterday. Michael Burke, Yankees' president, is at left. Story on Page 54.

For Roslyn and William Targ

So much my friends in a thousand
ways. Marianne Moore
April 11, 1968

Raymond C. Hagel relaxing with author.

One of my favorite Carl Sandburg photos, dated 1960.
(Photo/Dr. I. W. Schmidt)

FOG

In the hand of the poet . . .

The fog comes
on little cat feet.

It sits looking
over harbor and city
on silent haunches
and then moves on.

Hospitality in Gulbenkian country. A night in Obidos, at the Rex Tavern, with Eurico Fernandez of the House of Portugulia of Lisbon. 1970.

Formidable! The French publishing team of Isabelle and Robert Laffont. (Photo/Roslyn Targ)

Fritz Molden in Laffont's booth at Frankfurt, featuring *Le Parrain*.

Newsweek said of Robbins: "His work debases language, is false to life, and creates the very clichés it feeds upon. His novels insult truth, and that seems to be the reason people consume them—to escape not from their lives, but from truth."

About 150,000,000 people think that?

One category of HS fiction, the non-Gothic, nonromantic schlock, utilizes the essences and fantasies and 3-D extravagances of HS magazines such as *Vogue* and *Harper's Bazaar,* publications which, by the way, pose as arbiters of chic in all areas of culture and fashion. (Fact: they serve chiefly as advertising-space outlets for heavy sugar advertisers: the garment center, pantyhose, perfume, and hormone czars.) Their ad art is usually of some erotic interest or kinky robot-manikin chic, that is, bloodless and sexless. Which is also *trés* chic. The text is incidental; it's the bylines that count—HS symbols: names, places, wealth. The dress designers and perfume makers are featured as Personalities; department stores feature their pictures in ads as persons who are newsworthy. Design a line and become a VIP. This HS *merde* filters down into our cultural media, which includes books, films, TV. Talk shows feature HS personalities. One day *Viva* and *Penthouse* will move in on them and take the market away—their photography is more interesting.

Then, by way of contrast and illustration, there's the Low Schlock magazine. Recently, I read in one of these a dialogue between a woman interviewer and a New York call girl. A bit of the dialogue ran as follows (and remember, this is verbatim, and the interview was serious, informational, sociological):

QUESTION　Is it true that call girls have big dental bills?

ANSWER　Yes, they do.

QUESTION　Is that because of all the oral sex? I mean, is it really true about all that enamel being worn away?

For further questions and answers, see *Cosmopolitan,* January 1975.

HS fiction hooks you, titillates; feeds to the nervous system, the visceral, and the genital; and its dynamics involve S-M interraction. Plus action-adventure. The players are power-driven men and women who thrive on high-octane sex, violence, Big Decisions, narcissism, and wild fantasy. For added action, usually included in these novels are a few assorted nymphos; a stud playboy who also doubles in guns, garrote, or blackmail; plus a billionaire or two, a motion-picture tycoon, a super-sex-symbol star, and at least one

powerful eccentric who always wears shades and who can't get it
up, or find it. Shake well and add, as kickers, fun things like ejacu-
lating sperm into a lady's face (see Susann; it's good for the com-
plexion!), the cocaine ampule, "water sports," and other diverti-
menti. (Hallucinogens and barbiturates are old hat.)

We can wade up to our hips in a bog of clichés, trying to ra-
tionalize and anatomize HS. What we know for certain is that this
category of fiction offers deep-down orgasmic bliss: the ultimate in
lubricity, exquisite erotic tension, exotic delights, whips, nips of the
razor, baroque and flashy lifestyles, and characters who are larger
than life, and oh, so believable. Not forgetting story, story, story. It
is not kitsch. It is not literature. It is a commodity akin to the motion picture to which one opens the pores and allows the HS to
enter. (Mit *schlag*?) For millions of readers, HS offers euphoria,
and the indulgence is neither injurious nor costly to the body. In
time, it may possibly make the brain soggy. But no matter; look at
the people one meets! Many of them are *so* recognizable. It's fun.

It is somewhat degrading. But that's another day's discussion.

HS is a billion-dollar industry. It includes the "informational"
category; here's where the reader gets to zero in on life—big business, oil, gold, Arab billionaires, TV broadcasting, drugs. Then there
are the historical and biographical novels, the blockbusters produced by such old pros as Michener and Stone, where you *really
learn stuff*, the inside lowdown, with real dialogue (you can hear
Michelangelo muttering to himself as he's chopping stone in the
Italian quarries; you can hear dinosaurs talking about the ecology
crisis, and so on). The didacticism of Michener or Stone may put
you to sleep, but it can't *hurt* you. Now if only G. Legman would
turn to HS fiction—consider a 1,000-page work featuring a Linda
Lovelace.

Speaking of Michener, some of his HS novels achieve fame and
fortune for him through pure excess. He shovels out erudition with
minutiae beyond the call of duty. Take, for example, his 1974 novel,
Centennial. This 909-page book opens up some 136,000,000 years
ago and comes right up to the post-Watergate era. The author has
researched his work to a fare-thee-well, and gives the reader no
less than three-and-a-half pages of detailed acknowledgments. Talk
about turning over a library to make one book! As one reviewer of
the novel said, "It wasn't 'written,' it was compiled." Michener is
the ultimate HS scholar and, like Durant, has earned a vast fortune from his labors—with which we have no quarrel.

In case I neglected to mention it, those members of the HS school of fiction I've been privileged to know personally (Robbins, Michener, Wallace) are genuinely likable and generous people, as was the late Jacqueline Susann—and I hope this doesn't sound patronizing. There are, on the other hand, certain HS writers, less successful, who are too revolting to mention by name.

In a TV-glutted, politically polluted, and corrupted environment, where politicians in every level of our society are revealed as crooks, gangsters, killers, perjurers; where millions are dying from malnutrition and disease; where billions of dollars are stolen from the people through venality, taxation, manipulation, or inflation, or on "make-work" projects like space shuttles; who would dare to assume a "stained-glass attitude" over HS? In a world devoid of a moral center, a world of cyberculture, let's not give up on the few bubbles left in the seltzer. And didn't Harold Robbins say somewhere that "a writer is a filter for society"?

Historical footnote: It is interesting to note that two of the leading exponents of HS were first published by Alfred A. Knopf. The authors were Harold Robbins and Irving Wallace. I recall that Robbins' novel, *79 Park Avenue*, was originally entitled *69 Park Avenue*, and the author was asked to change the *number* to avoid any *soixante-neuf* connotation. I believe Robbins left Knopf after that book.

Etymological Footnote: The word "schlock" is of Yiddish origin, meaning "broken merchandise" or "merchandise of meretricious or obviously inferior quality." We have preceded the word with the adjective "high," so that no one may infer that we are calumniating the character of the merchandise. Also, I hope it won't appear anti-Semitic to point out that most of the leading practitioners, male and female, are Jewish. And then there was a gorilla motion picture made many years ago by Jack H. Harris, called *Schlock*.

Statistics Are *Out*

A confession: I have no use for statistics, or generalizations. Graphs and charts trying to prove something seldom convince. Mostly, they misinform.

The novel is dead. The novel is alive. Fiction doesn't sell, and that sort of thing. No editor worth his salt can make a judgment based on statistics, clichés, or so-called trends. Some of the best books, the most successful books, had nothing to do with trends or current taste. When an editor indicates a manuscript he's pushing is "trendy," I start to retch.

So while this book is in part a how-to book as well as an auto-biographical one, there will be no charts, few percentage figures, accounting facts, census data, financial breakdowns, overhead- and production-cost charts, and such. For this kind of information please consult the releases of the American Book Publishers Council, the *World Almanac*, or write to Arnold Ehrlich, editor-in-chief of *Publishers Weekly*, the official custodian of publishing information. He can tell you all about the rise in the number of books of fiction published last year, how many new books of poetry, textbooks, paperbacks, or whatever were issued, with comparative figures. What you will do with this information is beyond me. I don't know how any editor can be guided by such information. The fact that sixty-four books may be in print on a given subject will not deter an editor from publishing still another.

Production-cost figures are important of course; how else can one determine the retail price of a book? Overhead cost data is essential in publishing decisions. But these figures must not be confused with "statistics." Anyway, your production manager will tell you everything you need to know when a project is under consideration.

But for heaven's sake, don't spout or lean on statistics. They don't matter.

Quality

Many publishers work overtime to keep their standards low. (Just as New York's Seventh Avenue labors in the interest of low couture.)

High Schlock, nonbooks, coffee-table books, quickies, and skimmed-milk treatments of celebrities and superstars of the day, cookbooks and such—this output of "product" makes up the largest part of trade publishing. It bears no relation to quality publishing.

On the whole, though, it produces the revenue that sustains many publishing firms.

There are a few houses, however, who will, or can, bypass such publishing and try only for books of quality and purpose. This does not mean that quality books don't show up occasionally on the lists of all publishers. But the few who stick to high standards exclusively are the salt of the earth. I'll name one of them: *Atheneum*. Gold stars go to Atheneum for not only the quality of their books, not only because their typography and jackets are uniformly in good taste, but because they consistently publish some of the best poetry of the times.

From its founding in 1960, Atheneum has published poetry with annual regularity. Their first poetry volume was Randall Jarrell's *The Woman at the Washington Zoo;* it became a National Book Award choice. An auspicious beginning. They've published poetry ranging from two to ten titles each year. A number of these have earned the Bollingen, Pulitzer, Lamont, and National Book awards. Among Atheneum's poets are W. S. Merwin, Richard Howard, Mark Strand, James Merrill, Thomas Kinsella, George MacBeth, Osip Mandelstam, Philip Levine, Marvin Bell, Anthony Hecht, Howard Moss, Mona Van Duyn, Stephen Dobyns, Donald Justice, Peter Everwine, and others—all good-to-distinguished poets.

About one third of the titles (out of some seventy-five) have gone into two or more printings. Sales vary from over 10,000 copies per title to as few as 1,500 and 2,000. And some sell even fewer copies. To Atheneum's credit is the fact that they've never remaindered a book of poetry.

Harry Ford, a poetry aficionado, is now the editor of Atheneum's poetry list, and he tells me that he gets continuing solid support from the heads of his firm, Bessie and Knopf. Ford, also one of our best book designers, is responsible for the design of most of their books. (His preference seems to be for the more narrow format.)

Anyone interested in seeing how the high standards of bookmaking are maintained in America, year after year, should take a careful look at Harry Ford's books and jackets. The books provide another phenomenon for students of the anachronistic. For Atheneum's efforts on behalf of poetry, perhaps the Ford Detroit Foundation will one day attach a pipe line to their exchequer.

The Pebble in the Shoe; or,
What to Do about the Returns Problem

As you may know, all books sold to booksellers and wholesalers are returnable for full credit within one year following purchase from the publisher. We ordinarily refer to books as *shipped* rather than *sold*—the word "sold" is terribly final and becomes an actuality only after the date of return has expired.

The returns practice gives the publisher a hell of a problem. An author may think his book has sold, say, 8,435 copies, and then, after one year, he discovers that by discounting returns, he has really sold only 3,400 copies or thereabouts. Get the picture?

In 1975 and beyond, the returns situation will be giving the industry a severe case of colitis. Booksellers may be inclined to return every book they can, rather than pay scarce dollars for dubious inventory.

The publisher has a problem: the first printing is out of stock; should he order a new printing? How can he be sure that the first printing was sold in its entirety? He can't. He can't phone every dealer who bought three, five, ten copies. Half of the first printing may be sitting on shelves across the country, unwanted, unsold—and *returnable.*

Do you know what happens when an editor reports to his author a certain "sales" figure on publication date and then, one year later, tells the same author that the figure is now lower than the advance? The author blows his stack. Suspicion, anger, threats, despair.

There seems to be no solution, except that booksellers could donate their overstocks to charitable institutions—libraries, schools, churches, hospitals, prisons—and take tax credits. Publishers could invent an element (chemical-electronic?) to implant in their books, so that after one year they would self-destruct.

Cautious printing isn't feasible, no matter how carefully one behaves. There's no slide rule that will guide a publisher in ordering printings, no crystal ball, no wizard at the helm.

The other simple solution (simple!) is to cancel out the 100 percent return privilege and increase the dealer's discount. But is it possible? Increase the discount to what? Fifty percent? The dealer will cry, "Not enough."

If the publisher gets back approximately 17 to 20 percent of his hardbound books (the paperback returns are higher) what should he give the bookseller to avoid such a costly return? No one has come up with the solution because there is none that can be reached by logic. Someone must take the bull by the horns and do something on an emotional basis. Like what?

Over the Transom

It is easy to understand why certain publishers announce that they will no longer consider unsolicited manuscripts. Thousands of manuscripts come through our doors each year. I get at least twenty addressed to me each week. Almost all of them are unpublishable, hopeless.

How many do we accept? Speaking for myself, in over twenty years I have contracted for no more than three authors who came to me unsolicited, without benefit of an agent. One of these unsolicited authors has now published six books with me; each of his books has proved to be modestly successful.

An author should try to get an agent to represent him. Selling a manuscript cold is the toughest way I know to get published. It can be done, but the odds are against the writer. I insist that every manuscript or outline addressed to me be opened and examined, but after all these years, I must admit to having little remaining hope of that great lucky strike.

Who profits from all this writing activity? The manufacturers of typewriters and typing paper, of course. And the U.S. Post Office.

More about Advertising

Everyone seems to be an authority on advertising. Ask the switchboard operator, the mailroom clerk. They'll quickly point out *what's wrong* with an ad.

The trouble with advertising is not in its meagerness, but in its character, in its quality. Half of the book ads I see could be reduced in size and improved in both content and type arrangement. Almost no originality is to be seen in book ads and very few agencies or ad managers understand the meaning and power of white space.

The best trade-book advertising in American publishing is produced by Knopf, under the guidance of a true genius, Nina Bourne. She should write a textbook. She knows all about white space and type and how to wed them perfectly; and when she is out to get impact, she gets it—in spades.

I believe in using photographs in ads—authors' photos, even when the author is ugly, and many are, alas. Ugliness has a special power to attract attention, more so than a pretty face. If this were not true, why would so many unattractive people be employed on TV commercials?

The "Power" of Advertising

Here's an interesting case history from Michael Joseph, excerpted from his book *The Adventure of Publishing* (1949); it's an illustration that can be topped by many publishers, I'm sure:

Without reader-recommendation it is doubtful if any book can have a big sale. It is the one thing that can ensure the success of a book. The history of publishing can show many instances of books which have become best-sellers for this reason alone. If I quote one example from my own experience it is because I can be sure of the facts. In November 1941 my firm published a little book called *The Snow Goose*. It had only three and a half inches of advertising, listed with other books. Only twelve reviews appeared in the first six months of publication. The big national daily newspapers ignored it; no reviews appeared in the *Sunday Times, Observer, Spectator, Time and Tide, Evening Standard, Yorkshire Post* or *Manchester Guardian*. Of the twelve reviews nine were in provincial papers and the majority were short notices. Only one previous book by the author had been published in this country (*The Adventures of Hiram Holliday*) and that had a very moderate sale. It may safely be said that *The Snow Goose* owed nothing to advertising and that the influence of the reviews and of the author's reputation was negligible. Yet *The*

Snow Goose, after a slow start, sold merrily. As I write this, the book is in its 20th English edition, and including the sales of the separately printed Australian edition has sold to date 281,897 copies at the original published price. In addition, over 81,000 copies have been sold of an illustrated edition published in 1946 and a signed limited edition of 750 copies priced at three guineas was heavily oversubscribed before publication. Both the regular editions are still selling steadily.

A Sad and Familiar Story

The following case history can also be matched, I'm sure, by many publishers. Author publishes his first novel. It is decently written and well reviewed. An advance subscription of 3,200 copies depresses one and all. One *TBR* advertisement, one television appearance—and end of ballgame. No sales, no subsidiary money, no interest. The author accuses publisher of indifference, then proposes to invest his own money—$5,000 in consumer advertising—to prove that ads sell books. Thirty days after the $5,000 budget was exhausted, the sales were at the 3,450 mark.

Young novelists and editors, take heed. What conclusion can be drawn? Simple: the public does not want the book. Perhaps it will want his second or third or fourth book; but it does not want this one. Will authors believe this story? I doubt it. Authors will never accept rejection gracefully, and they often switch publishers after the foregoing experience.

If you have the answer, write.

Committees

Maxim No. 1: Decisions by committees are usually wrong. Give me one firm decision by an intelligent if eccentric individual with guts, anytime.

One editor can be right as opposed to nine in disagreement!

TV-Persuasion

Some day I expect to see George Plimpton on television squeezing books and doing dog-food commercials in doggie language. The men and women who squeeze toilet-tissue rolls on TV are probably worrying about their jobs, now that the literati are taking over. Plimpton, by the way, helped publish one of the finest magazines in the world, *The Paris Review*. I guess things are tough all over.

With all due respect, I must admit that Plimpton's magazine, (founded in 1952 in Paris' Montparnasse) introduced me to some of the best stories of my entire reading life. One in particular comes to mind: "Stones" by Samuel Beckett. I read this extraordinary "story" and later discovered it as a sequence in the novel, *Molloy*. It begins with, "There are people the sea doesn't suit, they prefer the mountains or the plain." Later, we get that fantastic business with the sucking stones, and so on.

It was in *The Paris Review* that I first encountered another well-known figure, the CBS–TV commentator, Hughes Rudd. His story, "The Fishers," will give you some indication of that man's hidden talents.

I've decided, after a weekend's study of magazine and newspaper advertising, that ads which are sexually underscored will succeed. A photograph of a well-filled bra, a sleek pantyhose model, a bikini that speaks a thousand words—these ads will sell almost anything. So why don't book publishers utilize this obvious means of promoting goods? Most authors on TV shows are not sexy or alluring but have rather unappetizing, tortured, and troubled faces; they are people who obviously are not fragrant or skin-cleansed—but thank heavens, there are some exceptions.

Movie Tie-Ins

As a rule, paperback publishers will pay a premium for reprint rights to a book when a "major" film is imminent. See the Movie, Read the Book used to be the slogan publishers carried in their ads. Almost no one seems to remember that in the early forties, long before paperbacks existed, we at World, and a few others (Doubleday and Grosset) published *cloth-bound* fiction at forty-nine and fifty-nine cents—unabridged texts with film stills. At World we published dozens of such editions (under the previously mentioned imprint, Tower Books) and exploited them with special "trade screenings." In those days, we invited booksellers and book wholesalers to the screenings, and we gave them "star"-inscribed copies of our editions.

Our list included *Mildred Pierce, Double Indemnity,* Traven's *The Treasure of the Sierra Madre,* and other well-known novels. For several years I concentrated on these Tower Books, arranging for photographic endpapers and jackets and, whenever possible, I would have the star of the film autograph books for distribution to hospitals, bookshop friends, and others. I had some interesting encounters while engaged in this activity; an outstanding one was with Humphrey Bogart. We met one afternoon in his New York hotel suite, and he signed fifty copies of the Traven novel, which was a great success for all concerned. We discussed the film, had gin and tonic, and I had the pleasure of meeting Bogart's wife, Lauren Bacall. (He did *not,* in my presence, call her "Baby.") I found him articulate, warm, informed, immensely likable. And sober.

I had a number of interesting tie-in film-star encounters, including one with Joan Crawford (she took an hour to make up her face before seeing me in her hotel suite after breakfast) and another with Ray Milland. The inscribed copies of their books were always welcomed by hospitals or the visitors to our screenings.

Warning: A bad book and mediocre film will do no one any good. For tie-ins to be effective, one must have top quality in both film and book. The public won't be cajoled into buying a book after seeing a lousy film, and vice versa. The ideal combination was *The Godfather;* in this case, all records were broken for film *and* book. Another good case history is *Jaws.* The film sold books.

Some film companies defy understanding. The Olympian minds in Hollywood, making decisions on high, are beyond me. For example, I read and responded to a screenplay written by Steve Shagan which Paramount had just bought. I asked Shagan to turn the play into a novel, which he did. It was entitled *City of Angels.*

Putnam's published it in the spring of 1975. The story is one of violence and is set in Hollywood. Paramount proceeded to make the
film, starring Catherine Deneuve and Burt Reynolds. They also
proceeded to change the title—while we were busy establishing the
book (and its title) as a best seller in California. The title chosen
for the film was trite, totally unrelated to the book in my opinion.
Obviously, the tie-in value was gone. Why did Paramount drop the
author's original title? See the Picture under One Title; read the
Book under Another—that might be the selling slogan. Meanwhile,
the author's wishes with respect to the title, not to mention the publisher's, are disregarded. Show biz.

At a private screening of *Mildred Pierce,* I noticed Mrs. Alfred
Knopf in the audience. After the showing, I asked Blanche how
she found the picture—did she like it? She replied, "Oh, I wouldn't
know. I never go to movies." But don't get me wrong, I admired
the late Mrs. Knopf's publishing acumen.

The Bookseller

A few friendly and biased comments on the personal
bookshop:
Will this book sell? asked Pontius the Publisher.
Who knows which book will sell—and why?
Is word-of-mouth the magical answer?
Yes. And it starts with the bookseller.
Every editor/publisher should have a favorite, friendly bookseller to whom he can turn for answers to questions, and I mean
straight answers. I don't mean to imply that every bookseller and
junior bookshop clerk is an oracle—far from it. But for me, a good
bookshop is like a touchstone, and if the bookseller or his staff are
on their toes, maintain professional standards, and are not too paranoid, then the relationship can be mutually profitable.
Precise information about rate of sales, reader-reaction, trends—
this is all part of the editor's meat and drink. While there is no
absolute in literary or publishing judgment, no Euclidean theorem
to guide one, there's an art—yes, art—in evaluating the market

potential of a given book, of all kinds of books. The bookseller's personal enthusiasm for a book is part of the evaluative scheme of things; his reflexes work in a magical way if he's a genuine bookman. And his enthusiasm is beyond the price of rubies.

Bookselling and publishing are within the realm of art; God knows science is not involved. A bookseller with a strong conviction or gut hunch based on experience, maturity, and certain divine sensibilities, is a valuable ally for a publisher. Cherish him. He's often capable of making a precise judgment. Booksellers know more than publishers in many cases, for remember, their job is to extract cash from the public for our wares. Each bookseller is, *ipso facto*, a magician, a VIP. He translates the editor's dreams into beautiful reality.

One of my favorite "touchstones" is the Gotham Book Mart. When you enter the shop you know that love of books is there, everywhere; it's the total ambience. Gotham sells most of the new books; it leans hard on contemporary poetry, most of the arts, film books, occult and mystical literature, used books, and modern first editions. Any member of Gotham's staff will give me useful "trade" information, solid opinions, and answers to questions by phone or in person. Sometimes I resist the opinions expressed, finding them painful and counter to my own judgment. But I get it straight. An important point: reciprocity is essential and one should try to give as well as take. Which means: become a customer, buy a book whenever you can. I am a good Gotham customer, of course, since I collect rare books, and my "dues are paid."

In 1940, Frances Steloff, founder of the Gotham Book Mart, issued a now-rare 90-page catalog called *We Moderns*. I own and treasure an inscribed copy, and as I leaf through it today, reminiscing, I can't help but wonder about this shop, it's durability and vitality, its services, and its founder; she is an authentic world-wonder.

Frances isn't the Colossus of Rhodes exactly, but she's indispensable to countless authors, booklovers, and publishers—and to me. She probably founded the shop right after the American Revolution (I never inquired as to the exact date, and she does look like George Washington's granddaughter) and she's still alive and well and visible on the premises almost daily, eating her sunflower seeds and honey, looking after her cats, and pushing the works of James

Joyce, Yeats, Henry Miller, Ouspensky, Krishnamurti (their best-selling author), Madame Blavatsky, Gurdjieff, Ramakrishna, and others. A heady literary cuisine administered by an extraordinary custodian who is definitely not wearing tennis shoes. She's also a nonstop enthusiast for good causes, books, people, life.

But the new owner—young, ebullient, sassy, and very canny Andreas Brown of San Francisco—is even bouncier; he's the brightest mover and shaker in Manhattan's book orbit, and I don't mean "celestial body." He's very terrestrial, although his literary tastes are anything but mundane. He's the final anachronism: a bibliophile-businessman. Ask for a price reduction on a rare book and be greeted with a granite stare; turn down one of his recommended rarities, and do penance.

One of the most dramatic stories of the book trade in 1975 was the sale by Andreas Brown of $485,000 worth of books from his shop to the New Mexico State Library at Las Cruces. It cleaned out a large percentage of the Gotham's stock—some 200,000 books were involved—mostly in the area of the arts.

Andreas Brown acquired the shop in December 1967. An old customer of the Gotham, he fell in love with the place; and when he heard it was for sale, he made a mortgage-pact with Satan and grabbed it. It was not unlike buying Fort Knox. The basement shelves were lined with gold (I know, I saw them shortly after he acquired the business). It was right out of the Arabian Nights. To mix metaphors, I felt like a boy locked in one of the Baskin-Robbins ice cream parlors.

Aside from having one of the best stocks of contemporary books, Gotham is a major outlet for modern first editions. Andreas is one of the shrewdest rare-book dealers around. He almost never issues a catalog because his turnover is too rapid, and the "good ones" get away as fast as he acquires them. If he buys a library, an archive of some famous writer, he manages to dispose of it *en bloc* to some institution. The lucky buyers are those who happen to drift in and ask, "What's new?" He'll reach into the twelve-inch clutter on his desk or into a carton on the floor and say, "This just came in; take a look." It might turn out to be an inscribed copy of Dylan Thomas' *18 Poems,* or Tennessee Williams' first book, or a holograph letter from Joyce, or Hart Crane's *The Bridge* (on Japan vellum, signed). When Andreas declares a book to be recherché, desirable, consider it an oracular statement.

The Gotham Book Mart's second floor, The Gallery, features frequent launchings of new books, with author signings and cocktails (Andreas has his own witches' brew or champagne punch, an all-purpose drink). The Gallery also features exhibits by such men as Edward Gorey, E. E. Cummings, and Marcel Duchamp. Gorey is one of the four-star attractions of the shop; his books are featured there throughout the year, and Gotham publishes an occasional limited edition of his work, too.

I had my first meeting with Gorey in the shop. As a collector of Goreyana, I grabbed at the chance to have him inscribe some of my books. Then my editorial wheels began to whirl and I proposed, on the spot, a large, one-volume anthology of his out-of-print books. Luckily, the idea took hold with him, and the result was the now-famous book, *Amphigorey*, one of the most beautiful and successful books I ever published at Putnam's.* It is now in its eighth printing. It was given an award by the American Institute of Graphic Arts, and *The New York Times Book Review* chose it as one of the five "best art books of the [1972] year." Andreas Brown is preparing a bibliography of Gorey's works, a formidable job; he is, of course, the foremost advocate of and expert on Gorey. Second only to Mr. Gorey, of course.

Gorey is a tall lean man, addicted to a full beard, ankle-length fur coats (I believe he has a total of sixteen), a large heavy ring on each finger, and other jewelry which, I suspect, is worn more to protect him from muggers than as ornamentation. He is one of America's foremost balletomanes, film critics, and authorities on the Victorian era. He is immensely opinionated, immensely likable, and about as close to genius as it is possible to be without being insufferable.

One of the bonuses (personal) of publishing Gorey was inducing him to make a portrait of Roslyn for a birthday gift, the first portrait commission he's ever accepted. It was a great surprise for her; she still hasn't recovered from the pleasant shock.

Gorey is now preparing an illustrated *Alice in Wonderland* for me, as well as the aforementioned *Amphigorey Too* volume—two plums for any editor in any season.

The Gotham catalog mentioned above, issued in 1940, is a museum piece, and will drive any book collector mad. The low

---

*As this book goes to press the second, companion volume, to *Amphigorey* will be published. It is entitled, naturally, *Amphigorey Too*.

prices are incredible by today's standards, and I cite just a few: The following are first editions, of course: Joyce's *Ulysses*, Limited Editions Club, signed by Joyce, $37.50; *Ulysses* in the twenty-two issues of *The Little Review* (a $1,000 set today), $37.50; Hemingway's *Three Stories and Ten Poems*, $100.00; Hart Crane's *The Bridge*, one of fifty copies, signed, $22.50 (a New York dealer listed it at $2,000 in 1945); Eliot's *The Waste Land*, $12.50; Faulkner's *Mosquitoes*, $7.50; Ezra Pound's *Cathay*, $5.00; Stein's *Three Lives*, $37.50; Stevens' *Harmonium*, $4.50; Dylan Thomas' *A Map of Love*, $2.75; William Carlos Williams' *The Tempers*, $2.50; Wolfe's *Look Homeward, Angel*, $20.00.

No point in belaboring the moral; the foregoing prices are an indication of the investment potential of rare books, and the Gotham catalog is enough to make a stony-hearted bibliophile weep.

Every city should be lucky enough to have the equivalent of the Gotham Book Mart with its splendid and intelligent staff, and publishers should help smooth the path of such booksellers when the going gets bumpy. A little extra personal consideration by a publisher goes a long way with the individual personalized bookshop; there are too few left.

The Gotham Book Mart is where one meets the readers and the writers. The Gotham brings back memories. When I was a bookseller in Chicago I made occasional bus trips to New York. I visited the rare-book dealers; also the shops on the Fourth Avenue "strip" and the remainder dealers. And Whitman Bennett, the bookbinder and dealer in "high-spot" first editions. (I bought many thousands of dollars of books from Bennett, and had a quasi-representation setup in Chicago whereby I sold his deluxe editions and fine bindings and rare books. Whitman Bennett, an original, a character, a fox; he taught me much about buying and selling rare books. He was a scholar; he and his wife would spend quiet evenings reading the *Britannica* for fun.)

But I was talking about the Gotham, which brings to mind the many writers I met there in the "good old days" and up through its present time under Andreas Brown's auspices. And I remember arriving in New York one day and coming face to face with a young, tall, handsome writer, two of whose books I had read and admired —Nathanael West (Pep to his friends). He was sitting in an alcove in the shop, visiting with Frances Steloff's husband David Moss, and David introduced us.

West's new novel, *The Day of the Locust,* had been just published that week. I bought a copy (less bookseller's courtesy discount, of course) and West inscribed it for me. I told him that I owned a copy of his first book, *The Dream Life of Balso Snell* (which I still have). He was impressed, and reminded me that only five hundred copies had been printed. *Balso Snell* is an outrageously funny and scatological story, heavy in Rabelaisian buffoonery, with numerous echoes of Cabell and Huysmans.

(Somehow, somewhere, and stupidly, I parted with my inscribed copy of *The Day of the Locust.* If any of you reading this know of the whereabouts of that copy inscribed to me, I'll gladly pay four times the price you paid for it.)

The Day of the Locust sold around fifteen hundred copies when it was published; Random House was its publisher, and I suspect Bennett Cerf and Nathanael West held no celebration party at the Stork Club on that publication. Cerf couldn't abide failure.

I met Nathanael West in 1939; within a year, he and his wife died in an auto crash. Like Camus', this senseless early death is one of literature's major losses. (Frances Steloff's young husband also died prematurely about that time, by drowning, I recall.)

None of West's four novels succeeded until long after his death. Today, *Locust* is an assured classic, a "collector's item." So, too, is *Miss Lonelyhearts.* Nowadays no one seems to write this kind of novel, or stories like *The Great Gatsby* or *Of Human Bondage*—stories with heroines and villains one can't forget. Maugham's Mildred Rogers, Fitzgerald's Daisy Buchanan, and West's Faye Greener get under the reader's skin and stay there. There are characters and episodes of grotesquery and poignancy one can't ever forget. They can haunt one all one's life, serving as constant frames of reference.

I recall a visit to Haiti a few years ago; we attended a cockfight in Port au Prince, the first I had ever witnessed. I detested every moment of it. I sat in that terrible, loud, humid, open-ceilinged hovel watching the sports fans—some were Americans—and the "game chickens" in action. I saw those deadly feathered creatures thrusting spastically with their tiny iron knives, clawing and pecking at each other's eyes and throats. As I watched, I suddenly thought of the cockfight scene in West's novel *Locust,* a scene so truly portrayed, so economically presented, that it would be hard to find its equal in any description of a bullfight or prizefight sequence in fiction. West had a genius for fixing an event. He could fix a scene, a landscape—and people—forever. The *impact* of his characters sets his writing apart from that of the majority of today's novelists. He simply had the knack.

Budd Schulberg spoke of this and other matters when he referred to "the satanic God-searching genius of Nathanael West." (Melville had it too.) West's vision of life was not one of joyousness.

But Schulberg's use of "genius" is apt. West was a craftsman, an artist, a storyteller. He was incomparably good in making us believe that he had indeed lived his story, known his characters. I don't think that his Tod, Faye, Homer, Miguel, Harry, Abe, and that extraordinary character and cowboy, Earle, are inventions. They're all alive and living—for me.

Read *The Day of the Locust* and you'll encounter pure American Gothic. (The film based on this book doesn't do it justice, I'm sorry to report.)

I have the Gotham Book Mart to thank for the chance to shake the hand of the writer called Pep. After reading four of his novels, I'm somehow curious as to how West's nickname was chosen. I must ask S. J. Perelman, his brother-in-law, one day.

―――――

Osmosis

One of the foremost rare-book dealers in the world, John F. Fleming, told me that if you put an intelligent, average dog into a bookshop, it would, in time, perhaps twenty years, learn almost everything one needs to know about the business of selling books. And Fleming was referring to rare books.

John was, of course, Rosenbach's apprentice, and started in the mailroom, wrapping packages. "Osmosis," said Fleming, is the explanation for the bookmanship he acquired. Rubbing shoulders with bookmen, handling books, smelling them, wrapping them— even looking within their covers—helps. When I threatened to repeat the above piece of information (about the dog) in my book, Fleming said, "Go ahead—it's true!"

Fleming, by the way, bought the Poe *Tamerlane*, at the Sotheby

Park Bernet sale in October of 1974; he paid $123,000 for it. Nice dog's work.

The press, generally, indicated that the $123,000 paid for the *Tamerlane* was a record price for an American book. Not so. I happened to have witnessed a sale at the same gallery, on January 28, 1947, of *The Bay Psalm Book* (1640). It brought $151,000, and by coincidence, it was John Fleming who walked up the aisle to claim it for his company. *The Bay Psalm Book,* incidentally, is the *first book printed in these United States.* The Rosenbach Foundation now possesses it.

The *Tamerlane* was sold by Fleming to the Joseph Regenstein Library at the University of Chicago.

Some of my key books came from Fleming's shop. But our relationship really began on an editor/author basis. Fleming and Edwin Wolf II wrote the biography of A. S. W. Rosenbach, which we published at World in 1960. It is one of the best biographies I've ever read and possibly, next to Jackson's *Anatomy of Bibliomania,* my favorite book about books.

When I'd learned through the late Lee E. Grove (of Oxford) of the availability of the manuscript (I am forever in his debt) I jumped at the chance and I went to Philadelphia to pick it up from Wolf. I returned to New York by railroad; I began reading the manuscript before the train pulled out of the station and continued reading straight through until three in the morning. Later that same morning, I phoned Ben Zevin, who was in Cleveland at the time, to tell him of my enthusiasm for the work, and his support was instant and unreserved. (An editor is fortunate when the head of his house has that kind of faith in his judgment.) The authors were astounded at both the speed of my reading and the alacrity of my decision. It was a record reading experience—approximately 250,000 words, nonstop.

Fleming and Wolf are among the world's great bookmen. Their book is an encyclopedia of rare books bought and sold, of great collectors; but mainly, it is the story of a very human merchant of books who surpassed all others of his generation. Rosenbach was highly intuitive; he read voraciously and collected rarities, as witness the Rosenbach Foundation collection in Philadelphia, which is a literary Fort Knox. Rosenbach loved wine, women, and books, as well as fine cigars and his own special salads. He was bawdy, deliberately ungrammatical, generous, shrewd—and a showman. The biography was for me a happy and exhilarating experience all the way, and the authors paid me a flattering tribute in the Preface. It ended up with: "The finished product will be his [my] labor of love for books."

The book was exceptionally well received, and opened with a front-page *New York Times Book Review* sendoff; it sold very well considering the subject and the price. A splendiferous publication party was given for the book at the Grolier Club, followed by a great dinner where most of the toasts and speeches were pure Sam Johnson. Among the guests were John Carter, the Donald Hydes, Louis H. Silver, Harrison Horblit, and Arthur A. Houghton, Jr., one of the world's foremost collectors—one of Rosenbach's and now Fleming's, great customers.

Speaking of Houghton: he provided me with the material for one of my usual faux pas. When I had been introduced to him some months earlier at a house party given by Harvey Breit and his wife Pat, I hadn't caught his name. On the occasion of the publication party he proceeded to speak kindly about my bibliophilic anthologies and I thanked him for his compliments. Then I asked him in what field he collected. His reply stopped me: "All fields."

Gulping, I continued, "You mean from Gutenberg to, say, Ginsberg?"

"Why, yes," he said, "I do have a Gutenberg Bible and I do collect in virtually all fields of literature."

I asked him for his name again, and when I realized it was *the* Houghton, I could have dropped through the floor with embarrassment!

Houghton, by the way, is Steuben Glass.

Huneker and Schma' Ysroel!

One of the rewards of browsing in antiquarian bookshops is the discovery of forgotten treasures. As a boy, when I first discovered the *Smart Set* magazine, I encountered the writings of James Huneker. He was the idol of Mencken and Nathan and all others who loved music and writing, the arts. Today his books are virtually forgotten. Ask the next person you meet about Huneker and you'll probably get a blank stare. Yet he published some twenty-five books.

Anyway, to return to the subject of browsing, I recently picked up a first edition of Huneker's *Variations,* published in 1921 by Scribner's. (I doubt that you'll find it in a paperback edition.) It has some wonderful essays on such subjects as Cézanne, Baudelaire, Chopin, Flaubert, Caruso, Ibsen, and others. But the real prize, the pure beautiful pearl in this collection, is an essay entitled *Eili Eili Lomo Asovtoni.*

Now most Jews and many non-Jews, know this title as the familiar and beloved Hebrew lament. Says Huneker, "Naturally I believed the melody to be the echo of some tribal chant sung in the days of the Babylonian captivity, and perhaps before that in the days of the prehistoric Sumerians and the epic of Gilgamesh."

But when and why do you suppose this beloved Hebrew song was composed? I'll tell you—and you may dine on the answer. *Eili Eili Lomo Asovtoni* was composed by Jacob Kopel Sandler in the early 1900s (he was still alive when Huneker wrote this essay), and the music was written for a historical drama, *Die B'ne Moishe (The Sons of Moses),* which deals with the Chinese Jews. It was produced at the Windsor Theater in the Bowery; Sophie Carp, a Yiddish actress and singer, first sang it in that musical play. The song, not the play, was a success.

It doesn't necessarily pay to go to college; but to second-hand bookshops, yes.

Sic Transit Michaux

Lewis H. Michaux, who founded the National Memorial African Book Store some fifty years ago, decided to close down his shop in December 1974. His age at that time—eighty-nine. Finances, rather than age, may have had something to do with his decision. Perhaps not. I don't know.

The shop was located in Harlem, at 101 West 125th Street. In case you don't know, Harlem is in New York. (Some New Yorkers may not know of its existence.) His bookshop was the hot center of black literature and black cultural activity, not to mention black political consciousness.

I met Mr. Michaux twice. In both instances I was accompanied by a black writer. The first was Richard Wright, which helped get me a rather warm welcome. Michaux was not famous for his love of Whitey; but he was most courteous to me, a publisher. My second visit was with Chester Himes, whose *Cotton Comes to Harlem* I was just putting to press at Putnam's. Michaux loved Chester, was kind to me, and most gallant to Roslyn, who was also with us. (Roslyn is Chester's literary agent.)

In his back room, where Michaux spent his spare time with cronies, was a floor-to-ceiling portrait of Malcolm X; there was also a giant-sized portrait of the late Mr. Nasser, of Cairo, Egypt. A few Muslims in fez and regalia were present, all very cool. There was another large picture on the wall: that old familiar engraving of an American Pilgrim, gun under his arm, walking with his family through the snow to church. Mr. Michaux "explained" that one to us. His interpretation: this is an example of the American white man out gunning for the black man. True, our forefathers did have a thing about Indians. The history books claim a number of red-skins were shot by our Pilgrim Fathers and others (and that red-skins practiced scalping on the white man—an art, it is said, he learned from Whitey). I offered mumbling excuses. I think I pointed out to Mr. Michaux that I, personally, had never fired a gun in my life. (That comment did sound stupid at the time, and still does.) Mr. Michaux came at me, nose to nose, and grinned. I recall that he said, "I believe in education."

Mr. Michaux is a good, dedicated bookman, and he has served his community long and well. The death of such a shop is an uncalled-for event, a tragedy. As this is written, I'm hoping that he'll find some angel and bookman who will decide to take over and continue the National Memorial African Book Store, for it should not be allowed to die. The people of Harlem need it. There is, somewhere nearby, a potential new Langston Hughes, a James Baldwin, a Countee Cullen, a Maya Angelou—they need that store. New York City needs it for many reasons.

Lagniappe and Negotiation

The dictionary defines the word "lagniappe" as "a small present or a gratuity." It can also be considered a "chisel."

Many buyers, at the point where a sale is about to be closed, will ask for something extra to be thrown in for good measure, the extra donut in the baker's dozen.

I'm reminded of the word when authors and agents make requests beyond the intent of the contract. The late Hiram Haydn, editor and scholar, told of the time Leon Uris asked Bennett Cerf for an outright gift of $12,000. The request had no bearing on his publishing contract with Random House. Bennett turned him down with Cerfing vehemence.

Many years ago, when Bobby Fischer won the American Chess Championship—he was then in his teens—he discussed writing a book on chess with me. We saw him and his mother occasionally. He was imperious in every sense. He dressed like a hippie long before the word was known: worn tennis shoes, a mouldy sweatshirt, and jeans were his dress. (Today he is a clothes sophisticate, and has his shoes, shirts, suits, and neckties made to order.)

I arranged for Bobby, his sister, my son, and Bobby's mother to meet me in my office at World for a "formal meeting" to discuss the terms of the contract. I wanted it to be businesslike. Bobby wouldn't sit still, but prowled around my office, bearlike. He'd pull down a book, grunt, then push it back on the shelf. I reminded him at one point, when he had taken down Biancolli's *Mozart Handbook,* that a recent *New York Times* article had compared him to the composer, calling him "the Mozart of chess."

Bobby rammed the book back on the shelf and asked, "Who's Mozart?"

Finally we were all seated and I proceeded to explain the nature of a publisher-author relationship and the terms of the contract I was proposing, including the advance payment and other details. When I finished, he said he wanted to ask a question.

I nodded.

"What are you going to give me?" he asked.

I studied him for a few seconds, then said, "I don't understand the question; I've outlined the terms fully." I turned to the others but they were watching Bobby.

"What I mean," he said, "is what will you *give* me, as a *bonus,* for the *privilege* of publishing my book? Ballplayers sometimes get a present—an automobile, a bonus check. That's what I mean."

He smiled and waited for my answer.

I was counting to myself and when I had reached twenty-five, I said, "No presents, Bobby, no bonuses. I think you had better try some other publishing house."

The meeting was adjourned. No hard feelings; merely a deeper understanding. Bobby was already on a big ego trip and knew precisely where he was going and what he wanted. And he knew, with deadly certainty, that he was going to get what he wanted. And he did, he did.

Another Bobby Fischer anecdote comes to mind. Years later, shortly before he was to go to Argentina to play the pre-Spassky match, he came to our house for lunch. Bobby asked Roslyn to represent him as a literary agent. He wanted some ready money and said he'd like to publish a book of his best games, together with some autobiographical details, but *excluding* his early years. We discussed the matter at length and he said he'd leave it in her hands, but that he wanted action.

Roslyn at once offered the project to a few publishers and was able to get some handsome, sight-unseen bids, one of them quite substantial. But when she was ready to propose a contract, Bobby had already left for Argentina. She phoned him there and gave him the details. She recommended that he take the substantial offer. His reply was characteristic; he said he'd like to think about it. She phoned him in Argentina several more times, and in each instance met with the same kind of vacillation: he still wanted to think about it. His money needs had eased up. Finally she gave up on the matter.

When he returned to America, and before going to Iceland, he spent a few months at Grossinger's, exercising and preparing for the big ordeal. He would phone us occasionally to discuss various matters, but in each case, when it came down to the line of action, he would back away. He was congenitally unwilling to sign a contract or commit himself to any agreement. At one time he asked us to secure the services of a famous lawyer for him. When I reported that we had the lawyer ready to serve him, he changed his mind.

Millions of books about Bobby Fischer and his games have been sold, most of which provided him with not one cent of royalty. Chess books, ever since the Iceland tournament, have been best sellers the world over. Bobby's book, if he had written and published it as he had originally planned, would have been a worldwide best seller with, perhaps, a million dollars in royalties for Bobby. His reluctance to act decisively on a simple matter cost him a fortune. Presumably he is aware of this and cares not at all. But I doubt it. I happen to know that championship and fame are not his only goals; *he loves money,* and the power of money. He once told me that his hero was Al Capone. He may have changed his mind since, but I do recall that he felt Capone had class—people moved when Capone spoke; he had power, fine automobiles, fine homes. Bobby did not follow through on his "game plan." Except in playing Spassky.

We have remained friends, but I suspect it is best that our relationship continue unencumbered by business matters. I don't think he distrusts us; he seems to prefer his frame of "inaction." He is the only true genius I have ever known and is, without question, the best chess player who ever lived. He may also be the best negotiator the world has ever known—unlike that amateur, Kissinger. We wish him happiness.

Censorship Is Not Beautiful

("If Mr. Clemens cannot think of something better to tell our pure-minded lads and lasses, he had better stop writing for them." Thus wrote Louisa May Alcott when an attempt was made to suppress *The Adventures of Huckleberry Finn* in Concord, Massachusetts.)

The word "censorship" is an abomination.

While one's stomach may turn, and the brain reel, at some of the books, films, TV programs, and printed matter to which we are exposed, I would not lift a finger to censor or suppress any of it. Freedom of expression still being one of the few rights left us, to censor would be to diminish something precious and basic, and this one must resist at all costs.

Time will take care of the offensive and the malodorous. The only kind of censorship that one can approve is *public indifference.* When the public turns its back on a book or shrugs its shoulders with a show of no interest, that is censorship. The natural, wholesome kind. Meanwhile, for gosh sakes, what the public does want, let it have. Let's leave the ultimate decision to time, not to self-appointed censors.

When we consider some of the good-to-great books and plays that were banned over the centuries, we should not be hasty in making censorial judgments—if only for the reason that posterity will most certainly laugh at our stupidity. Besides, our Constitution still grants us freedom of both speech and press, so we must keep reminding the would-be censors of the First Amendment. Also, we might urge more eager-beaver moralists to read John Milton, John Stuart Mill, and Thomas Jefferson on the general subject of "tyranny over the mind of man."

Which brings to mind the tyranny of the airwaves:

The greatest assault on one's nervous system and privacy comes from television and radio commercials. By and large, the *cost* of hearing a news broadcast is far greater than the service rendered. The offensive, vulgar, outrageous, and generally odious commercials (especially those with moronic players or singing children) which enter our homes ought to be stopped. Their perpetrators should be muzzled. Commercials are vile and have nothing to do with freedom of speech. Suppressing commercials is not a curtailment of opinion. If any kind of censorship is at all worth considering, I would put commercials up to a public vote, for partial or total outlawing. I would do what was done with cigarette advertising on TV—force them into printed advertisements which are easily ignored. Especially diaper advertisements on the morning TV news broadcast.

I would prefer to turn over the airways to the people and keep our lives free of the revolting clamor from the air salesmen. This includes book advertising. Most of the latter is ludicrous. I would also like to bar most authors from pitching their books on the TV airwaves. In the main, they are unattractive and unsuited to the role, and I think most of them do more harm than good. A particular abomination is the cookbook "author" who, by virtue of a pair of scissors and a pastepot, put a book together and found a willing publisher to make capital and publicity of the enterprise.

While I'm against censorship, I bleed for the millions of beautiful trees that are being destroyed to produce so many wretched books. Therefore, the problem is in part ecological. Let's save the forests; but let us also save our literature. There's a slogan for you. Write less, publish less—let the accent be on quality. La Bruyère said somewhere, "It is the glory and merit of some men to write well, and of others not to write at all."

As I indicate in more detail later, I have no quarrel with the four-letter word. But there are some writers around us today who would literally become speechless were they to stop using the sexual and scatalogical vocabulary which sustains them. Certain new poets in particular, including some undisciplined female militants, actually think that an excessive use of formerly taboo words such as "shit" or "motherfucker" add up to literature if used generously enough. These words are rendered innocuous by these writers, and their purposes futile, both as literature and as weapons for a cause. Someone must advise them, wise them up. But don't misread me— I'm opposed to censoring any of them. I'm also opposed to librarians censoring (denying) certain series books, and any librarian who refuses to give a *Nancy Drew* story to a child is killing that child's natural love of reading.

Where Do Publishers Come From?

Too many applicants for publishing jobs haven't the foggiest idea of what publishing is all about. They've heard about author luncheons and expense accounts, and how glamorous the work is. They've also read about the big six-figure advances paid to authors, and know one can meet interesting people in publishing offices. "Groovy" is (was) the word for the book business; it's show biz, literary style. But when you try to pin down an applicant concerning the job he is seeking, you get confusion and blank stares. "I want to *be* in publishing" is what they are saying, without realizing what the publishing business involves. Too few applicants know what they want to do in the field; they just "love books and want to be among them."

Therefore, a modest proposal:

The Association of American Publishers should finance the establishment of a school-employment agency to educate would-be publishing employees and to serve as a job-servicing agency.

The school-employment agency would serve as a nonprofit organization for the training/education of would-be editors and others wishing to become members of the publishing profession. Scholarships would be awarded to the brightest applicants on a test basis. Basic examinations would have to be passed before becoming a potential employee.

The school would teach a complete course in publishing, including editing, manuscript reading, production, design and graphics, advertising, publicity, promotion, book-shop liaison, accounting, and secretarial skills. Even mailroom clerks would be drawn from the pool of personnel provided by the school-employment agency. Typing and spelling would require tests. It is my contention that *everyone* working in a publishing house should know how to spell, how to use a dictionary, and how to type. A course in spelling seems to me mandatory in the curriculum; most college graduates can't spell.

Among the qualifications I suggest for an editor or publishing executive are an acquaintance with publishing history, starting with Aldus Manutius; a knowledge of printing and binding processes; some familiarity with paper manufacturing; at least six months' retail experience in a bookshop (the school-employment agency should operate a model bookshop to train candidates in the art of recommending books and taking cash in return); and a wide acquaintance with books and authors, by which I mean, the job applicant should have read widely most of his life.

Exams should be given in all areas, and students graded. The service would, of course, provide jobs without employment agency fees, a consideration not to be overlooked.

The courses could be run by a variety of retired executives with publishing backgrounds. I can think of no more honorable retirement for an experienced publisher than to teach young candidates who wish to make book publishing their life's work.

If the Association of American Publishers can't see its way to inaugurating such a school-agency, then some hardy private individuals might consider tackling the project. The important point

I'm trying to make here is that a job in a publishing house should be more than a job; it should be akin to a profession. A training course followed by a diploma or certificate could certify one's qualifications, and the assurance of a job should follow.

A Publisher Named Jim

Around 1937, when I operated my bookshop in Chicago, I was visited one day by a quiet, cultivated, handsome publisher's representative whose calling card read "James Laughlin." His firm name was the then comparatively new one, New Directions. His books were obviously *the* avant-garde literature of the time. The list was exciting.

We visited for about an hour; he showed me his new jackets and catalogs, and I may have ordered forty or fifty dollars' worth of books from him. He thanked me as though I had spent twenty times that sum.

As we continued to chat, I learned that he was the founder and owner of the business. My memory wheels whirred and suddenly I realized that the salesman caller in my shop was a member of a wealthy American family. I asked him how he could afford to bother with a bookshop as small as mine, and I recall his saying that it gave him pleasure to meet individual booksellers who cared about good writing. The size of my order mattered not at all, he said. I was flattered.

New Directions, founded in 1936, has published more first-rate authors than most publishing houses in our time. Among its authors are Tennessee Williams, Dylan Thomas, Ezra Pound, Henry Miller, Edward Dahlberg, John Hawkes, Vladimir Nabokov, Paul Bowles, Denise Lvertov, Pablo Neruda, Octavio Paz, Kenneth Patchen, Kay Boyle, Cyril Connolly, William Empson, García Lorca, James Purdy, William Carlos Williams, and many dozens more. Laughlin edits the splendid New Directions annuals and also writes poetry and essays. He works closely with his authors, and does not engage in splashy promotion or publicity; but his standards remain higher than most publishers. I doubt that he has ever issued a book in any category on which he'd be ashamed to put his imprint. New Directions is proof that quality can be maintained, that one can survive without compromising. Of course I haven't seen New Directions' balance sheets, but I suspect they make a little money. Today, New Directions publishes about twenty-five new books a year (Lippincott handles their selling and shipping). It keeps important authors in print and operates with a tight, efficient staff. Until his death in November 1974, Bob MacGregor, a gifted and all-around able publisher, was the all-utility manager.

Laughlin shows us that it's possible to run a modestly sized publishing house in America, despite the problems of the industry. His little craft stays sprightly and afloat, a beacon light for all those dreamers who are pondering the prospects of setting out for themselves for a try at small-scale quality publishing. It isn't easy, but it's possible—and should be encouraged. Bankers could do worse than to subsidize a few bright newcomers at good publishing, and I'm sure that some of the larger book manufacturers could afford to gamble for a few years on a newcomer or two.

Instant Immortality

A publisher, with luck and a million dollars' worth of judgment, can get into the Bookman's Nirvana quickly by imprinting his name on the right book. The right book is usually a great book of poetry. For example, lucky Horace Liveright had his moniker on *two* of the crown jewels of American poetry: *The Waste Land* by T. S. Eliot and *The Bridge* by Hart Crane. Any editor would turn violently green with envy at the sight of Liveright's list in his heyday, for no other publisher in our time has had Liveright's run of luck. Of course, he had authentic stars in his editorial department, including Lillian Hellman, T. R. Smith, and Louis Kronenberger.

Liveright died broke at forty-nine; some blamed his "reckless splendor," but Sherwood Anderson paid tribute to "his never-ending generosity and his real belief in men of talent."

Alfred Knopf made it when he published two of T. S. Eliot's earliest books; one wonders what happened to cause that author-publisher alienation. Meanwhile Knopf's name appears on two title pages, although one of them, *Ezra Pound: His Metric and Poetry* (1917), doesn't carry Eliot's name. Mysteries . . .

And think of having your imprint on the first edition of *Das Kapital* by Karl Marx (Otto Meissner) or *Alice's Adventures in Wonderland* (Macmillan in London) or *Psychoanalysis* by Sigmund Freud (Franz Deutcke) or *On the Origin of Species* by Charles Darwin (John Murray). Heady associations.

Of Mice and Men: A Pride of Publishers

Shoptalk and books about books—what bookman or publisher can resist the pleasure of exchanging views, gossip, experiences, relating to his colleagues? There are many fine memoirs and biographical studies of publishers which every newcomer to publishing should read or have some familiarity with. Some of these books are illuminating, honest, lively, thorny.

One in particular I'd like to commend to all is by Henry Holt, *The Garrulities of an Octogenarian Editor,* published in 1923 (Holt died in 1926). Read this book if you want to meet a civilized, talented man, a man with style and intelligence. Holt lived a good, rich life; read widely; translated from the French; played the cello; and published good books, among them works by Turgenev, Taine, Hardy, J. S. Mill, W. G. Sumner, William James, Lewis H. Morgan, Henry Adams, H. G. Wells.

The title of Holt's book is one of my favorites. I had at one time planned to borrow from it and call my own book *The Spewings of a Sexagenarian.*

Another beguiling and useful book is Michael Joseph's *The Adventure of Publishing*. His chapter, "How to Survive as a Publisher," is an honest, valuable account in which he makes the point that problems can't be solved in a vacuum.

Joseph was the publisher who discovered *How Green Was My Valley.*

Other publishing histories worth looking into are Michael Sadleir's *Authors and Publishers,* Sir Geoffrey Faber's *A Publisher Speaking,* and George H. Doran's *Chronicles of Barabbas.* And among my very special favorites is F. N. Doubleday's *Confessions of a Publisher,* one of the most forthright autobiographies by a publisher that I've ever read—a fine, old-fashioned success story that might have been written by Harry Truman if he had been a publisher.

My old friend and longtime associate at World Publishing, Donald Friede, published a book on his adventures entitled *The Mechanical Angel.* It's worthy of anyone's time, especially newcomers to publishing. He was one of Horace Liveright's boys, and a partner of Pat Covici. There are some great anecdotes in Friede's book. It's out of print, as are so many others, but seek it out. Donald was a gifted man and made valuable contributions to the publishing world of his time. Donald, while associated with me at World, brought in a great bestseller, *Andersonville.* Eleanor Friede is his widow.

George Haven Putnam's *Memories of a Publisher: 1865–1915,* is another good candidate for your publishing shelf. Which reminds me: when I told Walter J. Minton, head of Putnam's today, that while I was doing some research on the ancient founding father of Putnam's, I learned to my surprise that Putnam had once been Edgar Allan Poe's publisher, Walter replied, "Don't tell anyone, but Old Man Putnam drove Poe to drink!" (Putnam's also published Washington Irving and gave him VIP treatment: the gift of a beautiful writing desk.) I knew Poe was addicted to making small loans from his publisher and Putnam's made him sign very petty vouchers. I'd love to find one of those IOU's from Poe to Putnam's and frame it for my office wall. I wonder if they exist in any archive.

In an otherwise informative little book on British publishing, Mr. Anthony Blond, in *The Publishing Game* (p. 101), makes an error for which someone must correct him publicly. He says, "Mostly, New York publishing is lateral, air-conditioned and, with the strong exception of Scribner's, Jewish."

A glance through the *Literary Market Place,* which lists the top executives of America's publishing houses, might help Tony Blond find a clue to the Jewishness of the industry. The Jews continue to remain a minority, and though Jewish editors are highly visible there are many non-Jewish editors of distinction—probably the larger percentage.

In Charles A. Madison's book, *Book Publishing in America,* there's an excellent "Chronology of Publishing Events" (pp. 557–594), which, in a sense, comprises a history of American publishing which begins in 1638, preceding by two years the publication of the first American book ever printed, Stephen Daye's *The Bay Psalm Book* (1640).

Another useful book, though somewhat outdated, is Alice Payne Hackett's *70 Years of Best Sellers.* While we find here the top-selling books from 1895 to 1965, you'll be hard put to draw any conclusions from these lists. One thing you'll discover: there were enormous first printings of books in cloth bindings long before our best-seller lists were tabulating sales. Huge advances were not uncommon. Some titles, by authors totally forgotten today, sold like best-selling paperbacks of today.

The following novels, according to Hackett, sold *over a million* copies each, in *hard covers* (figures include book clubs): *The Robe* by Lloyd C. Douglas, *A Tree Grows in Brooklyn* by Betty Smith, *The Silver Chalice* by Thomas B. Costain, *Leave Her to Heaven* by Ben Ames Williams, *In His Steps* by Charles M. Sheldon, *The Razor's Edge* by W. Somerset Maugham, *The Call of the Wild* by Jack London, *Dinner at Antoine's* by Frances Parkinson Keyes, *Not as a Stranger* by Morton Thompson, *The Caine Mutiny* by Herman Wouk, *The Foxes of Harrow* by Frank Yerby, *Forever Amber* by Kathleen Winsor, *The Virginian* by Owen Wister, *The Harvester* by Gene Stratton Porter, *Mother* by Kathleen Norris, *All Quiet on the Western Front* by Erich Maria Remarque, *Strange Woman* by Ben Ames Williams, *Green Dolphin Street* by Elizabeth Goudge, *Lydia Bailey* by Kenneth Roberts, *The King's General* by Daphne du Maurier, *Annie Jordan* by Mary Brinker Post, *The Trail of the Lonesome Pine* by John Fox, Jr., *The Keys of the Kingdom* by A. J. Cronin, *This Side of Innocence* by Taylor Caldwell, *Before the Sun Goes Down* by Elizabeth M. Howard, *Desirée* by Annemarie Selinko, *Mutiny on the Bounty* by Charles Nordhoff and James Norman Hall, *Gentleman's Agreement* by Laura Z. Hobson, *David Harum* by Edward N. Westcott, *The Riders of the Purple Sage* by Zane Grey, *Rebecca* by Daphne du Maurier, *The Sheik* by E. M. Hull, *The Good Earth* by Pearl S. Buck, *The Rosary* by Florence

Barclay, *Love Is Eternal* by Irving Stone, *So Well Remembered* by James Hilton, *Pollyanna* by Eleanor H. Porter, *Lusty Wind for Carolina* by Inglis Fletcher, *Doctor Zhivago* by Boris Pasternak, *Topper* by Thorne Smith, *B. F.'s Daughter* by John P. Marquand, *The Sun Is My Undoing* by Marguerite Steen, *Scarlet Sister Mary* by Julia Peterkin, *Anthony Adverse* by Hervey Allen, *The Song of Bernadette* by Franz Werfel, *Yankee Pasha* by Edison Marshall.

Put these books and their synopses through a computer and what do you get? Well, entertainment and religion are high; adventure and the West; Gothic and suspense; serious views of the "human condition"; mystery, war, humor, nature, sex, the sea, dogs, history, horse trading. All of these subjects are treated in the above million-plus sellers. The moral is: Write the best book you can—and hope for a bit of luck.

As I said, we'd be hard put to draw any conclusions from the best-seller lists, and that applies to nonfiction, which I won't bother to list here. By the way, the greatest sales in nonfiction seem to be in cookery books, which depresses me no end.

Some Real Bookmen

I had the good fortune to know some of the giants (not many) in our profession. Although a very junior leaguer at the time, I met and spoke to, on many occasions, one of the great ones—the original George P. Brett of Macmillan.

I first encountered this bantam rooster of a man in 1925, when I began working for his company, and still recall the short, stocky proud figure; the thrusting chin; the father-figure. Our meeting was in the basement of The Macmillan Company building in Chicago's South Side. I was having lunch (sandwiches brought from home) with the building's superintendent, a crusty Scotsman. (He claimed to have read only one book in his life: the poems of Robert Burns.) Brett, Sr. came down, joined us, and proceeded to ask about the condition of the boilers, the consumption of coal, and other non-bookish matters. He was interested in every detail of his domain, including the royalty terms of every contract drawn by his firm. He was not much for conferences and publishers' associations; he kept his own counsel, conspired secretly, and acted with sound business judgment, literary taste, and a warm humanity. Brett, Sr. was famous for going after an author and wrapping up a deal by whipping out a checkbook and closing on the spot. Brett recognized three basic principles: to be a successful publisher you had to obtain good manuscripts, sell books efficiently, and attend to office work promptly. Simple? If he were alive today I don't think he'd be found lunching at 21, La Grenouille, or Elaine's.

At age seventy-three he became chairman of the board and let his son, George P. Brett, Jr. become president. I knew Brett, Jr., and while he had certain talents, he lived under the shadow of his father most of his life. When Brett, Sr. died in 1936, he was given his due by members of the industry. *Publishers Weekly* wrote of his accurate judgment, the force of his personality. "In spite of the careful departmentalizing of the business and able assistants, and in spite of the fact that the firm published six hundred books a year and reprinted many more, he was able to give his attention to all branches of the business. Every proposal had to meet the searching but rapid test of a man who knew every turn of a publishing contract, every competing line, every economy of production, every potential outlet."

It is my own belief that George P. Brett, Sr. was the best all-around publisher in American publishing history. His equal may be in our midst now, but I won't presume to name him here. A close examination of Brett's life and career will show you an individual who was the Total Publisher.

By the way, to avoid confusion, G. P. B. was not the founder of the American Macmillan Company; it was his father, George Edward Brett, who secured the American franchise in 1869.

His son, George Platt Brett, joined the firm at sixteen years of age, and made publishing history. Then came George P. Brett, Jr.

Another notable in the Publishers' Hall of Fame, and a personal favorite of mine, was Ben W. Huebsch. His story is one of achievement on the highest level in the editorial arena. He was among the first to introduce European writers (other than British) to America, including Gorky, Hauptmann, Jules Romain, Artzybashev, James Joyce, and others. Huebsch always spoke up with wit and forthrightness. He had humor, a twinkle in his eyes. And he had a special quality of savvy not often encountered among publishers of the seventies. We met frequently at the P.E.N. executive meetings (I was for a period an active officer in that organization). It was always a pleasure when he attended because he was sure to speak up, with wit, frankness, and a deep understanding of a given situation.

Huebsch's contribution to the welfare of the Viking Press is beyond measure. He was primarily a reader, an editor with a sense of quality, and he brought out numerous first-rate books, including works by D. H. Lawrence, Van Wyck Brooks, Thorstein Veblen, Sherwood Anderson, and many others of permanent worth. He fought censorship all his life; he did not believe in taking "refuge in silence."

The "three Alfreds"—Knopf, McIntyre, and Harcourt—were legendary for their commitment to books of quality and for their frequent "lucky strikes." And for their good business sense. It was Alfred McIntyre (of Little, Brown) who begged, in 1930, for a cutback in publishing. He believed that a reduction in publishers' output was a matter of urgency. He even urged booksellers to force publishers to reduce their lists, by threatening to boycott a good percentage of their titles. Nothing came of his efforts; today, nothing except the spectre of depression is persuading the publishers to be more discriminating. Publishers vie with each other for more and more manuscripts; whether good, bad, or indifferent seems not to matter. It was McIntyre who also saw, very early, that the book clubs were a blessing to the trade—not the evil some booksellers perceived them to be. His motto was Fewer and Better Books for his firm and others. I recall with pleasure several good visits with him in his Boston office, a quiet, twilight-dark room.

Alfred Harcourt was the original publisher of Sandburg, Frost, Keynes, and Sinclair Lewis, to mention only a few notable authors. I met him only once, briefly, at a publishers' gathering; I admired him from afar, as did every other envious editor. He died in 1954. His Bowker Memorial Lecture of 1937, *Publishing Since 1900,* is well worth seeking out and circulating among colleagues.

As for Alfred A. Knopf, he and his wife Blanche were superstars of their epoch, setting standards of quality and courage never before nor since matched. They published countless foreign writers; they introduced the colophon-consciousness, excellence in typography, beauty in binding dies; and especially noteworthy was the high quality of printing papers used in Knopf (or Borzoi) books.

Not too many editors are aware of the fact that the papers Knopf bought for his books made the special difference; nor were many of his authors aware of the fact that Knopf paid premium prices for his manufacturing—more than most trade publishers. His reason was simple: he detested second-rate work or second-best anything. He compromised less than any publisher I know. From every indication, Bob Gottlieb, the present editor-in-chief and president of Knopf, is carrying on the Knopf traditions. This should give Alfred much comfort in his retiring years.

Among others I had the pleasure of knowing was M. Lincoln Schuster, one of the founders of Simon and Schuster; a booklover in the old-fashioned sense, a reader, a worker. I often saw him on the streets with galleys and manuscripts under his arms. In his home he had a copy of every book he published, rebound in morocco. He loved each and every one. I also knew his gifted editor who died so very young, Jack Goodman, one of the early mainstays of S & S, and a best-seller "home-run hitter."

One of the rugged veterans, an individualist, a man I've known for over thirty years, is indestructible Nat Wartels of Crown Publishers. I think of him as the Spencer Tracy of the publishing world. White-haired (as long as I can remember), granite-jawed, but always with a ready smile, he's one of the last of the Mohicans. He is his own man and is owned by no one, including the banks. He runs his "shop" with an iron fist, but informally. He's considered a genius in the mail-order field, but he knows much more about books than merely how to sell them. He's a "bread-and-butter" publisher, whose lists are always filled with solid, "informational" works on a multitude of subjects, from collecting glass to American history—or the joys of sex.

Crown was started in 1936; Nat Wartels and Bob Simon were the original founders. Crown distributes for several small publishers, handles remainders in a substantial manner, and is very big in the oversize reprint book area, doing a tail-wagging-the-dog business with their Bonanza Books. They've had many best sellers over the years and have added hundreds of useful books to home and public libraries. Their fiction editor, David McDowell, has lent distinction to their list with his novelist discoveries.

Nat is the victim of many bachelor stories, including one you may have heard: Sitting in a barber chair getting a manicure, Nat says to the manicurist, "Honey, what are you doing tonight?" Her reply: "I don't know, ask my husband—he's shaving you."

No one knows how Nat managed to escape being swallowed up by some conglomerate. As to how Crown has prospered over the years, Nat told me that in 1936 his firm grossed less than $50,000, and in 1974 his volume was "well over a hundred times that figure." When I last saw him (at 21, where he usually lunches) he looked as though he was a stranger to pain.

And there was Whitney Darrow, guardian of rights at Scribner's; and Bennett Cerf, who was the most visible of all publishers; and Elliott B. Macrae of Dutton's, who came back from European trips each year with nets full of books; and Harold K. Guinzburg, co-founder of Viking Press, a man of standards and iron integrity. Bill Sloane, formerly of Holt, was the wunderkind (everything he touched turned to gold). Bill, who died in 1974, spent his last years at Rutgers University Press. When I was buying reprints for World, he sold me many fine books, including some by Ernie Pyle and Bill Mauldin.

I won't comment here on the newcomers, except to say that there are many bright contemporaries who exercise judgment and imagination in their daily rounds and who bring credit to their profession. Among them, there's a lot of virtuosity, fearlessness, and a willingness to examine new fields.

All of the foregoing is by way of emphasizing *people* and the conviction that today's young editor should know more about the men and women who make up our profession. They should, as I've suggested earlier, read about the struggles and achievements of the founding fathers, of individualist firms like Putnam's, Crown, Viking, New Directions. True, there are new developments, new techniques in selling, manufacturing, accounting, and warehousing that give the present-day publisher advantages over his predecessors. But not too much has changed in the editorial end of the game. Author and editor must meet and find common ground; a manuscript must be allowed to flourish under the encouraging eye of the publisher. The author must be regarded as the first asset of the publisher— not the packaging whiz kids, not the accountants.

Of Women and Books

Harriet Shaw Weaver, a generous and shy English-woman with a lifelong devotion to James Joyce and a major financial factor in the publication of *Ulysses,* was known in limited circles for her work on behalf of new writers through her Egoist Press. She published the archetype of the little magazine, *The Egoist,* and sponsored such writers as Pound, Eliot, H. D. Wyndham Lewis, Joyce, Robert McAlmon, and many others. It was she who published Marianne Moore's and T. S. Eliot's first books of poems. She was an ardent feminist, social worker, and "great lady." Her life story (*Dear Miss Weaver* by Jane Lidderdale and Mary Nicholson) is not only an inspiring literary biography but an important historical record relating to one of the richest literary periods of the century. Her private contributions, in both money and moral support, were unmatched. Understated, finding refuge in poetry and great literature, she gave completely of herself to advance others.

Caresse Crosby was another enthusiast and sponsor of great writers. She and her husband Harry founded the Black Sun Press in Paris, and published some of the most important writers of the period, among whom were Hart Crane, D. H. Lawrence, Kay Boyle, Archibald MacLeish, James Joyce, Ezra Pound. Caresse's autobiography, *The Passionate Years,* reveals that she and her husband led something of a Scott and Zelda-like existence, but their devotion to literature and fine publishing was unsurpassed. The quality of their books, the elegant printing and "packaging" in their famous gold-covered slipcases, gave Black Sun books a distinctive character never duplicated by any other private press. The Crosbys were patrons and publishers, but while unconcerned with finances, they were never amateurs.

On Agents and Agents

It has often been noted that amateurs are always making it tough for the professional. In the case of the literary agent, it is sometimes excessive professionalism that creates the problem.

There are agents and agents, and in my judgment, the best agent is primarily concerned with two issues: (1) making the best *overall* deal, and (2) working with the right house or editor. By overall deal I mean the guaranteed advance, plus the royalty terms, plus the basic rights due the author.

Obviously, the larger the advance, the more attractive the deal to agent and author. When a publisher extends himself with an abnormal cash guarantee, he is often entitled to *quid pro quo* consideration.

It is the bookkeeper mentality of an agent that gives the profession a bad name. An author wants a competent and trustworthy agent, not an accountant. Accountancy is a special profession and I think that an agent should not try to be both. Nor do I think that lawyers are the best suited to deal with an author's agency needs; they are not, as a rule, sufficiently qualified to do so. True, the lawyer is often called in for special problems; but he should not, with rare exceptions, substitute for the agent.

Notable among the exceptions is Paul Gitlin. He is both an astute lawyer *and* a literary agent, with a deep-down knowledge of taxes and international literary law. He represents such big guns as Harold Robbins, Irving Wallace, and other six-figure writers, and is unique in the industry for contract sophistication. Unlike most lawyers, Gitlin knows what motion picture, trade, and reprint contracts look like. He knows the custom of the industry. He eats contracts with his breakfast cereal.

Bella Linden, Eugene Winick, Harriet Pilpel, and Barry Lee Cohen, four able lawyers, are other exceptions; they've been bred in the literary vineyards and know the vocabulary of publishing and contracts with authors.

Many literary agents are my friends; at least I look upon them as such. One of my favorites is Max Gartenberg, a sturdy, independent operator. His "shop" is small, but he is totally committed to each of his clients. He's interested in getting a good deal for his authors, not in impressing them with his cunning.

I asked him at lunch one day (facetiously, of course) whether he really thought agents were necessary. He reminded me that I was married to one, and then said, "One might ask the same question about any group of professionals. Doctors, for example. There are many ailments that can be cured simply by sitting in a tub of hot water, and you can even get rid of an inflamed appendix if you have a steady-handed friend who owns a penknife. Just as some people never see a doctor from one year to the next and keep healthy, so some writers stay in financial good health without ever making the acquaintance of an agent."

Then I asked him about the agent's primary function, and his answer was: "From the publisher's point of view the agent's primary function is that of a screen. Winnowing good books from bad, the agent saves the publisher money he would have to spend on readers going through a lot of gibberish. Apparently this is worth the better terms an agented work gets compared to an unagented one. And some publishers now are simply not looking at so-called unsolicited manuscripts.

"From the author's viewpoint, the agent's function is more personal and complicated. Primarily, the agent is supposed to get the author the 'best deal,' whatever that may be. But a lot precedes and follows every deal, and no author-agent relationship is the same as any other. Some authors need editing and critical advice; some need a good deal of hand-holding; some would just as soon not hear from their agents except when there is a check to send. Naturally, the agent tries to conform his side of the relationship to the needs of the particular author. If the author wants no advice, the agent doesn't give it, unless he thinks the author needs it—which is when the latter brings in a manuscript that is less than it should be."

Speaking for myself, I must record that there are more good agents than bad. By bad I mean those agents who will send along anything that is typewritten on 8½- by 11-inch paper. It is hardly a secret that many of them don't read the stuff they send to editors. A few of them seem not able to read; nor do they care about reading. They are solely "operators," deal-makers. Not only do they dislike books, but they dislike their authors, too. But they do like —and often make—handsome dollar deals. Hollywood peddlers are most guilty of offering sows' ears as silk purses; they simply don't read *books*. (Spare me from the type known as "Hollywood effusive.")

A number of agents—happily, not all—abuse the multiple-submission auction system by submitting cats and dogs that barely merit two minutes' consideration. The one- and two-page outlines that some of them submit, on marginal subjects written by unknowns, would not be believed by an outsider. A large percentage of submissions for auction are not acceptable on any terms, and the hoopla and drum-beating that accompany some of these scarcely help the image of those particular agents offering them.

Another example of the "bad" agent is the one who fidgets over commas and semantics and forgets the basic deal and the intent of the agreement. Constipated, paranoid, uptight, these agents waste time trying to chip away at the publisher's profits, wrangling over language and small type. They fail to realize that legitimate publishers use standard language that is accepted by most agents and authors and their lawyers. The amateur challenges every word and is a pain in the ass. He negotiates with belligerence, as though the publisher were an enemy. He puts on a performance for his client.

There are many agents with whom I can conclude a deal on the telephone—and I do this often with some of the biggest in the business. I often have the pleasure of negotiating and processing contracts within a total period of forty-eight hours, and that includes getting the author's signature when he happens to be in our city. Then there are those that take weeks, months, to conclude—

Still another example of the "bad" agent is the one who harasses an editor day after day about matters which are none of his business. Agents sometimes drive an editor up the wall with telephonic raillery and repeated questions about sales, reviews, and ads. "What was your first printing?" is a question often asked by an agent, and my reply is usually, "Sorry, it's confidential." My contention is that in most cases, as long as a book is in print and available, the quantity printed is solely the publisher's business. When a publisher is unable to fill an order for a book, then it is proper for the agent and author to ask questions. There are exceptional cases, of course: if a motion picture company is negotiating for the rights to a book and asks about printings and sales, the agent is entitled to this information. Any editor will bend over backwards to help the agent close a film sale.

The good agent takes a live-and-let-live attitude. He knows how to walk the fine line which earns him the respect of all parties concerned, and is easily worth the 10 percent commission he receives. My advice to authors is never to begrudge the commission paid to a good agent. If one feels the agent is not doing his job, then of course some action must be taken. But sometimes an author will blame an agent for failure to sell his work even though rejection follows every submission. Some authors just can't believe that certain of their babies aren't pretty and that no publisher really wants them at any price. It does happen—alas, often.

I must add to the above a vignette of the type of agent who represents the worst of his profession. He is the man who renders only dissension and confusion, the agent who should have been a district attorney or an IRS investigator, for his is the soul of a mean prosecutor or accountant. A Dostoevskian character. He also tries to preempt certain prerogatives of the publisher, and aids and abets the author's paranoia. If this agent won't approach the negotiation in good faith and with a view toward establishing a wholesome partnership, then he should take his manuscript and shove it. He is unlikable—deliberately, I think—and should be avoided by both the author and publisher.

Much can be said on both sides, but the best deal can be achieved without the irritating tactics of this particular type of agent. Luckily there are very few such ones, and I suspect their identities are known. They would render the profession a real service by joining some accounting firm and forgetting the literary world.

P.S. I showed the foregoing two paragraphs to an agent friend and asked if I was being unfair, too rough. "No," she replied, "and I happen to know exactly who that prick is!"

Donald MacCampbell has no Pulitzer or Nobel Prize authors. He is one of the more rugged individualists in the agent field, and he likes to sell books that make money. He works hard, is successful, and specializes in the sale of paperback originals. He's a defender of the author, but intolerant of the temperamental and demanding prima donna. He admits to being snobbish about choosing his clients, but lacks no objectivity where a sale is involved. He doesn't nitpick; when he wants the deal, he sees it through with dispatch. To him a "name writer" is someone who makes money. What makes MacCampbell unique among agents is that he is totally unpretentious. But he's tough, and there are few mysteries in the business for him. One of the books he wrote has been known to offend (deliberately, on his part); it is called *Don't Step on It—It Might Be an Author.*

I like his forthrightness.

Some time ago, I commented in a public interview about several literary agents who had proclaimed their position with regard to a *certain kind of author*. Specifically, they said they would not represent an author they did not respect. I said that this was hogwash —that no intelligent agent would pass up a productive, money-making author, unless he were named Adolf Hitler. The superciliousness of the statements made by these several haughty and holier-than-thou agents brought laughter on their heads by others than myself. One very special agent, a friend named Robert Lantz, wrote me to say that he "did not know of any agent who was interested in anything but art—certainly not money."

I know that most readers of the foregoing are going to be disappointed by my failure to list the names of the "good" agents, but that's impossible for obvious reasons. I never recommend a specific agent but suggest that you check the Yellow Pages of the Manhattan telephone directory—the literary agents are listed right after Liquor Stores, in alphabetical order. A dowsing rod will help you locate the perfect one.

In case I've failed to make the point: an author *needs* an agent, and if he succeeds in getting a good one to represent him, he should count himself lucky. Agents, like friends, should not be abused or taken advantage of.

A good agent, in three words, is *one who sells*.

Footnote to agentry There's a loathsome aspect to the subject and I was reluctant to touch on it, but a few friends suggested that I discuss it, since "it's in the air."

The subject is that special cockroach* who bilks unsuspecting writers of their money. This breed of vermin pretends to have serious literary critics on his staff who will read, appraise, and render judgment—striptease advice—for a fee. He solicits manuscripts to read for a stiff price, knowing that not one manuscript in several hundred has a chance of being published. He knows that most of the stuff is hopeless, but he pretends to render sound, critical advice. Most of the manuscripts are skimmed over rather than read. The critical reports are "personalized," boiler-plate forms that can be sent to a variety of writers. He hands out clichés, oblique and homey promises, phony advice—and false hope. Boiler-plate hope. They are genuine, hand-typed, ink-signed letters. All pure bullshit.

I think the fees run around $150 for an average 300-page manu-

---

*Cockroach: "Although these insects are usually viewed with disgust, they are not devoid of interest."—ENCYCLOPAEDIA BRITANNICA

script. Short stories probably run to $50 or a $100. This agent handles many hundreds of manuscripts a year, and grinds out the reports like a factory. Young editors or hacks work at this labor, but soon get wise to what they are doing, and quit. Their stomachs can't take it.

There are some honorable private readers who charge fees, legitimate and capable critics who make a modest living from such work. But I would warn any newcomer to writing to avoid, or at least be on guard against, all fee-demanding agents. If your manuscript has merit, it will be sold—either through an agent or to a publisher directly. Publishers never charge for reading a manuscript, and I don't believe that agents should, either.

David Higham

This British literary agent is one of my favorites in the world. He is my senior in age and experience, and has represented some of England's most prestigious authors.

On each visit to London he is my host at his favorite Soho restaurant, L'Etoile, and his table is, of course, at the window.

He is alert, aware of the market, eager to sell, but a low-pressure salesman. I always leave Higham with an outline or manuscript. He is a practical, thoughtful man. He knows that an editor from New York is in London to *acquire*. Some agents will come to lunch and just *socialize*.

Youngsters entering the agency business can learn from David Higham. There are no mysteries for him in negotiation or in the art of selling. And, always, he is a gentleman.

I hope he never retires.

Drugola/Payola: Dire Prediction

We in book publishing can boast of the fact that we are free of the vicious payola problems that plague the phonograph record business. We do not bribe book reviewers, as is alleged to

be true of disk jockeys, with drugs and/or money. But I can foresee a time when bribery will be employed to get on the best-seller
lists, and on big-time network TV shows; cancer hits at every level,
sooner or later. Of course, books can't match the dollar volume of
records and tapes which, I understand, exceeds two billion dollars
annually. But the time may come . . . And who would not pay
heavy money to be at the top of *The New York Times'* Best Seller
List?

Please don't answer that last question. Before that occurs, I hope
all best-seller lists are abolished.

Vanity, Vanity

I've been asked whether I would speak up "candidly"
on the subject of the vanity press, that is, the publishers who charge
the author to publish his book. Some sanctimonious publishers consider them a blemish on the industry, parasites, a disgrace and dis-
credit to a noble profession, and all that.

To which I say, not really. If a man wants the pleasure of seeing
his name on a printed book and can't find a legitimate publisher
to take it on standard terms—well, why not?

Consider the small-town banker, schoolteacher, barber, kitchen
or bar philosopher, minister: they all want a touch of immortality,
a bit of public recognition, some of the limelight before they die.
What's wrong with spending a few thousand dollars to indulge oneself, if one can afford it? The money spent on a vanity press book
is better spent than, say, on horses, booze, or at the Vegas gambling tables.

The major vanity publishers declare their proposition in clear
enough language in their brochures. I've read some of them and I
don't consider them dishonest. They give you the facts of the deal:
they produce a book, they advertise it, they send out review copies.
The terms are spelled out clearly. Any lawyer can check out a vanity
press contract.

These publishers never lose money on a book; they can't. But
I don't believe they cheat their authors. I think they do give them
a fair shake, and they also give the author *hope*. Admittedly, vanity

publishers are the pygmies, or mice, in the publishing field (if one wishes to so view them), but they are neither villainous nor reprehensible. If I wanted desperately to be known as a poet in my community but had a book of poems that no one cared to publish, I think I'd spend the money to see the book come alive. Didn't William Faulkner, Edward Arlington Robinson, Cather, Stephen Crane, Poe, Whitman, and hundreds of other authors pay to get their first books published? You bet they did.

In my bookshop days, doubling as a publisher through my Black Archer Press, I was guilty of a bit of vanity publishing—publishing anything (well, *almost* anything) to make the rent. I had a customer who worked in a factory. He bought used books from me on history, geology, astronomy, and such. One day he told me that he had written a book whose title was to be *The Rhymed History of the World*. He yanked the manuscript out of a paper bag and handed it to me.

"Publish it; make it into a book," he said, "and I'll pay whatever it costs."

I told him I'd look the manuscript over, and that I'd have my answer for him the next day.

It was a wretched work. But he did indeed, in simple rhymes, relate the history of the world, beginning before recorded history and ending with a rhymed couplet dealing with the then-current American Depression. I told him I could produce a thousand copies of the work, totalling sixty-four pages (the history of the world in sixty-four pages!) in hard covers, with a two-color printed jacket, for $750. It would take about six weeks. He pulled out a checkbook and said, "It's a deal."

I never sold a copy of the book. I had them all delivered to his home. He was a bachelor. Later he told me that he was now *a somebody* in his factory and neighborhood. He gave the book away as wedding, birthday, anniversary, Christmas gifts, and even got a review in his neighborhood paper. He was a local hero. An author! He even brought me a bottle of bourbon as a gift, in appreciation, and we celebrated with Wild Turkey, neat. I think my total profit on the transaction was about $150.

Another vanity press job I took on was a book of love poems. The author, a middle-aged nightclub singer, an ex-musical comedy tenor, rather overdressed and overmannered, said he wanted to publish the book as a birthday gift for his boyfriend; it was a "make-up present." Presumably the book—very elegantly designed in black and silver, with silver on the title page—had its desired effect. The profit on this deal was a bit larger than the first—about $250.

One of my Chicago friends, E. A. Van Steenwyk, a founder of Blue Cross (he died in 1962, most tragically) wanted to surprise his young bride with a unique wedding present. She was a poet and he decided to give her a *printed* book of her own poetry. I designed and produced an attractive little 68-page book of her poems. It was entitled *Brittle, Bright* and appeared in 1931. No emeralds, no pearls, could have made Marion happier. We printed three hundred copies. The poetry was quite good, in no sense the work of an amateur.

My profit on this transaction was minimal, and everyone concerned was pleased. Vanity press books can bring joy to everyone involved; certainly they do no harm.

One more recollection: A retired scholar, whose sole interest was in John Keats, asked that his book-length essay on the poet be published. He was a man of means. The book was richly illustrated and rather expensive to produce, but he footed the bill. We sold some copies and there were, I recall, a few good reviews.

Again, what harm? A vanity press publisher doesn't have to worry about returns! And on occasion, he does manage to publish a good book. The vanity press that issued Willa Cather's *April Twilights* had something to boast about, as did the publisher of Robinson Jeffers' *Flagons and Apples*.

Publishers on Publishing

I once spent a year preparing a 600-page anthology dealing with publishing and publishers; World Publishing gave me a contract for its publication. Shortly before I completed the manuscript, along came a book on the same subject. It is *Publishers on Publishing*, edited by Gerald Gross. The book is almost 500 pages long and is the best single volume of its kind that I know of. It deals with the history, personalities, problems, and processes of publishing, a true one-volume course in the field. Grosset published

Publishers on Publishing in 1961 and I urge everyone to buy and read it, providing it's still in print. If it's not, call Jerry Gross and ask him about it. Needless to say, I shelved my own manuscript on the subject. Jerry's is the best.

In *Publishers on Publishing* there is a fine, short Preface by the late Frederic G. Melcher, whose friendship I was proud to share. One of his comments in this piece helped to free me in working on the present book. He said, "What we would most wish to hear from publishers is the records of their *personal experiences* in publishing and some suggestion of the ideals and purposes which they have brought to their work." I hope I've made some sort of contribution in that direction. Of course, ideals and purposes are only a part of the publisher's concern; there's also the matter of survival.

Penguins Are for Reading

If all the books in the world were destroyed except the titles now available in the British Penguin series, life would go on and little harm would come to our cultural life. One might add a few other paperback collections such as Capricorn, Harvest, Schocken, Anchor, and Vintage to the Penguin list, and the totality would be formidable. But taken by itself, Penguin is the Everest of paperbacks. Or, if you wish, it is *the* desert-island library. It affords those of every possible taste enough books to read. More than enough.

Penguin publishes originals and reprints, as do most paperback houses today. It started out with titles by such writers as Mary Webb, Ernest Hemingway, André Maurois, Beverly Nichols, Agatha Christie, Dorothy L. Sayers. At once, you get the level of its standard. Penguin Books Ltd., founded as a private firm by Allen Lane, with a capital of £100, is a perfect illustration of Ralph Waldo Emerson's aphorism that every great institution is the lengthened shadow of one man. Of course, Allen Lane, later Sir Allen, was a remarkable man. He had not only a taste for literature and a feel for what the public wanted to read, but a sharp business sense. He had sound ideas about manufacturing, good taste in design and, most importantly, an understanding of distribution. From the start, his books were sold in every possible outlet: in bookshops and stalls, department and chain stores, and other mass outlets. Lane's list grew rapidly and included titles such as *South Wind, A Passage to India, Crome Yellow;* books by Conrad, Shaw, Lawrence, Sinclair Lewis, Evelyn Waugh. Later, original works in the arts and sciences were written and published by Penguin. They also commissioned important works on music, philosophy, history, painting, and biography, which were published successfully.

Penguin branched out into other areas, including books for children (which list would, in itself, make up a successful publishing company), and for students in specialized areas of education such as archaeology, physiology, natural history, astronomy. In some forty years they have grown to so incredible a size that Penguin Books may be bought in almost every city in the civilized world.

Penguin's director, Peter Calvocoressi, tells me that there are some 4,500 Penguin titles in print today and that they sold about 43,000,000 books in one year, 1974. A formidable figure. They publish approximately 365 titles annually, of which 98 are Pelicans (self-improvement), 137 Penguins (fiction and lighter nonfiction, poetry, and the like), 100 Puffins and related children's series, and 30 more expensive specialist books of a serious nature. About half of their Pelicans are originals rather than reprint. Calvocoressi predicts an increased sales volume in the coming years.

As for printing today, Calvocoressi says that they "now use the full range of book types suitable for rotary printing from rubber or plastic plates." Invariably, the name of the type-face is indicated on the copyright page, in the best tradition of publishing.

Penguin Books is much more than a success story. It is a saga of quality surviving in the toughest business in the world. Great care was always given to quality of paper, and typographic design (Times New Roman, designed by Stanley Morison, was for many years the favored type), and covers were designed with simple felicity.

What is so special (at least to this typophile) is the fact that the interior of every Penguin book is given its own typographical treatment; they don't adhere to the usual standardization of design, with the dreary monotony found in most paperbacks. Penguin designers *worry* about title pages, headings, illustrations, ornaments. As Sir William Emrys Williams said of these books, "The Penguin product looks good, it bears the mark of aptitude and congruity, and is the appropriate physical expression of the belief that inexpensive books can be good books." Most paperback publishers devote most of their money, time, and energies almost exclusively to the cover design. It is no accident that one of Penguin's earliest books was Oliver Simon's *Introduction to Typography.*

There are all sorts of conclusions to be drawn from the Penguin story, but the most obvious one is that quality pays off; another is that having a genius to found and run your business helps. Many years ago I met Allen Lane in New York; we spent an afternoon in his hotel room at the Waldorf (with Ben Zevin) talking about— what? Literature, authors, royalties? No. His interest and reason for visiting America was to study packing, shipping, and warehousing systems. He was going to Gerard, Kansas, to inspect the firm of E. Haldeman-Julius because he was interested in the fulfillment techniques of that firm. I suspect most readers of this book have never heard of Haldeman-Julius. Well, in a sentence, he published countless millions of Little Blue Books that sold for five cents each, chiefly by mail order. (*The New Yorker* magazine, in its first issue on February 21, 1925, carried a full-page ad for Little Blue Books —twenty for a dollar, plus postage.) Part of my education as a reader is based on the hundreds of Little Blue Books, which ranged from writings by Mark Twain, Oscar Wilde, and George Bernard Shaw to Voltaire, Shakespeare, Zola, Thoreau, and Ibsen—you name the author, and if he is a renowned figure, his name will be on the Little Blue Books list.

Though to my knowledge, no other paperback collections measure up *completely* to Penguin, America has several series that emulate the Penguin qualities. I'm thinking specifically of Doubleday's Anchor Books, which Jason Epstein founded in 1953. He started with twelve titles, then left the firm five years later, having established the base for a great paperback list. (I once asked Jason why he had left Anchor and he said he couldn't remember.) Epstein pioneered quality paperbacks in America—not only books of scholastic interest, but also those with appeal to educated audiences. He managed to come up with an occasional best seller when he published original works in his series. Anchor won the Carey-Thomas Award for creative publishing in 1955.

Another impressive series is Vintage, part of the Knopf complex, run by Epstein and Anne Freedgood, also an ex-Anchor editor.

Many of the mass-market imprints such as Bantam, New American Library, Popular Library, Ballantine, Fawcett, Berkley, Pocket Books, and Dell, have some titles that are comparable to the quality found in Penguin, Vintage, and Anchor; but their real thrust is in mass audience literature, from low schlock to Nobel Prize material.

The future of the book industry is, of course, in the paperback. More and more, general (trade) titles will appear as paperback originals; copies in cloth will be issued simultaneously for the shrinking cloth-oriented market and libraries. The industry will *live* and thrive through paperbacks, like it or not. But anyone planning to enter the paperback publishing field should have, not Allen Lane's original founding capital of £100, but at least several million dollars. A lot has happened in publishing since the thirties. The reprinter, or tail, will soon be wagging the dog.

Spacemanship

At the end of this book I'll devote a few words to the subject of the *TBR* (*New York Times Book Review*), a subject that recurs (rears its ugly head) in book-industry conversations daily. Nothing raises blood pressure and hackles more readily or provides greater frustration to book editors, publishers, and writers, than the *TBR*. The most common complaint is, of course, *no review*. One of the several reasons often given for the pass is lack of space—too many books published, not enough space to accommodate them, and so forth.

I've been a student of the *TBR's* spacemanship for some years, and continue to be astonished each week at its uses and abuses of space. It runs the gamut from wild and generous space allotment for certain titles, down to a stick or two of type (or none) for others more or equally deserving.

I'll provide one example here:

In the February 16, 1975 issue of the *TBR* more than two full pages were devoted to Brendan Gill's *Here at the New Yorker*. The book was most favorably reviewed, as it well deserved to be. My quarrel is not with the book, nor with its author, nor with *The New Yorker*, which is still my favorite American magazine (and its editor, William Shawn,* is still the best editor in New York—and that includes those in both magazines *and* book publishing offices).

But all that space! Gill's book could have been covered handsomely in one page. If it was the *TBR's* plan to *celebrate* the Fiftieth Anniversary of *The New Yorker,* I think they were out of order. The *TBR's* job is to *review* books, to present *book news.*

Any junior editor armed with a ruler can see that the *TBR* is quixotic in its disbursement of space. The Brendan Gill review was a piece of self-indulgence on the part of the *TBR's* editor. In an expansive, post-Christmas mood, the *TBR's* host was handing out largesse while other good books, new to the season or ignored in the recent past, were suffering neglect. Which makes this a case, not so much of bad judgment, but of inequity of a serious nature. The munificence is not the *TBR* editor's to give if authors and publishers are to get a fair shake.

But, to repeat, more on the *TBR* later.

---

*William Shawn's *New Yorker* celebrated its fiftieth anniversary at the Grolier Club with a fine bash on February 21, 1975. One day, a week before the affair, I asked Shawn (we always sit in opposite corners of the Algonquin's Rose Room for lunch) if I'd be seeing him at the party. He replied, "I'm not sure I'm going; it's a black tie affair and I don't own a black tie." He didn't show up! But Brendan gave a peppery talk, startling the more conservative element of the SRO audience with some earthy (non-Grolier) remarks about the *New Yorker's* founder, Harold Ross. Among Gill's epithets for founding father Ross, was "ignoramus." I doubt that Shawn would have agreed. I met Harold Ross just once, and he was *rude.* Very. That was when Carl Rose once tried to introduce me to him. He barely raised his head and I heard him grumble, "I know too many people already." But I wonder about "ignoramus." He did have the good sense to surround himself with some of the best writers of his time, and he paid them handsomely, thereby keeping their loyalty. This is not consistent with the epithet "ignoramus."

4 Lo! The Editor

You ask for the distinction between the terms "Editor" and "Publisher": an editor selects manuscripts; a publisher selects editors.

—M. LINCOLN SCHUSTER

The Editor: Is It a Bird, a Plane . . .?

I'm often asked, "What does an editor do?" The questioner could be someone from the shoe manufacturing business, the mortuary profession, the sports world. Or a nosy IRS investigator.

What is an editor? Can the profession/*calling* be defined?

No matter what the dictionary tells you, it isn't possible to nail down the precise role of the editor. In a sense he is a publisher. An entrepreneur. It's a cliché to remark that editing is neither an exact science nor a skilled profession. Some opprobrious epithets are used in describing editors, especially when it's realized that one of the major qualifications of an editor is the ability to *procure*.

In the following pages you'll get a composite picture of the book editor: at worst, a caricature and slavey, a working fool; at best, a saint or lucky devil, a home-run hitter. Some editors are happy, carefree; some, disgruntled. Speaking for myself, I think I'm all of the above at various times, with luck and good reflexes close to the top of my qualifications level.

So what does an editor do?

The best way to answer this question may be to describe my own activities. Let's take the year just past, 1974, as an example:

In 1974 I produced (processed) thirty new titles for Putnam's. These books had been negotiated and contracted for by me through solicitation, submission, old-fashioned negotiation with agents, authors, and European publishers. None of these came to me "over the transom." Each book had been presented and discussed at editorial meetings. Each had been given a sales and subsidiary income examination before a contract was issued, a house (collaborative) enterprise.

These thirty books were handled (edited, processed, published) by me with the aid of one secretary-assistant (Chuck Finberg) within twelve months. Of course there were many other hands involved in the overall operation, including the accounting department.

To produce and publish a book means that one has read the manuscript, worked with the author (discussions relating to textual changes and other pertinent matters), turned the manuscript over to a copyeditor to check for errors, grammar, inconsistencies, repetitions, and the like. The book must be estimated for cost and approximate retail price, based on a minimum sales expectancy. The rights department comes up with an evaluation of income. Then the manufacturing department gets the manuscript. The book is placed on a production and publication schedule, involving about six to eight months from start to publication date. And the editor is involved in each of these steps; the book is his baby all the way.

The physical book, the jacket, the typographical treatment (sometimes), jacket blurbs, and the author's photo and biography are also the editor's concern. He must look after each of these details. He must prepare an "editorial presentation"—a description of the book for use by everyone: the publicity, sales, rights, promotion, and library departments. The editor also "presents" his book at the company's sales conferences—*sells* it to them, verbally.

The editor must hold the author's hand when the going gets bumpy. He must keep author and agent apprised of all matters of concern, including sales, publicity, and income from rights. Discretion is sometimes essential; certain information such as a bad review might be withheld temporarily. Certain sales information might also be held up when it could be erroneous, premature. Intelligent censorship is advised. The author's spouse is also someone to consider when tension builds.

The editor must try to wheedle advance comments from VIP's. A statement by Saul Bellow, for example, proclaiming your novel almost as good as *War and Peace* will do the book a lot of good. A limited number of reading copies, sent in advance to key booksellers, will help, too.

While the editor is working on his various books for publication, he is also reading—searching for *new* material—and considering manuscripts and proposals submitted all during the year. (Last year

I received and examined over 250 manuscripts and about the same number of outline-proposals. I contracted for 18 titles from these submissions, and these books, with luck, will materialize in the next year or later.)

The editor usually reads manuscripts "on his own time," which means away from his office. He reads nightly, weekends, holidays. If this sounds like medievalism, or cottage industry, it may very well be; but that's what editing is—a full-time job with an occasional break for relaxation. Somehow, too, an editor manages to read books published by other houses.

An editor travels as part of his job, and obviously it isn't all unpleasant work, especially if one's author lives in London, Malibu, the south of France, or Paris. But long, hard, grim hours of reading manuscripts and proofs are the editor's destiny, and there's no substitute yet known for reading a book. Getting someone else to read for you is not the answer because, in the end, your decision to publish is based on your firsthand knowledge of the book under consideration. A rave report from a "first reader" is not enough on which to make a publishing judgment.

Manuscript reading is rarely done in one's office except in emergency situations. I usually sample a manuscript from an unknown before taking it home, to make certain the book is not illiterate, hopeless, or out of my range of interest. But I repeat, manuscript reading by an editor is *homework*, in the old-fashioned sense.

What else must an editor do in his job?

He must think up ideas for books. Then he must find authors to match the ideas. This subject is discussed elsewhere in this section.

The editor must present and convince his firm's editorial board of the merits of his book, the book under submission. He may be wildly enthusiastic about the work and eager to sign a contract. But after discussion with his associates, he might discover a number of things: the author's reputation is that of a loser; the book is similar to one recently published or about to be published; the asking price (dollar advance requested by the agent) is risky, too high for the particular book. Finally, the sales and rights departments may express negative views on the project—which means, in basic English, no support. To buy a book in which very few of one's colleagues has any faith is hazardous. It is possible to be a minority of one and come up smelling like the proverbial roses; but it takes nerve, experience—and luck.

An editor often writes some of his own letters because no single secretary-assistant can handle all of the correspondence.

Handling galley proofs (for authors, agents, and others) is important, calling for "good housekeeping." Likewise the physical movements of manuscripts to and from the author, printer, and copyeditor requires maximum security-type care. An original manuscript that is lost is a disaster situation, especially when no carbon or Xerox copy exists. Scrupulous care and vigilance are called for. A sloppy editor gets into trouble sooner or later.

Ken McCormick, grand old-young man of Doubleday, once said, "The most important change in an editor's job today is that he has slowly acquired the publisher's responsibility." (Ken, by the way, started his career in a bookshop; today he is a very active "consultant" at Doubleday with a personal stable of authors as large as ever. And he's still waging war against censorship.)

Of the thirty books handled and published by me in the 1974 fiscal period, ten were novels. Thirteen were by authors I had published before, such as Simone de Beauvoir, Art Buchwald, Harry Golden, Ashley Montagu. Fourteen of these authors appeared on my personal list for the first time at Putnam's.

The thirty books included memoirs, anthropology, history, humor, fiction, medicine, occultism, psychology, and so on.

A few were taken by book clubs; about 30 percent were contracted for by paperback houses. There were no art books or technical works among them.

We may have lost money on seven or eight of these thirty books; as of this writing, the final figures are not yet in. We made a good profit from subsidiary income: one title alone brought in a gross of $300,000 for reprint rights, plus a good five-figure advance from a club. Others went to reprinters for figures ranging from $50,000, $35,000, $25,000 and less. One book went for a modest $3,500. Because of a depressed (cyclical) paperback inventory situation, we were unable to place every title with a reprinter, but this doesn't preclude a sale at a later date. There's always a reason for a delayed subsidiary response. Sometimes, however, a book simply isn't wanted, has too little appeal, or is not the best of its kind. In a few cases, we earned income from foreign rights—where there was no agent involved.

Some editors can produce more than thirty titles in one year, while some veterans handle less. Years of involvement in publishing are needed in order to develop a "stable" or acquisition rhythm. I know some young editors, gifted men and women, who can't come up with more than eight or ten books a year. But they will increase their productivity in time.

Now that you've read some of my comments on "being an editor," I'd urge you to get a copy of Sir Geoffrey Faber's previously mentioned book, *A Publisher Speaking*, published by Houghton Mifflin in 1935. (Probably you can borrow it from the public library.) He headed the house of Faber & Faber in London, and died in 1961. In this book you will find much solid information about the editor's and publisher's role, and more on "what an editor is." He sums it all up in a short, unflattering sentence: "In the first place, we publishers are middle-men."

Advice

Giving advice to newcomers to the publishing business reminds me of what Flannery O'Connor once said to a class in writing where each week a new writer-instructor would hand out advice: "What you hear one week from a giraffe is contradicted next week by a baboon."

The long and short of advice-giving is: Try to be practical and understated; follow instincts, not textbooks.

An editor should sleep on it, that is to say, let a few days or a week pass after reading a manuscript. It may provide a better perspective. In the end, the editor's decision to accept or reject is as lonely a role as the writer's. It's got to be his decision, and he's got to stand on it. If it turns out to be a mistake, admit it and write it off.

The Education of an Editor, Part 1

The need to reject manuscripts turns an editor into a judge-executioner, an uncomfortable role for any sensitive person.

With the knowledge that an author will suffer from rejection, knowing that some writers will be devastated by a cold and impersonal letter, the editor has no choice but to say no in cliché terms: "Sorry, not suited to our present needs." This is the message that will protect the editor though it is a coward's way.

I recall a letter from Ezra Pound to an aspirant. Pound, who was anything but shy, opened up by saying, "Come now, you can do better than that!" I cherish that sentence as a perfect opening for a rejection letter, but am reluctant to use it.

Don't get involved editorially or show paternal anxiety unless you intend publishing the author's work: that's the best advice I can give to an editor. Offering gratuitous editorial advice usually leads to heavy breathing on the part of the author—and in the end, hostility.

A British publisher sends the following rejection slip, which, on unsolicited manuscripts, seems to me humane:

"We regret having to say 'no' to your manuscript. The fact that it proved not to our taste does not necessarily mean your work is unpublishable, but all we can do, under the pressure of submitted books, is to wish you better luck elsewhere."

I don't think a publisher has any further obligation to the author of an unsolicited and unwanted manuscript. In fact, he can't afford to indulge in correspondence. Ask an accountant what it costs to write a critical letter, stamp and mail it, and file the carbon. Of course, cost is not the only factor. Getting involved with a writer on a work of no interest to you can have no small effect on the nervous system.

On a wistful, personal note   I read and declined a manuscript one day in October 1972, a book by the New York call girl-madam, Xaviera Hollander. Her story begins with her childhood in Holland. Her doctor father has sexual relations with a nymphet patient, and witnessing the act of fellatio between them triggers Xaviera's sexual saga. Fellatio becomes her lifelong passion-avocation, and vocation. She is expert in it. Some of her disclosures are more than heady (pun intended) and she tells of services rendered for which a fee of up to $1,000 for an evening's work is charged. A phrase in the text caught my eye, "the paradise stroke," referring to the final, preorgasmic thrust of the penis. Vivid, poetic, certainly accurate as a description of the divine moment.

I declined the manuscript with the usual excuses. But not because I was opposed to it. I would have, quite frankly, enjoyed publishing the book. But none of my colleagues agreed. Most of them viewed it with horror. Some began to wonder about my sanity. The head of the house was abroad, so I didn't have his judgment. One executive said, "This cocksucker's story may bring us a lot of money but we don't need money that badly."

My reply was, "I don't want to publish this for money but rather for sentimental reasons—I'd like to look back on it as one of my more memorable publishing acts." As history shows, Dell published the book, sold millions of copies, and made Miss Hollander's fortune. I record this manuscript rejection because I know that in the long run it would not have been such a mistake, editorially, to have published the book. Financially it would have been sensational.

Why do publishers get sticky and righteous at the wrong time?

Writing of Miss Hollander recalls to mind a tender anecdote. George Jessel was leaving for Israel and was saying good-bye to some friends at a party. Xaviera Hollander, his date, kissed him farewell and George said, "Now you be true to me, honey, you hear?"

Editors don't usually speak of their lesser achievements, but remembering Jessel reminds me of a book I published with him, a minor book called *Hello Mama!* What saved the book were the illustrations by the late Carl Rose, *The New Yorker* cartoonist and a personal friend. Truthfully, good as the drawings were, the book wasn't "saved." But I recollect that Georgie was not only a sentimentalist, as indicated by the above anecdote, but he had the world's most pronounced supply of chutzpah. He came to my office on publication date of his book and asked, "Did the Sunday *Times* review my book yet?"

I hesitated and he pushed ahead, "They didn't, eh? Who's the editor?"

It was Francis Browne and I told him. Jessel snatched the phone from my desk, asked our operator to get him Brownie *tout suite*. Believe it or not, Brownie came to the phone, and when Jessel ended up asking, "So when will my book be reviewed?" he was told, "In a few weeks." And it was! And not a bad review either.

One day Carl Rose and I were visiting with Georgie in his hotel suite. Suddenly Jessel put his hand to his head; I thought he was going to scratch himself. But no, he removed his toupee and disclosed the "big secret" of his life: he was bald. Jessel is/was not renowned for his shyness.

Many good talkers are lousy writers; never judge a prospective author's work by charm, vocabulary, diction, or "verbal music." I've found that most good writers are mumblers, deficient as speakers, and seldom witty in person. Insist on *reading* something by the author before a meeting. Don't let an author con you into a conference or serious discussion of his work (there are exceptions of course) before seeing something on paper. When an author has to *explain* his work, caveat emptor. Needless to say, the above does not apply to a writer with a publishing history.

To Be or Not To Be The nightmares and indecisions that plagued Hamlet are nothing compared to what an editor suffers when trying to make a judgment about a troublesome manuscript.

He found that he enjoyed reading it but his conscience told him it had no future.

"It's a loser," says one part of his brain.

"But what about the wit and elegant style?" says another part.

"Yeah, but there's no story."

And so on. I've often awakened during the night, wondering what decision I would render the next day. Sometimes one is deliberately imprudent. Or else too logical. Very often the illogical prevails—and succeeds.

If you toe the party line and lean hard on the track records of "similar" books, you're lost. The rip-off book, the careful imitation, riding the coattails of a successful genre book, can lead nowhere. The intuitive editor can go farther than the cerebral slide-rule editor. In the end, the big successes are surprises to everyone. For example, there's the story about a little book dealing with a seagull that most of the publishers in New York turned down and which Macmillan signed up for a $2,000 advance . . .

Get Carried Away An editor *must* do something reckless at least once a year: outbid everyone for a book; overadvertise; fire an employee for purely personal reasons; take a lover/mistress; demand a raise out of hand; print a book in white ink on black paper (figuratively) in order to shake up the scene. Life is short, and an editor takes too much abuse not to deserve some indulgence.

Occupational Hazard   Most editors drink too much. Liberal expense accounts are responsible in part. And tension. Alcoholism sneaks up on the unwary drinker and by post-middle age the effects are visible—and a problem. *Show some character!*

Advice: Lay off all drugs; they can give only temporary relief, and the dependency grows.

To cure a headache or ease tension, I've found a simple remedy: a glass of chilled Pouilly-Fuisse taken with two aspirins.

As for hard liquor: take only *one* drink at lunch and *one* before dinner. Don't wind up a sot, with cirrhosis of the liver or worse. And a reputation to match.

The Education of an Editor, Part 2

A working, qualified editor of books must read. He must have read from the earliest days of his childhood. His reading must be unceasing. The *lust* for printed matter is a biological thing, a visceral and intellectual necessity; the urge must be in the genes.

An editor must read everything—newspapers, magazines, advertisements, labels, encyclopedias, novels, history, short stories, poetry, lectures, essays, editorials, speeches, political oratory, plays, and all other written matter. Even the *Congressional Record*.

As a rule, schools don't provide the incentive to read. An antiquarian bookshop or a library can be the basis of an editor's education. You'll find books, old and new, including forgotten masterpieces of literature that are not as yet available in paperbacks.

A publisher's editor should know something of the fiction of the past. Take, for example, Balzac. There are at least twenty of his novels one should have read, among which are *Eugénie Grandet, Le Père Goriot, Le Cousin Pons,* and *César Birotteau.* I read some twenty-five of Balzac's novels in my early twenties and many of his characters (there must be about twenty-five hundred in all) still remain in my memory. For years Balzac was my idol; I read his books and dreamed of France—and Paris. The pictures of Parisian and French provincial life drove me out of my mind. Balzac embraced all of society. He wrote like a demon and even when he took time off to make love he "cost-accounted" the event, noting that to fuck a woman could cost him as much as a chapter. I read Balzac with a frenzy, as I did Zola and Dickens. Those were novelists. The story—and character—were their concern. And their novels did "make a statement."

In my teens I bought the works of Théophile Gautier and Zane Grey and Edgar Rice Burroughs. At nineteen I read all of Ibsen and I suspect that no one on my block has read the *Works,* including his *Julian the Apostate.* I read that play with a passionate involvement. The play, I think, is unknown today.

I have always read indiscriminately. I was a reading machine, just as later, I became a book-making machine.

I recall that at thirteen, as a bar mitzvah gift, I received the works of Jack London from my cousin Max. I devoured these books —twelve volumes—in as many days. Among them were *The Iron Heel* and *Martin Eden,* two books that shook me up. My mother was furious with me. "Couldn't you stretch it out a little longer?" she asked. "You *used up* your present so fast." I promised that I would reread some of the books later.

No one in my family, except my mother, cared about books. (She devoured romantic novels in Yiddish.) My father loathed the whole idea and said that reading anything but the Hebrew prayerbook was a waste of time, and *goyish.* (Could one make a living from them?)

Gautier I've already mentioned. He was an early enthusiasm, but don't ask me why. I moved like a Sherman tank through his "collected works." I loved his *Captaine Fracasse,* and of course, the wicked and forbidden *Mlle. de Maupin,* which I read at least three times. (My earliest encounter with sexy literature.)

Emile Zola was another enthusiasm in my early reading years, and the *Rougon-Macquart* series was virtually popcorn to this reading incinerator. I read his first book, *The Dream;* then moved into his major works: *L'Assommoir, Germinal, Nana, La Terre, La Curée,* and others. Some twenty volumes succumbed to my assault. To this day, some forty years later, I remember each and every one vividly. Who writes such books today? And why not?

I also devoured Upton Sinclair.

And then came the English: Dickens, Austin, Trollope, Thackeray (much earlier I had downed a dozen Hentys). Next, the Russians: Dostoevski, Turgenev, Chekhov, Tolstoy, Goncharov, Gogol, Pushkin. Later came Hermann Sudermann's *Song of Songs,* which

I read twice. Likewise Wassermann's *The World's Illusion* (which I still think is a very great novel. Jakob Wassermann died in 1934; his other books, also well worth knowing, are *Casper Hauser* and the *Maurizius Case*). Most of the Italians left me cold. For me, Dante is still a bore and unreadable. (Yes, despite T. S. Eliot's admirable essay on the poet.) I know the fault is entirely mine. I like some of the contemporary Italians, and I think Italo Calvino is the best. (I also like visiting with him when we are in Paris; he and his wife Chichita are two of the non-French citizens of Paris whom we adore.)

I was delighted not too long ago to find Erica Jong saying: "When I was a ten-year-old bookworm and used to kiss the dust-jacket pictures of authors as if they were icons, it used to amaze me that these remote people could provoke me to love. Once I discovered that some author I loved had been dead for *years*, and my response was astonishment. Love beyond the grave! Love from people you will never meet! Love seeping through paper and parchment and ink!" Jong goes on to say, "Here was the solution to loneliness. A piece of paper would be the magic mirror through which I stepped to join the imaginary friends who really loved me. Through the looking glass. Narcissus finds her one true love. Papagena finds Papageno."

As I began by saying, an editor must read all his life, and start early. Read Jean-Paul Sartre's *Words*. He said, in speaking of writing, "It's a habit, and besides, its my profession." This is how I view reading. Sartre's book, by the way, is one of the really tolerable memoirs of a young writer; most preadolescent confessionals are boring.

Sell: The Editor Gets Out of the Ivory Tower   What I'm about to say here is fairly basic, perhaps overfamiliar. It may be that you are a veteran for whom this is elementary stuff and therefore boring. In which case, feel free to skip.

Until an editor gets out of the ivory tower and into the selling arena, he's only *half* a publisher. He must understand, through personal experience, how a book is exploited, sold, "noised around."

Signing up the author's book is Step Number One, and in itself is as important as the creative act from the publisher's standpoint.

Once the contract is signed, the book written, and the manuscript is about to emerge as a Book, the editor's selling job begins—

long before the salesmen get to work on it. At this point the editor's worth begins to become apparent; it is here where we see how much he really cares about the welfare of his book.

Step One: *Start by being shameless.* Try anything within reason to get your book noticed. Galley proofs should go off to key sales-men. (Some salesmen can do better by *not* reading a book.) Copies should go to a select group of booksellers (over the sales director's signature), to certain writers, and to those persons with access to the press or the air—persons likely to respond favorably to the book. *Publishers Weekly* should be given brief running stories about the book or its author.

The foregoing may seem like the publicity department's job, and in the final and larger sense, it is. But first the editor must start send-ing up flares, writing letters and memos to all concerned, and *talk-ing,* so that the baby about to be born gets enough oxygen, *atten-tion.* Advance comments from readers who are influential in the trade or in the press are the lifeblood of the book. Stories in the press about a book can often produce wonders. Word-of-mouth press agentry is important, much more so than paid space adver-tising. Please write across your memo pad: *Word-of-Mouth Sells More Books than Printed Advertisements.* (Your author won't be-lieve this of course, but it is the truth.)

To put it in the crudest of terms, an editor who wants to make it must get off his ass and *do* many things *himself,* and that includes delivering proofs, advance copies, urgent and personal messages to the VIP contacts who will help get that book on the escalator. Tak-ing a book-buyer to lunch sometimes helps, but please—no hammer-swinging, no ear-bending. Easy does it. Book-buyers are intelligent as well as sensitive.

Selling is a creative business if you take the job seriously. One of the first commandments in selling is: Never lie. Liars get found out, and to be known as a liar in the book trade is suicidal. Honest en-thusiasm is enough.

Keep an eye on all publicity releases, the review- and gift-copy lists, copy and layouts of the ads, and the mailing pieces sent to the trade. Check out jacket and biographical blurb copy with your author.

There's nothing easier than printing a book. Next to writing a book, there's nothing tougher than selling it. If you're inclined to believe in miracles, then consider every best seller a miracle. Think of the odds and you'll see why.

An editor can help along the realization of a miraculous act, but it's a sixteen-hours-a-day job. Is it worth it? It's almost as good as sex when it works!

One of the essentials in an editor's training is learning what the customer wants. Taking money in exchange for a book. This is why it's important to work in a bookshop for at least six months.

Any editor can do a bit of moonlighting to get the experience by working, say, as an extra on Saturdays or evenings. The pay is far from princely, but consider the job educational. Observing a customer making up his or her mind about a book is an experience.

Persuading a customer to part with $7.95, $10.00, or $15.00 for a new book is an act of magic, in my opinion, and any bookshop salesperson who understands the art of prying money out of a reader is beyond price (and is probably underpaid). Intelligence, taste, and salesmanship—that's a combination to cherish.

———————

For many years at World, I sold our books to the big wholesale accounts—Baker & Taylor, American News, Bookazine, Dimondstein —as well as to the Walden chain, Doubleday's, and Brentano's. I also sold to Scribner's and a few other shops. From these various firms I learned some of the bread-and-butter facts of publishing life. The Baker & Taylor buyer (Allen Hood in those days) was my "El Exigente"; his reaction was crucial. If he bought a thousand copies of a new title, I knew we were in; if he frowned and bought, say, twenty-five copies, I saw trouble ahead. The wholesalers' initial orders really told us where we were and what the score was.

Bill and Ted Epstein of Bookazine are major factors in the health of a new book; they too knew, almost instantly, whether we had a big book or a marginal one. The Epsteins, in a few decades, built a giant-sized book business out of a hole-in-the-wall-beginning. Bill was one of my best teachers in those learning days of the forties and fifties. Today he and his brother Ted are among the wholesaling giants. Of course, several other important new distributors have emerged—Ingram, Raymar, Brodart—but the Epsteins and the Dimondsteins of the old days taught me much about this business when I was calling on them each month. The editor should get to meet some of them; watch them buying and selling books. One of the best wholesaler's salesmen in America is Julie Spinner of

Dimondstein, a canny, enthusiastic superstar bookman who can often *make* a book if he likes it. An advance proof or copy of a new book to Julie is the best investment imaginable in our business. Lou Klepper, another veteran bookman, is a force in the selling arena of New York.

Doris Laufer, Bill McCarthy, and Carl Kroch of Kroch-Brentano in Chicago are three of the most aware and influential book people in America; the Kroch-Brentano store is probably the best of its kind anywhere. I watched it grow; I remember when Carl's father Adolph founded it on Michigan Avenue many, many years ago. Carl took it and *ran*, building it into *the* giant book outlet of the Midwest. Doris, one of the brightest women in the book business, is someone to talk to for bookselling enlightenment. And so are Lillian Friedman and Trudy Laub, in New York, both seasoned bookwomen.

Shelley Stein, among the leading publishers' reps in Chicago, is an inspired, indefatigable "old school" book peddler who rolls up fat advance orders for new books for Putnam's by putting his personal reputation on the line. Booksellers love and trust him, as do his colleagues.

I always found Scribner's Igor Kropotkin uncanny in his initial order for a book. His instant evaluation of a book's market potential was shrewd and usually hit the bull's eye. He'd study a jacket briefly. He might say, "Ten copies"—or "Two hundred and fifty"— and he was invariably right. He was intuitive; he seemed to need no guidance from the publisher's salesman, no background coaching. I miss those old contacts with the trade. The big-city merchants can teach an editor plenty about his trade. So can the Marboro remainder buyer.

I often think nostalgically of my monthly visits (during the World years) to the Walden Book Company, whose home office is in Stamford, Connecticut. Visiting with Larry Hoyt, the company's founder, and his buyers, was always a picker-upper for me because these bookmen were such feet-on-the-ground realists; they simply *knew* what the public wanted to read, and they were so well organized: almost daily, the reports from their hundreds of stores across the country told us more than the best-seller lists.

Toby Wherry is one of the best-liked, most respected veteran bookmen on New York's publishing scene. He is also the leading sales representative for Putnam's in the East. He's sophisticated, articulate, widely read, and independent-minded. I cornered him one day and got him to talk. I wanted his overall view of the publisher-bookseller/wholesaler relationship today, a few insights into some of the problems that exist. Following is an edited extract from our conversation:

Said Toby: "At about the time I came into the business, in 1947, the relationship between trade publishers and their retail and wholesale outlets underwent a radical change. Heretofore books had been sold outright, and if the stores and jobbers could not sell them they had to mark them down and take a loss."

I pointed out that the British publishers don't have this problem of a no-return policy, but their advance subscription is therefore usually much smaller.

"I know. The American publishers' representatives tried to load up their accounts, and the accounts in turn tried to unload on their customers. So, in those bygone days, both salesmen and booksellers had a very direct and immediate influence on book sales."

"Do you recall who conceived the return policy?" I asked.

"I'm not certain, but I think that in 1947 Viking and Simon and Schuster, among other publishers, began accepting unlimited returns, attaching a small penalty, usually ten percent, to cover handling. Book outlets had finally convinced publishers that they could not survive under the old economic conditions and that the publishers, being more affluent, must bear the major responsibility for a book's failure."

"In my book I've covered the subject of returns in part," I told Toby. "I'd like to get on to another subject; let's talk about selling, and, yes, what do you (the generic you) think about the publishers' editors—on or off the record?"

Toby had no compunction about speaking *on* the record.

"Being a book salesman or publisher's rep," he said, "can be a rather odd and confusing way to make a living. Publishers and editors try to fire his enthusiasm by encouraging him to read what he sells (a device which often backfires), while the salesman, in order to maintain the mystique of his job (otherwise he might lose it), goes along with the game. When actually face-to-face with his customer, the salesman, if he is any good, finds himself in an entirely different situation—trying to help find out who the people are who would enjoy a particular book and devising ways to reach them.

Since all merchandise is returnable for full credit, trying to agree on a suitable quantity of each title is a problem."

I asked about salesmen competing with each other for the customer's budget dollar.

"Most salesmen in the same industry," said Toby, "compete with one another: Proctor and Gamble does not tell Colgate-Palmolive. Not so with books. Except for items like cook and reference books, each title is a separate entity. The novels of Herman Wouk do not compete, even on the same shelf, with Vladimir Nabokov. Where competition does exist in the publishing business is in the editorial departments."

"How so?" I asked. "Do you mean for *status?*"

"No. Where acquisition editors compete is in the area of the agents—they vie for material among the agents. These editors are bundles of psychological and aesthetic contradictions. Most of them are well educated and have come into the business in the hopes of becoming another Maxwell Perkins, without whom, according to publishing myth, Thomas Wolfe, F. Scott Fitzgerald, and Ernest Hemingway could not have made their marks. Once hired, however, these editors find that they are employed reading manuscripts, most of which are rejected, and their taste and vision undergo a profound change. Naturally, if you spend most of your days reading poor material, your aesthetic standards are going to be lowered and you are apt to believe you have found another *Light in August* in a quite ordinary novel of southern life."

I interrupted. "That's one of my old arguments, already hinted at in my book—the lowering of standards, the editor's compromises, brought about by the shortage of decent material."

Toby continued: "I know that once an editor has committed himself to a book by accepting it, he usually manages to convince himself that it is not good compared to what he has been reading, but that it is intrinsically worthy. He becomes angry if the book is not reviewed well, even though, were it to be issued by another publisher, he might not review the book favorably either. This possessiveness toward a manuscript he has accepted, which now becomes *his*—the poor author having long been forgotten—is what causes the editor to try to convince salesmen and booksellers to read the book, forgetting that they have no such commitment. One would think that they were oversensitive authors, not business-minded distributors."

I interrupted to say that he, Toby, was rather shrewd in his appraisal of the editorial mind and behavior. He went on:

"Though their functions often overlap, even in this era of increased specialization, acquisition editors may be distinguished from the editor who works with an author to improve a manuscript. This person, today often a woman, is not so well paid as her fellow, but the job should be more satisfying creatively. Even so, all book editing as it exists today is a twentieth-century creation, and the question has to be asked whether authors who lived before 1900 would have found their work materially improved by today's editorial ways. I rather doubt it. I imagine few editors today would allow the inconsistencies in *Hamlet* to pass; yet those inconsistencies contribute, and some might say are responsible for, *Hamlet's* greatness."

I said that in Great Britain far less editorial work was done by the editors than in America, that many manuscripts went to the typesetter almost untouched by editorial hands.

Toby responded: "I believe a good case can be made for the contention that today's publishers act less as a conduit from the writer to the reader than as a censor. Who, one may ask, gives these people the authority to sit in judgment on a writer's work?"

My answer was based on the professionalism of the editor (and especially the copyeditor) and the less-than-professional work being submitted by authors to the publishers. Too many people writing today are without talent or lack genuine qualifications.

Changing the subject, Toby noted "the decline in influence over sales of individual titles by booksellers."

"So what, in your wisdom, makes a good bookseller?"

"Good bookstore management. Imaginative merchandising, the use of creative displays, the ability to identify and keep clientele, keeping up with reviews, trying to keep one step ahead of trends, noting the authors who actually can translate their appearances on TV talk shows into sales of their books. All authors think they can; few are able to do it."

Then I asked one of the key questions, the one dealing with *his* customers and their buying methods.

"The most intelligent buyers of books are the wholesalers, also buyers for retail chains and remainder houses. They all have to operate on a quick cash turnover, and what with low-profit margins, cannot afford too many mistakes.

"Publishing, book wholesaling, and book retailing are not professions as many would have us believe, but they form a complicated, interlocked business that takes its style in part from the commercial theatre and in part from the garment industry. As in the theatre, no one can really predict success; most books fail, but the successes are so huge as to make the gamble a constant lure. The publisher, like his neighbor on Seventh Avenue, stands or falls on his current list, or line; tries to anticipate trends; and copies his competitors who have done so, by riding fashion as long as he can."

(I interjected that certain good publishers can coast on their backlists.)

Said Toby: "A business for gentlemen, a business for aesthetes, a business for scholars? To quote Liza Doolittle, 'Not bloody likely!' "

"Toby," I concluded, "you are a gentleman, a businessman, an aesthete, and a scholar—and no bloody doubt about it!"

Selective Morality, or Old Whores Never Die   A few basic facts for junior editors only:
One must begin with the premise that book publishing is a business.

Back of every business is the profit motive.

Cash flow plus profit make the business world go round.

Regardless of one's passionate zeal for beautiful letters and the dissemination of learning, business principles must prevail. (Obviously, it is recognized that no one takes a job in publishing if one is devoid of some interest in, or love of, books. Some aspect of publishing, one or many of the publishing processes, must interest one.)

Young editors and also so-called mature adults are sometimes unable to make publishing judgments because of certain emotional or mental blocks. The question of values arises. Integrity. Morality. Taste. Aesthetics. Standards. These virtues are sometimes obstacles to an editor's business judgment.

Let me give an example. A "Gothic novel" comes across one's desk. It is a formula piece of fiction, with the usual trappings. The editor is bored with such material, doesn't consider it serious writing. Recalls du Maurier's *Rebecca*, Bronte's *Wuthering Heights,* and sighs. This manuscript on his desk, awaiting his decision, is an offense. He declines it. What he did was turn down a book that probably would have sold at least 7,500 copies and produced a paperback contract of anywhere from $3,500 to $25,000 or more. Because of any one of the editorial reasons cited above, the editor's judgment

was out of order. He failed to recognize the simple business responsibility placed before him. He was bored with, or contemptuous of,
the book, its author, the genre.

Young editors are sometimes inclined to forget the name of the
game. It's easy to sneer at second-class goods. Standards and pride
will often force an editor into an eventual dead end; he will become
one of the nonproductive ones. He will bring in books, books which
he likes but which have no basis for existence in a commercial publishing world. I knew one editor who spent a lifetime losing money
for his publisher employers because of his "standards."

An editor can be an angel soaring in the stratosphere of Literature; he can also be lower than a pimp in hell, a procurer. He can
be a "moral fool"; he can echo Cicero's "O tempora! O mores!" as he
struggles with his conscience in the abattoir of publishing each day,
compromising for the sake of sweet commerce. His dilemma is
that he *must* make decisions that violate his personal, sacred ethos
and his sensibilities.

The editor must cajole, flatter, kiss hands and cheeks, praise extravagantly, even when it hurts. What is sad is that he does all this
while often involved with hacks and *drek* writing. If he's lucky, 5
percent of the books he publishes (and their authors) will give him
pleasure; if he's *very* lucky, 50 percent of the books will make money.
If he's one of the anointed, he will get one of his books on the best-
seller lists once a year. (I know editors who have never had a book
on the best-seller list after more than fifteen years in publishing.)

Does morality enter into all of this? Is there a moral issue, a moral
attitude we must adopt in this profession? When a first-rate author
with a first-rate book comes along, life becomes beautiful; then the
editor contemplates his mirrored visage and his soul with a smile
and equanimity. So we must ask: What manner of man is he?

It's all very simple. An editor must be a realist, must be able to
avoid taking himself seriously, must be able to laugh often. If not,
then alcohol, Seconol, and the other assists become his lifestyle. If
the dual role, the selective morality, becomes an issue, a problem of
functioning or "living with oneself," then one must get out of this
particular arena and look elsewhere for a way of life and a livelihood.

Having made numerous flights abroad, visiting publishers, editors, authors, and agents in quest of manuscripts and co-publishing
deals, I must report that most of the books I've secured and pub-

lished are not, could not, be labelled prime goods. (I'm not apologizing.) And lest I be misunderstood, the same holds true of the books I've signed up on American terrain. A lot of these books could be called anything from wretched to publishable; some are pride-filling books, books I'd want to remember and perhaps fondle in my years of inactivity. I refer to books that could be said to justify my existence by association. But I have no illusions and I'm trying here to differentiate, for the young editor, between commerce and the occasional lucky strike.

Many of the books I've contracted for over the years resulted in handsome profits for my publishers, and a respectable income for myself. I prefer not to mention titles or authors here. I'm not anxious to play a look-how-good-I-am role. I enjoyed my work most of the time, ate in fine restaurants, slept in good beds, had my cake, enjoyed the publishing fellowship in Europe and America. Many of the European publishers and agents were amiable, interesting, fun to be with. A few were bores, sticks. A few others were alcoholics; two notable agents were outrageous liars. Some were merely stupid. Ditto a few American agents.

I bought some books in London that made their authors rich, mainly by virtue of six-figure paperback sales here. In most cases the books were nonsense, fake passementeries, embarrassments. I suppose one will wonder how a devotee of good books and decent writing can play this dual role, how endure working year after year with so much second-class goods. The answer is this: There are not enough good books coming our way. The noble book, that gleaming chimera in every editor's fantasy, is not something one sits around and waits for. It does happen to some editors named Alfred A. Knopf, but not too frequently of late. (*That* golden epoch has ended.)

The toughest part of the editor's job is playing psychiatrist to a third-rate writer: that's "overtime" work. Trying to provide comforting words to an otiose novelist whose latest book has been destroyed by Martin Levin—that's no fun. Taking an ego-tripping author's tantrum (or his agent's) in stride should justify time-and-a-half pay.

I repeat my question: Is morality an issue here? Does the editor, in compromising his values and his self-esteem, do himself injury? Is there scar tissue to show for the violence to one's psyche? I don't think so, not if you laugh enough. When you begin to wonder and brood, then it's time to look at your assets, your bank balance, your lifestyle, your wine cellar, and your working conditions. If you aren't getting your just compensation, then you are a fool. But if you are getting yours, including some of the kudos properly due you, then grin and bear it, and order another very dry martini. (My physician once told me to take a very dry martini and two aspirins for my aching, arthritic shoulder. If that didn't help, he said, take another. "But," added this sage old man, "don't do anything drastic.")

My advice is the same to all editors whose authors and books are giving them a pain in the neck: be sure the martinis are extra dry.

Robert T. Wood, who worked for the CIA for some seventeen years, speaks of the term, "old whore," in referring to a worker in the Central Intelligence Agency. He says "old whore" is a term to describe an officer "so experienced, so devoted to his trade, so loyal to his organization, and so accustomed to following orders that he will accept and do a creditable job on any assignment without regard for moral, ethical, or possibly even legal considerations. Within the Agency it is a high compliment to professionalism."

One final word (and you might stick this up on your wall over your desk): *Publishing Is a Business, for Gosh Sakes!*

The Education of an Editor, Part 3

Becoming a book editor, a publishing executive, or head of a publishing house is a good fate for any man or woman of intelligence and taste. It is fulfilling in the extreme, it provides (forgive the word) status and opportunities for a very interesting life. There are worse fates. But one of the penalties of the good life in books is the necessity of dealing with neurotic and anal-erotic men and women—people with talent but insufferable behavior patterns and hangups. This group, by the way, includes editors and agents as well as writers.

It must also be said for the record that a great many editors are worse than their so-called difficult authors. A problem of vanity and identity crisis. Many of the new breed of editor confuse their role with that of their authors. They often take on the coloration of their famous writers, going so far as to wear the same kind of clothes and to adopt their eating and other habits. The new breed is a boastful peacock, letting the world at large know how he/she single-handedly "saved" a manuscript from disaster by putting some "creative pencil work" into the project. "I spent a month rewriting Joe's book," says the editor, sighing in martyrlike fashion, "but it was worth it. Look at the paperback sale we got." And so on.

The simple truth is this: no matter how skilled an editor may be, he can't write a first-rate book. If he can, he leaves his job and writes. He can't do both. There are, of course, a few exceptions; Costain is one that comes to mind.

But to the young editors who are in the majority, I say: Don't turn into a frustrated writer and start competing with your authors. You can't win. Unless you have unmistakable talents, don't try to write. Edit and enjoy!

Etiquette for publisher   It is essential that an editor and publishing executive remember his *humanness*. Here are some rules of etiquette to enable one to survive and function decently, a few *reminders* relating to values and good business practice:

1. The author and his manuscript are the most important elements in your professional life. Let the author know this. Everything you do, every action you undertake should be with this in mind. Carl Van Doren once said to me when I was getting sticky about some publishing detail, "Everything other than the manuscript is *bubbles on the horse piss.*"

2. Treat the author with every possible courtesy; remember, he's palpitating from blood-drain, from the efforts expended on his book, and needs encouragement and friendship.

3. Answer all authors' letters and calls promptly. Be available.

4. Never keep your author waiting beyond reason for a report on his new manuscript; you are probably the first reader of the work and your response to it is vital.

5. Keep your author informed regularly as to sales and any interesting news, especially good news.

6. Return the original manuscript to the author promptly after publication. It has sentimental and archival value to him, and it is his property. Likewise original art.

7. Most royalty statements are hard to read; help the author out

by clarifying some of its mysteries. It is his "bank statement" and pretty important to him.

8. Be sure the author gets press clippings promptly.

9. Take your author to lunch or dinner at least once a year.

10. Your author must know in his heart that you are always levelling with him. If you don't like something, tell him/her; if you are pleased, speak up. Your author must trust you, and must know when you are bullshitting.

11. Don't promise your author anything you can't deliver.

12. Speak respectfully of your author's agent.

Echelon   The editor-in-chief is "responsible" in most trade houses for the entire list. He not only acquires books and processes them, but he also presides over editorial sessions, confers with editors, reads or examines submissions to various editors. The lists— and the bottom-line results—reflect in a large measure the talents of the editor-in-chief. It is to him the head of the house goes for an overview of the "shape of things to come," including an estimate of the big books' potentials in the market and their subsidiary income. The editor-in-chief keeps in close touch with the sales, promotion, publicity, and rights departments.

If an editor-in-chief vetoes the wrong books enough times, his head rolls. If he allows too many marginal books to appear on his lists, eyebrows will be raised. If he permits unjustified extravagant advances to be paid too often, he will put his company and himself in jeopardy. The editor-in-chief must develop the best possible public relations; agents and authors must respect him, trust his judgment. He should represent the house everywhere in the world of books and should be visible at all important literary functions. A once-a-year trip to Europe is mandatory for the maintenance of contacts. He must be a reader, a bookman in every sense. His judgment should be reflected in the jackets and physical books, and in the company's advertising.

Next to the head of the house, the editor-in-chief ranks highest insofar as the outside world is concerned.

The senior editor is primarily concerned with his own books and authors, his personal stable. He is available for consultation with editors and should appear at all editorial meetings. A senior editor is a responsible executive who, through years of experience and maturity, is useful as a sounding board to the staff. But he must first and foremost pull his own weight by bringing good and profitable books to his house.

The above two editorial executives, plus a staff of alert and informed editors, make up the editorial department. The copy editing department is an adjunct, and makes no editorial acquisition determination.

Bringing home the bacon   The game is *acquisition.*

Acquiring a publishable, salable manuscript is what publishing is all about.

Cocktail parties, literary luncheons, junkets, film screenings, socializing on behalf of your company—a lot of it can be fun. But unless a contract for a book results, it is a sleeveless errand you are on, and the name of your game is *kinderspiel.*

Acquisition of a manuscript is the first order of business. Nothing else deserves priority. Turning a manuscript into a publishable book is the next step. What follows is publicity, sales, and getting the author to produce another book. (Keep him occupied with the *next* book and he'll understand why he should "leave the driving to us.") A lot of executives in publishing houses (and especially in the offices of owner-conglomerates) often forget that the author sweating out a manuscript in the loneliness of his home or office or penthouse is the heart of the matter. The book is all, the whole game. In the beginning was the manuscript . . . Try not to forget it.

An acquisition editor is at least as valuable as a home-run hitter on a baseball team. If his percentage of home runs is decent, then he is a major factor in the welfare of the company. He should be spared the stresses and tensions of corporate problems; he should not be checked out and scrutinized in matters of hours spent in the office, on his expense reports, or on his numerical contribution to the manuscript stockpile.

The pretentious, "literary" editor who talks unrealistically about "better books" should be forced to prove his worth in dollars and cents. I don't hold with the principle of auditing an editor; his efforts, if meaningful, are evident to all. But the blowhard who scorns the commercial book and makes light of the popular best seller must be put into focus. Editors with taste and high standards should be supported and encouraged, obviously; otherwise the publisher's lists would be embarrassing, and get damned little respect in the book trade. Booksellers must take a publisher seriously, and if one issues only shoddy goods, he will waste away. Possibly go broke.

In short, the acquisition editor who takes his job seriously should go after both the big popular book as well as the book of quality. He should seek out fresh talent, first novelists, poets who show genuine talent. And authors who sell! So, bringing in the bacon means publishing money books *and* books of distinction. The good acquisition editor will try to avoid the stereotype book; the tired, overfamiliar theme; the marginal book that is at once publishable but unsalable. Originality often pays off. Admittedly, luck is a factor in bringing in the successes. Luck, interestingly, follows the avid and eager worker.

How to Get a Book   Being seen in the Italian Pavilion or the Four Seasons, the Algonquin, 21, or Lutèce will not, *per se*, bring you manuscripts. How, then, does one get a manuscript?

Keep a file or card index of book ideas. When talking to agents, find out which of their authors are looking for assignments. Matching a good idea with the right author is a reasonably safe procedure. My colleagues and I have processed dozens of good, salable books by studying the works of authors who could be approached with the "irresistible book idea." One example that comes to mind is the biography of Al Capone, which I had for years believed worth nailing down. One day I was told by the William Morris Agency that John Kobler, a veteran *Saturday Evening Post* and *New Yorker* writer, and author of several books, was eager for a book assignment. I discovered through scanning a few dozen of his articles that true crime interested him. I proposed a definitive life of Capone. Kobler accepted the proposal with high enthusiasm and produced a first-class book. The book was on the *TBR* Best Seller List for a number of weeks. It was also a best seller in France and in Germany.

Another case history: In the spring of 1956 I approached Marchette Chute to ask if she'd write a book in which the plays of Shakespeare would be retold for today's readers. I had read her books on Chaucer, Ben Jonson, and Shakespeare and had responded to her scholarship, style, and feeling for the Elizabethan world.

Serendipity helped. I had met Miss Chute by accident at a P.E.N. dinner; luck got me seated next to her and I fell in love with her instantly. The opportunist-editor within me also responded, and editorial brain cells began to click. The next morning I phoned her, reminded her that we had met the night before, and said I had an inspired book idea for her.

"I never accept book assignments," she replied.

Silence. Then I asked if she'd care to hear what my proposal was, anyway. She consented to listen. When I finished there was a pause. Then she said that I did indeed have an interesting idea, but that she would have to think about it and discuss it with her mother and sister, and her publisher, Elliott Macrae, of Dutton.

The next morning she called to say she would take on the job. She agreed that Charles Lamb's *Tales from Shakespeare* was a bit creaky for the readers of our time. I know that Macrae hated me ever after for having presented a book idea to his star author.

The point of this story is, by "exposing myself" to a P.E.N. dinner, and acting on a social encounter, I secured a book that is now a minor modern classic. It has sold well over 100,000 copies in its trade edition, many more in the Book-of-the-Month Club edition, and countless thousands in the NAL paperback edition. It is also published elsewhere in the world.

There are many good, professional writers who are "between books," and looking for projects. Seek them out, but first do a bit of "creative" homework.

Public exposure is essential for an editor. Parties may bore or tire you, but inevitably you will meet someone who will lead you to a manuscript or to an author. The more time you spend among people, the better your chances.

Read the newspapers and magazines; watch TV and listen to radio. When you encounter an interesting personality or a story that might be built up and shaped into a book, pursue it. Keep alert, on top of public events. The book *Alive* is an example of follow-through by an editor. Waiting for a good manuscript to fall off a tree is not the way to acquisition. Acquisition is the heart of publishing life, and all it takes is energy and imagination.

Book Ideas: Creativity-Can-Be-Fun Kit Let's begin by admitting a fact: there are no *new* book ideas. Taking the name of Creativity in vain is sacrilegious. But there's always room for a *good* new book on a basic subject.

Actually the key word should not be "basic" but "better." The new one should supplant the previous work on the same subject and have a real justification for existence. In my opinion, a new book on a familiar subject that doesn't add anything to the category, or to the enhancement of human knowledge, is a *glut-book*—a who-needs-it-book.

The object is to find the *right* author for the *particular* book idea. There are writers who can write good books on given subjects, but you've got to be sure they understand the specifications of the job. Each book must have a fresh slant, an honest-to-God purpose.

I'm thinking here of several book ideas that call for good writers who are expert in the areas indicated and who are also able to write in a certain vein, *sans pedantry*, for the broadest audience or for the audience for whom the subject is important.

For example, consider VIOLENCE and CRIME: these are common-enough subjects, and there are thousands of books on the general theme. But why can't a book be written in Basic English, dealing with the subject of capital punishment in the light of what is happening in the world today?

I happen to believe in the death penalty for first-degree murderers, kidnappers, and hijackers of planes. Capital punishment has not, it is true, been a crime deterrent; but there is nevertheless a price to be paid for taking a life or taking possession of another human being against his will.

A book should also be written outlining the kind of punishment *we should* hand out to criminals, punishment other than putting men and women into cells like cattle. Why cannot we establish farms or desert camps, where they can *work* and perhaps become rehabilitated? We must punish the criminal, the antisocial person, who is guilty of premeditated acts of violence. But we need not treat criminals as a subspecies: there are really no morphological differences between the criminal and the noncriminal. But crimes must be punished; they must be noted, recorded.

RAPE: Special courts should be established for rapists, ensuring privacy to the victims who are obliged to appear and testify. Too many rape victims fail to report assaults out of fear or shame. The big American cities are today overrun with rapists. They should be tracked down and punished with minimal delay. A book dealing with rape and the law, in simple but tough terms, by an outstanding *legal humanist* would have a purpose and a market. Why is it not written? It is a subject for a genuine writer, a John Hersey. A good book on the subject, by Carol Horos, does exist, but I think there's room for a more stern, practical, legalistic, and militant work. Rape in America is reaching an epidemic dimension; not enough people are talking about it, doing something about it.

DRUGS: A book dealing with the pushing and dissemination of narcotics, that is, illegal peddling of cocaine and heroin, is needed— also written in Basic English. It should call for the establishment of special drug courts and new laws for handling drug criminals, with utmost speed. The subject should be dealt with by an authority who can write simple declarative sentences, by someone who is respected by officialdom as well as the public. Why don't United States senators, presidents, write such books?

MUGGERS, STICKUP MEN: These vile creatures should be given punishment on a rapid-fire basis, with minimal courtroom delay. There should be mugger courts to process the growing number of these lawless and desperate men. A book is long overdue on this international problem.

ARMS: I'd like to see laws passed allowing men and women of proven civic responsibility to carry arms. Women in particular should be allowed to defend themselves with pocket weapons— side arms, if you will. Brass knuckles and stilettos should be available to all citizens. If the criminal has easy access to knives and guns, why not the rest of us? There is a war going on in our cities, and one army—the victimized army—is without arms. A small how-to book on the subject would be welcome. And a few new laws.

The editor's duty is to get intelligent writers who are prepared to drop literary and pedantic pretense and get the essential ideas across so that laws and action can be implemented. Too much legalese drowns meaning and good intentions.

Turning from the criminal world, we might look at another subject—THE AUTOMOBILE AND AIRPLANE: Let's have a good, simple book showing the world how evil the gas-consuming engine is, how we are destroying our health and resources through immoral use of nature's gift, oil. Why cannot the world go on a real oil-austerity program? Let's cut down on our use of oil by, say, 75 percent. Let's walk, hike, bicycle—go back to using a horse and buggy! Let's fly less, drive less, pollute the air less. Tell the people the truth about oil and the need for universal conservation. A low-fuel diet is the program we should be on now. But nobody is listening; we'll run out of oil in a few hundred years anyway, they say. Perhaps a small, clear, truth-telling book will help do the job that needs to be done. Let's have an end to the excess of words and get the message across in crisp, to-the-point language. A book of sixty-four pages should do it easily.

Another subject: COPYRIGHT. This subject is of interest to millions, since so many men and women are now writing, composing, painting pictures, making sculpture and graphics. Why can't we have a simple copyright law that makes sense for all and is easy to comprehend?

I once told my old friend, the late Jacob Blanck, a bibliographer, that I could draft a copyright bill that would fill not more than one 8½ by 11-inch sheet of paper. He challenged me to do it, but I let the opportunity pass. But here is the deal: in a 24-page booklet, in Basic English, one could write a new copyright law covering every possible base.

How would it go? Well, why not simply say: let's give fifty years' maximum protection, covering reproduction and performance rights, to all literary, artistic, musical, dramatic, and graphics works throughout the world, with all rights to be reserved exclusively by the creator-author and heirs, and permission to make use of such material to be secured from the copyright owner in writing under certain financial considerations. No mechanical copying permitted (now hear this, Xerox); no cassette, television, or anthology use; no motion picture or dramatic performance without approval and payment to the copyright holder, his representative, or heirs. After fifty years, the property goes into public domain. All countries possible should be signatories to this proposed new bill.

Let's not entrust the writing of this bill to lawyers; instead, give it to a good high school English teacher to draft. It will work.

One final subject for the editor: a small book, a sane, well-reasoned case *for* legalized prostitution, state-supervised, with its taxes and revenues turned over to VD research or, perhaps, the cultivation of good English among politicians.

Happy Hunches   The acquiring editor must be as nimble-footed as a gazelle. As I've already said, he must be the ubiquitous traveller, attending parties, meetings, public-affairs sessions, symposia, and the like. He must be available and approachable. He must be a well-mannered eager beaver, and he must never show impatience.

While I abhor cocktail parties, I've attended many over the

years. One meets new people, promising writers and established ones who are sometimes ready to make a change (author-publisher disaffection does occur).

A typical case: At a small house party my host asked if I would like to meet "that woman over there." She has a son, I was told, who is completing a novel, "a first novel that just may be something for your firm."

I met the woman; I found her charming and cultivated. She said her son, just returned from Spain, had completed the draft of a novel and would I care to look at it. I promptly invited submission.

The next morning our receptionist called to say I had a visitor; it was the party-lady's son. I spent an hour with him, discussing Spain, writing, publishing. I promised to read his book at once. I took it home that evening, read it until about three that morning. When I got to the office I phoned him to come in to see me.

"I read your book," I said, "and I like it very much. It needs some work, as you yourself volunteered. But we'll publish it." I then outlined the terms of a contract.

"Is that a firm offer?" he asked and I assured him it was. (At World Publishing Company I had total autonomy in such matters.) He accepted and returned to Spain.

Two months later, after many exchanges of editorial letters, the book was ready for publication. It was entitled *A Place Without Twilight*. The author: Peter S. Feibleman. It was very well received. As of this writing, in 1975, it still seems to me his best book. (Today, as John Updike has intimated, more and more authors do their best work early in their careers.) I published two other Feibleman books, and rendered him some favors beyond the call of duty, as do so many editors. But when I left World to go with Putnam's, he was the only author who wouldn't follow me. He said he did not like some of the authors on Putnam's list, and did not want to appear among them. Obviously, there were other reasons which he wouldn't express.

I've never forgiven him this display of no-loyalty. He may have had some very personal reasons, but they hardly matter. I learned something about the author-editor relationship from this; happily, he proved to be the only exception. Feibleman went to Atheneum with his next book, but I note that he has now moved on to another publisher with his upcoming book.

Getting back to the main theme—be gregarious and be available to potential new writers. But don't expect lifelong devotion from young novelists. Consider the relationship as one might a marriage —and then think of the divorce rate.

There are too many examples of serendipity in publishing to make a case for the importance of being available.

Small risks are worth considering, and if one encounters a fine book of poems or essays by an unknown, it is not a bad thing to gamble on occasion. Although the chances are slim, a great literary career is sometimes preceded by a modest book of poems.

One of the most valuable "properties" acquired by E. P. Dutton is the work of A. A. Milne, a perennial gold mine. The *Winnie-the-Pooh* books have brought millions of dollars to that firm. It all began many years ago, when John Macrae, head of Dutton's, was in London and happened on a modest book of essays by an unknown writer. The book was entitled *If I May*, and it appealed to Macrae, who had a soft spot in his heart for essays. He imported a few hundred copies in sheets. In due course, along came the author's next work, *When We Were Very Young*, and later, *Now We Are Six*, and others. I know of few publishers today who will take on a book of essays by an unknown writer in the hope of striking it rich some day. I doubt that Macrae had any great expectations; he simply *liked* the essays and wanted to publish the book, modestly, in America.

Ironically, it doesn't always work out that way. Harper's published John Updike's first book, a volume of poetry called *The Carpentered Hen*. But when he wrote his first novel, it went to Knopf. I haven't inquired as to the whys and wherefores, but my sense of fairness tells me that any publisher of a writer's first book of poetry is entitled to that writer's first novel. Possibly Harper's declined it?

Monkey Business   One day, while reading about the Yerkes Primate Center of Emory University in Atlanta, I learned that they had the largest collections of apes, chimps, gorillas, and monkeys in the world. I telephoned the director, Dr. Geoffrey H. Bourne, and asked if he'd like to write a book on his Primate Center to let the world know what goes on there. It turned out that he had written numerous books, but none for the general reader.

"But," said Dr. Bourne, "I'll not sign a contract with anyone unless he comes down here and spends a day with me, seeing for himself what I am going to write about. No one can imagine what this place is like unless he visits us."

I agreed to fly down the next day. The Center, surrounded by beautiful, landscaped grounds, was most appealing, and Dr. Bourne and his wife and staff were cordial in the extreme.

When I left Atlanta, I swore I would never again look at a primate closeup. While the Yerkes Primate Center is a model of modernity and cleanliness, and is equipped with every conceivable mechanical and electronic device for testing purposes, and so forth, I could not shake the eyeball-to-eyeball experience for weeks. Staring into the privacy of the chimps' and gorillas' lives, watching them undergoing tests, seeing them in captivity (though comfortably so), pained me. Of course these animals were well fed, well housed, cared for in every way. But it was all too much for me. And when I got back home, I could hardly wait to unclothe myself and get into a steaming shower—with lots of cologne at hand.

Two fine books resulted from the trip, and a third one (on gorillas) is in progress. I'm glad I went to Atlanta, and it has been a pleasure working with Dr. Bourne. But as an editor, from now on, all contact will be at a distance, lovable as some of those chimps are. I'm just plain delicate.

Special Dividends   One of the special bonuses in this editing profession is the unexpected chance to work with an author one has admired over the years. Writers often change publishers for one reason or another (money, paranoia, insufficient promotion and advertising, menopause, and so on), and when a major writer switches allegiance, it's a happy day for the lucky editor who inherits him.

I'm not referring to authors secured by direct solicitation; no self-respecting editor will make a direct overture to any author who is presumably happy and established with a publisher. Editors know directly or instinctively when an author is unhappy and ready to make a change. The word gets around or the author himself speaks up.

I've had a number of such experiences—lucky breaks, I call them. Among them is John Collier. (I've referred to him earlier.) I had read his early novels, *Full Circle, Defy the Foul Fiend,* and *His Monkey Wife,* and most of his short stories that appeared in *The New Yorker* and elsewhere (see *The John Collier Reader,* Knopf, 1972). Collier is one of the masters of the macabre and magical in fiction, and he writes solely for our enjoyment. Anthony Burgess says it well: "He [Collier] makes literature out of the intrusion of fantasy, or quiet horror, into a real world closely observed. . . ."

Like Saki, Collier is for exotic appetites, for the devotee of Charles Addams, for those with a passion for fiends and angels interacting in our midst. Collier is also a master screenplay writer; notable among his scripts is *The African Queen.*

One day in the spring of 1974 an unproduced screenplay of Collier's, *Finding Ernie,* was brought to my attention by Shirley Collier, his ex-wife. It was a good play. Unlike some editors, I don't approach screenplays with a jaundiced eye. I've found that some can transform into novels successfully. (One of my hunches that paid off handsomely was in urging Herman Raucher to novelize [a word I dislike] his screenplay, *Summer of '42.*) I felt that Collier's script would, with certain rearrangements and additions, make for a viable novel. I wrote him and told him so. We signed a contract for the novel (through his agent, Harold Matson, who is part angel and part fiend).

Other experiences: In 1937, while still in Chicago, I first read Lin Yutang's *The Importance of Living* and was enchanted by it. Here was *my* cultivated man who espoused my "philosophy" and articulated it in a civilized and winning manner. I found an instant affinity here, for I recall his saying that he despised claims to objectivity in philosophy and that "the point of view is the thing." I read the book twice, talked about it everywhere, and sold countless copies in my bookshop. I wrote Dr. Lin a gushing fan letter but never mailed it. Many years later we met in New York. I was with World, and he had just left John Day, his publisher. To this day I don't know why he and Richard Walsh of John Day parted company; if he told me, I have forgotten. After a good meeting with him we proceeded to publish his novels and essays.

Interestingly, Lin Yutang wrote his books first in Chinese, then translated them into English himself. The English texts required some close editing, but nothing of consequence. Where he was weak in syntax he more than made up in charm and a natural style. We published seven or eight books together, both at World and later at Putnam's, where he followed me. Finally, I was rewarded with a dedication—the ultimate compliment an author can pay to an editor. It was in the book *The Pleasures of a Noncomformist,* published by World in 1962. The title derives, of course, from Emerson, whom we both admired: "Whoso would be a man must be a nonconformist. . . . Nothing is at last sacred but the integrity of your own mind." The book is a delight and I'm proud to have been involved in its publication.

One of the fringe benefits of my relationship with Lin Yutang was a monthly luncheon, always Chinese gourmet-style, in one of his favorite restaurants. It was great fun watching and listening to him ordering in Chinese, often scolding the waiter in advance to make sure his wishes would be carried out to the last detail. Lin was a chain smoker and ate very little. He would order elaborately, then pick at the food and sit back, awaiting the next dish. A big event was an invitation for dinner at his home, where his lovely wife and daughters would cook and serve extraordinary meals that were often far beyond my plebeian taste, visually and otherwise.

Moral Courage Required   Madeleine B. Stern, bibliophile and scholar, brings our attention to a book on phrenology (!) published in 1874, *What to Do, and Why,* by Nelson Sizer, from which we offer you an excerpt—a bit of philosophy and also some guidance for editors:

> An editor should also have courage—no position needs greater; having a selfish world to deal with, he should be willing to utter the truth when justice demands that an unpleasant truth be spoken, and then to back it up. *A want of courage in an editor is as bad as a lack of courage in a soldier* [italics mine]; for while cowardice or treason in a soldier may cause the loss of a battle, a lack of courage or conscience in an editor may poison the public morals, and, perhaps, contribute to the loss of a battle as well. . . . We would not give him excessive Benevolence and Ideality; while lack of Combativeness, Firmness, and Self-Esteem renders the editor pusillanimous, and leads him to soften the truth until its very back-bone is withdrawn; but there is such a thing as manly courage, unyielding determination, serene dignity, and unflinching justice, combined with kindness, affection, and proper consideration for the rights, prejudices, and even the ignorance of others.

Phrenologist Sizer's observations and values seem to hold up after a hundred years, but who's listening!

Faux Pas   I was pursuing a chimera: the love letters of a famous author, Thomas Wolfe, to his mistress, a woman famous in her own right, Aline Bernstein. After months of phoning and writing her, she finally granted me an audience. I met her in her Central Park West home and had a warm reception, with an elegant tea served me. She was now a grandmother, wearing a hearing aid. Plump and delightful. (Not the "mistress type.") As we talked, I spoke of the dream book I was hoping she'd make possible.

She smiled as I spoke, and then suddenly the phone rang. It was on the coffee table before us, so I rose and walked away discreetly so as to avoid eavesdropping. Standing before a wall of books, I noted that two or three shelves contained nothing but the works of Henry James.

When her phone conversation ended I returned to the sofa where she awaited me. I remarked that I was surprised at the large number of James' books she had and asked if James was one of her addictions. She admitted that she loved Henry James, that her family and friends always gave her Henry James' books as gifts. Then she turned to me and asked which of James' novels I liked.

Without pausing to think I blurted out, *The Aspern Papers.*

She smiled. I left shortly afterward.

I did not get to publish the book I was after, of course. The love letters from Wolfe to his mistress were given to Yale, I believe, to be held privately until a certain fixed time. My pursuit of these letters came to naught. But on my way home I suddenly knew why she smiled when I said *The Aspern Papers* was my favorite James story.

End of story; end of pursuit.

━━━━━━━━━━

Take thy beak from out my heart, and take thy form from off my door!   Quoth the Raven, "Nevermore."

—E. A. POE

The Meanest Author in the World   There have been several difficult authors in my life; one of them could have easily doubled for the Marquis de Sade. But the meanest of all was the late Oscar Levant.

Levant was brilliant, witty, vitriolic, and a splendid musician. He was a fast man with the one-line gag. But he was not lovable. While editing his last two books, *Memoirs of an Amnesiac* and *The Importance of Being Oscar,* I endured mental cruelty and obscene vituperation beyond belief. His language in private reminded me of what Groucho Marx once said of Fanny Brice: "Her language was that of Pier Six." I suppose some of his friends will think me ill-mannered, unkind, or perhaps an oaf, for speaking thus of the dead. But I suspect Oscar would not have hesitated in doing so were our positions reversed. I can't care less. I think there are occasions when it is salutary to speak candidly of the dead.

While working with Levant on his manuscripts he was literally on my back all the way. I received countless calls at home; he would awaken me at all hours of the night. Phone calls at my office came with a deadly regularity, and in all cases the calls were complaining and demanding, ranging from the unreasonable to petulant to insulting. When I phoned Levant to report some good news, such as a large paperback sale, he responded with, "There's something mighty fishy about that deal." When I wired him to tell him of a fine serial sale, he replied by telegram: "I'll have my lawyers look into your shabby machinations." He once called me at three in the morning to give me a humorous anecdote for last-minute inclusion in the *page proofs* of his book. I failed to break up with laughter at his story on the phone; later, he was reported to have told friends in Hollywood that his editor had no sense of humor.

When I refused to allow certain outrageous, obscene, and libelous anecdotes to appear in either of his books (he accused a famous playwright of being coprophagous and also cannibalistic), he threatened me with the law, accused me of being in league with the enemy and hell-bent to destroy Levant.

On the day of my marriage, during the afternoon celebration at home, the phone rang. It was Oscar. He opened with a torrent of sulphurous abuse. I interrupted to say, "Excuse me, Oscar, I have guests. I got married an hour ago and we are having a reception." There was a slight pause and then he said, "Congratulations. As I was saying . . ."

I hung up on him.

No editor should be obliged to endure an author as profane, abusive, and intrusive as Levant. Why did I get into it in the first place? Out of a sense of loyalty to my firm and my job; it called for hanging onto an author who was profitable. When I signed Levant up a second time, Walter Minton said I was assuredly a masochist.

I had been a fan of Levant's during the years when he reigned as the supreme quiz kid and court jester on the radio program called "Information, Please." I had heard him in concert, and I had most of his Gershwin recordings. Also, I had read with much pleasure his first book, *A Smattering of Ignorance*. All of this added up to a great interest in the man and his future work. I approached him and he "succumbed." I thought it would be great fun working with this unique man; there was no question about his gifts, and I do happen to enjoy men with the "gift" of acid humor. Levant was the devil's own. Perhaps I should have realized very early that his neuroses, his vicious libelling of friends, his addiction to pills, his need to beat up on everyone around him, would be too much for me to endure. I suppose I was too stubborn to give up once I had begun the job.

Finally, having had as much as I could take, I said to him, following an especially gruelling telephonic session, "I'm hanging up on you, Oscar, and I don't ever want to talk to you again—ever! I'll work on your book but only through June [his wife]." A minute later he phoned back and said to my wife, who picked up the phone: "Why is Bill angry with me? Doesn't he know I'm an incurable paranoid?"

Oscar's wife June was as likable as Oscar was not.

Another mean author comes to mind, a classic example of the totally self-consumed and selfish writer. He is a famous writer, prolific, rich. He would be the model actor for a plantation slave owner in an antebellum film.

At any rate, he was in a writing-and-selling slump one summer and invited Roslyn and me to visit him. He was depressed and worried. He hadn't sold a story in many months and simply could not work up the energy to write a book. Did I have any ideas?

I dreamed up a project for him and proposed certain terms that might be feasible if the book worked out right. Finally, with much maneuvering and difficult footwork, I got him a *large, six-figure cash advance* for a novel, a novel of which not a word was yet written.

The manuscript was eventually delivered and I read it with sick dismay. It was a disaster and totally unlike anything he had ever written. I prepared a brief of particulars and begged him to make certain revisions and additions. I emphasized the fact that the book needed a great deal of work, that in its present form it would be a disservice to him to publish it. I pointed out that it would not only *not sell* but that the reviewers would *clobber* it. I begged him as a friend, as a well-wisher, as a professional editor, to consider my critical suggestions. He replied: "I'm not going to make any changes for you or anyone. No one is going to tell me how to write a novel at this stage in my life."

I replied that a few of my colleagues had read the manuscript and agreed completely with me. I added that I was literally losing sleep over this whole problem, and as a rule, I was a sound sleeper. I had committed my firm to a huge sum of money and I was terribly worried.

His reply—which I will never forget—was: "I'm not making any changes in the book, and as for your losing sleep, too bad; I'm sitting pretty."

By which he meant he had an iron-clad contract, not dependent on the manuscript-acceptance clause which we usually require. My mistake, of course, was in assuming that his track record would assure me of a satisfactory performance in this instance.

The book failed on every front: no sales to speak of, few reviews and all exceedingly bad. *The New York Times* made mincemeat of the book and his reputation. Financially, he was "sitting pretty."

There is a moral in the foregoing true case histories for young editors: Set up ground rules carefully before stepping into difficult situations; protect yourself. There are, or should be, Marquess of Queensbury rules to cover both situations described. No editor should be obliged to take abuse from a writer or to be "had" as I was in the second instance.

My publisher, Raymond Hagel, and Mario Puzo—both of whom read the foregoing, in manuscript—urged me to reveal the author's name. I've decided to withhold it. He and his family and a few others will know to whom I'm referring, and for the present, that takes care of my needs. It isn't fear of legal action. It's really between the two of us, I guess.

And then, I once had lunch with Jed Harris . . .

Alacrity   Every literary agent respects, and shows partiality toward, the editor who turns in an early decision on a manuscript.

Get a reputation for alacrity. Don't keep an author waiting. If a delay is unavoidable, send in an interim report or indicate in some manner that you are not simply *sitting* on the manuscript.

Good manners require promptness. I know some agents who

have blackballed, and properly, certain editors because they were notorious for sitting on manuscripts for three, four, or more months, and for being inaccessible. A reputable agent is entitled to prompt attention. And an editor must never forget where his bread and butter (or cake) comes from.

There are many editors who have almost no stock in trade, and without alacrity they are damned close to bankruptcy as acquisition editors.

Some books come to an editor through recommendation from other "satisfied customers." Just recently (in February 1975) Irwin R. Blacker, an old friend of mine and the author of several novels, including a 14-karat classic of the Southwest, *Taos,* which I published at World in the mid-fifties, phoned from Hollywood to recommend a writer and manuscript to me. The agent, Timothy Seldes, sent it over—some 725 pages—and I read it in two nights. Entitled *Audrey Rose,* it is a novel in which the central characters are two little girls. The theme: reincarnation. The author is Frank De Felitta who wrote one earlier novel, *Oktoberfest,* and a number of award-winning television plays. I think the time involved, from Blacker's phone call to me and the execution of the contract, was less than ten days. *Alacrity.*

Of course the book hooked me at once, and a long telephonic conference with the author (who lives in California) resolved the minor editorial matters.

The Pay-Off   Many editors must wait until they get to heaven for their reward. Some never get there! As I've already pointed out, most employees of publishing houses are underpaid, certainly underpaid by living-wage standards and by special qualifications, such as education and creative potential.

The turnover rate among editors is scandalous, and the reason is apparent: not enough pay. Editors with decent credentials can be easily wooed and won by competing firms which offer more money.

Publishers should take a hard look at reality, which includes the cost of training a new employee, getting him settled into his job and becoming a meshing member of the organization. At least three months is the minimum for orientation. Publishers should offer a bonus incentive to every contributing and creative employee —that is, a percentage of the profits on books acquired. A best seller should certainly provide a payoff for the procuring editor. Any employee who shows loyalty, diligence in his work, and a lively intelligence that results in moneymaking books or books of distinction, deserves careful money consideration.

So, publishers: if an editor is a credit to your firm, pay off! Cherish your worthy employees in a tangible, palpable way by surprising them occasionally with unrequested increments.

There are always a few goldbricking editors who earn more than they are worth, riders of coat-tails who sweet-talk their way through their jobs; phony intellectuals with a certain cultivated style who deceive their bosses—for a while. In the end, of course, their lack of real production (*production* is the operative word) catches up with them.

In a publishing house a woman can do anything a man can do— even selling on the road. To suggest that a woman be given equal pay is not enough. Discrimination because of sex is immoral, unethical, and possibly a misdemeanor.

Publishing heads: If you get the urge to sell your company to a conglomerate or some other organization, take care of the loyal employees who helped build your business. Don't let them drift for themselves. Consider the possibility of selling the business to *them*, first. Publishing houses are simple entries on the balance sheets of conglomerates. The employee's name is less than a cipher. Take note!

They Want to Be Alone   One or two successes often can transform an editor from an eager and avid pursuer to a character who "wants to be alone."

From a private study, I've learned of more than a dozen top editors who won't take phone calls or manuscript submissions seriously except from a few very select agents and friends. "The arrogant ones," we might term them. I know heads of houses who answer their own telephones; but not many top editors can be reached even through secretaries and assistants.

The legitimate business of the editor involves communication, and while the telephone is often a menace and a burden, it is the instrument by which a vast amount of our business is done. (I must confess that I have a Pavlovian reaction—negative, that is—to answering the phone at home. Nevertheless, I take calls and return calls quickly.)

The First Novel   All editors want to discover a Thomas Wolfe. Some publishers encourage their editors to publish first novels.

Editors seek out the first novels with the seductiveness of Don Juans; the pleasure of discovery is one of the obvious reasons. I've always been a sucker for a first novel, although I must admit that very few of those I've taken on—very few—have made any profit for us, and only a handful of the writers have gone on to writing careers. There are countless first novelists who never turned in a second work; most are not hardy; they dry up and blow away.

First novels are challenges to the sales and publicity departments. How do you get the TV and press to arouse themselves over first novels, novels that have excellence but are not sensational? The editor beats his small drum, bores his friends, begs for advertising money, clutches lapels of famous writers, pleads for advance comments. He scrutinizes each bit of publicity in the hope that a fire will ignite. Meanwhile, the new author is on the verge of hysteria or suicide. Of course the editor and his publisher shoulder the blame when failure is the end result. Often, if the first book fails, a first novelist will turn to another publisher with his second one. (First-novel paranoia: we're out to destroy the new writer; we hate first novelists, etc.)

When a first novel hits the jackpot—clubs, big paperback sales, and the best-seller lists—then life can be beautiful. It can also be a time of trial for the publisher because other publishers begin to seek out and woo the lucky newcomer.

Without a true zeal for first novels, American fiction can't thrive. It's the obligation of every publisher to issue as many publishable first novels as he can. In the end, the payoff will come in one way or another.

Shifting Taste   Market (or audience) changes occur so rapidly that it's not always easy to keep up with the shifts. For example, Western fiction, long a standard category for trade publishers, declined in popularity, with the exceptions of works from a few of the big names. But I expect to see a turnaround in this situation and I can easily foresee a big market for Westerns in the near future. The

Westerns will be more permissive, and cowboys will be kissing not only horses, but women (and other cowboys) with greater frequency. I predict the emergence of superstar newcomers to the genre, new Zane Greys and Max Brands.

Heightened sophistication can't rule out even the old-time romance fiction, and I can well imagine the return of Harold Bell Wright and Jeffrey Farnol and Gene Stratton Porter and Booth Tarkington—and Jack London, who is long overdue for a comeback.

The publication of *Lolita, Candy, Fanny Hill,* and Henry Miller's *Tropics* helped to break the censor's barrier. But now that freedom of language is ours, there are many who want surcease from red meat. Stand by for new Ethel M. Dells and Faith Baldwins, and religious fiction of the Lloyd Douglas school. Science-fiction will also gain a huge increase in public interest and some major new writers should emerge in this area of writing in the next decade.

But Is It Art?   Photographs, like diagrams and other illustrative aids, are important in many kinds of books. But beware of the book dependent entirely on pictures. In any twelve months I'll have examined and declined about a dozen photographic book projects: collections of photos dealing with such subjects as horses, dogs, sports, babies, ships, automobiles, jazz, billboards, "the American scene," slums, and nude men and women.

Attractive and intelligent men and women come in with portfolios. They are photographers and want to be "authors"; that is, they want to see their photos reproduced in book form. The quality of the photos run from good to excellent, but none of it adds up to an affirmative publishing decision.

Over the years I've watched the proliferation of pictorial books and witnessed the industry-wide development of pictorial "treatments" of biographical, scenic, social, and historical subjects. Actually, this is not a new trend. Big illustrated parlor-gift albums were popular a century ago; they were the forerunners of our coffee-table books. Christmas gift books, profusely illustrated and gussied up with gold embossing and gilt edges, were a holiday commodity, like neckties. Publishers would assemble collections of engravings, then send them to authors (usually famous names) for captions or running commentary; it was easy money for the authors. Some of these books were sold by mail order, some by subscription. There was a lot of loot in this enterprise for everyone. There still is, but the percentage of successes by title has been substantially reduced because there is a superabundance of such books, more than the market can absorb. The excess lies also in the amount of subject-duplication. Name a famous historical event or biographical figure and I'll show you several books on the subject. The upcoming Bicentennial will probably result in a few thousand extra candidates for the remainder counters, in a plethoric situation that could bankrupt many small publishers foolhardy enough to get into that swim.

I've been involved with some of these books; but as an editor I dislike the category intensely. The books are okay for the magazine addicts and for children. Many of them are pure kitsch; ersatz. My dislike is personal and, I believe, stems in part from my resistance to the scissors-and-paste kind of book and also to the notion, promulgated by photographers, that photography is an "art form." My attitude has lost me a few friends, but I still maintain that while photography is a craft calling for skill, a selective eye, sensitivity, and professionalism, art has nothing to do with it. It's machinery and hardware put to work, with the aid of chemicals.

Anyone handling a camera, still or motion picture, considers himself an artist today. Film directors are also artists. I've discovered recently that there is an aggregation of Polaroid photographers that considers itself in the "artist" category. There must be fifty million "artists" in America operating cameras, and there are hundreds of thousands making home movies and porno films and amateur films and videotapes. Each proclaims his product a work of art, an art form; each is an artist. Then there are the millions of Japanese and German tourists with cameras . . .

The Marboro bookstores, where millions of remainders are sold each year, specialize in pictorial books, coffee-table books, books with photographs and illustrations in which the text is secondary. They are sold at discounts of 50 percent or more. It is hard to explain to photographers that, while the pictures they make are attractive, they are not necessarily book material; that photo books are very expensive to produce today and that the market—at the high publication prices—is limited. There are great exceptions, of course. I'm referring here to the majority of such books that sell off about 30 percent in the normal market and 70 percent to bargain-book clubs and to Marboro. A lot of these are nonbooks, hardbound magazines at best, suitable for an hour's browsing or for dentists' and psychiatrists' reception rooms.

With costs about 25 percent higher than they were two years ago, these books are, financially, both a nuisance and a hazard. The temptation to publish them is great, because very often they are produced abroad, minimizing effort and time for the American publisher's staff. They are packaged to bedazzle the editor. And when a season doesn't produce enough attractive books, the allurement of picking up a few of these imports, with comparative ease, is great. This, in my judgment, is not sound publishing. But the editor's problem, speaking very subjectively, is in dealing with the photographers and their pictures.

Anne Shanks, a dear friend and highly skilled photographer and cinematographer, is still on speaking terms with me, but probably worries about my intelligence. I told her at dinner one evening, after watching some avant-garde films, "But photography is not an art form." She nearly speared me with her fork. We had been listening to Jonas Mekas and Warhol.

Anthony Burgess, a short time ago, said, "Film, seeming to have all the resources, and more, of literature, still cannot produce anything as great as a work of literature." And I read just recently, in one of Robert Craft's diary entries, a remark made to him by the poet W. H. Auden: "Photography isn't an art form—any claim for the cinema as an art is rubbish."

From Auden! That settles it.

5 *Special People—*
And a Few Others

Brigid Brophy

She may be the greatest punster alive, the best since Louis Untermeyer was in his prime. (Louis once said, "I delivered a talk for Dallas so that I could pay my Texas.") This London-born Irish woman is dear to my heart and viscera. I had the honor of publishing some of her novels, among which were that baroque beauty, *The Snow Ball* (which someone should film); *Flesh;* and the deliciously (also baroque) wicked *In Transit.* And of course I've read her much-maligned book on Mozart, the earlier stories, and her profound *Black Ship to Hell;* not forgetting her study of Roland Firbank, a vast labor of love and scholarship.

In the spring of 1969 I had luncheon with her in London at the Connaught, following a dramatic Pan Am flight. (I had passed out from trying to break a record consuming splits of champagne and paté, and was declared a possible coronary case. The Viennese doctor on board insisted that I must not move a muscle, although I swore to him that it was low blood pressure plus too much bubbly. Anyway, I had the usual airport hospital checkup and was declared "tip-top." A pretty Pepsi Generation stewardess was all attention until I told her I'd be phoning my wife in New York, at which point she dropped my wrist and vanished.)

At noon Brigid Brophy arrived. She looked cautious, interestingly sullen, but friendly. Also on guard, I thought. I don't think she knows too many Americans, although the *TBR* uses her on occasion when kneecaps need breaking in their front-page feature reviews. It's her eyes that hold one, and one had better pay close attention to them if her message and mood are to be received.

I brought her a gift of the latest *Don Giovanni* recording (with Marilyn Horne, Leonardo Monreale et al.—the London album). Next to punning, I gather Mozart is her chief preoccupation. I spent too many nervous moments talking up the Connaught's great cuisine, then suddenly was brought up short when she reminded me that she was a vegetarian. How many Irish-British birds do you know who will turn down a steak or pheasant? Anyway, we both ended up eating chaste omelettes.

Plain, pleasant, and quietly spoken, she still gives the impression of being a dangerous adversary. I'm told she has the impact of Muhammad Ali when sparring verbally on the BBC.

Brophy is, as indicated, a marvelous punster, not averse to the utilization of genital references in her punning. (She calls the Irish air line *Air Cunnilingus*). She is also wicked in the filetting job she does on her betters. For example, she had just published a front-page review in the *TBR* of Simone de Beauvoir's *Force of Circumstance*, of which I was the editor. (I planned to see de Beauvoir in Paris the following week.) Brophy's review was a personal and extremely bitchy attack. I recall her saying, among other uncomplimentary things, that de Beauvoir was the most overrated writer in France. Also, at that precise period, I was editing Nelson Algren's book, *Notes from a Sea Diary* (also for Putnam's) in which de Beauvoir did not fare too well. Algren, in case you didn't know it, can be ungallant on occasion. He had given me some rough moments in New York a few months earlier because of de Beauvoir's *Force of Circumstance:* she had reproduced in the book certain of Algren's highly personal letters to her without his permission. I recall taking a long walk with him one night in the Village, literally begging him to grant permission to Putnam's to include her letters, so that we could publish her book. He finally yielded, but most unwillingly.

Anyway, I found Brophy's reserve puzzling. Her novel, *In Transit,* is precious to me, as is she; however, she may not reciprocate my feeling for her, since I had the unhappy duty of declining two of her subsequent works.

In Transit was not a commercial success in America, and no paperback reprinter or club took it. But I loved publishing the book, and hope she writes more such stories and that I'll be allowed to serve as editor. *In Transit* is a wicked maverick of a novel—surreal, polylingual, with exquisite puns in five or six languages. It may very well be the wittiest British novel of our time.

I do hope the next photograph she takes shows her smiling; I'm sure she's capable of it.

Corwin

One doesn't usually commission a book-length poem. I tried it several times and failed. But once I did succeed. In 1962 I met Norman Corwin, the playwright and screenwriter. Among his best-known works were *Thirteen by Corwin, On a Note of Triumph,* his opera *The Warrior,* and *Dog in the Air.* I had admired him for years; he stood for bold, voluble opposition to McCarthyism and other social anomalies. He wrote beautifully; he was a *mensch.* In 1947 he received the Wendell Willkie One World Award.

We met in my office at World in New York and found ourselves discussing the atomic bomb. What to do about it? Should we play ostrich? Should we run? What were its merits, its dangers? Finally I asked him why he didn't write something about it, declaring his innermost feelings, his passions, about the bomb.

"I'd like to do it in the form of a poem," he said, "but who would want to publish *that?*"

Then and there I said that we would be proud to publish it.

We did, in 1963. Entitled *Overkill and Megalove,* it is a poem on the subject of nuclear war or peace, on fallout and other related matters. It has been performed on radio and in large public arenas. It's now out of print, I believe, and shouldn't be.

Corwin and I met again in Malibu in 1974; it was a joyous reunion. He is unchanged—a bit older perhaps, but still beautiful; one of our great ones. I'm proud to have been involved in his little book.

Saul and Lillian Marks printed an exquisite book of Corwin's in 1972, entitled *Prayer for the 70's.* One hundred copies were produced, and Norman sent me an inscribed copy. One sentence in that book sums up Corwin: "That man should love his kind in all his skins and pigments/ and kill no more."

What did you say our current military budget was?

Sui Generis

In 1968 I published at Putnam's two writers, both women, who happen to be the best of their kind: Kate Simon, the travel-book writer, and M. F. K. Fisher, the writer on food and the pleasures of eating. The books were *London* and *Paris* (by Kate Simon) and *With Bold Knife and Fork* by M. F. K. Fisher.

Working with these two writers (personally fascinating women) was a frustrating experience since there was very little I could contribute to either as an editor. They are both perfectionists as writers and supremely self-critical; and their standards are impeccable.

But I did make two contributions. To Kate Simon I introduced one of my then (not now) favorite London restaurants when we both happened to be in that city at the same time. We ordered, I think, some twelve entrees between us, so that we could sample as much as possible. She refers to some of that meal in her *London* book. To M. F. K. Fisher's book, I was able to lend some modest assistance to her chapter on tripe. (Her favorite food? Potato chips and caviar—and Dom Perignon.)

Kate Simon, in strolling with me through the streets of London, taught me how to *see* architecture, to look *up*, where there is so much usually unseen beauty. Though I've been to London many times, she showed me some bypaths that I would have missed. She also pointed out some of the joys of omnibus riding, a means of transportation I'd never explored.

These two women are among the most felicitous and cultivated writers and civilized people I have known, and when I tote up my "stable" of authors, I count them among the most enduring. Both get four stars in my private Guide Michelin.

―――――――――

Harry Golden

On June 16, 1974, Harry Golden and I had a luncheon meeting at the Algonquin. He handed me the manuscript of his new book which he entitled *Leben Zul Columbus*. I asked him if we'd better not call it *Long Live Columbus!* and use his Yiddish version as a parenthetical subtitle. He agreed. The manuscript ran to over five hundred pages.

This was the fifteenth book he and I had worked on together— our relationship has spanned some seventeen years. We had published his first book, *Only in America,* at World, in July 1958. I called his attention to the fact that in all these years and during the processing of fifteen books we had never had a quarrel, never raised a voice against each other.

Only in America came to me in the form of a large box of clippings and yellow tearsheets, mostly from Harry Golden's own newspaper, the maverick among American newspapers, *The Carolina Israelite,* published by him in Charlotte, North Carolina. It is now defunct. I had not previously heard of Golden or of his paper, but Ben Zevin, president of World, was a subscriber and ardent follower of Golden's. He felt there was a book in these articles and anecdotes from the *Israelite.* I read them, expressed mixed feelings about some, and asked Golden to make the final selection himself. My job was to shape a cohesive book out of what he chose. My choice for the opening piece was the now-famous "Why I Never Bawl Out a Waitress." We gave Golden an advance of $3,000 against the usual terms; our first printing was 5,000 copies. None of us had any notion as to the size of his audience, and we were nervous. Golden said that if we didn't sell out our printing he would come to the rescue by buying a few hundred copies and using them to hustle *Israelite* subscriptions.

On publication day, we had some 3,500 copies advanced to the trade and the wholesalers. Harry was sitting in my office in New York that morning; later he was going to have lunch with me to celebrate the book's publication. As we sat there, the phone began to interrupt us, and frequently. Wonder of wonders, the calls were coming from booksellers and wholesalers. They had run out of stock on *Only in America*—on publication day!—and could we rush them more copies? Golden appeared to doubt what he was hearing and witnessing. Could his book, unheralded and virtually unknown, be selling? Who was buying it, and why? To make this saga brief, the final total sale in the clothbound trade edition was 250,000 copies— the biggest selling trade book in World's publishing history.

We had lunch that noon at the Plaza's Oak Room. Shortly after we sat down, Victor, the maitre d', came over and asked if we would allow (allow!) Mr. Richard Rodgers to join us. Rodgers, a regular of the Oak Room, was sitting at the other end of the room. We thought it pretty odd, but said of course we'd be honored, and words to that effect. Neither of us had ever met Rodgers.

When he joined us, Rodgers proceeded to compliment Golden for the "marvelous book." He said he had bought three copies already, and two had been "borrowed" by Edna Ferber and Ilka Chase, and that Golden was little short of a genius. He kept on, exclaiming over the merits of Golden's book, his famous "plans" for achieving civil rights, and said he shared Golden's Lower East Side reminiscences. Golden stared at me and I returned his look, wondering if this was really happening. Later, we found the acclaim repeated in the bookshops and elsewhere. It was intoxicating, unbelievable.

After lunch we walked over to Scribner's Bookstore on Fifth Avenue and were greeted by Igor Kropotkin, the store's manager. He said they had sold out their entire stock of fifty copies and needed more books at once. He didn't know what it was all about and assumed there was a mammoth publicity and advertising campaign at work. Of course there was no such thing. The demand for the book was pure "word of mouth"—the only true method yet known for selling books. As we stood talking to Igor, clerks came over to ask when they would have more stock, that customers were clamoring for *Only in America.*

We had a best seller and no one could explain it. We had been exceedingly modest in presenting the book, and the advertising was minimal, almost nonexistent.

There was obviously some ingredient in the book, in its title and contents, that fired the American public. In Miami, I was told, the book was seen in large numbers at all the pools and beaches. It was *the* book in Miami Beach. At Grossinger's there were dozens of copies visible. Subway and bus riders carried it. Every hospital room seemed to have a copy or two. It was the gift book for all!

I still can't understand what happened and why the book was such a success. Of course we all know that genuine humor is a rare commodity and when it is good, when it is right and well timed, it is pure gold. And that, I suspect, is what we had.

Subsequently, as mentioned, other books of Golden's were written and published. They were all successful—none was a failure—but none matched the sale of the first book. Golden's biography of Carl Sandburg, his close friend, went through several printings, as did his *For 2¢ Plain, So Long as You're Healthy,* and others.

Harry Golden and I often met for lunch, dinner, or a drink, almost regularly, every six weeks, at the Algonquin.

Golden had problems and wrote about a major one in his autobiography, *The Right Time*. I refer to the period in his life when he served a prison sentence. Since it is all recorded in detail in his memoirs (G. P. Putnam's Sons) there's no need to repeat the story here. But I must say I will never forget the tension and trauma of that period in our lives. Briefly, Golden had never told us of his prison sentence, so when it became public, it hit us with the impact of a bombshell. We were pretty startled to learn that our Number One best-selling author had been a jailbird.

Drama galore! Eleanor (Kask) Friede, at that time publicity and advertising director at World, and probably the best writer of publicity releases in the business—had the job of holding Golden's hand and keeping him "under cover" while the heat was on. (Incidentally, Eleanor later achieved fame as editor of several great best sellers at Macmillan's. Now she is a VIP editor at Delacorte, with her own imprint—another woman who has "scaled the heights" through her own efforts.)

Eleanor did a great job helping Golden to relax in his Hotel Warwick suite. Read about it in his biography, *The Right Time*, still available, I hope, in a Pyramid edition. A short piece on this episode, written by Golden for the book, *Long Live Columbus!* is reprinted below:

THE PRESS GIVETH BACK

Forty-five years ago, I heard a judge sentence me to five years in jail. I spent three years, eight months, and twenty-two days in prison, during which time I catalogued the prison library at Atlanta.

In the years that followed, I told only three men in the South about this episode. I told Josephus Daniels, Woodrow Wilson's Secretary of the Navy and the publisher of the Raleigh *News and Observer;* Frank Littlejohn, the Charlotte chief of police; and Hermann Cohen, a Jewish textile merchant.

In 1958, when my book *Only in America* had made me a celebrity, an anonymous letter to the editors of the now-defunct *Herald Tribune* revealed this prison record.

I remember repeating my story with a dry throat to reporter Judith Crist in the offices of my publisher.

For the second time in my life, I made the front pages. When the story appeared on September 19, 1958, I thought I was a dead man.

I was wrong. Many editors said in their columns that the past was over with, that the only reason to hold me in contempt was if I let this exposure keep me from functioning. The moral of my story is: *The press taketh away and the press also giveth back.*

That was not the end of the story, though.

In early December last year [1973], when dusk was falling, I had a call from the White House. The call was from White House Attorney Leonard Garment. The President had granted me a full and unconditional pardon. Legally I was never in jail.

For any man who's ever been in prison, a pardon never comes too late. Not only has the President restored my vote to me, he has freed me to run for the Charlotte City Council, a prospect I make more as a threat than a promise.

(Why did he go to jail? He ran a bucket-shop on Wall Street in 1928. Everyone was gambling in stocks. Harry took the rap, though many others just as guilty were never punished.)

What not enough people realize today is that Harry Golden played David against the Goliath of southern bigotry in his day. He was one of the earliest, most forceful advocates of civil rights in our time. He worked and fought for the blacks' rights, spoke up vigorously against oppression and discrimination. His home was bombed by the Ku Klux Klan to warn him to stop his "nigger-loving" activities. His books, gnomic and entertaining, were on target; he was one of the first to kid the pants off the segregationists in his own southern-Yiddish idiom. His Swiftian proposals for the solution of racism in the South are now classics, particularly his "vertical plan." His books are a testament to his commitment to the South and to human rights. He helped decontaminate areas of bigotry in many areas of intolerance. He has delivered thousands of lectures across the country and abroad, and in most of his talks he has carried the message: enough already with bigotry. Surprisingly, few blacks I meet today, especially the writers, educators, and activists, give Harry Golden his due. Some have been known to deprecate his activities privately and publicly, but we know their motivation: anti-Semitism. Some of the white intellectual establishment have made light of his writings. I've discussed this with Golden and he smiles, pointing out that the blacks need their whipping boys too; as for the Jewish intellectuals—well, why should a few buzzing flies bother him?

Golden has had ample rewards, including honorary doctorates. His full reward he'll have waiting in heaven—a certainty.

Recently, in early 1974, I was visiting with Harry. I asked him what he thought was in store for the Israelis; what about the "Jewish problem," the rising anti-Semitism, the Arabs, oil, the United States, and other related matters.

Smiling, he replied, "Bill, one thing you can count on—the Jews. Don't sell them short."

I don't intend to. But let's face it, Kissinger is no Moses.

Marianne (Craig) Moore

When the Ford Motor Company decided to enlist the help of this poet in selecting a suitable name for its latest model, a lot of people held their breath. Naming a new automobile is no small matter. The correspondence that ensued between Miss Moore and Mr. Robert Young of Ford's Marketing Research Department is preserved in a book* so I'll be brief about the matter.

Miss Moore labored valiantly and wittily, hoping to find a name suitable for the *wundercar* about to be launched by Ford. This all took place in 1955. She proposed names such as the Ford Fabergé, Astronaut, Taper Racer, Andante con Moto, Dearborn Diamanté, Regna Racer, Mongoose Civique, Chaparral, Cresta Lark, Pluma Piluma, and others. Her suggestions were not accepted, though Ford's representative was patient, polite, literate, respectful. In the end, Ford chose the absolutely right name for their car—a name which the Ford people found all by themselves; a name they thought had "a certain ring to it. An air of gaiety and zest." The name they chose was Edsel.

Marianne Moore was a poet's poet, "a mischievous moralist"; when asked about poetry she said, "Poetry is all nouns and verbs."

T. S. Eliot wrote of her work quite early, in 1934: "Miss Moore's poems form part of the small body of durable poetry written in our time; of that small body of writings, among what passes for poetry, in which an original sensibility and alert intelligence and deep feeling have been engaged in maintaining the life of the English language."

*Letters from and to the Ford Motor Company, The Pierpont Morgan Library, New York, 1958. The Ford letters were actually by David Wallace, all but one, but transmitted over Mr. Young's signature.

After many years in Brooklyn, Miss Moore (out of St. Louis and Bryn Mawr) moved to Greenwich Village, just a few blocks from where we live. She became our most glorious neighbor and our friend. She brought a new dimension of light and glory to the scene.

I had been a reader and collector of her poems for a number of years, and owned her first book, *Poems,* which was published by the Egoist Press in London, in 1921. It was published without her knowledge, by H. D., Robert McAlmon, and Bryher. Just recently, in 1974, I acquired a copy of her very rare little second work, *Marriage,* a pamphlet published in New York by Monroe Wheeler in 1923. In it, among others equally striking, is the statement, "Psychology which explains everything explains nothing." I bought the book from Bob Wilson to celebrate the opening of his posh new Phoenix Bookshop on Jones Street in New York City. The copy was signed by the author. Bob overcharged me outrageously, but I couldn't resist it. I would have chosen it over any jewel at Cartier's.

Marianne Moore came to our house, and we visited in hers. She was brittle, bright, and always unpredictable. I never heard her say anything in cliché terms. Her choice of language in casual conversation was as selective as in her poetry. She was a *rara avis* indeed.

One day she phoned me to ask if I would sell her a copy of a book we had just published at Putnam's, a little book dealing with exercise. I think it was the *Canadian Air Force Exercise Book.* I asked her why she wanted it and she said it was for herself. She was bothered—in her eighties—by rheumatism and felt that she should "limber up some." I sent her the book. A week later I visited her and she said, "Watch this." I watched as she suddenly jumped up from her seat. "Jumped" is not quite the word; she sort of *levitated* from her chair.

"See," she exclaimed, "this is the result of reading your exercise book."

Another phone conversation I recall began: "What do you think of miniskirts?"

I was taken aback by this question out of the blue. "Can you tell me why you want to know?" I asked.

"Well, I'm writing a piece for the *Times* on women's fashions, and was curious about a man's view. Also," she added, "what do you think of women in *slacks?*"

I asked, "Don't you want to ask Roslyn?" and she said, "Oh no, I want *your* opinion." I think I replied that I felt miniskirts and slacks were great on certain females, or some similarly inane statement. She thanked me politely. I didn't find myself quoted in her *Times* article. But it did please me to feel that I could contribute to Marianne Moore's fund of fashion information, that my opinion would matter on such a recondite subject.

I treasure the memory of this rare, fragile, original woman who has been called many things, including *objectivist*. And while I had no particular interest in animals, I savored certain of her jewel-like poems which they inspired. I think she was the most meticulously observant poet of our time. Somewhere I remember her saying, "I work in classified disorder."

I have a color photograph of her in her black tricorne taken by Arnold Weissberger in our house one evening. The photo shows her luminosity, her wisdom, and her shrewd view of life—all of it is to be seen in her eyes and in the tilt of her head. (I also have a memory of her in her last weeks, lying in bed, with pink plastic curlers in her hair, preparing for "a date.")

She once wrote a special poem for Roslyn for me to take back to the "beautiful princess."

She inscribed my copies of her books and loved to make corrections of typos in ink. She shared some of my prejudices, and could show real indignation over sloppy printing or poor book design. We both liked Jon Vie butter cookies, fresh-cut flowers, books with color illustrations. She died in her eighty-third year. We miss her, this "felicitous phenomenon," as does the world.

One Saturday evening (November 4, 1967), we had a reception at home for Bosley Crowther, *The New York Times* film critic (Florence and Bosley are among our dearest friends); we had just published his book, *Fifty Golden Years*. Among our guests were Lillian Gish and Marianne Moore. In their behavior and radiance, they were the youngest women in the room.

These two beautiful women sat side by side on a sofa in our crowded living room, chatting away like old friends, and almost everyone in the room felt the need to eavesdrop, to catch a few phrases exchanged by these wondrous creatures—two immortals relaxing at a Greenwich Village party on a wintry night, unaware of age or time or place; each aware only of the magic of the other. They sat as though under a special, impalpable spotlight, real, yet etherealized.

Following is a letter we got in the mail the following Monday from Marianne. It's reprinted in part, to indicate some of the quality of her prose and person:

> The French tea-cakes are an event [we gave her a parcel of cookies as a souvenir to take home with her] and should have remained with you. . . . The party was superb and it is a long time since I was so dazzled as by Mrs. Targ, and delighted by a writing figure as by Bosley Crowther. Have always loved Lillian Gish but had not met her; true angel lent by Heaven she is. I am not saving the party cakes for someone worthy—am eating some *now*, and your parting with what you could make use of yourselves, is an example for me—cakes and books, and time—giving that I venerate. May blessings rain on you. . . .

One of our favorite photos of Marianne Moore, from *The New York Times*, is reproduced in this book; the whole world knew her as New York's Number One baseball (Dodger) fan. (She inscribed the newspaper clipping for our "collection.") She had "perfect pitch" in everything she did. I never knew her to throw a curve, but she could surely throw a fast ball.

Footnote to Intellectual History

I once had the pleasure of lunching with Elliott Cohen. (You probably never heard of him unless your name is Podhoretz.) He came from Mobile, Alabama, and was the founding editor of *Commentary* magazine. He died in 1959; a suicide, I believe. I recall approaching him with a view to getting him to write a book for World. I had read (and saved among my scrapbook treasures) something of his that struck me forcibly: "Each Jew moves, consciously or not, in the context of a long and special history and a religious-ethical tradition that lays upon him, whether as a burden or a badge of pride, the sense of being *chosen,* and so creates in him the tendency, even the obligation, to carry himself 'with a difference.'"

I had clipped the above and used it as the basis of my luncheon discussion.

Cohen was a nervous but witty man, an articulate and authorita-

tive editor. What saddens me is the impermanence of a man's reputation; he's probably forgotten except by a handful of old-time intellectuals. I was later told that he was "sick, sick" for some years.
In many ways he was a man of gold and, now, a loss to the world of
ideas and letters. I recall sitting with him in the old Barbizon Plaza
dining room, across the street from World's offices, studying him and
concluding that he was a manic depressive; I don't recall what
prompted this "diagnosis." I liked him and wondered what was
troubling him.

I suppose he was simply born when the moon was not in the
right quarter. A *festschrift* would not be amiss.

The foregoing is out of context, of course, a note from the old
memory bank.

———

Abel

For some twenty-five years I would meet with Abel
Green for lunch at 21, the Algonquin, or the Forum. We met perhaps
once a week. He was a friend whose absence I'm reminded of with
painful, weekly regularity. He died at seventy-two, on May 10, 1972.
Roslyn and I both saw him at lunch the very day of his death. The
next morning's obituary in the *Times* really threw us for the well-
known loop. His widow Grace had been unable to phone.

Abel was the "architect of showbiz prose" and editor-in-chief of
Variety. He wrote the Stix Nix Hix Pix headline and countless others.
Eyeglasses gleaming, hair black, with the familiar bowtie and dark
suit, and always smiling, he could light up any room. His curiosity
about everyone was unbelievable. Pencil and pad at hand, he noted
everything down for his paper, a kid reporter on the make in his
seventies. At seventy-two he was still rich with vitality (we attended
an afternoon porno screening a few months before he died and he
chuckled through it all, although he was old-fashioned about explicit
sex). He had the energy and bubble of a young man, and a warmth
that radiated.

Abel was a great ad-libber. One day as we were leaving 21,
Bennett Cerf waved to him. We went over, exchanged the usual

comments. Bennett said, "Abel, why don't you sell us *Variety*—is it for sale? We're looking for acquisitions."

Abel said, "Sure, it's for sale—fifty cents on any newstand, Bennett" and off we walked. I think he was hurt that anyone would consider his *Variety* "available."

Abel was no respecter of confidence, and I say this without malice. *The story* came first—always. Anything said to him of newsworthy interest might appear in next week's issue of *Variety*. He was always after *that story* morning, noon, and night. On several occasions he had me upset, when he published some confidential piece of information I had given him at lunch. Everyone was fair game and the ground rules were, "Watch your step."

Abel was generous to me and my wife; he provided us with opening-night seats to hundreds of Broadway plays, concerts, ballets. He also contributed to my record library. Abel could take a set of galleys and read the pages like a professional proofreader. He often phoned me at home on a Saturday or Sunday afternoon, opening with, "Get a pencil out, Buster. I've got about a hundred factual errors to correct in your galleys." His memory was prodigious for dates, spelling of names, attribution. He also knew the tag line for about a thousand jokes.

When we went abroad, his secretary, Norma Nannini (one in a million) would get my itinerary; and notes, invitations, theatre tickets would be awaiting us in our hotel rooms. Even in South America he had friends to look after us, entertain us in Rio. I'll not forget his getting us the Number One table at Maxim's on Christmas Eve, when I decided to "give Paris" to Roslyn for Christmas. We had a five-hour supper there; that Maxim's affair was an event never to be duplicated.

Everyone who knew Abel loved him and misses him, as does *Variety*. And that goes for every subscriber *and advertiser*.

Morley

Not too many readers of the seventies know Christopher Morley's books. And yet he was beloved by several generations of readers who cared passionately about books, about good writing, and bookshops. His *Parnassus on Wheels* and *The Haunted Bookshop* are two classics that turned thousands of young people into collectors and readers. His novel, *Kitty Foyle*, published quite late in his career (1939), brought him great financial success, but his real talents lay elsewhere—in his poems, plays, and casual pieces. For almost twenty years he breathed wit and life into the *Saturday Review of Literature* (before they dropped *Literature*).

While Morley was from the East (Haverford, Pennsylvania), he fell in love with Chicago. I met him there a number of times; he loved to prowl in bookshops. The Argus Bookshop was his favorite, of course, and Ben Abramson did much toward making Morley a collected author. Ben also got him to write that "love letter" to Chicago, *Old Loopy*.

In 1944 World persuaded Morley, via his friend Louis Greenfield, to let us publish a good selection of his works in one large volume. We called it *Morley's Variety*. In it you will find his "play" on Walt Whitman, a sympathetic and moving portrait of the poet and some of his friends. The book runs over 630 pages and is a plum pudding, providing weeks of great reading chosen from his best works.

We met on occasion in New York, a few times in his studio. I also attended some of his public appearances. He was warm, always with some bookish gift in hand. There is no one around like Chris Morley. No one seems to look like, laugh like, or *feel* like Morley. His laughing, bearded countenance could light up a hall.

As a selfish collector, I regret that Chris died in 1957, several years before I finally acquired a copy of his first book, *The Eighth Sin*, one of the scarcest of all modern books of poetry. It carried the name of C. D. Morley as author, and was published at Oxford by B. H. Blackwell, in 1912.

A Touch of Gallic

Robert Laffont is one of my favorite people and publishers. His bustling offices in Paris are always a haven for Roslyn and me. She introduced me to Robert on our first trip to Paris in

1965, and I was taken with him on sight, not forgetting Jean Rosenthal, his editor, and certainly not overlooking Robert's beautiful daughter Isabelle.

I contracted for a few books through Laffont over the years, among which were Pierre Rey's high-schlock novel, *The Greek*, and Fernand Fournier-Aubry's *Don Fernando*. (I met the real, living Don Fernando in Laffont's office one day. He was about six feet, two inches tall, about seventy-two years old, endowed with a great chest, a handsome tan, and a small stiletto which he carried in his belt. He pulled it out and thrust it at me to make a point [it was sharp, razor-honed]. I asked him what he planned to do or write next, following the adventures related in his book. He said he was going shark-hunting, by which he meant he would hunt them with his bare hands. How did he do this? When he caught them, he said, he would break them in half over his knee, then pull out their livers. He would sell the livers to hospitals for medicinal purposes. "I am doing this for humanitarian reasons," he said to me, through our interpreter. A French Baron Munchausen. Alas, he died a few months later and never got to follow the sharks.)

My relationship with Robert Laffont was strengthened when, one Christmas evening in his home, awaiting dinner, he asked if we had anything exciting coming along at Putnam's, something for his firm. I suggested that he buy *The Godfather*, which we were publishing the following March. "Tell me about the book, Bill," he said.

I gave him a few sentences of description and said, "Just buy the book—read it later." He asked what price he should pay for it and I replied, "Whatever the agent asks."

He searched me with a strange look; Rosenthal's expression was also quizzical. Then Robert turned to his editor and said, "You heard Bill. Call tomorrow—yes, on Christmas—and buy the book. Do as Bill says; pay whatever it will cost." A vote of confidence. Then Robert relaxed in his red velvet jacket, pulled out his pocket harmonica, and began to play "Home on the Range" and some other tunes which he loves.

Laffont acquired *The Godfather* and it became the second biggest selling book he ever published. He also bought Kobler's *Capone* and it, too, proved a great success, almost matching our own sales.

Robert Laffont is one of the most imaginative, totally alive publishers in France; he is an attractive man, exceedingly modest and understated in public, but bold in his business behavior and judgment. He has a special zest for publishing, and in some respects is "very American" in his sense of the trade-book business. He gets a good share of the major American and British books, and he publishes best sellers frequently and without bluster.

His wife is one of the best cooks in Paris and their home is always a delight to visit. He is, in fact, one reason why Paris has come to be our second home.

H. D.

We never met, but I was a fan of H. D. (Hilda Doolittle) and her poetry for many years, and I still collect her first editions. (She died in 1961.) Harriet Monroe, who published her "Imagist" poems, did not consider her major. Regardless, I held her in high esteem and it may have been due in part to her unique personal history and background. One evening, dining with John Schaffner, the literary agent, and his wife Perdita, I happened to mention H. D. and my fondness for her work. What a pleasant surprise it was to learn that Perdita was H. D.'s daughter! I sat there speechless. Then shamelessly, I said, "I wish she were here to inscribe my first-edition copy of *Sea Garden*" (her first book, published in 1916).

Chester Himes, Native Genius

Chester Himes, a writer who has been shortchanged by the American public, is someone to consider on several counts. He is an authentic genius in his genre, the crime novel. He is also a comic artist; and finally, he is both a serious novelist and autobiographer. I published some of his books, beginning with his major novel, *The Third Generation;* also his *Cotton Comes to Harlem, Run Man Run, The Heat's On,* and *Pink Toes.* I declined a few of his books (which I liked enormously) for the simple reason that his books were not selling well enough to justify a decent commitment to the author.

I know that Chester, whose friendship I value highly, is puzzled and annoyed by the comparative indifference of the American public to his books. At World and at Putnam's, we paid him modest advances. We recovered our investment, not from hardback sales, but from the paperback reprints. But the reprints, in turn, did not fare well. It is very hard to find any of Himes' paperbacks in the bookshops of America, although most of them are in print. Luckily, this is not true in Europe, especially France. The French readers love him. Gallimard, the foremost publishing house in France, publishes Himes' books with profit. Chester Himes is a VIP in Paris as anyone can see who visits the French bookshops. This is also true in Barcelona.

Himes has talent to burn: he has wit, a fine comic sense, an understanding of scenic values; he's an inventive plotter; his characters are alive and easy to become involved with: his stories have action, animal heat, tension. He also usually has something vital to say. Added up, he should be popular in America. But he isn't.

Himes attributes some of the indifference to a kind of racism, with which I can't agree. Any writer who is fun to read and who succeeds in making important statements while so doing, is someone to take seriously, as an artist. Himes is an artist. Why is his native land not supporting his books? If you have the answer I would welcome it; I'd like to pass it along to Himes who, working in Alicante, Spain, wonders where the action is. We owe him an explanation.

Roslyn and I have many glowing memories of times spent with Chester and Lesley: a mad drive in his super Jaguar from Paris to Brussels, to catch a plane to Rome during the "1968 revolution"; evenings in Paris at LeRoy Haynes' in Montmartre for spareribs and black velvets (champagne and Guinness); a leisurely drive from Nice through the south of France into Spain; picnics along river banks; a visit to Van Gogh's Bridge in Arles; Barcelona and "Gaudi hunting"; in New York, at Chez Targ and at the Chelsea, good evenings of fellowship. Especially memorable was our stay at the house he built in Alicante—a writer's dream house.

As an author his reward must come soon—I mean his American reward. Meanwhile, his *critical* reception continues good; the critics and the aficionados love and understand him and his worth. When his autobiography is completed and published (possibly in 1976) some dramatic changes may occur for him—for the better. Sam Goldwyn, Jr., who filmed two of his books, may decide to film more of his Harlem "domestic" classics.

Sir George

In the mid-forties, when I was busy trying to build up a trade list for World in New York, I was visited one day by a British publisher named George Weidenfeld. (Victor Gollancz, with whom I had lunch a few days earlier, had said, "There's a strange man in town, an English publisher from Vienna, I believe, and he's stirring up things; he doesn't have a dime. Do you know anything about him?") At that time I hadn't yet met George—I only knew his name.

Weidenfeld, I recall, reminded me instantly of a European (Viennese) stand-in for Willie Loman: his blue suit was unpressed and shiny; in his hands he carried two heavy, shabby suitcases that were bulging with "dummies." His brow was gleaming with perspiration. He was overweight, intense, balding, but withal, appealing, eloquent. He was, I later learned, quite young—under forty. Charm, as the cliché goes, was "oozing from every pore." He was terribly bright, informed.

George came to London as a refugee from Hitler. He was well spoken, educated, nimble, familiar with the Great Names of Academe. He was looking for American support (financial) for certain projects which were still, at that moment, a gleam in the eye. Among them was an ambitious collection of books to be called *The World Civilization Series*. Each book would be written by a leading scholar in a given area; for example, Sir Michael Grant would write on Rome; Friedrich Heer on the medieval world; Maurice Bowra would write on Greece. He would deliver the "big names," each in his own field. And he did.

The plan appealed to me as well as to Ben Zevin, and we made a long-range commitment to George, putting down fairish sums of money as advances on the various contracts. We bought many other books from him on the same basis: always money down on the presentation of a brief memo or outline. At one time we managed to secure a sizable lump sum of cash for him from a paperback publisher who wanted to get into the act and was willing to help subsidize George's program.

George has several passions, but *one obsession*: Selling. Not books, but *selling* books. He likes to invent books, to make a deal, but only for the purpose of selling. If Moses were to approach him with his autobiography and an eye-witness account of the parting of the Red Sea, the first thought in George's mind would be, *To whom shall I sell it?* His real skill as a salesman is that, while trying to persuade you to buy a certain book, he has, in the back of his mind at all times, another prospective customer, in case you decline his offer. In short, a rejection doesn't offend or disturb him because his reflexes are so lubricated that he has moved to client Number Two before you've said no. He is a master of the controlled emotion.

Among George's other characteristics is his ability to walk two sides of the street simultaneously. For example, he is known to make two breakfast appointments, two luncheon dates, two dinner dates, and possibly one or two late-supper dates. In between, usually at the restaurant table, he will take a half dozen phone calls. He is Mr. Hyperactive. In a restaurant, usually a three-star establishment, when you think you're having a good, quiet conversation with George it suddenly dawns that George is only half listening. He's keeping his eye cocked for celebrities, VIP newcomers to the restaurant, to whom he can bow, wave, or table-hop, if possible. In short, George's motor is always racing.

Eventually, George became a figure in British publishing, a legend in his time. He married handsomely (the daughter of one of America's richest women), and set up a splendid residence in London. He travels widely, pursues society more avidly than ever, but always, his eye is on the deal. He secured a great plum in the *Memoirs* of Golda Meir (Putnam's secured the American rights), and later, Moshe Dayan's. He publishes one of America's greatest living novelists, Saul Bellow. And Norman Mailer, too.

His lists (with the exception of the American VIP's) are a montage in my mind: oversized books in full-color jackets on subjects dealing with great houses, major but dullish great names, historical episodes, and in particular, British aristocracy; he loves association with men and women of social or historical eminence. *Names.*

I suspect Sir George is secretly planning to top the Coffee-Table-Book-of-the-Year (Winter 1974), McGraw-Hill's $750, five-volume set entitled *The Madrid Codices*. George was obviously upstaged in this incident and there's bound to be bad blood. George is King of the Coffee Table and must not be pushed into second place. I'm sure he's thinking up a real topper, and it wouldn't surprise me if he came up with a facsimile of the original Ten Commandments, the stone tablets, of course.

For the record, George told Roslyn at a Kay Graham party in New York in 1974 that he was indebted to me for "giving me my start and for many kindnesses in the early years." So he had not forgotten. I'm grateful and say, "Thanks for the memory. You've come a long way, Baby, and I salute you, Sir George!"

L. C. Powell, Librarian and Man[*]

One summer afternoon in 1951 I was first introduced to the delights of Lawrence Clark Powell's world. It was in Philip C. Duschnes' bookshop in New York. Duschnes handed me Powell's *Island of Books,* and indicated that no self-respecting bibliophile should be without a copy. How right he was! It was through the pages of this book that I first encountered the master essayist, bookman, the evangelical bibliophile. Later, in 1954, I discovered Powell's handsomely printed work, *The Alchemy of Books*, on the shelves of Bob and Anne Levine's Publix Book Mart, in Cleveland. It was then that I began to make serious enquiry about this ebullient librarian who preached the devil's own gospel: the notion that books were fun to read and own.

As a publisher's editor, I could not rest until I had made the author's acquaintance and secured his signature on a contract for a book. What followed, over a period of six years, were three volumes of Lawrence Clark Powell's essays which I had the pleasure and honor to publish: *A Passion for Books, Books in My Baggage*, and *The Little Package*.

Knowing and working with Lawrence Clark Powell was a unique

[*]Revised and abridged from the Introduction by William Targ, ed., *Bookman's Progress*, Ward Ritchie Press, 1968.

experience. He is a renaissance man. His enthusiasms include Mozart, Haydn, sports cars, travel, history, the arts, fine printing, the Southwest; books of every imaginable sort and period, including paperback reprints; rare manuscripts and autograph letters; authors such as D. H. Lawrence, Robinson Jeffers, Henry Miller, Lawrence Durrell, Walt Whitman, Herman Melville, Austin Wright, Raymond Chandler, Rabelais, Dobie, Joyce, Steinbeck; his home in Malibu, collectors, libraries and librarians, bookshops and booksellers—and the good life, meaning really the world of the mind and the heart.

A former jazz musician, then a student at the University of Dijon where he received his doctorate of literature; a bookshop assistant (with Jake Zeitlin in Los Angeles); world traveller, teacher and lecturer—and last but not least, a great librarian—Dr. Powell's bibliography of published writings is formidable, an astonishing record of one man's zest and industry, one man's lifelong love affair with books and bookmen.

Just as A. Edward Newton fired the minds of booklovers in the '20s, so has Powell set ablaze the passion for books and reading in the present day. As a librarian and teacher of library science, he has set new and higher standards and instilled a special sense of "calling" in the men and women who have chosen librarianship as a way of life. In this respect he has been at once a stormy petrel and respected doyen, and all who have been privileged to know him or cross his path have profited from the experience.

Now retired Dean of the School of Library Service and Director of the Clark Memorial Library at UCLA (where he spent twenty-eight years), Powell continues to write and travel and lecture, as avidly as ever. In his Porsche, with his beloved wife Fay—and with a bagful of books and fig bars—he cruises about the country, especially visiting and revisiting the highways and byways of California and the Southwest. And wherever he goes, this perfervid and charismatic man leaves his mark, brings joyousness and understanding, and the message that the fellowship of books and music is good and most enduring.

Note: Just the other day I received in the mail, a copy of L.C.P.'s latest book, *Southwest Classics*, published by Ward Ritchie Press. What a treat this book is for anyone who loves Cather, Haniel Long, Dobie, Mary Austin, Mabel Luhan, Ross Santee, Erna Fergusson, and others who have devoted so much talent to the heart of the

Southwest. Powell's essays on these writers will bring delight and sunshine to the reader, and I urge you to get a copy if you care about beautiful letters and some very special American lore.

Palinurus (1903–1974)

Another great one gone; one of the best.

Just recently, we lost Edmund Wilson. Now Cyril Connolly. He died in November of 1974.

Connolly, like Wilson, was one of a kind. And who's going to replace him? One asks this kind of question whenever a good or great man dies—an Auden, an Einstein, a Toscanini, a Stravinsky.

Connolly's presence was felt wherever new writing had meaning, a special value; where the innovator's force was welcome. He was an advance man, an opener of doors, an enthusiast; an ironist, too. His reviews and essays, his pensées and satires and witty maxims—all set our juices flowing, as did Huneker's and Mencken's in an earlier period.

I discovered Connolly in his novel, *The Rock Pool* (a first-edition copy which I still own). I had met him once (he looked like a plump bartender) and the meeting was a simple handshake and a dumb, mumbling exchange of amenities at a publisher's house in London. (A social crush in a British living room is no place to meet a Cyril Connolly.)

This year I was looking forward to a real meeting with him, in the spring of 1975. He was due for a visit to New York, for the launching of his *Evening Colonnade,* his latest collection of essays.

Connolly was among the first to write about Joyce, Gide, Hemingway, Huxley, Fitzgerald, and Sitwell. During his Paris years he got to know the Olympians and he wrote about them brilliantly. Following his *New Statesman* period, he founded the magazine *Horizon.* This periodical lasted for nine years, then ran out of funds. (A familiar story.) Wise collectors will try to put together a run of that magazine; if it doesn't enhance in dollar value, your cultural quotient surely will.

I read and reread Connolly's *Enemies of Promise* and *The Con-*

demned *Playground*. Then I encountered his *The Unquiet Grave—
A World Cycle*, an extraordinary little 150-page book which he
chose to publish under the pseudonym of Palinurus. (A good deal
of it was beyond my understanding, and a French dictionary was
called into use frequently.) It was published in 1944, and may still
be in print with Harper & Row.

On a special and personal basis, Connolly means so much to me
because of his book *The Modern Movement* (1965), where he lists
and discusses over one hundred landmark or influential books from
England, France, and America. The roster begins with Henry James'
novel *The Portrait of a Lady* (London, 1881) and ends with William Carlos Williams' poem, the five-volume *Paterson* series (1946–
1958). Through *The Modern Movement* I was introduced to a body
of literature that literally made me grow up. Until 1965, when I
discovered it, I fancied myself a well-read person. I had read some
of the titles in his list, but a number were unknown to me. Connolly
got me to read Flaubert's *Bouvard and Pécuchet*, and works by
Apollinaire, Villiers de L'Isle-Adam, Alfred Jarry, William Plomer,
André Breton, and so many others. He had me plunge into a pool
of literature I was only dimly aware of, had me meet "life-enhancing
writers," writers I would probably never have otherwise encountered, considering the pressures of my editorial job.

As a collector, I began to hunt down and assemble his *Modern
Movement* books in their first editions—a tough challenge that I
haven't yet met completely, although I do have at this moment
about 80 percent of the titles.

Connolly was responsible, as I said, for part of my education.
For the past decade his *Modern Movement* book was my bible. In
March-December 1971, there was an exhibition held at the Human-
ities Research Center of the University of Texas at Austin, where all
the *Modern Movement* books were displayed, together with manuscripts and autograph material, plus some *recherché* association
copies. The catalog is handsomely produced, and copies may still be
had from the University of Texas.

Hail, but not farewell, Palinurus. I hope this brief notice (and
most inadequate it is) will bring you and your works to the attention
of a few new readers.

Certainly, serious bookmen—trade-book editors—should be
familiar with Connolly's critical writings. He knew good writing and

what it was all about; and he approached literature with a gleam in his eye, a zestful sensuality, and a healthy expectancy. He was a bull's-eye hit man most of the time.

It is ironic to note that the 1962 edition of *Encyclopaedia Britannica failed* to include Connolly. Interestingly, it also neglected to include the greatest book collector the world has ever known, an *Englishman* named Thomas Phillipps (1792–1872), whom I discuss at greater length in Chapter 8.

———————

Pat Covici

I first met Pat Covici in Chicago, in the mid-twenties. He was *the* local publisher, and also ran a bookshop. He was really the red-hot center of culture in Chicago. His publishing firm struggled without capital and published some lively books, among which were works by Ben Hecht and translations from Europeans, including J. K. Huysmans. He had color and flair, a piratical gleam in his eye, and while he may have been involved in some vanity press publishing (as who hasn't?), his taste was top-notch and his enthusiasm for books always ran high.

I once wanted him to publish a collection of my poems, when I was about seventeen. He was kind. He took me into his office, looked at me closely and said, "Go home, son, read some of Lascelles Abercrombie and think about the kind of poet you want to be." To this day I don't know why he chose Abercrombie for me to study. Luckily for me, my poems were never published. I've enough between book covers to live down; *that* collection of poems would have been too much of a burden to bear today.

When Covici came to New York, he was able to show his true talents; together with Donald Friede, he established a fine and colorful publishing house. More so than most, Covici-Friede always approached publishing with courage and imagination. They published deluxe, limited editions, some quite ambitious, such as the Samuel Putnam translation of Rabelais. They published Clifford Odets, John Strachey, Gene Fowler, Ben Hecht, Radclyffe Hall, and some of John Steinbeck's early books including *Of Mice and Men*. Friede left the firm when finances became a problem; and when Covici found it rough sledding, he joined Viking Press. Steinbeck followed him, and his *The Grapes of Wrath*, published in 1939, sold almost a half million in the trade edition. Covici became Steinbeck's editor in the fullest and most intimate sense; there are many moving and illuminating letters on record between them which editors should study, to see what a true author-editor relationship means. In *Journal of a Novel: The East of Eden Letters*, a posthumous work by Steinbeck, we see the extraordinary relationship at work. Without Covici, I doubt that *East of Eden*, Steinbeck's most ambitious novel, would have seen publication. Covici sustained Steinbeck as both friend and author. Pat also served as editor to Marianne Moore, Arthur Miller, and Saul Bellow. Miller said, "I think of Pat as the great listener. . . . Pat stood rather alone, superbly himself, eager to be moved by something true." And Saul Bellow said of Pat: "Like an old prospector, he rose every morning to look for treasure, never doubting he would strike it rich. . . . His calling was to find books and put them in print. . . . He loved writers and he lived for literature."

I think Bellow summed him up accurately.

―――――――――

Another Incomparable Max

I first made contact with Maxwell Evarts Perkins in 1951. I was still a bookseller in Chicago and was operating my Black Archer Press. Having a strong yen to publish something by Thomas Wolfe, I got permission from Perkins to issue a small limited edition of Wolfe's *Gentlemen of the Press*. Perkins was terribly nice to me, and the deal went through without a hitch. I note that the book brings a fancy premium in the rare-book market today.

It's about twenty-eight years since Perkins died. No one approaching his stature has since appeared on the publishing scene. I got to know him when I came to New York, but never intimately. We did have two very good luncheon visits (at Cheerio's) and I learned from him the joys of the extra-dry, perfect ("Upright, please") Gibson. It would be pointless for me to speak of his personality, talents, influence. I interviewed him for a weekly column I once wrote for a Cleveland paper, and he answered some fairly dumb questions of mine most graciously. (I can't locate the clipping and perhaps it's just as well.) I recall his prophesying, at a time when F. Scott Fitzgerald's books were not selling, that Fitzgerald's time would come, and he told me to watch out for the "big revival."

Perkins never acknowledged his title; he found it embarrassing. He turned down all invitations to speak in public or on the air. We all know of his famous dictum—that editors should not be seen. But despite his equanimity he was human, and responded to some of the abuses to which an editor is sometimes subject. He once said, after the departure of an author, "What sort of madhouse is this, anyway! What are we supposed to be—ghost-writers, bankers, psychiatrists, income-tax experts, magicians?"

He was the best of them all.

J. C. F.: RIP

A special virtue attaches to editors who were poets; and John C. Farrar was a poet, among other things.

One of the best editors and publishers I was to meet—about five years after I came to New York—was this convivial and informed bookman. I was glad to make his acquaintance, for I had read his famous rejection letter (*The Writer*, January 1948), in which one of the things he said was, "I prefer not to see an author until I have read *something* he has written." I had also read his autobiographical essay on publishers (*Colophon*, Winter 1938), in which he admitted that "modesty is not one of my prime characteristics . . ."

Some considered Farrar a character because, in his later years, he seemed to become addicted to eccentric behavior, non sequiturs, and explosive outbursts on many issues (some rather trivial), and because he was easily irritated. But he also had a sharp sense of humor; he caught a point quickly. I suspect he suffered from hypertension induced by pressures in his business, hostile influences, or sheer emotional expenditures. His voice, often high-pitched, showed edginess.

We had occasional luncheon visits which I always enjoyed. He gave me sound advice on judging manuscripts; lectures on the nature of authors and their special perceptions, especially the novelists.

He spoke of having faith in one's own instincts or hunches; the importance of keeping one's perspective. He had some lively if cynical comments to make on the "new criticism" and the highfalutin lingo of the book reviewers and book editors. He hated phony, ornate writing. "Those critics are going for baroque," he once put it.

Farrar was a first-rate editor, an admirer of Maxwell Perkins. While he was among the top half-dozen best editors in New York, he was not always fully appreciated, and he was frequently deprecated by his inferiors.

Farrar was a "working stiff" who spent his days and nights with a pencil, laboring over manuscripts. He loved young writers, encouraged new talent. He had more than one man's share of literary and commercial success. Two of his books that come to mind are *John Brown's Body* and *Anthony Adverse,* almost enough to justify any editor's existence on a publisher's payroll. A literary man right down to the ground, his feet *were* on the ground. He hated the snobs, the pretentious element in publishing, the swaggerers; also the hucksters and vulgarians.

John Farrar died at age seventy-eight. Most of his working years —following his six years as editor of the magazine, *The Bookman*— were devoted to editing and administration jobs in publishing houses, the first being Doran, followed by Doubleday and others. But he was active in other areas as well. He loved poetry and wrote it from time to time; he enjoyed controversy and spoke with excoriating candor, attacking hokum, and especially censorship, with destructive energy. He was an enthusiast. He liked to take chances, to toss an egg into an electric fan.

I met him often at the P.E.N. meetings, and recall his forthright, sometimes fiery, comments on many subjects, especially during his tenure as president of P.E.N. He was a hard-working president and was responsible for many innovations, including the weekly cocktail sessions. He also initiated the Breadloaf Writers' Conference at Middlebury College, in Vermont.

We had drinks together once, in Chicago, during an American Booksellers' Convention. We may have both been a bit loaded. As we sat at the bar I couldn't help observing that the week-long meetings were becoming a bore. In all seriousness, I asked why was he bothering to be there in Chicago, wasting a week of his valuable time listening to complaints of booksellers—the old "playback" speeches we had been hearing over the years. (It was the week in which Bennett Cerf put his foot into his mouth—yes, again—by giving a gung-ho speech, calling the book clubs the greatest blessing ever to befall the American bookseller. Joe Margolies, then manager of Brentano's bookstore chain, had been doing his David-vs.-Goliath battle with the clubs on behalf of the booksellers, and Cerf's speech was inept and somewhat worse than badly timed—and he was booed.) Anyway, Farrar said to me, "Bill, always remember, bullshit is part of our business, as well as art."

How could I forget that honest remark?

I also remember discussing the matter of simple writing, and the diminution of decent English and the clean declarative sentence in books. And he said, smiling, possibly with mind roaming: "There are a lot of other things besides nouns."

I thought, *that's* a queer non sequitur. Then he continued, "That's from Gertrude Stein, you know."

"What do you mean?" I continued, perplexed, feeling stupid.

He replied, "What it means, Bill, is that we should have another drink."

A lot of writers are going to remember John C. Farrar. He was a credit to his profession, a giving man, an original. If he was at odds with the world in his later years, let's think of the total lifespan of the man, his life-force, his worth and contributions. I hope one of his colleagues or his wife Marguerite will write his biography for my further personal edification—and yours.

Portrait of a Publisher as a Shit

Right off I must say that my subject here is portrayed from a distance; I don't know him well at all. I've observed him mainly from afar over the years. I've never had a meal with him, nor been to his home.

He's one of a kind to the best of my knowledge; and I know a good many book publishers—and a great variety. There are Publishers and publishers, just as there are Men and men. The individualistic publisher is not uncommon: the profession attracts mavericks, eccentrics, intellectuals, entrepreneurs—even genuine lovers of literature. There are also some nonliterary businessmen in publishing who find the associations inviting, exciting. There are a few visionary empire-builders in our book world, too.

My subject can't resist making himself observed, which is, in part, the reason for this "study." His type can be found in many businesses, especially in the garment or show business; some Hollywood agents resemble him. He uses the film-biz lingo, the "kiss-kiss" etc. He prefers "suck off" to "fuck off." He can't help propositioning, in bluntest terms, eligible women he meets or speaks to on the phone, with an invitation to fuck. I use the word because he does himself. It is his hallmark, his special signature. I have no idea how successful he is in his offers, nor have I enquired. Scatalogical allusions are common in his speech. "Shit," of course, is the obvious epithet and expletive. What interests me in this man's behavior is that there's no way to correlate the high level of his publications (the belles lettres) with the man. He cultivates elegance and quality in his books, but he has the manners of a longshoreman or pushcart hawker. (No *beautiful letters* aura about him!)

Consider the following "true to life" scene: Six of us were standing together talking, at a literary reception. There were four young women in our group, one a fine poet. The above-unnamed publisher approached, moved right into our little circle and said, "Well, hello, motherfuckers." Then he walked off, grinning. End of scene. An exotic social approach you will admit.

We all did doubletakes; two of the women were appalled. One said, "What a distasteful clown." The poet said, "I wonder how far he will go to attract attention. He's obviously got some deep-seated needs."

This publisher has built a list of authors by the simple process of hiring editors away from other houses, editors who have distinguished authors who will most likely follow them. (A not-uncommon practice to be sure.) He probably loses money each year, but his social status, due to his literary facade, assures him a place in the sun. He's no ornament to society, but he's determined not to be ignored. And he succeeds admirably. He may yet expose his genitals publicly to ensure getting the ultimate recognition; I hope there'll be a camera around. I would suspect that his fantasy is *being surrounded by the paparazzi*.

In reviewing the publishers of the New York fraternity, those I've known personally, I can't think of another one remotely like the one I've been describing. There are several I don't admire, but the fault may be mine. Certain hard-nosed, hard-working, but gross, book publishers are not always my dish. Then there are strong, rugged personalities, always with the best possible credentials, whom we all know and like. Some are slightly fey or madly visionary or hypercritical of almost everything. Some are isolationists, loners, and some are just too big to mingle—except with bankers. But I know of only one man of the above anachronistic character, and I suppose, in terms of industry percentage, one is tolerable.

A friend of mine who read this piece asked if there was any real purpose in introducing the man in this book. I said yes. He's an irritant, a bit of dust on the eyeball; he can't be ignored. Perhaps there's some biological reason to explain why he's like he is and why we must endure his presence. After all, meeting him is only a harmless, a chance, encounter. All buffoons provide copy and seasoning for gossip. Meet Mr. X. He may be your publisher!

Bennett

Probably the best-known individual publishing figure of his time, Bennett Cerf deserves a full-length biography. I'm sure there are a number of first-class candidates for the job, including his partner, Donald Klopfer. Millions of Americans knew his face, due in part to his weekly TV appearances.

Bennett's public image was that of a punster, a jokester, and celebrity hound. He spoke to hundreds of clubs and business groups each year. He could always be seen table-hopping at the old Stork Club, at the 21 Club, and the Plaza Oak Room. The entrance of a famous movie star or politico would galvanize him into action: his glasses and entire face would light up; his famous grin would go to work, and he'd leap to his feet. He always had a ready quip, never told an off-color story, and wouldn't listen to any. (I once tried a fairly crude sexual pun, with a biblical origin, on him, and he winced.)

Random House was his achievement, and his acquisition of the Modern Library from Horace Liveright in 1925 gave him the start, the foundation for his business. His list was heavily indebted to

Liveright, since he later acquired Jeffers, O'Neill, Faulkner, and other Liveright stars.

One of his greatest single coups was publishing James Joyce's *Ulysses;* he fought the censors and got the right to publish the book in unabridged form. The case is historic, and Judge Woolsey's ruling is one that all publishers should read. To the best of my knowledge Cerf gave Joyce an advance of $1,500 for American publication rights.

When I served as reprint editor for World, I would visit Random House regularly to get rights to certain of their books. I often ran into Cerf and he was always warm, cordial. Several times he offered me a job; his approach was not what could be called felicitous. He would say, "Say, Targ, I could use you. Want a job at Random House?" The word "use" bothered me. I guess I didn't want to be "used."

In 1945 I was modestly involved with Cerf, as an editor; he was preparing a collection of short stories by American authors for World for our low-priced anthology series. While the job was fairly simple as editorial involvements go, I recall Bennett's screams on the long-distance phone from time to time; he'd disapprove of a certain story choice, or the jacket flap copy, or something. His disapproval was always high-pitched, and certainly never relaxed. The book—384 pages, clothbound, for $1.50!—was fairly successful. And the contents included works by Hemingway, Steinbeck, Faulkner, Thurber, Welty, Saroyan, Lardner, and others of similar quality. It's out of print and certainly merits a paperback reprint.

I will always have a special warmth for Bennett Cerf, if for no other reason than that he treated his editor, Saxe Commins (who worked with O'Neill and Faulkner), humanely and brotherly. I had heard rumors, following Commins' heart attack, that he was not going to continue working at Random House. So I invited Saxe to lunch and proposed that he work for World, on his own terms: hours and compensation would be his decision. He smiled and said that he was flattered, but Bennett Cerf had already given him the same proposition—a job to suit his convenience and needs for the rest of his life. Cerf meant it and followed through.

It is hard to believe that I was around when Random House was founded—in 1925. As a footnote to my own personal history, the firm was started the year I joined Macmillan. And I bought one of their first books out of my $18 salary—Voltaire's *Candide*, illustrated by Rockwell Kent.

Bennett summed up himself and his career one day at the end of a speech: "I am in the publishing business because I love it. They are going to carry me out of Random House feet first!"

6 *Prejudices / Personals /*
Proposals / Predilections

Song of Myself (No Apologies to Whitman)

(The following assortment of chitterlings, grits, turnip greens, et cetera, may help you get a fix on me, if you've failed thus far; and in the end you may find me understandable, perhaps not insufferable. I can plead innocence on many counts, since I frequently fail to practice what I preach.)

At this juncture, I can exclaim, and thank my luck, for a beautiful and devoted wife who, in her joy of life, transmits it to me each day; for a comfortable nest in Manhattan with a good view of the city; for a decent digestion that can accommodate delicatessen food; for almost enough cash to pay my taxes; for my son, his lovely wife, and my three beautiful grandchildren. I sing gratitude for friends; for more books than I can possibly read; for the makers of beautiful recordings; for Beefeater Gin, J & B Scotch, Stolichnaya vodka, Preparation H, not to mention a dependable wine dealer, Jack Lang, of the "67 Wine and Spirits Merchants" who never lies to us. I envy no one.

Why Women Should Be
Imperious Chauvinists

Without question, the most potent word in the English language is "cunt." (Even when used as an expletive or in some pejorative sense.) Women possess it exclusively. Most dictionaries fail to define it. This is a form of censorship or ostrich-thinking, or else a continuation of the conspiracy to maintain its mystique. If you can't find the word, in your dictionary, then seek out "pudenda," a reasonable synonym, but lacking the basic word's real impact.

Snapshots

Imperishable Memories from My Friendly Computer, with the aid of photographs from the Targ Instamatic Archives: some shared views and experiences of the past ten years:—Watching Roslyn go at some giant grilled sardines in a Lisbon *estaminet,* while a Portuguese girl sobs her heart out doing her *fado* number; I seem to remember some of Roslyn's tears mingling with her sardines . . . attending a midnight mass at Christmas in Guadeloupe, with an all-black congregation and one white French priest presiding . . . orgiastic shore dinner in Istanbul, with five-foot lobster, courtesy of our friends, the Kesims, Turkish literary agents . . . dinner at the White House with the LBJ's, attended by Humphrey, McNamara, et al., followed by hamburger snack at two A.M. in a D.C. greasy spoon with Nathan Cummings as our host . . . our first view of Gaudi's unfinished cathedral towers in Barcelona . . . watching Nureyev and Fonteyn in *Romeo and Juliet* at the Met—Roslyn in an orchestra seat, I in a box—sharing each moment apart but together . . . our entrance to Martinique at three in the morning under the cobalt, billion-starred sky, with the air filled with the effluvium of rotting sugar cane . . . view of ancient Greek and Roman ruins from the top-floor balcony of the Dominican Palace Hotel in Taormina, with Etna as a backdrop, while Roslyn and I tore at a freshly roasted chicken, drank local wine, and gorged on giant peaches—in the nude under the hot Sicilian sun . . . the two of us sitting in the middle of an Arab household in Casablanca, eating couscous while eight members of the family stand around watching us . . . Roslyn, Lesley, Chester Himes, and I having a river-side picnic in the south of France, using a boat-bottom as our table . . . treasured evening with Jane and Ledig-Rowohlt downing gimlets at the Plaza Oak Room . . . watching a sunset on Botafogo, Rio . . . our first view of the stained glass windows in Chartres Cathedral . . . relaxing over a pasta feast on a Friday night at Mary

Adams' Greenwich Village Grand Ticino . . . Roslyn and I sharing our "Roman bathtub" in Antigua, while tiny yellow birds fly in and out of the open-work wall . . . experiencing *Les Troyens* at the Met together . . . dinner at "the world's greatest restaurant," Maison Arab, in Marrakesh . . . a cheese-blintz breakfast on Sunday morning at the old Rubens . . . the white peacocks in Lisbon . . . champagne and hot dog supper at the John Stevensons' . . . first view of the Bosphorus from the Istanbul Hilton terrace . . . Botticelli's *La Primavera* in Florence's Uffizi . . . a performance of Mozart's *Abduction from the Seraglio,* in the Topkapi Palace gardens—sung in Turkish! . . . and the Acropolis at sunrise . . .

Retreat

One of life's pleasures (for a bibliophile) is to have friends among booksellers. One recent afternoon, following some pressing and troublesome business with an author, I fled from my office and went to visit with my old friend, Lew D. Feldman. His home is also his bookshop. Treasures surround us, and he hands me a folio volume which I notice bears a price mark of $360,000. It is an illuminated manuscript—Chaucer's *Canterbury Tales,* on vellum (circa 1455). I open it carefully and can't resist reading aloud from its opening page the familiar "Whan that Aprille with his shoures soote . . ." What an opulent manuscript this is to look at, to hold. I'm next privileged to hold an original watercolor painting by William Blake—a Crucifixion, *The King of the Jews,* for which Lew is asking $50,000. I would have bought it at once, finances permitting. Ten years from now it will prove to be a bargain. I finally did buy a book from him, a copy of Vachel Lindsay's first book, *The Tramp's Excuse and Other Poems,* printed in Springfield, Illinois, in 1909.

Other shops I love to visit as retreats are Fleming's in New York; Loliée's in Paris; Rota's in London; also the Gotham, the Phoenix, and Black Sun in New York.

tuary, when survival is the issue.

For me, the bookshop is the escape hatch, the cathedral sanc-

Cosmology: Rumblings in the
Solar Plexus and Elsewhere

- Everything is concept—and refutation.
- There is no absolute—except pain.
- The human being has only one purpose: to live as *both* the lower and higher animal.
- Man's greatest disease is acquisitiveness.
- Art is aesthetic excrescence, likewise the book.
- Idiot's Delight: the camera.
- Supreme Anachronism: the Nobel *Peace* Prize.
- Ultimate vanity: hair transplant.
- Christ and Thoreau gave us all the answers, but who listens?

* * * * *

Memo to Gloria S.: What do we do about *Ambassadress?* Ms. Ambassador?

More Rumblings and Non Sequiturs

- Never confide in a newspaperman, even if you love him.
- One should be imprudent at least once a year.
- Racism is universal and irradicable; it is a blood disease for which there is no remedy. Even the victims of racism are racists.
- Prurience exists in all of us; life would be flavorless without it. I'd hold suspect anyone who denies this.
- There's no such thing as a *simple* pleasure. Smoking a fine cigar; looking at a sunset, a Rembrandt, a rolling sea, an Ingres drawing: all call for a most complex and sophisticated nerve mechanism. Can a dog respond to any of these, to a Beethoven sonata?
- Someone once said that "hatred is self-punishment." Bear this in mind next time you find yourself putting down a man or woman.
- Why don't authors write stories like Stephen Crane's *Open Boat* or Dostoevsky's *Notes from the Underground?*
- No American musician has yet demonstrated the genius equal to

that of Stravinsky or Shostakovich. Why? Or for that matter, why has America produced no Van Gogh, no Picasso, no Matisse?

- Herbert Marshall McLuhan represents a new breed of man who gets away with semantic nonsense while being handsomely paid. It is a new profession in our time: getting away with intellectual murder.
- Laugh as often as you can.
- More white women are attracted to black men than one might imagine. And vice versa. Why does society resist this fact? (Why doesn't a novelist use this notion as a theme?)
- We are virtually all second-rate. Why do most of us posture about and refuse to believe it? If we are not second-rate or inferior, how equate ourselves with Mozart, Aristotle, Shakespeare, or the author of the Book of Ecclesiastes?
- Everything can be explained, but explanations are not answers.
- Soul-saving and religious evangelism are the highest form of arrogance, usually practiced by idiots, rogues, or worst of all, dangerous hypocrites.
- There is no literary elite in New York—nor a literary clique.
- I hold all majority-opinion in question. I hold coterie opinion in doubt as well. Make up your own mind. Dare to be wrong.

Scraps from the Journal: More Cosmology

In my brief tenure on this bit of dust in the infinity of the cosmos, I've seen the development of the automobile, the telephone, the airplane, radio, penicillin, talkies, TV, jet planes, the A-bomb, Elvis Presley, the bikini; I've seen the moon-walk live on TV; I've gawked at the vaginal color photography in *Penthouse* magazine. In my time I've seen the emergence of some great writers: Kafka, Joyce, Faulkner, Eliot, Beckett. All of these within a bare few years. (And I can remember when gas lamps and horse-drawn buggies were used in Chicago.)

I console myself that there are two roles for each of us to perform: creator and/or consumer. I am the latter. I come home after a day at the desk and phone, remove my shoes and put on Mahler's Fifth Symphony; I may listen to the *Adagietto* and sip a dry mar-

tini. Or it may be Scott Joplin and Scotch on the rocks. I rational-
ize: *I am as great as Mahler or Joplin; without my response they
are nothing.* I pick up a book and consume it, digest and expel it in
one form or another. I may steal something from it, or utilize it in a
constructive way. The book would be less than common paper were
it not for my eyes and brain cells. As I read Mr. Eliot's poem,
"Gerontion," I too am a poet, certainly the poet's surrogate.

The reader may stop and ask himself: What was *this* editor doing
at the time he made the foregoing banal notations; what book was
he editing, working on? Something profound? A philosophical or
sociological essay? Was some tremendous intellectual project rubbing off on him?

Well, I did check back on my calendar-record, and the foregoing
notes were recorded in my journal while I was editing Vidal Sassoon's autobiography, *Sorry I Kept You Waiting, Madam* (1968).
Nothing terribly cosmic about *that* project. But editing Vidal's book
was an educative enterprise for me, and I learned considerable about
the world of high-style hairdressing and the superchic in that
strange galaxy. I discovered that it bears almost no relation to reality; that it provides a lot of loot if you're nimble and clever, as is
Sassoon. Someone called the beauty business "packaged hope," and
that certainly applies here.

My only quarrel with Vidal during the production and publication of his book was with his need to have a full-page photo of his
wife Beverly in the book. She's good to look at, but I felt it was an
editorial indulgence putting the author's wife's photo in his book. In
the end, I yielded to the pleas of young love.

Richard Burton's ex-wife Sybil (pre-Elizabeth) arranged a publication party for the book at her discotheque, Arthur. One of the
most overworked, pointless activities for a book publisher in New
York is organizing a party for The Beautiful People. My secret to
you, dear reader, is that The Beautiful People don't exist except in
the imagination of magazine and newspaper editors' minds. As I
watched the dancers on the discotheque floor, the only thought that
crossed my mind was—were there any buyers for Vidal's book at the
party? I concluded that there were few.

If you're looking for a connection between my ramblings about
life and literature and Sassoon, don't. I just thought of the Sassoon
book as part of my "life's record" at that particular time. Sassoon,
by the way, is immensely likeable.

Speaking of pointless "celebrity parties," we attended the opening of a Hirschfeld gallery-showing in November of 1974, in Greenwich Village. Al Hirschfeld is a clever (*New York Times*) theatrical caricaturist, but how anyone could confuse his bloodless drawings with Art and pay high prices for cartoons of actors and actresses, except for professional reasons, beats me. (I know he's represented in many museums.) Hirschfeld postured about, looking older at seventy-one than Titian at ninety-nine. (They are look-alikes, in beards anyway.) The "opening" brought out The Beautiful People. In this case we were glad to see Gloria Vanderbilt again; she's always warm and genuine. As her ex-publisher (I was responsible for her book, *Love Poems*), I have a deep-down nostalgic empathy for her. Sam Marx was there as a guest, and we brought him home and talked about the book he is going to write for Putnam's—the dual biography of Rodgers and Hart. A warm, richly endowed, anecdotal man, Marx. And so to bed.

Husbands: Beware of Poets

The male, heterosexual poet is, more often than not, a menace. Don't invite him to your home if you're married. He will have his hand up your wife's skirt before you can say Dylan Thomas. He'll finger every vagina, proposition every female, including nubile maidens and grandmothers, at every opportunity—certainly after his second vodka on the rocks.

He is afflicted with Don Juanism (satyriasis) for reasons that elude me. It may have something to do with the Lord Byron-syndrome. He's on a perpetual high in any gathering of adoring readers; he sees himself as a cross between Richard Burton and Dylan Thomas, unless he's of another gender—in which case, housewives, en garde!

Speaking of poets: I received an invitation from the Gotham Book Mart to attend a reception for the publication of a new book of poetry. Since I collect modern poetry, I planned to attend. When I checked my calendar on April 29, 1974, the day of the reception, I read the invitation and discovered that the book, published by The

Kulchur Foundation, was entitled *Rhymes of a Jerk* by one Larry Fagin. I never did get to that party but must remember to ask Andreas Brown to show me a copy of the book one day.

More Snapshots—and Some Memorable Moments

Meeting Carson McCullers (1943) in her publisher's office in New York (Hardwick Moseley introduced us) while securing reprint rights to her *The Heart Is a Lonely Hunter,* and remembering her short, little-girl white socks and Alice-in-Wonderland slippers, her bobbed hair, large teeth, shyness, and southern accent, and her just discharged-from-the-army husband . . . Yehudi Menuhin performing godlike at Carnegie Hall a solo evening of Bach, unaccompanied . . . my first reading of *Crime and Punishment* . . . the opening night of *Hair* . . . a Charles Ives concert in Venice, at the bejeweled Teatro Fenici, as the guests of the Bela von Blocks (who preferred Mozart) . . . handling three Gutenberg Bibles simultaneously at the Morgan Library . . . my first reading of Mario Puzo's first draft of *The Godfather* . . . acquiring the first, unfinished holograph draft of Dylan Thomas' poem, "Do Not Go Gentle into That Good Night" . . . the wild black and orange sunsets over Antigua . . . first airplane ride in a *hail*storm . . . first transatlantic flight with two continuous hours of turbulence . . . the little old lady who asked for my autograph, insisting that I was Barry Goldwater . . . first view of Picasso's *Guernica* at the Museum of Modern Art . . . lying on Eugene Braun-Munk's purple bed in Nice and feeling terribly decadent . . . luncheon with Jenny Bradley, the French agent, in her sun-drenched apartment, on my first visit to Paris . . . editorial session with George Burns and learning about being eighty years old . . . first view of Hieronymous Bosch's *Le Jardin des Delices* in the Prado, Madrid . . . receiving a large, prize-winning photograph of George Bernard Shaw, fully inscribed—and without charge! . . .

Me and William James

Very few book editors (if any) can boast of a literary relationship such as I've had, an experience without precedent as far as I know. It was with no less a person than William James. Yes, *the* William James of Harvard, one of our most eminent philosophers and psychologists and dabblers in parapsychological matters. He died, by terrestrial standards, in 1910. But there was nothing mundane about our professional kinship.

It happened this way:

Susy Smith, the writer on psychic matters, a woman highly receptive to the supraphysical world and with whom I worked on several books, proposed a book which I found irresistible. It was a work to be called *The Book of James,* comprising a series of messages *from beyond the grave* that had been coming to her over the years. Susy took dictation (automatic writing) from William James on her typewriter, and the result was an astonishing book published by Putnam's in 1974.

Naturally I was curious as to the content and style of these communications from this singular man, and during my reading of the manuscript, I made certain editorial suggestions. Eventually I received the following comment from Susy Smith: "James was very pleased with your editing. There are a few pet whimsicalities, or 'folksy' terms, that you removed that he was rather interested in keeping. He realizes that his dignity as a communicator is more important than having a colorful text, and so he bows to your better judgment . . . James thinks this thing is in very good shape now, and hopes you agree." Susy Smith also reported that William James "says to tell you that he admires you and your work and has great respect for you . . . and is grateful for the efforts you are making in his behalf."

I know of no other editor who has had the unique experience of working with an author beyond the grave, and I'll cherish this memory always. Along with P. T. Barnum, William James is one of my favorite Americans. To have his fascinating and gentle assertiveness, his goodwill, and cooperation from beyond the grave made my cup run over.

I wonder if James knew that I had once published a new edition of his book, *Psychology*, when I was with World, a handsome Living Library edition. And what I neglected to ask was whether William's brother Henry might want to dictate a new work of fiction.

———

About Money

Question: What's the most important thing in the world.

Answer: Cash flow.

Also Sex.

A lot of people lie about both.

Most of us (about 99 percent) are interested in having as much sex and money as possible. If you don't believe this, then you may not believe anything else I have to say here.

The constant preoccupation with either is injurious to the nervous system. There must be intervals when neither sex nor money is on your mind. As when fishing, or feeding squirrels.

But getting back to money: I am for the profit system, and for having just a bit more money in the bank than I'll ever need. I don't want to leave a fortune to anyone. Whatever I happen to have left over when I'm gone, my family is most welcome to use. I hope the Pentagon and its military budget doesn't get its bloody hands on it first.

Money: get as much of it as you can but don't kill yourself doing it. Don't kill others, either. Having it to spend is one of the sweetest gifts of life. Being *very* rich is offensive. To be very rich one must commit shameful, desperate, sometimes terrible acts. Most very rich people behave despicably. (Just observe them.)

Van Gogh painted some of the most beautiful pictures in all history. He was lifelong poor; did not sell a painting while alive. But his genius could never be outmatched by the combined wealth of all the Rockefellers. Don't misunderstand—I'm not opposed to money; simply don't fret your life away worrying about being rich. Be comfortable and civilized about money.

Probably the most urbane comment on the subject was made by John Kenneth Galbraith. In his admirable book, *The Affluent Society*, he said, "Wealth is not without its advantages, and the case to the contrary, although it has often been made, has never proved widely

persuasive." I like that, too. I've also frequently called young writers' attention to this sentence, to prove the power of ironic understatement.

Query: Why are so many U. S. senators multimillionaires?

―――――――

Wino

Sitting in the Zurich pub, the Kronenhalle, with the
Rainer Heumanns in the very booth where James Joyce and his
family took meals and drink . . . recalling the many fine impressionist paintings, the photo of Joyce on the booth's wall . . . recalling
a dinner at the Curtis Cates' in Paris, where I was seated next to
Stuart Gilbert. I had asked Gilbert "What was Joyce really like?"
since he was an intimate of his and worked closely with him for
many years. Gilbert leaned over and whispered in my ear: "Joyce
was a wino; he'd sip white wine all day, so elegantly; but he was
usually smashed. A real wino."

―――――――

Longevity

I've observed that dealers in antiquarian goods—for
instance, old books, old furniture—outlive the joggers, tennis players, and bicyclists. It's my belief that the longevous individual shuns
health foods and exercise and makes sure that no day passes without
a modest portion of wine or whiskey. George Bernard Shaw was the
exception, but he was bullheaded; he also laughed a good deal,
which is the other secret ingredient in the longevity formula.

―――――――

Modest Proposal No. 16847

There are hundreds of good-to-fine books of poetry
published each year; there are at least fifty excellent *little magazines*
in which poetry is published. They all need financial support. There-

fore, it is proposed that every poet who submits his work for publication must first give proof (cancelled checks?) to the little magazine, showing that he is a bona fide subscriber to at least a dozen little magazines. To be a genuine, franchised poet, he/she *must* support the magazines. We must equalize our little magazines with readership and subscriptions from the poets themselves. I think that fifty dollars a year is not too much for a poet to invest in his own market. Don't let the little magazines die. They matter!

Liberation Statistic, Pioneer circa 1960

In 1967 a little book of poetry, *Word Alchemy* by Lenore Kandel, was published. Earlier, Lenore had published a poetry book entitled *The Love Book*. (It is undated; possibly 1960?) Both of these books created waves. They are concerned in the main with sexual love, and Lenore moves on erotic high wires rarely before traversed by a woman for public viewing. Candid and lyrical, I think Lenore Kandel was one of the earliest to break (crash) through the erotic zone of quiet; also, she happens to be a fine poet. She says, "My favorite word is *yes!*" Look her up—you'll find her on Grove Press' list.

Lenore Kandel preceded Germaine Greer, Sandra Hochman, and Kate Millett and Gloria Steinem; she put female sexuality on the line when it was kind of lonely. I doubt that anyone in America, male or female, has written two more erotic books of poetry.

Trouble is, I think Lenore Kandel likes being a sex object.

Gallant Ladies of Letters

Janet Flanner, Lillian Hellman, Simone de Beauvoir, Eudora Welty, Katherine Anne Porter, Jessamyn-West, and Mary McCarthy. There are others who belong in this charmed and charming group. As I think of them, it comes to mind that there is no similar group among the male writers of my time.

The Public Conscience

John Simon, the theatre critic, is the conscience of our community and we should be grateful for at least one totally honest observer in town. While he is often the minority of one, count it a plus, an asset. He is the one voice that will utter "shoddy" or "*merde,*" without fear of retaliation from the Establishment or "interests." I often disagree with him—my tastes are sometimes low; but I find his dissent stimulating, and more than that, a force that compels me to examine my own responses more carefully. This is his chief merit and we must cherish him for that. The book review, fashion, and sports media could use a John Simon; more visceral integrity is needed in reporting and reviewing, and he has plenty!

P.E.N. Forever!

I love the organization called P.E.N. Its members are writers, translators, editors, publishers; its purpose and works are good. It takes a stand when necessary, and makes itself heard around the world.

In 1973–1975, under the guidance of Jerzy Kosinski, a gifted novelist (*The Painted Bird, Steps,* to name but two) and energetic humanitarian, the P.E.N. achieved a healthy record of "getting there with help" in many important SOS situations. Kosinski speaks up and masterminds the cable and letter protests to countries where authors are persecuted, tortured, suppressed, or worse. Kosinski is involved and concerned with all writers' problems and author-publisher relations. A man of goodwill, firm opinions, and a track record as a writer, he's been a great asset to P.E.N. Every professional writer should be a member even if he has no intention of being a joiner in the corporal sense; the P.E.N. *Newsletter* is a lively publication and alone worth the annual membership fee. While I seldom attend their meetings I find their *Newsletter* most worthwhile, and I am with the organization in spirit. (Address American P.E.N. 156 Fifth Avenue, New York, N.Y. 10010 for information.)

Three of my favorite women in the whole world are Marchette

and Joy (B. J.) Chute, and Elizabeth Janeway, all active workers in the P.E.N. vineyard. Their weekly cocktail receptions (until 1975 at the Hotel Pierre), are often a delight, a social bee for out-of-town writers and lonely locals seeking fellowship. (They honor newly published authors—give them carnations and a free drink.)

But why do all those starchy little ladies and ditto men insist on cornering every editor who comes to its meetings, with their musty manuscripts for sale? The meetings should be for good-fellowship, not business. They approach one with shining hope in their eyes, knowing full well their stuff will never see the light of day. Perhaps colonic irrigation is all that is required.

And then there are certain literary penguins who confront one with resonant clichés, pontifical pills; they move about with their martinis in hand, mincing and menacing. One children's book author advanced on me one day to propose "an enchanting book for children," and I had to respond with a protective reflex, "But I'm opposed to children's books."

I love the P.E.N., but there is a sense of "time warp" I feel every time I attend their parties. I hope this confession doesn't get me excommunicated.

Recollections of a P.E.N. dinner meeting: Elizabeth Janeway reading aloud the entire contents of Edward Gorey's book, *The Curious Sofa,* as an example of one of "the most shocking works of pornography of our time." A marvelous actress, she kept a straight face all the way. At the same evening's dinner, another glorious stalwart and soldier for free speech, Marya Mannes, got up and gave a fiery talk advocating phalluses and vaginal designs for the facades of some of our "boring cigar-box skyscrapers." (What lovely evenings we've had at the P.E.N.) And Barney Rosset, who was at the focal center of that "obscenity" dinner meeting, just sat there and grinned, knowing full well that he had done more than almost any other American publisher in the cause of liberating literature. And the spirit of Henry Miller hovered over us all.

From the Journal:
Remembering a Great Lady

What about religion?

I think of religion when I remember Zora Neale Hurston, and lunching with her at the Algonquin in the spring of 1959. She and the meeting stand out in my mind in a very special way. She was a vital, marvelous woman, and her death the following year was premature, tragic. A great spirit lost forever.

At lunch she gave me an inscribed copy of her book, *Tell My Horse,* in which a great many issues, including religion and creation, are discussed and resolved in simple fashion. I quote from the chapter on voodoo in this book, and must say it sums up my own views on religion and other related subjects. Please don't expect more on this subject from me; Zora covers it most adequately:

> Dr. Holly says that in the beginning God and His woman went into the bedroom together to commence creation. That was the beginning of everything and Voodoo is just as old as that. . . . Thus the uplifted finger in greeting in Voodoo is really phallic and that means the male attributes of the Creator. . . .

When you read the "Voodoo and Voodoo Gods" chapter in *Tell My Horse,* you will have experienced a profound mystical and religious experience.

More about Zora: I remember taking her to a Chicago South Side nightclub once, and dancing with her. I was the sole white male on the dance floor and she pointed this fact out to me with a chuckle, thinking I'd feel awkward. I know several other such vital and richly endowed black women: Gwendolyn Brooks, Maya Angelou, Rosa Guy—gifted writers, joyful, with sound digestions.

—————

Mad about Mozart

With Brigid Brophy, Lawrence Clark Powell, and about a few hundred million others, I am devoted to Mozart. I

would urge writers to read his letters, which Emily Anderson translated. Pure genius . . . indecent pleasures. To indicate the gross
earthiness of this *wunderkind,* I suggest you read some of his letters
to Maria Anna Thekla, his cousin (*The Letters of Mozart and His
Family,* p. 358). You'll never forget them. Shades of Rabelais and
Henry Miller!

Brigid Brophy, a lady totally mad about Mozart, said: "Our century, which will surely be the most execrated in history (provided it
allows history to continue so that there is someone to execrate it)
has this to its credit: it is recognizing Mozart." (This from her
Mozart the Dramatist, Penguin Books.)

Just as no home should be without a few thousand books, one
should have *all of* Mozart's quartets and quintets on hand; they are
really quite inexpensive—balm for the bleaker hours.

This extraordinary composer died at the age of thirty-five, having
made the world infinitely richer, as had Shakespeare. Do we cherish
our treasures enough? How many of Mozart's 626 compositions do
you have? Most of them are available on LP records.

Fantasy: One night in 1974 Roslyn and I were celebrating our
ninth wedding anniversary by attending a Mostly Mozart Festival
concert at Lincoln Center. On the program was the Cleveland
Quartet, featuring Misha Dichter the pianist and Gervase de Peyer
the clarinetist, two extraordinary performers. Twice during the program I began to have powerful extrasensory vibrations; there was a
large folding screen behind the players on the stage, and every so
often I had a premonition that young Mozart himself, dressed in the
wig and concert plumage of his day, was peeking out at the audience from the edge of the screen. I kept staring at the corner of the
stage where I felt certain he was standing. I also had a strong hunch
that he would suddenly pop out, take a bow, run to the piano, push
aside Dichter, and take over. MOZART APPEARS ON AVERY FISHER
HALL STAGE ran the headlines in the following morning papers.

But sanity was restored.

One of the special privileges of being the editor of an author
who is a music or play critic is getting the chance to be invited to
concerts, opera, ballets, and opening nights of plays. I especially
enjoyed the friendship of Louis Biancolli, who was a New York
City critic of music for the now-defunct *Telegram.* He often gave

me tickets, sometimes an hour before curtain time. Since I lived in the Village, I could get to any of the concert halls or theatres within thirty minutes of his call.

Biancolli was working on his *Mozart Handbook* for over a solid year, and during the gestation period, I must have read a million words dealing with the composer, his family, friends, and his times. Selecting and rejecting material was the big job. One of the great dividends of this particular project was free tickets to almost every Mozart concert and opera while the book was a-borning.

I miss the exhilaration of publishing that book and the intense musical education I received in a period of one year. Biancolli almost never sat during a performance; he was a pacer. So I would often sit alone, and then, during intermission, he would rush up to me and deliver one of his very Italian lectures in capsule, filling me in on the quality of the work and the particular performance of the soloist or the conductor. For a while I was *the* Mozartian on our block. I may still be, since I play Mozart quartets often while reading; he is one of the few composers whose work I can enjoy while occupied with a book.

―――――

Something Happened?

Egged on by high expectations, do-or-die devotion (or angel dust), the reviewers—most of them—sort of perjured themselves in the fall of 1974. Got carried away. They canonized Joseph Heller, hailed and acclaimed his first novel in twelve years, *Something Happened.* They sent the book soaring, like mercury in a fever thermometer, to the top of the best-seller lists.

If these reviewers are the custodians of American literature, then I say they're Keystone Cops and had better turn in their tin badges. Because Joe Heller's novel is one soporific epic—overlong and boring.

Mr. L. E. Sissman of *The New Yorker* (an exception among the Establishment) opened his review of the book by saying, "I'm extremely sorry to say that *Something Happened* is a painful mistake." And he went on to tell us why, in honest, cogent language. I simply couldn't believe Sissman. I went out and bought the book, and after struggling with the first eighty pages, put it aside and proclaimed Mr. Sissman in a class with the lad who declared that the emperor wore no clothes. (Wilfrid Sheed seemed to admire the book, but also referred to its "droning repetitions.")

In the main, the reviewers took to the book like kittens to catnip. The question is, Why? Why did so many praise this dreadfully dull and hopelessly unreadable book? And why did it sell so well? I have no ready answers. *The New York Times Book Review*, in its annual summation of Best Books of the Year, featured *Something Happened*, recommending it to its entire readership. Mr. Heller should send in a lifetime subscription to the *TBR;* and to its editors, a few cases of Dom Perignon.

Footnote to the above: One of the natural philosophers, and all-round great storytellers in America today is Isaac Bashevis Singer. He's always a delight to meet, to listen to, to read. When honesty and no bullshit responses are wanted, try Mr. Singer. Israel Shenker quotes him as saying, "If a book was boring, we used to throw it away. Now it is considered that a book must be boring to be good." Singer also says, "Some authors are so good-natured they will give you quotes saying your book is a masterpiece no matter how bad it is. . . . If they would give such quotes about food or medicine they would be put in prison."

He may have something there. In any event, I declare Mr. Singer Man of the Year for forthrightness.

La Vie Intellectual

Seated at dinner at Anne and Bob Shanks' home was David Susskind, New York's leading intellectual and authority on everything, and he spoke of the joys of breakfast in bed on Sundays.

I volunteered the fact that I prepared breakfast at our home on Sundays. Whereby he dropped his fork and stared at me. "*You* make breakfast on Sunday morning?" he asked in an astonished tone that might have implied something gauche.

"Yes," I said, "and I enjoy it. Roslyn works, you know, and does most of the cooking during the week."

Susskind ignored my explanation and turned to his dinner neighbor and reported my confession. The fact that I made breakfast on Sunday was soon known to the fourteen persons having dinner that night. Then he turned and stared at me, shaking his head.

I wonder what he thinks of President Ford's fetching his own morning newspaper.

Would you like to know what I make for Sunday breakfast? Smoked salmon with onions; cream cheese on toasted bagels; and scrambled eggs with onions. Roslyn makes the coffee, an art I've never mastered.

A Few Favorites That Didn't Make It

Some of the best books don't often make it in their time. I have more than a few favorites—books I sponsored, in which I invested time and high enthusiasm, that never reached the goal line.

When I was in Paris in early 1968, the city was experiencing a political upheaval far more alarming than anything we were witnessing in America at the time. The French students and workers were whipping up what looked like a spontaneous Marxist revolution. The city's facilities were crippled; banks were closed; airlines were out; public buildings were swarming with students, paintbrushes in hand, who were slapping slogans in red paint across the facades—a situation that had the city fathers reeling and the tourists scared spitless.

I arrived in Paris on the "last flight," with no ground crew at Orly to shepherd the plane safely in. I got a taxi by hook and by crook (mostly the latter), and drove to my hotel where Roslyn was to meet me. As I taxied through the streets I was by turn fascinated, then alarmed. I was exhilarated in that I was witnessing history in the making (I thought); I was on the reviewing stand of history; I was an observer of a great human and political crisis. But it stopped being interesting when I saw hundreds of black, ominous trucks loaded with armed police and soldiers. They were everywhere, looking grim and murderous. The French intellectual was delivering a real seismological jolt to the Establishment. *La goose!*

As a publisher I began to drool; I wanted the story in book form, and first! The whole story, the record for the American audience. I also wanted the full details for my personal edification. I was fortunate in getting two authors, Patrick Seale and Maureen McConville, two top-flight journalists of the London *Observer* staff, to collaborate on the book. It was signed up, written quickly, and published the same year, 1968. It was entitled *Red Flag/Black Flag: French Revolution 1968.*

The book was authoritative, based on eye-witness knowledge and a deep awareness of French politics. And it was well written—dramatically, enthrallingly written. The opening page begins: "Two hours before dawn on Monday, March 18, 1968, a left-wing student commando crossed the Seine to the fashionable Right Bank, and, with small explosive charges, blew in the plate-glass windows of the Paris offices of the Chase Manhattan Bank, the Bank of America, the Trans World Airlines."

The narrative continues like an adventure novel. It was well reviewed, well advertised, and rather widely displayed. But the end result was a modest trade sale, perhaps less than 7,500 copies. (Happily, Ballantine brought the book out in paperback, helped to find a good audience for it, and enabled us to recoup our advance.) The book is a valuable, important, readable account. Why didn't it sell?

Another notable book I brought to Putnam's (the William Morris Agency handled the contract) was Robert Vaughn's *Only Victims* (1972), a study of show business blacklisting. It was well documented, fearless in reporting some of the ugliest aspects of the period. It presented the names of all the players and exposed their cowardices, and betrayals as well as their heroism, in the face of McCarthyistic terror.

For those unfamiliar with the subject, it is a study of the activities of the House Committee on Un-American Activities, authorized on May 26, 1938 by the United States House of Representatives. Its purpose: to investigate subversives in the American theatre and other cultural areas of American life. It was a period of witch-hunting, naming of names, incrimination, perjury, accusation, lying, betrayal—friends turning on friends. It was a fearful time when the "phantom of communism" was across the land. The author, an actor on television (*The Man from U.N.C.L.E.*), films, and the legitimate stage, was the first person in his profession to publicly criticize the

United States involvement in Vietnam. Gore Vidal once called Vaughn the "factual William Buckley of the left." The great American woman and playwright, Lillian Hellman, replied to questions asked of her by writing to Chairman John Wood of the Committee; her letter, reproduced in the book, is worth the price of admission. One sentence remains clearly in my memory: "I cannot and will not cut my conscience to fit this year's fashions . . ."

The book sold modestly and never made the clubs or paperback. I'm still glad to have been its editor.

Another book I was proud to sponsor and publish was Clark R. Mollenhoff's *The Pentagon,* published in 1967. I considered it a daring exposé of the power-madness prevailing in Washington and the ineptness of the defense secretary, Robert S. McNamara. I was shocked at some of Mollenhoff's disclosures, particularly those relating to contract-granting, the mythology of Pentagon efficiency, the false claims, and judgment errors on a grand scale.

This important, 441-page study also sold only modestly, and no paperback reprinter took it on. It illustrates how power corrupts and absolute power corrupts absolutely. Anyone interested in the American war machine should dig up a copy of Mollenhoff's illuminating book. Despite its failure in the market it is still, today, explosive stuff.

Getting Away with Murder

The TV programs—talk shows, interview shows, and panel discussions—get away with murder. Every VIP (some are considerably less than VIP) who has written a book is invited to appear and give of himself—for *free.* If he or she is witty, personable, or controversial, the viewer gets free entertainment and enlightenment; but most of all he gets the zoological thrill of seeing a celebrity, live, on the tube.

The book publishers and their publicity people pat themselves on the back every time the "Today Show" or Johnny Carson or Merv Griffin allows an author to appear on their shows. But the shows pay nothing to many of the author-guests. The question is, Why not?

The TV people argue that an appearance on one of their pro-grams is great publicity for the author and his/her book. Yet musi-cians and actors who perform on the shows also reap the benefits of wide publicity, and *they* get paid. In essence, the author is also a performer when he appears on the TV screen; if he had no public appeal or entertainment value, he wouldn't be allowed anywhere near the show. Publishers, therefore, should stop handing over their celebrities to TV without charge.

The fees paid by TV shows to the author-celebrities could, if necessary, be put into a common fund and used to pay for news-paper ads for new young writers who are without budgets. Every young writer, every first novelist, should be given a few thousand dollars from this fund to publicize his or her first book.

Of course, this proposal will never be accepted and I will be put down as an impractical dreamer. But remember, you heard it here.

A greater offense than not paying the guest is the rudeness of the interviewers. Guests are often treated like freaks. One of the worst abuses is the interruption for a commercial—usually for a dog food, a deodorant, or a denture cleaner—when the interviewer cuts into a speaker's thoughts, often in the middle of a sentence. I've wit-nessed this indignity countless times and suffered with the speaker for the bad manners of the TV interviewer. *Advice:* If this happens to you, please speak up with the following two words: "Fuck off" or the equivalent. The interviewer will never forget you.

I recall one incident when Moshe Dayan was speaking earnestly and was about to make a very cogent and personal point. His sen-tence was cut into for a commercial. Apparently he protested, be-cause after the commercial the interviewer apologized for interrupt-ing Dayan's comments and read the conclusion of Dayan's state-ment to the public. Dayan must have anticipated my advice. Am wondering how one says "fuck off" in Hebrew.

As of this writing, I've appeared once on television. It was at the urging of my author, Liberace, whose autobiography we were just publishing. I was absolutely averse to the idea and argued that I had nothing to say. Liberace disagreed and said he would "like to discuss the process of writing my book with my editor on television." The studio also urged me to appear and I finally yielded.

I must admit I was neither nervous nor forgetful; we did talk at some length, and judging from the calls and mail, my appearance was satisfactory. But—I was not paid. And though I deferred to

Liberace on that one occasion, I will never again appear on television unless I am paid standard rates. There is no vanity in this decision. Nor is it a matter of greed. The TV people have fantastic budgets and can well afford to pay anyone they think enough of to invite to appear on a show—especially a network show.

Just a week ago, as a matter of fact, I was phoned and invited to appear on a program to discuss rare books and answer questions. "What are you paying me?" I asked.

The reply was a shocked pause; then, "But we have no budget."

I hung up quietly.

My Favorite Story

My favorite story is the one of Tolstoy's dealing with the question, How Much Land Does a Man Need? Even though you may know the answer, it's well worth being reminded of again, because this particular story applies to everyone.

The answer to the question is, of course, "Six feet of ground."

Envy of the rich denotes a sickness and a distortion of values. Aim high, say I, but remember, Tolstoy's answer stands. One can fulfill oneself on a $12,000–$15,000 annual income; likewise, one can feel deprived or impoverished with $100,000. Aping the follies of the rich leads to ulcers.

An editor who turns green with envy over another editor's success is pitiable. Envy leads to nothing. What matters is to make a decision, decide what you want, then try your damnedest to let it happen.

So Who Needs the Moon?

The numerous books on the moon-shot were failures. Countless thousands of books on the subject were remaindered; ditto numbers of dollars were lost by publishers. Norman Mailer did all right with his book on the moon; his advance was, to pun deliberately, astronomical.

When are we going to try for Jupiter? We *know* that's where the action is.

A number of planets may possibly have organic and other forms of life. Why our astronauts have not tried for them, instead of the moon, is a logical question; we all knew the bloody moon was dead. A billion dollars spent in exploring the mysteries of Antarctica, the South American jungles, Australia, or Portugal would prove more rewarding, I think, than visits to the moon. Let's subsidize a giant archaeological digs department and explore. "Old men should be explorers," said Yeats.

Speaking of Sex

Speaking of exploration—no one really knows much about the mysteries of sex. Of course we all have ample assistance from the manuals on how to achieve "joy" and orgasm, and all that. But the mystery of sex, the real mystery and truth of sexuality, should be investigated—the arcane biological aspects, that is. Does anyone have a key to the *true* structure and nature of the sperm and the ovum? The male hormone, testosterone? Spermiogenesis, as an intellectual and scientific pursuit, is far more interesting than, say, Indian mysticism or biofeedback. Next to the business of food and liquid intake, fertilization is certainly the single most important subject in the world.

The Last of the Libertarians

The publication of native Chicagoan Elmer Gertz's *To Life,* in May of 1974, brought back for me—and pretty vividly as an ex-Chicagoan—the memory of a man of a special breed. There aren't too many Elmer Gertzes around any more. What's so special about Elmer? "Well, dammit," as Carl Sandburg would have said, "he's just crazy enough to always be telling the truth." And remember, his profession was the law.

Gertz preceded me on this earth by about a year. I often ran into him when I lived in Chicago, and I often think about him and about his activities in literature. For instance, whatever happened to that manuscript of his dealing with the life and times of Colonel McCormick of Chicago? Eh? At any rate, he stopped the suppression of Miller's *Tropic of Cancer*—for which, gold stars!

Elmer Gertz has done too much good for one man's lifetime, and he's still at it. As a lawyer he spent more time defending clients in civil and constitutional rights' cases than he did in individual "commercial" cases for fees. He battled like a demon for free speech. He helped get Nathan Leopold out of jail. He fought and still fights for public housing; and he wasn't afraid to tell off Joe McCarthy when that kind of bravado called for guts.

Chicago should proclaim an Elmer Gertz Day; he's one of the last of the Mohicans, an honest lawyer.

Gertz was described by his publisher as a Don Quixote. To my way of thinking (and I love Don Quixote) that appellation is a canard. Like Sam Ervin, he simply dotes on the American Constitution, which includes the freedom to read, the freedom to speak.

───────────

My Favorite Recipe

I've admitted to a loathing of most cookbook writers. But I can't resist giving you, free of charge, my recipe for preparing *tripe*.

Now when you ask most people if they like tripe, they're probably unable to answer because they think tripe is some sort of exotic fish. (Critics use the word to characterize certain books.) But tripe is *meat;* it comes from the stomach of a cow and was once the cheapest of all meats, eaten by peasants. When you find that you enjoy tripe, you will always long for it in a special way, almost as one longs for sex.

Tripe, which must be thoroughly, carefully cleaned, takes a long time to cook and prepare; about five hours of cooking is necessary. (Or you can buy it precooked, which will save a lot of time.) Iron pots are recommended for cooking, never aluminum.

Tripe should be cut into narrow strips before cooking—finger-width. Plenty of butter must be used in the cooking water; also thinly sliced onions, garlic, chopped mushrooms, chopped fresh dill, ground peppercorns, *and in particular, bay leaves.* Without bay leaves an important element is missing. Salt generously.

The tripe should be scalded and the water drained off; remove black parts. Tripe *should be served very hot,* in simmering sauce, and mashed potatoes dipped in the tripe gravy provides the extra Lucullan touch. Be sure you have a sofa on which to collapse after eating your fill of this extraordinary dish.

The foregoing is not a professionally presented recipe, but any cook book of merit will give you more technical details. But be sure that bay leaves and enough seasoning are introduced, and give it ample cooking time.

Please write me if you feel I've given you a bum steer.

Reincarnation Department

In the late sixties I worked with Eileen J. Garrett, the medium. She was writing her autobiography, *Many Voices.* We had corresponded, spoken on the phone, and I had negotiated through her assistant, Allan Angoff. (He also wrote an Introduction for the book.) I was most eager to meet and talk with this internationally famous psychic, one of the "aristocrats of the psychic world," and finally, we had our first luncheon meeting.

When I sat down at the table, she leaned toward me, studied me for a moment, then said, "Aren't you one of my former lovers?" She had the eyes and monolithic look of Madame Blavatsky, at least judging by the *photos* I've seen of the Theosophist.

I've heard interesting opening gambits, but this one took me off-guard. My reply finally was, "I'm certain, but in a previous incarnation."

That seemed to set well with her, for at that point she proceeded with the business of ordering a three-star luncheon for all of us. Putnam's published the book in 1968.

Eileen Garrett was much more than a psychic; she was a scholar, a great reader, a friend of William Butler Yeats, H. G. Wells, Sidney and Beatrice Webb, and countless other notables in literature and world affairs. And important, too—she had one of the best chefs in France working for her in her St. Paul-de-Vence headquarters, that is where the Parapsychology Foundation met annually.

She was born in Ireland and did indeed see fairies at the bottom of her garden. Or did she? I was never sure. She was not one easily led into making absolute statements.

The late ex-movie vamp, Dagmar Godowsky, always greeted me at New York parties with the line, "Excuse me, but aren't you one of my former husbands?" I suppose that if every man to whom she said this were to come to Madison Square Garden at the same time, it would be filled to capacity. But it made for a bit of relaxed "social intercourse."

One day, out of perversity, I took Arthur Ceppos by the arm and led him to her. (He's a publisher of sex and psychological books.) I said to her, "I want you to meet the foremost authority on female orgasm in the world," and left the two of them, abruptly.

Prejudices and Very Private Adores/Abhors

Lists of likes and dislikes can be a bore, but they can, if honestly presented, also serve as an inventory of one's makeup. In case you're interested:

I ABHOR: liberals . . . calorie-counting and health foods . . . literary workshops . . . jewelry on men . . . "ballsy" women (except Bella Abzug) . . . cookbook authors (except three) . . . pollsters . . . hair "stylists" . . . Barbra Streisand . . . "best-dressed" women . . . country music . . . young panhandlers . . . raw fish . . . blue eye shadow . . . Keystone Cop mustaches . . . politicians . . . British cooking . . . political oratory . . . British television serials . . . name-dropping . . . porno magazine shops . . . trendy male dressers . . . borax furniture . . . TV talk shows . . . Hare Krishna dancers . . . the Duchess of Windsor . . . airport customs . . . TV and radio commercials . . . stylish people . . . telephonic solicitation . . . fundraising letters . . . evangelists . . . juvenile actors . . . automobile horns . . . "limited editions" of coins . . . the word "alienation" . . . overstylized personalities . . . cocktail parties . . . liars . . . glass sculpture . . . porcelain birds . . . alcoholics . . . film bigshots . . . the word "goober" . . . newspaper "celebrity" photos . . . schlock rock . . . ear benders . . . snakes . . .

I ADORE: radicals . . . Paris . . . San Francisco . . . Mozart . . . Sex . . . Chagall . . . Garbo . . . delicatessen food . . . chili con carne . . . cold vodka . . . I. F. Stone . . . Norman Mailer . . . ice cream . . . *Turandot* . . . feminine women . . . Robert Moses . . . Fellini . . . Colleen Dewhurst . . . movies . . . colored socks . . . the Museum of Modern Art . . . style . . . William Shawn . . . burlesque . . . French bread . . . Matisse . . . Jane Fonda . . . Scott Joplin . . . classical guitar . . . tripe, properly cooked . . . poetry . . . paté . . . Sophia Loren . . . walking . . . limericks . . . sitting . . . chamber music . . . Vanessa Redgrave . . . stage magic . . . good pornography . . . Dory Previn . . . motoring . . . Lina Wertmuller . . . corn on the cob . . . cotton clothing . . . the Frick Museum . . . Firenzi . . . Kurt Vonnegut, Jr. . . . *Mad* magazine . . . sunrises . . . J & B Scotch . . . Shirley MacLaine . . . green grass . . . super pizzas . . . *Don Giovanni* . . . Olivier . . . Vivian Vance . . . Laurel and Hardy films . . . Mick Jagger singing "Going Home" . . . Doug Henning, the illusionist . . .

7   *Lo! The Writer*

Verbosity

People talk too much; writers often write too much. The present book would have been much shorter if my contract had called for fewer words.

What prompts the foregoing are two very small books that happen to catch my eye—bedside books. Both are treasures. One is Eudora Welty's *On Short Stories*, a 53-page book that every short-story writer should read a few dozen times. Miss Welty writes well and makes sense all the way. Her book is full of apothegms relating to the craft and aesthetics of writing. For example: "What's seen is what we're interested in." And: "The plot in many instances is quite openly a projection of character." Or: "Don't we after all want the same thing? A story of beauty and passion and truth? When we are in the act of writing we are alone and on our own, in a kind of absolute state of Do Not Disturb."

I met Miss Welty in the dining room of the Algonquin one day and found her a great and modest lady. I brought her my copy of *On Short Stories* the following day and she signed it. What a treasure for bibliophile and editor.

The other little book I refer to is gold—unalloyed gold: *The Elements of Style* by William Strunk, Jr., with revisions, an introduction, and a new chapter on writing by E. B. White. In a sense, this book (71 pages) and a good dictionary are all a writer needs. Concise, witty, intelligent, this book tells you everything you ought to know about writing. The original was published in 1918; the edition with White's material, in 1959.

Strunk makes the rules of grammar fascinating; he must have been a marvelous teacher. As White says, Strunk's attempt was "to cut the vast tangle of English rhetoric down to size and write his rules and principles on the head of a pin." White adds, "Its vigor is unimpaired, and for sheer pith I think it probably sets a record that is not likely to be broken."

I must give you one example of the good sense that is prevalent throughout this little book:

> Vigorous writing is concise. A sentence should contain no unnecessary words, a paragraph no unnecessary sentences, for the same reason that a drawing should have no unnecessary lines and a machine no unnecessary parts. This requires not that the writer make all his sentences short, or that he avoid all detail and treat his subjects only in outline, but that every word tell.

It's unthinkable that any publisher's editor would not have read this little book; but on the chance that my reader may not have heard of the book, I render him/her a service by urging the immediate acquisition of the book, *The Elements of Style*.

Another small book in another area and in an altogether different vein—a short work that proves again that brevity and high quality often go together—is John Hersey's masterpiece, *Hiroshima*. It runs to 118 pages. It is about a half dozen people who witnessed and survived the first atom bomb dropped on Hiroshima on August 6, 1945. All the elements that make for an enduring work of art are here. William Strunk would have been pleased with the quality of Hersey's prose style. James Michener would have taken a thousand pages to do the same job. Hersey's book, published in 1946, will endure. No one has written a finer historic "report" in American literature.

In a time when printing papers are scarce and expensive, the practice of being brief in books should be encouraged.

To Be a Writer:

1. Learn to light small fires so that you can burn your early drafts.

2. Discipline yourself not to read stories aloud to friends; if your editor is willing, read to her/him;

3. Develop a geiger counter for the detection of clichés and platitudes, tired and ineffectual words and phrases. To be a writer

of fiction you must employ a third eye; you must tell a story—and *see* it in the telling—and keep telling a story, if a story is your objective. If you have an idea, don't smother it to death with verbiage, keep it clean and pure and breathing all the way.

Most would-be writers will never be published because they haven't the necessary strength and patience. Authorship is a fantasy, a dream of most aspirants. It's a glittering notion, a mirage with their name on the title page. Writing demands self-conspiracy, sweat, and humility—a touch of madness, too. But most importantly, writing means rewriting and rewriting. And rewriting.

Writing a first-rate book is no easier than climbing Mount Everest.

I think Everest is easier.

Character: Without it there is nothing. A brick wall, a face, a sidewalk, a tree—they all have character. Cézanne saw it in a dish of apples. If you are a writer you will bring character to life in your work.

Writer: describe a wall.

What is a good age to begin writing? I think about age ten. By twenty, one should have sold a few stories or poems. Truman Capote started writing at ten or eleven and got his first acceptances at seventeen. (His Madame Récamier photo helped him get his first book launched.) F. Scott Fitzgerald published his first novel when he was twenty-four. A good time, too. But not too soon.

Originality, Wherefore Art Thou?

Why do so many novelists beat the same old bushes in plotting their stories? Why so many glaring examples of theft from current successes? Why must one smasher of a novel beget a dozen imitations within a period of a year or so? Category fiction with the trite situations, overfamiliar and soapy themes written in trite and soapy fashion—who needs them? Why do publishers rush to take them on? Or commission them?

When someone comes along with a story idea that is fresh, or freshly handled, the world takes notice, even applauds. Peter Shaffer's play, *Equus,* could have been a great novel; it's the perfect example of what I mean by originality. It is a play embued with boldness and imagination and impact—greatness. I say this despite the carping of a few ineffectual though highly placed psychiatrists and play reviewers.

One of the reasons for the appeal of *Equus* is that it doesn't have the genre tarnish. To quote the author, "It's not a crime story," a whodunit. Shaffer accepted the characterization, "*why*dunit," but added that "the shadows that fall on the play are deeper."

Category fiction is usually boring, except to insomniacs, although the stuff continues to prove a dependable commodity on a small scale (it does a bit better in paperbacks). The average Gothic novel sells around 6,000–8,000 copies in hardcover. We could do with a reduction of that output.

As is true of most great stories, the play *Equus* is based on a true incident: a stable boy in England did indeed blind a number of horses. But the imagination at work, not the bare facts, is what gives the play its power and meaning—and yes, its greatness. *Watership Down* by Richard Adams is another example of getting away from the stereotyped category.

There are dozens of fresh areas to explore, and writers should seek them out or employ a fresh vision in *re-creating* themes that are currently in vogue. Editors shouldn't encourage authors to trudge down old weatherbeaten roads. I don't agree with John Wain who said that "small writers seek for novelty, either in gimmicks of presentation or in the itchy search for a 'new' theme." Originality leavened with imagination is not to be confused with gimmickery. A fresh note, a new insight, is always welcome in fiction. But in the end, of course, it all comes down to the word "art." The individual writer's talent, his gift, will be the determining factor of its "originality."

Adjectivitis

It's a disease. It is one of the author's natural enemies. Like the weather, everyone talks about it, but few do anything about it.

I'm naturally leery about adjectives and avoid them whenever possible. Gertrude Stein said it all: "Adjectives are not really and truly interesting."

Steve Shagan is the only novelist with whom I worked who bothered to thank me for removing some twenty adjectives from his novel, *City of Angels*—his doing so was the sign of a professional and a man with humility. Most writers fight to retain them.

If you find excessive adjectives in the present book please feel free to excise them.

Etiquette for Authors

The following is offered in the friendliest spirit; the purpose is to educate the newly published author and help to achieve a harmonious relationship. I once suggested devoting an evening's discussion to this subject to a P.E.N. official, a lovely woman who is also a well-known writer, and she replied with, "You mean 'etiquette for publishers,' dontchu?"

1. Don't drop in on your editor without an appointment.

2. Stay away from the advertising, sales, and promotion departments.

3. Don't phone on publication date and tell your editor your Aunt Mabel couldn't find your book in her local bookshop in Sioux Falls, or for that matter in Doubleday's, Kroch-Brentano's, or Pickwick.

4. Don't ask your editor, "How come my book wasn't reviewed in *The New York Times?*" or elsewhere.

5. Don't phone your editor at his home unless the problem is too urgent to wait; remember, your editor may be taking a well-earned nap, or he may simply be smashed and not able to respond.

6. Advertising is the touchiest of subjects and I would not push

for more space, more frequent TV appearances, or comment abrasively on the physical appearance of the ads.

7. Don't contact or date paperback reprinters and book-club editors with the idea of doing some behind-the-scenes selling of your book. Wining and dining club and paperback personnel is the rights director's job; don't try oily-oozy charm tactics because they will not work.

8. Don't bug your editor about the book jacket art; that's the publisher's domain.

9. Don't ask for more free copies of your book than you are entitled to by contract.

10. Don't annoy the booksellers with queries about sales and displays; they will probably lie to you anyway. Unless you are Linda Lovelace, they aren't interested in live authors. (Gotham Book Mart is one of the few exceptions.)

11. Keep your editor posted *by letter* on the progress of your book under contract; if delays are expected, give him an approximate new delivery date.

12. When your editor reports a six-figure reprint or book-club sale, buy him/her a lunch.

(If I should suddenly leave the publishing business, the reason will probably lie in the fact that my nervous system is no longer able to cope with authors' queries about advertising and reviews.)

How to Write a Bestselling Novel

I can handle this question readily.

The secret, in one word, is *identification.*

Examples in proof:

1. When 240,000 hardbound copies of *Portnoy's Complaint* were sold at $6.95 retail, it came as no surprise to me. I had already read the great "liver scene" and knew that Mr. Roth had hit a gusher. The highly publicized element, *masturbation,* did the trick. *Reader identification.* Need I belabor the fact that almost everyone (except a few of my friends) identify with masturbation—especially today, when women are widely encouraged to practice it? Philip Roth had the genius to recognize this truth, and he employed this "secret"

element in a most artistic and telling fashion. Incidentally, he wrote a comic classic.

2. The enormous interest in, and great commercial success of, the book *Alive* (the Andes crash story by Piers Paul Read) is due to the secret ingredient, cannibalism.* Millions of people everywhere in the world will not admit to it, but inherent in our taste buds is the appetite for the forbidden—human flesh—in one degree or another. *Identification.* Kissing and sucking and fondling of human flesh, not forgetting biting—how far removed are they from cannibalism itself? "Succulent" is a word often used to describe an attractive female. Nureyev once said of the dancer Lucette Aldous, "She has nice legs, *edible* legs." I pursue this no further; Krafft-Ebing and others have covered the subject too well. The film, *The Night Porter,* came mighty close to being a story of cannibalism.

Make no mistake, it wasn't the disaster aspect of the story that sold *Alive;* check *Portnoy* again, for the *eating* elements.

3. Mario Puzo's novel, *The Godfather,* is a perfect example for our identification thesis. *Power and crime.* We all identify with Don Corleone who exemplified both elements. Crime fiction and true-crime narratives, when done with skill and strong narrative power, will titillate the reader like catnip; most readers have fantasies about committing the perfect crime, solving the unsolvable crimes, or exercising power of a supernatural order. In *The Godfather* we also find the element of *magic.* Everyone, from the kiddies to the geriatrics, enjoy magic: the Don can grant any wish; he can pull a rabbit out of a hat or secure a major film role for a has-been. All he requires in payment is some "service" at some undetermined date. Payment deferred.

So there you have it: *Identification.*

You are wondering, What about *sex?*—aren't you?

There is not quite enough mystery about sex any longer; we are swimming in it. Sex is provided in one form or another in every kind of book. You can get it in either explicit or subtle form. John O'Hara and Frances Parkinson Keyes and Taylor Caldwell provide it in their fashion, as do Robbins and Wallace in theirs.

John Updike, a talented and horny novelist, who writes with wit, perception, and high style, is the best purveyor of *literary sexuality*—something not easily achieved by your everyday fiction-

---

*Flesh and Blood, A History of the Cannibal Complex by Reay Tannahill, touches on the theme fully.

izer. As an interesting tangent, and obviously unable to contain himself, Updike recently published a poem, entitled *Cunts*, in a limited, signed edition of 276 copies at $25 per copy. It is ,handsomely printed, comprises sixteen pages, starts with: "The Venus de Milo didn't have one, at least no pussy/that left its shadow in the marble, but Botticelli's Venus . . ." There is some splendid poetry here, and a few sequences that make one gulp with surprise ("I pulled a Tampax with my teeth," for example). As poetry it is top-level; as a subject, its appeal is obvious. The point, however, is this: Sex *per se* is not the answer for a would-be best-seller novelist, though it may nevertheless be apropos to quote Cyril Connolly, who, in writing about Henry Miller, said: "Art is larger than sex, although without sex there would be no artists."

Examine the first three themes above, and consider which path you will follow: masturbation, cannibalism, crime. But in utilizing any, or all, of these themes, be sure you are telling a story; be sure your characters are not faceless, that they are, in fact, recognizable forever after, once introduced. Can you do that?

There is one other universal theme—*constipation*. Everyone is at some time or another concerned with that subject. *Identification*. Whether constipation is suited to the novel is a moot point. Still, it served well in a John Osborne play dealing with Martin Luther; in play and film it was highly successful. Perhaps a novelist seeking a new theme might consider it. Felicitously treated, it just might make the best-seller lists, especially if all comes out well in the end. Catharsis through peristalsis!

And then, too, there's this theory about seagulls.

And rabbits.

———————

Telling It Straight

I love simple, simply presented facts. For example, Brigid Brophy says in her book on Ronald Firbank, "Psychology certainly existed in 1900, which is the date on the title-page of the original edition of *The Interpretation of Dreams*. But few people knew it did. That original edition consisted of 600 copies and took eight years to sell out."

What a lot of information to assimilate in those three short sentences. The simple declarative sentence is at a premium today. Almost no one makes a statement without preceding it with "to tell the truth," or "in point of fact," or "the fact of the matter is," or "I want to tell you about . . ."

Why a prefatory opening is needed beats me. Why can't we tell it straight? For example, you are late for dinner; your explanation is, "I stopped in at a bar and had a drink and that's why I'm late." Most people start out with, "The fact of the matter is, I stopped at a bar . . ."

You may be sure that when someone starts an explanation with "to tell you the truth," a large portion of bullshit is sure to follow.

And there are words and phrases originating and used in Washington, Hollywood, and New York that mark a man instantly as someone to be on guard against. I refer to the following pungent samples: you better believe it — no way — input — conceptualize — finalize — psychovaluation — wind-down — meaningful — evaluative — insightful — decisional — emergist — paradigm — cognitive — feedback — cost-wise — multidimensionable — enthuse — ruling elite — vibes — dig — mixed media. There are at least a hundred others.

When I encounter any of the foregoing in a manuscript, I want to stop reading. An editor who isn't stopped by such bilge is wasting his time and his employer's—unless he's working for IBM or on computers. An author who is obliged to use such language should be sentenced to life at ITT.

The Expletive and I

Some editors worry about expletives or obscenity in books.

There is today some general confusion about the word "expletive." It was made famous during the Watergate tape discussions and disclosures. Most people believe the word to mean something obscene. Yet "expletive" once could refer to a sacrilegious word or phrase, an insulting word such as, say "idiot." Or it could be a parenthetical remark, totally innocuous.

Perceptively, obscene words are now beginning to appear with frequency in the press and are now used more often in "polite society." And while an expletive could be a mild exclamation or an oath, such as "goddamn" or "hell," we now think of it in terms of something scatalogical or sexual. Or physical, such as "asshole."

Expletives of every variety are now common on the American motion picture screen, not to mention all manner of sexual behavior. When we can watch, in closeup shots, sodomistic and other sexual acts, why become alarmed over a word or two making reference to such acts in serious, humorous, or *expletive* fashion? These words, by the way, are called "linguistically unconventional English" by the lexicographers. Soon, I suspect, these words will be heard on the TV screen.

The film *Shampoo* (in case you haven't seen it yet) will give you most of the words, and the visual action to go with it. (As did *Night Porter.*) At a private Columbia screening of the film in February 1975, the audience—mostly publishing and show business people—seemed to tense up and laugh nervously, particularly when one of the actresses in the film, Julie Christie, says to the star, Warren Beatty, "I want to suck your cock." And she makes a valiant attempt to do so in a crowded bistro filled with Republican fund-raisers and politicos of high order, all on their best behavior. She failed in her attempt, but the scene and dialogue were not forgettable. Remember, this was not a hard-core film; it was one of Hollywood's better, legitimate efforts. It was given an R rating, which entitles anyone over eighteen to admission. Of course the word "cocksucker" is no longer a closet expression; the film *Lenny*, starring Dustin Hoffman, utilizes it numerous times, in clear and loud tones. And then, there are such films as *Sometime Sweet Susan, Emmanuelle, Defiance, French Throat, Flesh, The Devil and Miss Jones, The Life and Times of a Happy Hooker, Deep Throat,* and dozens of others, which, though rated X, are available to one and all for around $5.00 admission. New York City must have at least twenty-five porno films showing as this is written.

You'll find the words and actions in these films. In another few years even these will stop being X-rated, and teenagers will be yawning (or masturbating) as they view the raunchy, no-holds-barred nonsense coming to us from the filmmakers. The best producers and directors will gravitate to where the money is—and porno is where it's at. The transvestites and lesbians, the freaked-out nymphomaniacs and high-camp artists, the deep-throat stars will take over. So what are we talking about here—*expletives!*

Women are using the words freely. Just the other day, in a Manhattan restaurant, I overheard a woman say to her friend, "Shit, this martini is piss warm." And why should women not use these words? Some of our best writers—Shakespeare, Henry Miller, Genet, Steinbeck, Hemingway, Norman Mailer—have used them with great effect, as have the Elizabethans, who used them with great originality and gusto. Somewhere in Shakespeare I recall reading, "He fenced by day and foined by night." Check Partridge's *Shakespeare's Bawdy.*

As an editor I became actively involved in permissive language when Earl Wilson and I were working together on his book, *Show Business Laid Bare.* For the first time, I was putting a book to press that employed, in abundance, language on its lowest level. Earl and I had attended a Friar's "roasting" of Henny Youngman. I had never before attended one of these sessions and was startled to hear Milton Berle, Red Buttons, and other well-known comedians talk dirty: I mean lowdown, insulting, scatalogical, and sexual stuff that had even the waiters blushing.

To my surprise, Earl planned to include a verbatim transcript of the entire proceedings in our book. And he did. Frankly, I was surprised at his courage—and foresight. He simply knew that we were on the threshold (this was in 1973) of total permissiveness. The copy chief at Putnam's gave me some strange looks when I turned the manuscript over to her. Rumors around the office of "Bill Targ's shocking book" came back to me. One executive said to me, in worried confidence, "I hope you know what you're doing; I hear the language in the Wilson manuscript is horrendous."

I replied that it was very entertaining.

There are a few sequences in the book that did give me pause, but not for long. When Earl Wilson interviewed the actress Carol Lynley, he quoted her as calling Red Buttons "a cunt." They were discussing the film *The Poseidon Adventure,* in which she and Red were appearing. She said, "Red is basically a master of ceremonies, and he's a great MC, but sitting around on a movie set, he's a cunt."

Earl admitted that he lost his aplomb. "I'd never heard a man called that before . . . ," he said. Then he added, again quoting Carol: "That's what he is, a cunt!" And so on.

Show Business Laid Bare was a commercial success; a few of the reviewers expressed surprise at the frankness of the language and the daring of his reportage: Earl was interviewing strippers, burlesque and topless performers, hookers, singers, famous actors and actresses. What seemed bold no longer is; the paperback edition (New American Library) is getting a great national acceptance, giving the *silent majority* a bit of an education. *But it's too late.* For a dollar, at your favorite newstand, you can buy the tabloid paper, *Screw,* in which advertisements covering every form of sexual accommodation appear, classified ads dealing with unimaginable opportunities are printed, photos show every sexual act in the most explicit detail, and "Fuckbooks" is a feature in which Michael Perkins reviews current books of porno interest. And yet, I have no quarrel with *Screw;* it serves a definite purpose, a social purpose if you will. And at the risk of appearing in a punning mood, it does not pussyfoot around the subject. *Screw* is the greatest buy in porno anywhere.

Where do I stand on the expletive?

I'm for it—foursquare. The profane or obscene oath is part of our heritage and language and life. So what's the problem?

Simply this: There is room for the expletive or epithet or obscenity or "filthy word" on certain occasions—to characterize a situation or person, as an exclamation on experiencing sudden pain, in extreme anger or frustration, or as an essential element in the telling of a humorous story which might be scatalogical or sexual. Some of these anecdotes are educational.

What's really wrong with the expletive is its use by the president of the United States while conducting official business in the White House. Richard M. Nixon gave the expletive a new meaning —he vulgarized it, *fucked it up* as he *fucked up* the country. If anyone can think of a more apt expletive to describe what Nixon did, I'd be glad to hear from him/her, and possibly substitute the synonym in the next (next!) printing of this book.

Happily, books continue to be free outlets to literary men and women, and with the exception of certain types of textbooks, the book is and should be the repository of all the riches of the English language. Grace and discretion are essential factors in all prose and poetry, and bearing that in mind, I insist that the obscene or gutter colloquialism has its wholesome place in human interaction.

I doubt that any brain or nerve damage was ever caused by calling a spade a spade, and if you wish to characterize a certain bit of nonsense as "bullshit," where's the harm? Besides, no one has yet adequately defined obscenity.

The editor and the publisher must not attempt to censor or in any way hinder the serious writer in his use of these words. (Unless the general effect of the statement is *cheapened,* lowered.) If the book or article is bad, then judge it in its entirety. But I would urge the editor to keep his hands off the particular word or phrase on the grounds of "propriety" or "decency." The question is: Does it work? Is the word or phrase being used properly, in proper context, and is it effective?

Text lesson: If you were the editor of this book, would you excise my anecdote on page 345 relating to the woman and her martini? If you tried to delete it I think I'd protest violently and probably use an expletive to make my point.

The Novel Is Dead: Death-Wish Department

When I read articles that begin, "The publishing industry can no longer support quality fiction," I want to reach for my letter-to-the-editor pen and sound off. Talk about death wish!

About twice a year someone writes a jerk-off article on the imminent demise of the novel. There are also individuals and groups (co-ops) who announce plans to publish "serious fiction," since it appears that the commercial publishers, the Establishment, will not be interested, or able, to recognize art.

My threshold of boredom is reached quickly when I hear from scrubby ineffectuals along these lines, or when I get letters and phone calls from rejected authors who declare that the literary artist is being deprived of his inalienable rights and audience.

Bullshit.

Look at the number of new novels that are published each year. Almost all of them lose money. But publishers continue to invite and publish them, and the good-to-fine novels that appear with regularity on the trade lists each year do credit to the Establishment. If more *major* novelists aren't showing up, it's simply because there are damned few major writers. Every editor dreams of discovering or launching a new I. B. Singer, Mailer, Didion, Faulkner, Welty,

Pynchon, Bellow, Baldwin, Kerouac, Oates, Hawkes, Barthelme, Potok, Updike, Saroyan, Solzhenitsyn, Vonnegut, Steinbeck, Hemingway, Wolfe, Wright, Greene—you name them.

Most novelists drive a bumpy road all their lives, trying to make a living from their work. Only a lucky few hit the paperback, club, and film jackpots or the best-seller lists. But don't blame the publishers. The publishers take their lickings on fiction like soldiers; look at the remainder counters.

If you know a publisher, ask him to show you a few cost estimates and some financial audits per title, in fiction. Despite the fact that fiction is a drain for publisher and bookseller, the number of new titles continues heavy; the publishers keep dropping them each week as cats drop kittens. Why? The gambler's instinct compels them to keep playing that "wheel."

I insist that any new writer with *talent* and a decent regard for his craft will find a publisher—in the Establishment. There's room for originality, quality, humor, entertainment. Any good publisher will gamble on talent. A good story, well written, will make it, and that includes the Becketts and Steins and Barthelmes. Sometimes it takes longer for the Gertrude Steins, but in the end acceptance comes.

I don't subscribe to statistics and charts—I detest all those figures in six-point type—but I recommend that anyone who doubts the fact that the novel is alive and kicking in America should check out the facts in *Publishers Weekly;* the number of novels published each month will astonish you.

The novel is alive; all we need are a few new Tolstoys—and fewer weepers.

A novel, to be more than just a novel, must be more than a diversion. Perfect example: Dostoevsky's *Crime and Punishment*.

Are Authors Human?

Many authors should be shunned socially. Some are almost not human.

There are perhaps no more than a dozen living authors I would care to know intimately, socially. I can't think of more than a dozen I'd care to be left alone with on a desert island. On the other hand, I can list about three hundred living authors whose works I would like to publish.

Why can't we have authors who look and behave like Sophia Loren, Vanessa Redgrave, Ingrid Bergman, Catherine Deneuve?

On second thought, everything said above could apply to editors and *publishers*.

A Book Is Born

The manuscript gestation process is the most delicate one and it is the most crucial period in the editor-author relationship. Extreme care, courtesy, and toleration should be exercised on both sides. Remember, push leads to shove and loose lips sink ships, et cetera, et cetera. If the author asks for a jar of pickled watermelon rind at three in the morning, get it for him or her somehow.

More Book Ideas

Almost any newspaper or magazine will contain at least one article or item that will provide the kernel of a book idea.

The following "Milestones" story appeared in *Time*, October 21, 1974:

> *Died*. Athina Niarchos, 45, fifth wife of Greek shipping baron Stavros Niarchos and ex-spouse of his arch rival Aristotle Onassis; of

an apparent heart attack; at the Niarchos town house in Paris. Blonde, willowy Tina had already been through two marriages (14 years with Onassis, ten with John Spencer-Churchill, now the Duke of Marlborough) before her sensational 1971 wedding to Niarchos: it was just 17 months after the death of her older sister Eugenie, Niarchos' third wife, from what was officially ruled to be an overdose of sleeping pills. Tina's death was discovered by a maid as she brought breakfast to her bedroom, while Niarchos was asleep in another room.

A novelist could take this and run with it. Here's a modern Greek tragedy. Pierre Rey, in his novel, *The Greek*, touched upon one aspect of this story. I offer it to one and all as proof that stories exist everywhere around us. Somerset Maugham could have handled it. He knew something about the art of the story.

Trollope and the Writer

Many young writers give me a pain when they complain about how hard writing is and how tough it is to make a living out of it. They talk too much, bellyache too much. Of course everyone knows that good writing is the most difficult of all occupations; but it is a self-imposed one. Writers should be writing instead of talking.

I often direct writers to Anthony Trollope's *Autobiography*. It was published in 1883 and is as pertinent now as it was then. He published over fifty books. He never complained, worked hard, was unexploited, unglamorized, and for many years, unrewarded. (He never queried his publisher about advertising.) He worked by schedule, as did Arnold Bennett much later, and though he was ignored or scorned by his colleagues and the critics for many years, he triumphed in the end.

His autobiography tells the story—a simple account of his progress as a writer, his earnings per book, and the like. An honest picture of a man possessed of genius involved in plain industry.

Trollope believed that "a novel should give a picture of common life enlivened by humor and sweetened by pathos."

Dear reader: read Tollope's book and conspire with yourself.

Michael Sadleir's book, *Trollope, A Commentary,* published in 1927 and reissued in 1947, is also a work to note. Sadleir called Trollope "the voice of an epoch—mid-Victorian England." He was that and much more, and in our time his true worth is again being recognized. TV is helping, too, thanks to our BBC cousins.

Talking

The true writer is not a talker; at least he doesn't talk about his writing. Or shouldn't. The blood runs out of his writing veins if he spills, orally, what he is doing, or sounds off about his problems. The only one he should discuss his work with is his editor or surrogate editor.

Faulkner, the model writer in terms of self-discipline, said, "I am too busy writing. It has got to please me and if it does, I don't need to talk about it. If it doesn't please me, talking about it won't improve it, since the only thing to improve it is to work on it some more. I am not a literary man but only a writer. I don't get any pleasure from talking shop."

Honesty in Journalism

I think Al Goldstein, publisher-editor of *Screw,* the weekly tabloid, merits some sort of historical notice for candor—a candor not be found among any journalists or book-page editors known to me. He said in an interview, "*Screw* leads the league in tastelessness. Our photos are filthier, our articles more disgusting. Our stock in trade is raw, flailing sex. The word 'love' is alien to us. Who needs love? Yuch!"

He also said, "After my review of *Deep Throat,* it became a huge hit. Later I interviewed Linda. Then she went down on me. I ran the photos and my description of it. It was a paradigm of personal journalism."

In my years of reading and studying the works of journalists,

I've observed a lot of peacock posturing and pretension. But nothing like Mr. Goldstein's honesty has come to my attention. It may be due in part to the fact that he is totally himself, without aspirations toward intellectual or literary recognition (to my knowledge he has not written or published a novel), and though loathsome in many ways, he is nevertheless genuine.

The Writer-Teacher

The good writer is a member of a nobility, if "nobility" is the word. But, before the writer, comes the *teacher*.

A good teacher comes before anyone. And it seems to me that a person who chooses writing as a serious profession should try to combine the two: writing and teaching.

To teach, to open up minds, to pose ideas, to make one think or try to think—this is the first of the arts. A dedicated teacher, a communicator of ideas, is really our first citizen.

The writer-teacher must be 75 percent individualist, 25 percent academician. He must be both disciplined and free-wheeling. He must have his feet planted firmly on the earth, but his mind should be free to soar. He must know the ground rules and also how and when to ignore them. The writer-teacher must avoid banality at all costs, even at the risk of appearing outrageous.

Being a good reader (reading aloud) is also being a teacher.

The writer-teacher earns less money than most politicians; many earn less than barbers, taxi drivers, insurance salesmen. Which is ironic and certainly something one must try to remedy before the writer-teachers move into other professions that are more lucrative. We must not, cannot, afford to lose a single good teacher, for they and our youth comprise our chief assets. Good writers should be encouraged to devote part of their time to classroom work. Everyone gains.

For a perfect example of the ideal writer-teacher at work, read W. H. Auden's Introduction to *The Portable Greek Reader*—a door- and eye-opening piece for readers of every age and background. Love of his subject is felt in every sentence.

The foregoing is simply my attempt to indicate what a good writer is all about. Even when it appears that he or she is "merely" entertaining you, you are being taught. All schools should encourage the presence of writers who understand the teaching art.

To write/teach by indirection—I think that is the ultimate art; also, the greatest civic act.

Gilbert Highet's book, *The Art of Teaching*, is still the best book on the subject in the last twenty-five years. He asks you to "cultivate a sense of wonder . . ."

Teacher vs. Popularizer

The late Jacob Bronowski, who became an international public figure when he began to broadcast his TV series, *The Ascent of Man,* is the prototype of the Teacher. This Polish-English scholar and humanitarian exemplified the best qualities of the Teacher, carrying the torch of knowledge with dignity and a sure hand. The quality that also emerges in his narration of man's progress through the centuries is *love* of knowledge.

Sadly, the opposite is true of another TV-culture exponent, Lord Kenneth Clark (the TV Will Durant), who became famous (and rich) through his TV and book successes dealing with civilization and "the romantic rebellion." Clark is a *popularizer,* and somehow one feels his facts are glibly presented and his own persona given theatricality unbecoming a true and dedicated teacher.

Bronowski was a Renaissance man, and I don't use the term lightly; he was a mathematician, scientist, and poet, and one of the great exponents of human knowledge. I hope his "performance" and humane comportment are studied by writers and teachers everywhere.

How to Write a Novel in One Easy Lesson

Get a good opening sentence.
The rest will follow.
Most readers will know of the opening sentence in Laurence

Sterne's *Tristram Shandy*, "I wish either my father or my mother, or indeed both of them, as they were in duty equally bound to it, had minded what they were about when they begot me . . ." Who can stop reading after this sentence?

For another example, here's how William Faulkner's novel *Sanctuary* opens: "From beyond the screen of bushes which surrounded the spring, Popeye watched the man drinking."

All sorts of dramatic possibilities are open to the author after that sentence; and of course the name, Popeye, is irresistible. It's the book that first got Faulkner off the ground.

And how about "Lolita, light of my life, fire of my loins." Mr. Nabokov had us hooked at once. *Lolita*'s literary and publishing history is too well known to comment on here.

There are a hundred and one examples of the *opener* that grabs you and says, "Stick around." Study some first sentences in great and famous novels and you'll see what I mean. Getting a good opening *page* is even better. If your reader (publisher) has trouble with page one, beware.

Under no circumstance should you speak of toilet training or sibling rivalry on page one. Introduce mystery, terror, passion, but avoid adolescent portraiture unless your name is Charles Dickens.

One of my favorites is: "It is a truth universally acknowledged, that a single man in possession of a good fortune must be in want of a wife." Jane Austen said that in the opening of *Pride and Prejudice*. No woman reader would put the book down after reading that sentence.

Superstar

Five years ago Viva's novel, *Superstar*, was published at Putnam's. I loved editing and publishing that book, and I'm still enchanted with it. I dipped into it last night and found no reason to change my regard for the book and its author. It was rough going, getting the book to materialize; but overall, it was a great experience for both of us. And the book is a milestone in the literature of the period.

While some reviewers excoriated it, others loved it. Gore Vidal called me from Rome to say, "Not since Mary McCarthy's *Memories* has any book so beautifully and poignantly described the hazards and results of a Catholic girlhood in America." When I asked if I could print that on the jacket flap, he said, "Certainly." And I did.

Viva's *Superstar* had an impact on our time, though in a modest fashion. It sold better in France than in America, and it did quite well in England and Germany. The book is an honest portrayal of Viva's world and mind, and has given many women and men a vision of American life not to be found elsewhere. Viva told me, shortly after *Superstar* was published, that she got many phone calls at the Chelsea Hotel (where she formerly lived) from runaway girls. They had read her novel and left home. Some came to New York penniless, and called from the bus station for help and advice. She had "changed their lives." One earnest young girl said, "I want to live freely, to have the freedom to fuck, and your book gave me the courage." Viva had her hands full; but she was up to her responsibilities and gave generously of her money, time, and love.

Viva never dealt in bullshit terms (Warhol training?) and always spoke her mind. While she sometimes seemed shockingly plain in calling a spade a spade, it always made for a healthy understanding.

Her daughter Alexandra will forgive me, I hope, for turning down her mother's invitation to witness the videotapes of her birth, filmed by her father Michel Auder. Roslyn and I were at Viva's hospital bedside the very morning the child was born and we toasted the event with champagne. But I had no wish (or stomach) to see the film. Alexandra today loves to see playbacks of the tape.

By the way, one of the finest fan letters I've ever seen was sent to Viva by G. Legman, the foremost authority on erotic literature. He declared it a masterpiece. And he's not alone.

One night at a party in Shirley Clark's Chelsea penthouse, I was talking to Andy Warhol about Viva's book. He said the one mistake we made with the book was in the title. His view was that it should have been called *Super Cunt*. I explained that the librarians would have resisted it and that few newspapers could handle *that*. He looked wistful.

Memo to Mr. Fellini: perhaps there is a film project here, to be entitled *Superfigone?*

The H – – K Writer

Once—and only once—I was invited to speak to a group of writers at a dinner meeting of the Society of Magazine Writers. They were and are a lovely and lively group. But they proved highly flammable when I got up to speak and used the word *"hack."* I thought I would be lynched. Dozens of men and women rose from the floor after my talk, raised their hands (fists?), and challenged me to prove that publishers and editors were not indeed the real hacks.

Well, my thoughts on the subject are clear. There are writers who will turn in a one- or two-page outline to a publisher, hoping to get a book contract for almost any subject under the sun. If you don't like his proposal for a book on the history of submarine warfare, how about a book on collecting seashells, or on lesbian activity in Outer Mongolia, or on the art of writing Haiku? And so on. What is wrong with these all-utility writers is that they seldom deliver publishable book manuscripts—or anything!—and the publisher must write off the advance. The day of my talk, I had experienced a "write-off session" with our comptroller: some $20,000 had to be written off on outline projects that had never materialized. Needless to say, their would-be authors never refunded the advances.

Talking about hacks—as I've already indicated, I dislike cookbook publishing, despite the alleged big profits. There is more fraud in the cookbook-writing business than in any other area of publishing and writing. It is an annoying literary (social) pretension to announce that you've "written" a cookbook. If all but six existing cookbooks were destroyed, it would prove no loss to society or gastronomy. Actually, three books I know would more than serve for every possible occasion. Movie stars and TV celebrities and socialites with time on their hands turn to "writing" cookbooks. Every half-assed social climber and literary pretender tries his/her hand at a cookbook. There must be thousands of these books, each living off the other, editorially. Why are they published? Who buys them? If I had dictatorial powers, I'd ban all publishing of new cookbooks for ten years. Maybe forever.

So Where's *Moby Dick?*

The question is often asked: Who are the leading living novelists in America now that Faulkner and Hemingway are gone? And what about the Great American Novel—isn't it overdue?

For me this is an easy question to handle, and I would begin by putting Philip Roth and Saul Bellow at the head of the list. Roth has more talent per thousand words than most readers realize. His performance to date has been varied, but almost always brilliant. His Great Opus is yet to come and I suspect it is due soon. He's young enough to produce a half dozen more good books; a super-major book is already in the works, I would venture. I *know* it's in his genes.

Re Saul Bellow: The author of *Augie March* and *Herzog* is still productive and perceptive, and alive enough to come through with a book that will top all of his previous books. This is a prediction I'll stand on, providing Bellow remains in decent health and is around for another decade.

Malamud and Mailer—these are two more literary artists of the first rank, and both will be heard from before long—I mean, in a big, resounding way. Mailer is a sure bet, so long as he doesn't dissipate his energies with marginal exertions and journalistic projects. (He's probably hankering for a Jupiter-shot as this is being written.) If it were up to me, I'd give him a comfortable cell, a thousand-volume library and a two-year sentence (deadline) to come through with his *Moby Dick*. He could do it, too.

The prospects are good; why the wringing of hands? Meanwhile, *Portnoy's Complaint* may very well be the Great American Novel, circa 1900s.

The Big Payoff

There are many ways for an author to make it.

The idea, of course, is to write a great book. More often than is realized a great book will make it commercially as well as critically. Obviously, *The Valley of the Dolls* will get faster results for an

author than, say, a novel like Thomas Pynchon's *Gravity's Rainbow,*
John Hersey's *The Wall,* or John Gardner's *The Sunlight Dialogues.*

Fat subsidiary sales—films, paperbacks, serials, clubs, foreign-
language sales—these can add up in a large way, *if* the book is
right. But few of us can predict which one is.

The ultimate payoff is, of course, the Nobel Prize. This, however, is given for one's total output rather than for an individual
work. With the prize comes a substantial sum of money as well as
worldwide respect, not to mention a place in literary history. Actual
book sales don't follow, necessarily; there are dozens of Nobel Prize
winners whose books you never heard of; many of them have been
long out of print.

The only prize that really pays off in immediate *sales* is the
Goncourt, in France. This award is coveted and fought for somewhat like the Hollywood Oscar. Sales sometimes run up to a half
million copies when the Prix Goncourt is given to a book. Ironically,
the Goncourt publicity means or does almost nothing for the book
in America. Many of them are bypassed in the American market.
Which is curious. Why should a book of great interest to the
French reader be of no interest to the American audience? Well,
alas, such is the case. And vice versa. Many bestselling American
books fail to find British or French publishers.

The American Pulitzer and National Book Awards likewise do
very little for a book in terms of sale. Naturally, the prestige acquired is welcomed by the author, but the bookseller and publisher
gain very little tangible reward. The dollar payoff is simply not
there. And again, no one seems to know why, except that frequently
the American prizes are in dispute, and the books honored are considered less than worthy or important or of general interest. Some of
the choices are indeed bizarre. Attached to many American awards
is the suspicion of clique support, quixotic decisions made in smoke-
filled rooms. As this is written there is doubt that the National Book
Awards will be continued beyond the spring of 1975.

Some day an American millionaire—a Rockefeller or a Ford—
will establish the equivalent of the Nobel award, giving a good
sum of money and recognition to an American writer for his total
output. But in taking a hard look at the matter, I can actually
think of damned few Americans, still alive, who are worthy, who
have the staying power and track performance to merit the Big
Payoff.

Meanwhile, I'd like someone to explain why the French respond to their Goncourt with such rousing enthusiasm; the books aren't really always *that* good. Maybe they have national pride. Or as the *Fiddler on the Roof* phrase goes, "It's tradition."

I had the pleasure of publishing only one Goncourt award-winning (1954) book, and it was indeed a happy choice: *The Mandarins* (1956) by Simone de Beauvoir.* This novel is of classic stature; many of its characters are recognizable: Camus, Jean-Paul Sartre and his friends, Nelson Algren, and others come to mind. I recall that I urged a 50,000-copy advance from our salesmen at World when I presented the book at our sales conference. They thought my figure impossible, but they brought the subscription in and its sale went far beyond that figure. Intellectual novels often do sell in America—on a par with tinselled schlock. Which makes publishing *more* than a business. We had a number of best sellers during my tenure at World, but *The Mandarins* gave me the greatest personal pride, as publisher.

Descent of the Man

Three of my favorite American novels of this century are Fitzgerald's *The Great Gatsby,* Dreiser's *An American Tragedy,* and Henry Roth's *Call It Sleep.* I have other favorites by authors such as Mailer, Bellow, Farrell, West, Philip Roth, Styron, and Updike. But looking over a two-century range, no American novel compares with Melville's *Moby Dick,* in my opinion.

Some years ago I wrote a bibliophilic-cum-literary appreciation of *Moby Dick.* In examining it recently, for possible inclusion in this assemblage, I found little fault with the piece beyond the fact that it offered very little that was new, and it was a bit Callow-Stylish. It didn't belong here, and I'm sure Max Geismar or Randall Jarrell or Alfred Kazin could have done it better. It can be found in my *Bouillabaisse for Bibliophiles,* if you're interested. As the lady in

---

*As a footnote to the history of censorship, there was one sentence in the French edition of *The Mandarins* that might have offended the postal authorities and we wrote to the author, asking permission to delete it. Simone de Beauvoir was amused and granted permission. I won't indicate the precise sentence but the subject area was *pubic hair.* We've come a long way since 1956.

Wonderful Town said, "It's worth picking up again . . . it's about this whale . . ."

What prompts the above is the following:

About forty-six years ago, Lewis Mumford published his biography of Herman Melville. (In case you don't know Mumford, and haven't had the pleasure of meeting this great writer, historian, teacher, and philosopher, get a few of his books; he's never written a poor one. Start with his *Sticks and Stones,* and continue with *The Culture of Cities* and *Technics and Civilization.*) The Melville book (an early Literary Guild selection) had all the elements of a great biography. In rereading it recently, I found it worth the time and effort and was especially glad to see how it had endured. I recall my *first* reading of the book and I'm prompted to relate a modest and sad incident:

Mumford mentioned in his book that Melville, in his last years, lived on Twenty-sixth Street—104 East, to be exact. In Manhattan.

Mumford says: "Every morning a grave, firm, square-bearded man leaves Number 104. A little slow and reflective in gait, as if deliberately setting himself apart in pace as well as inward gesture from the world about him, Melville turns west toward Madison Square, passes through its green, and follows Fifth Avenue, whose ranks of trees are just beginning to be broken, down to Fourteenth Street. . . . He follows the broad thoroughfare clear over to Hudson Street, and turns to the block below, where the Gansevoort Market and the customs office lie, touching the river."

This tantalizing account of Melville's daily walk to work hooked me. One evening, Roslyn and I went to 104 East Twenty-sixth Street, eager to touch the stones of the house in which Melville spent his last years. Reader, will you believe this? Number 104 East no longer exists. So much for reverence of historic landmarks in Manhattan.

Saroyan

Since 1934, when his *Daring Young Man on the Flying Trapeze* was published, I've been a fan of this man. "I'm great and I'm proud to be great," he says. And I have no quarrel with that statement. Whitman might have said it, too.

William Saroyan comes from Fresno, California, and his writings often relate to that part of the world. He wrote some beautiful plays, got a Pulitzer Prize for *The Time of Your Life;* he's written over a dozen others, and his stories and novels are out of one great big Armenian barrel with most of the apples mighty edible.

To writers, he says, "Don't expect to write with intelligence, just write." He writes from the heart, the head, and elsewhere. Most of it works beautifully. He loves the racetrack, is indifferent to money except when he really needs it. He's one of the few men on earth I would care to be shipwrecked with, because I think he'd get a big laugh out of it and make do, somehow. He's a life-lover.

I once pirated a short essay by Saroyan, and he forgave me. It was a modest piracy. I invited him to write a piece for my *Book Collector's Journal,* a tabloid I once published in Chicago. He wrote me a fine article called *Those Who Write Them and Those Who Collect Them.* While in the printshop checking the proofs, it occurred to me that I ought to make an offprint up to fifty copies, as pamphlets, and sell them for a dollar a copy. This was in 1936. I had them bound in colored paper wrappers. The printing quality was probably an all-time low, likewise the paper. But the fifty copies disappeared quickly. I may have a copy somewhere in my library; it's pocket-size. I ran into Saroyan in the Algonquin lobby a year or so ago and I said, "You don't remember me," and he interrupted with, "Sure, you're Bill Targ; you pirated my stuff." What a memory. He put his arm around me and said with a leer, "I hear it's a collector's item." It certainly is: I've seen it listed for $50.

Saroyan is a "gentle genius," and he's also been called "a kind of American Buffalo Bill." I doubt that he's ever written anything he's ashamed of, and as a lifelong reader of his, I can't recall anything he wrote that I didn't like, though some of the writings are better than others, of course. He and Vonnegut and Brautigan and a few other guys are among our national treasures. Make a note, please. Every would-be writer of short stories should study Saroyan, particularly the tales in *The Daring Young Man.*

When an Author Gets Mad—

Some years ago, in the late forties, the famous author Count Maurice Maeterlinck, at the age of eighty-five, decided that his publisher, Dodd, Mead, wasn't doing him justice. Authors often feel that way about their publishers at some time or other. But Maeterlinck (a Nobel Prize winner, no less) decided to sue the publisher for $250,000 for making "no reasonable effort to sell and market the books," which included the famous *The Life of the Bee*, *The Blue Bird*, and other best sellers. Luckily, he withdrew the suit.

This may seem like a pointless anecdote, but it isn't; an author often develops a feeling of frustration due to a diminution of sales and income, and builds up a hostility which can only be directed at one person—his publisher. How can one blame, or sue, the *public* for gosh sakes? And the public decides what books are going to sell—not the author, not the publisher.

Cummings

I met him twice at Village parties, but had no real contact.

I wish I had *known* this man. He lived about two blocks from my present home. I'd been reading him since he wrote his first book, the war novel, *The Enormous Room* (Liveright, 1922), up through his final *Collected Poems*. His novel, about World War I and the *schrecklichkeit* of prison life, is the kind of antiwar book that should be in print and available everywhere.

Today I own most of his first editions, and I must note, for the uninitiated, that his association with the printer, Sam Jacobs, was fortuitous. Some authors aren't so lucky.

The Golden Eagle Press (Mount Vernon, New York) who printed many of E. E. Cummings' books among countless others of great distinction, stands alone in many respects. Sam Jacobs, its chief factotum, seemed to be the only typographer who could set Cummings' poems to accommodate the poet's special needs, among which was omitting space between commas and adjacent words.

Said Jacobs: "A comma creates its own space. Mr. Cummings knows exactly what he's doing."

Cummings dared to express himself in favor of Pound when Ezra was in the doghouse. He said: "Everybody in my generation is in debt to Ezra Pound. He was to the poetry of this century what Einstein was to physics. He was the guy with the broom."

If Cummings, "one of the inventors of our time," is an unknown quantity to you, dip into his poems; they hold up as well as the best, and the newcomers to the game can learn from him. Start with the poem "Epithalamion," in his *Tulips and Chimneys;* in those first eight lines you'll get some measure of the poet and man.

Simenon

I've long had a vacation fantasy: taking a full year off to read Georges Simenon. This Belgian-born author has written more than two hundred novels, about fifty of which are about Inspector Maigret. When I ran the reprint department at World, I published some of the Maigret novels but found them less successful than the traditional American police novels. But I developed a taste for Simenon that will, I hope, be satisfied one day. I plan to immerse myself in the full body of his work because I feel that he is incapable of writing a poor book. I must satisfy my curiosity.

After I've read a hundred or so of his books I'd like to go to Switzerland, meet the man, ask him a few questions, and get him to inscribe some of the books. At this writing, Simenon is seventy-two years old. I gather he's most careful of his health, takes long walks each day, sleeps, and devotes only about one-third of his time to writing. And I'm told he still produces three or four books a year, which appear in some twenty languages.

This is obviously a writer with no writing block. He also has a profound understanding of human behavior. A blueprint study of his working method might help aspiring writers in programming their careers. Of course, one must also discover the *combination* of the safe that shelters his mind. He's much more than a detective-story writer; he's an intuitive psychologist, and his stories unfold not only with the ease of a camera's lens following the action, but with a tape-recording fidelity for dialogue and language tones. No seams show in his story structures, and there's a kind of human omniscience, an intelligence, that ensures a satisfying tale with unabated fascination for the reader. The Scheherazade gift.

Simenon discovered early in his life that the best kind of stories are detective stories; that inherent in a good crime novel is what most listeners and readers respond to—a puzzle and a solution.

It may be that Georges Simenon is the wisest of all writers. He thinks of a book as a play, something to be consumed and enjoyed in one evening, one sitting.

Says Simenon: "My books are written by intuition alone . . . before I start a book, *I clean the desk.*" Also: "In one man, or in one couple, or in one family, you can find the whole world."

A clear-headed, uncomplicated man.

8 · *The Collector*

The Virus

The book collector's virus attacked me early in life. I was never to recover; in fact, the malady became aggravated with the years. It was in my eighteenth year, while working at Macmillan, that a friend introduced me to a Dickensian character who owned a coffee shop near our office on the South Side of Chicago. One day this man—some devilish instinct prompting him, no doubt—handed me a thick paper-bound catalog of rare books. I had never seen one before. He told me he collected Trollope, but there were other books in the catalog that might interest me. It was issued by Maggs Brothers of London, a quarto volume, expensively printed and lavishly illustrated. Some plates were in color.

I spent many nights studying its contents (I didn't buy anything from it, of course) but I resolved that I must have more of the catalogs which Maggs so invitingly offered in a list on the back cover. I wrote that firm and before long found myself a regular recipient of their catalogs. As each new one arrived, my sense of guilt increased. I felt like a con man, for I could not afford to buy any of the books they offered. But I did read the catalogs and came to learn something of old books and bibliography and a great many other related things.

> Like some small nimble mouse between the ribs
> Of a mastodon, I nibbled here and there.

I suppose I became insufferable because of the odd smattering of knowledge I was acquiring. I became, overnight, an "expert" on Elizabethan literature, color-plate books, rare medical and scientific works, books on exploration, history, and such. I became a repository of information relating to incunabula and early printing. Points and variant bindings became my daily diet. At eighteen I was talking glibly about Dickens in "parts" and Scott in "boards," about trial issues and the 1865 *Alice*. The vocabulary of the bookbinder became mine, and I rolled on my tongue such phrases as "silk doublures" and "gilt dentelles." The Maggs catalogs became, over the years, my university. And of course, I scrounged catalogs from other dealers in Europe and at home. Ultimately, I began to order books from them. Packages with foreign stamps began to arrive— and is there any excitement to compare with the opening of a fresh parcel of books? It was inevitable as funds became available that my library began to expand, from cheap subscription sets and twenty-five and fifty-cent bin books, until it boasted of press books, modern first editions, Beadle Dime Novels, fine bindings, small runs of books by such then-favorites as G. K. Chesterton, Lafcadio Hearn, James G. Huneker, Theodore Dreiser, and others, plus a number of books about books (one of the first I read was Pearson's *Books in Black or Red*). Gradually, the subscription sets and bin books were eased out of the house. I was a collector. I was always broke!

And of course my collection of book catalogs grew, and I have never ceased regarding them with special affection. Eugene Field termed it "The Malady Called Catalogitis." I can only add for emphasis that catalogs, and books about books, are the backbone of any good collector's library. They are the fuel that keep the bibliophilic temperature at boiling point, or near it.

As a footnote to my Maggs Brothers catalog experience, thirty years after getting my first one, I made my first trip to London. I proceeded at once to Maggs Brothers, 50 Berkeley Square. I won't attempt to relate the sense of exhilaration and aroused sentiment that was generated within me as I entered the doors of this establishment. My wife stood at the foot of the stairs leading to their door and aimed her camera at me. The snapshot, with the Maggs plaque behind me, is one of the precious mementos of my first European trip.

I visited many other London bookshops—shops whose names were as old friends to me through numerous catalogs I had received over the years. And I bought books from many of them, none of which failed to give me satisfaction.

A book collector has friends everywhere. The bookseller from whom you buy books is, more frequently than not, your friend. There is a bond between you that transcends the commercial transaction. For you've established *something* (call it rapport) between you that is personal, almost spiritual if you will. He understands your interests and your needs and the compulsion which brings you to him. (And let it be freely admitted, his magnet is as compelling to the bibliophile as the bar is to the boozer.) The bookseller becomes inextricably identified with you, your library, your intellectual life.

First Principles: Collect What You Like

Collecting the great names, the milestones of literature, is child's play; all it takes is a checkbook and some indoctrination. But collecting a young, fledgling author—that's the game!

Did you ever hear of, or read any of, the poems of Patti Smith?

Well, one day, while browsing at Gotham Book Mart, I picked up a copy of a pamphlet entitled *Seventh Heaven*. I was attracted by the photograph of its author, a young woman who looked as though she had just come in out of the rain, or just back from a swim. I began to read the poems in her little book, which was published by Telegraph Books in 1972, and was instantly taken by them. One of the two people the book is dedicated to is Mickey Spillane, one of my favorite authors. So I bought it.

Later, I acquired other works by Patti Smith, pamphlets called *Witt* and *Kodak* and a four-page thing entitled *One of Us Is the Stronger—Early Morning Dream*. She also published, in holograph reproduction, *Devotions to Arthur Rimbaud,* a broadside which ends up with the words, "He was so damn young." Someone described her voice and delivery as a "quivering quickness, like the quail that lights down so fast you almost miss."

Gotham had a party for Patti and I went, bringing along my various Patti Smith artifacts. I met her. I found her enchanting. Shy. Self-effacing. Embarrassed by all the attention. She inscribed each of my books and the *Rimbaud* broadside. I let her borrow my Parker fountain pen which, I told her, Samuel Beckett had used to inscribe my *Waiting for Godot*. She genuflected and kissed the pen.

Patti Smith appeared at Max's Kansas City, and elsewhere, but I missed her "act." I want to continue reading her poetry and shall buy each booklet as it appears. Some day I will be able to say I recognized her talent way back—that's collecting. If she doesn't become famous, no harm. I empathize with her and her poems. I hope you make the discovery one day.

One day, in a long coffee-shop visit with Patti, I learned of her deep interest in flying saucers; of her ability to see and sense the proper placing of a word beside its destined mate; that she once listened to a half-hour discourse by a tortoise—all of which I earnestly believe. She understands, too, a great deal about the sexuality of extraterrestrials and other arcane matters. She will surely write (based on a deep regard for William Burroughs' writings) a major novel, and I hope to serve as her editor.

———

Closeup of a Collector

Carl Sandburg, in his *Lincoln Collector,* has much to say about collecting, and in particular, about that prototype of the great collector, Oliver R. Barrett.

Sandburg tells this anecdote about Charles Gunther, the candy manufacturer-collector, and Barrett—an anecdote which offers a classic portrait-in-miniature of the true collector:

In another session, when Barrett saw a manuscript in the handwriting of Robert Burns—the verses of "Auld Lang Syne"—he said, "I want this 'Auld Lang Syne.'" Gunther replied, "I know how you feel. I went over to England and I got it and I had to pay a lot of money."

Barrett: "I want it now. You know how it *feels* to have it, and I *don't* know how it feels."

Gunther: "I will sell you this 'Auld Lang Syne' and you write out the receipt and put in the receipt that any time I want it, I can buy it back at the same price."

Barrett took it home. A week later Gunther was on the phone, saying: "Bring back the 'Auld Lang Syne.' You know, I haven't been able to sleep. I hear the waves of Lake Michigan pounding at night and I think about it. I walk down Michigan Avenue thinking about it, and now it is gone and I am not going to last many years. Let me have it back."

The World's Greatest Book Collector

When I was visiting with Ben Glazebrook of Constable in 1966, he mentioned an upcoming book that pulled me up short. It was a one-volume condensation of the five-volume work on Sir Thomas Phillipps (*The Phillipps Studies*) adapted by Nicolas Barker.

The prospect of publishing, for Putnam's, the story of the unparalleled account of the most fanatically dedicated book collector in all history, was a great prospect. I was delighted to learn, on reporting the project to Walter Minton, that he was all for publishing the book, although he held out little hope for sales or profit. (The virus had reached him!)

Phillipps was the ultimate bibliomanic. He said somewhere that he wanted to own one copy of *every book printed*. He was the illegitimate son of a rich Birmingham merchant, and was never allowed to see his mother. Lawrence Clark Powell conjectures that this was the cause for his bibliomania—an unfulfilled need for affection. Whatever the reason, he was insatiable. He filled two large mansions with books and priceless manuscripts. No one knows how many printed books he finally did get to own. He begrudged his wife the space occupied by her dressing table—because it could have accommodated another book case. I believe, in the end, he had more than 60,000 *manuscripts* which he cataloged. In today's terms, his library could be valued at perhaps a hundred million dollars, possibly more. He often neglected to pay his bills and sent some booksellers into bankruptcy (or to the madhouse).

Bookseller, librarian, publisher, collector—all will respond to this fantastic story. The man was detestable, personally. But so admirable in his genius for collecting. If you can find a copy of this now out-of-print book, treat yourself to something *recherché*.

I believe I have some of Phillipps' genes in my makeup; alas, what is lacking is his income. He was damnably rich.

Book Collecting for the Smart Money; or,
What the Disillusioned and Bewildered
Stock Market Speculator Can Turn to for
Solace, Culture, and Some Profit

A publisher I know told me, in utmost seriousness, that anyone who couldn't take a complete break from his daily interests was suffering from soggy brains.

I disagree. Editors and publishers do read manuscripts after hours; they also see authors and fellow publishers socially, at home. Somehow, I think they should have decent libraries, *aside* from the usual reference miscellany, the haphazard stuff assembled over the years. I mean they should have a *collection*, put together with plan and purpose, a cohesive collection.

The investment factor is also there, and that is, in part, why the following article was written. It first appeared in *New York* magazine (November 11, 1974) in somewhat modified form, when the subject of inflation and investment was on everyone's mind; when a president was up for impeachment and a secretary of state was double-talking and making protests over accusations such as wire-tapping and other indelicate behavior; when it *appeared* that only gold had an intrinsic value and bread was going to cost a dollar a loaf. It was a time of fear and depression-talk, and stocks were unpopular and going to hell. The article was also intended to indicate what was going on in the rare-book world and I wrote it with the hope that it would suggest as well a perfect escape hatch for the troubled, escape from the routines and pressures of work and the rigors of social life.

As a rare-book watcher for over three decades, as well as a some-time collector, I've come to a few drastic conclusions. One, that the possession of a rare book beats owning a deflated stock certificate. Also, that there's no contest when the choice is between curling up with a good book or a Wall Street engraving. However . . .

If you're going to take to books with the single crass purpose of making money, then please turn to another page. The prospect of lending voice to the sole practice of making money out of bibliophily gives me the horrors. This is not my intention here.

What I want to enunciate here are a few not-too-well-known facts about rare books and collecting. First, rare book prices are skyrocketing in America, England, and France; literary "stocks" (which include autographs and manuscripts) have gone inflationary, and the climb appears to continue steadily Everestward.

First editions are *in* among many hundreds of college and university libraries where collections of rare books are being avidly assembled. Scholars use them! The emphasis appears to be on contemporary literature as well as the milestones of the past. The great rarities will soon be out of circulation because of institutional buying. (Where does one find a first-issue copy of Whitman's *Leaves of Grass* or Rimbaud's first little book, *Une Saison en Enfer,* which he published at his own expense—as did Whitman. Or Camus' first book, *L'Envers et l'Endroit,* printed in Algiers in 1937.)

It's plain to see that it's folly to sell one's books in haste.

A home library of, say, 1,000 good first editions, could represent a pretty impressive estate or nest egg for any modest family. And what glorious reading!

"How do you know it's a genuine first edition?" That's the most common question asked by book owners. There is no simple answer; there are many rules and guidelines, and also many variations and contradictions, and publishers do not have a uniform style for indicating first editions, alas. Some trade publishers will indicate "First Edition" or "First Impression" on the copyright page. But not always. Some publishers put reprint information on the copyright page, which quickly answers the question as to whether it is a first edition. Some publishers put the publication date on the title page, then remove it in reprintings. In short, bibliographies must be consulted, as well as booksellers. Instinct and rule of thumb are called into play. In the end, your memory and rule-of-thumb sense will guide you. A bookseller will of course guarantee any book he sells to you.

If you have a wall or shelf of books at home, take down and examine those by famous authors such as Steinbeck, Hemingway, Tennessee Williams, and others—books you bought when the books were first published. The chances are that some of them are first editions—that is, if you bought them around the time of publication. The books which seem to you to be first editions should then be checked out through rare booksellers' catalogs, bibliographies, guides, and auction records. Use the public library as much as possible. Catalogs are valuable guides.

Don't expect your bookseller to be on tap for endless questions; to earn his attention and service you must first prove yourself a customer and a reasonably serious collector. If you simply badger him with questions and fail to buy, you'll alienate him quickly. Courtesy and good business manners must prevail. Remember, the bookseller has rent to pay and an overhead. Don't bring in boxes and bundles of books for appraisal; if you want to sell them ask for an offer. If you think you can get free appraisals, guess again. No professional dealer will hold still for that. Many dealers charge a fee for appraisals and properly so; what they have to offer is a lifetime of experience and study.

What is a rare book and what is it worth? How high is up? The first question is easily answered: A book is rare when the supply is short and the demand long. Its value is what one is willing to pay for it in a competitive market. Often, a rare book is rare by virtue of its limited first printing. If one hundred copies were printed and most of them landed in institutional collections, the chances are the price will be prohibitive.

For example: James Joyce's *Ulysses* (Paris, 1922), one of 100 copies, signed by the author, bound in blue paper wrappers as issued, could have been bought for around $1,500 in 1964. Today it would cost you anywhere from $7,500 to $10,000 (a copy sold for $8,000 at auction in February 1975) if you can locate a copy. In 1935 the Limited Editions Club reprinted the book and got Joyce to sign around 250 copies. The book was issued at $15 plus $5 for the autograph. Today the book fetches $1,500, $2,000, or more.

Hart Crane's great poem, *The Bridge* (1930), was issued in Paris, with 50 copies on Japan vellum, signed, at about $50. Today it is probably a $1,500 to $2,000 book; and the American trade edition, issued the same year, is also a great rarity and may very well be in the $500 area.

On a personal note: Nine years ago my wife Roslyn expressed the desire to buy me a present. I suggested that a book would be very nice and proposed that we visit John Fleming's ducal book emporium on East 57th Street in New York. As an old devotee of Doves Press books, I asked if there were any in stock. Fleming showed us a few titles, including Emerson's *Essays,* one of 25 copies printed on vellum. The price was $225. My wife generously bought it for me.

In 1974, a copy of the Doves *Emerson* on vellum was sold for $2,600, at the Parke Bernet auction gallery in New York. (Paul Getty, Jr., was the buyer.) Shortly after the sale, Fleming encountered my wife and asked her if she thought I would care to sell my copy of the book back to him. He suggested that his customer might pay $3,000 for it. Of course we wouldn't sell the book. But we were pleased with the "appreciation" this little book enjoyed in some nine years—an appreciation unheard of in Wall Street.

Do you like Robert Lowell's poetry? You might—he's possibly our best living poet. Anyway, if you want to collect him you'll be interested to know that his first book, *The Land of Unlikeness,* published in 1944 at around $2, might cost you $1,000 today—more if inscribed. William Faulkner's first book, a little volume of poems entitled *The Marble Faun,* printed (not published) in 1924 at about $1.50 a copy, now costs between $3,000 and $5,000, depending on whether it has the original jacket and is inscribed by the author.

Samuel Beckett's famous play, *Waiting for Godot,* was published in Paris, in 1952. It was first written and published in French and its title is *En Attendant Godot.* There were 35 copies printed on a paper called Velin; it retailed for about $25 when published. Today, a copy, if available, would fetch around $5,000. Ezra Pound's first book, *A Lume Spento,* printed in Venice in 1908, brings around $7,500 today. It was privately issued and first offered for a few dollars—or given away to friends.

Are there many commercial stocks with comparable histories of growth?

And what about that "sure thing," gold! Eh?

Here's another interesting rarity: John Hawkes, one of our finest novelists, issued a small paper-covered booklet of his poems in 1943; it was entitled *Fiasco Hall.* It could have been bought at that time for $1. Dealers are currently offering it for $250. A "fiasco" in reverse.

There are more collectors for such first editions than there are books available. Every collector of Stephen Spender would love to own a copy of his first, privately printed book. Spender himself printed it on a crude hand press. It was called *Nine Experiments by S. H. S.,* and was issued in Hampstead, England, in 1928. About 18 copies were made and I've never seen a worse piece of book printing. A copy of this book would bring well over $5,000 today, and alas, no Spender collection can be complete without it.

As a collector, my personal preference is in the poetry area, and I've been watching the price-climb on certain key books by Auden, Betjeman, Eliot, Plath, Marianne Moore, Robert Frost, W. C. Williams, Dylan Thomas, Allen Ginsberg, and others. A fine copy of Eliot's *Prufrock and Other Observations* (London, 1917), might bring over $1,000 today; likewise Robert Frost's *A Boy's Will* (London, 1913). Certain key French books, in particular Baudelaire's *Le Fleurs du Mal* (1857) with the six suppressed poems intact (a black tulip if there was ever one) might bring a few thousand dollars today. Wallace Stevens' *Harmonium,* published by Knopf in 1923, with the striped boards binding in dust jacket, might justify a $200 price today *if* you can locate a copy. A fine but tough poet to collect, William

Carlos Williams, is worthy of any serious collector's attention, providing he has the funds and patience to follow the labyrinthian paths leading to a complete collection. Of course there is no more difficult author to collect in his entirety than Samuel Beckett—but the course is worth the time, money, and energy. Poets and playwrights—a broad collection in these two fields—are highly recommended to new collectors; poetry is enjoying a renaissance today, with more works being published than ever, and many of the new poets are top-notch. Happily, they are finding favor (and pleasant loot) on university campuses.

(Speaking of poetry, the monumental *Leaves of Grass* by Walt Whitman [Brooklyn, 1855], was cataloged by Dawson's of London in January of 1975 at £5,500 [or around $13,500]. There aren't too many copies of this book [in its first-issue binding] lying around.)

Does a book have to be ancient to be valuable? As you can see above, the answer is no, definitely not. Age has nothing to do with dollar value. Allen Ginsberg's two books of poems, both issued in paper wrappers in 1956 (one was mimeographed on board a ship) *Siesta in Xbalba* and *Howl*, are rarities; the first may be worth about $500 today, and *Howl* might fetch $150 today. It was published at 75¢. Norman Mailer's novel, *The Naked and the Dead*, published in 1948, is currently offered for $150 in the paper-covered advance copy. Thomas Wolfe's *Look Homeward, Angel*, with its dust jacket intact (1929) brings between $250 and $350 today. There are numerous titles from many areas of literature published during the past fifty years which bring premiums of 100% to 1,000% and more over their publication price. To repeat, supply and demand plus "collector's condition" determine the price. A book without its dust jacket could be worth up to 50% less. It is part of the book regardless of logic; so never throw a jacket away, and when you read a first edition, remove the jacket first so that you don't soil or tear it. And please read all first edition copies with care. Keep the book as clean and close to the original condition as possible. No soup stains on the pages; no dog-eared pages; no glass rings on the cover or jacket. Don't open your books carelessly so that the spine is cracked. Handle a rare book gently—as a delicate and valuable object. And—don't lend your first editions to anyone.

The literary explosion in America, brought on in part by the so-called paperback revolution, explains the widespread interest in books. The book clubs (club editions are *not* first editions) have helped to heighten the possessive interest in books. The auction sale record prices have animated many newcomers. Students and young executives are learning something about the pleasure (and status) of a good home library cum collection. Some of them are listening to the siren songs emanating from the auction rooms, and they're responding.

More and more, we see shelves with books as background decor in newspaper and magazine advertisements. *A house without a library is not a home*. And books are so easy to acquire. The taste for books and reading is leading more and more to collecting, and once the step is taken, the investment factor rears its beautiful head. And when this happens, rules of the game must be studied and followed. It can take years to master the intricacies, not to mention the vocabulary of the hobby. But it's all great fun, and all it takes is a love of books.

How and what type of book to collect? The answer usually is: buy the books and authors you like best. But of course if your taste runs to soap-opera fiction and nonbooks, forget it. Quality is the prime consideration in collecting—in collecting anything for that matter. The author must be gilt-edged. Schlock literature may be fun, but will get you nowhere in the investment sense. There are no hard and fast rules, and each season turns up surprises. Many of the "beat" writers, the "outsiders," and avant gardists of not too long ago, who were suspect insofar as durability goes, have won their permanent place in the "market." Among the notable ones are Jack Kerouac, Michael McClure, Gregory Corso, William Burroughs, and others. And let us not forget the perdurable Henry Miller. Michael McClure's seminal play, *The Beard*, issued in pictorial wrappers, small folio size, in Berkeley, California, in 1965, may one day become a major collector's item. Today it is worth around $40.

And then there are many exciting comparative newcomers such as: Richard Brautigan, John Gardner, Thomas Pynchon, Harold Pinter, Robert Creeley, John Barth, Gary Snyder, Kurt Vonnegut, Jr., LeRoi Jones (Imamu Amiri Baraka). These are all worthy of the collector's attention, and some of their books are already way out of reach.

As for the modern solid-gold standbys, I cite at random: F. Scott Fitzgerald, John Steinbeck, Truman Capote, Robert Frost, Theodore Roethke, Anaïs Nin, Sean O'Casey, William Saroyan, Robinson Jeffers, Graham Greene (his first book, *Babbling April* [Oxford, 1925], might cost you around $400 today), Richard Wright, Katherine Mansfield, Randall Jarrell, Nelson Algren, Tom Wolfe, Richard Wilbur, James T. Farrell (his *Lonigan* and *Danny O'Neill* series are, with Dreiser's novels, among the best novels of our century), and so many others—they will all give the reader immeasurable pleasure and satisfaction in the collector's sense.

There are several levels of book collecting. The top plateau (where collecting is really "a sport of kings") comprises the deepest blue of blue chips: manuscripts, incunabula (books printed prior to 1501), literary and typographic milestones of the 16th and 17th century; highspots of literature such as Boswell's *Life of Samuel Johnson*, Gibbon's *Decline and Fall of the Roman Empire*, Jane Austen's *Pride and Prejudice*, etc. Then there are the great examples from the fine presses: the Doves, Kelmscott, Ashendene, Gregynog, Grabhorn, and other presses. First folios of Shakespeare, Caxtons, early examples from the press of Aldus, illuminated manuscripts, Elizabethan literature, colonial American and Western Americana rarities—all of these are for the serious, long-view collector, and invariably, they are sure-fire investments. A single leaf from the Gutenberg Bible (I bought one for $500 about twelve years ago) now brings around $4,000 or $5,000—if you can locate one.

Then there are the first editions of Dickens, Thackeray, Melville, Poe, Hawthorne, Shelley, Byron, Keats, Coleridge, Wordsworth, Whitman, Twain, Thoreau, etc., etc. These authors' books are always in demand, particularly so when signed or inscribed. Autograph material by any such authors—and that includes all important contemporary writers—is also in our category of good investments. Good holograph letters and manuscripts by notable writers as well as celebrated public figures, are spiralling upward each year. (What would you pay for a letter from Charles G. Rebozo to Richard Nixon relating to gambling casino or real estate matters? Or a love note to Jackie, signed "Ari"?)

Specialization is recommended to new collectors. Concentrate on an author or category. There are many collectors who now buy only *first books* of famous writers. Others want everything an author has produced, including the ephemera and juvenilia—and in the case of playwrights, theatre programs and posters. Do not confuse a rare book collection with a library.

If you have very limited funds and can only spend five or ten dollars a week, I'd suggest buying first editions of the new poets, as published. It just happens that some of the best writing today is coming from poets such as Erica Jong, Muriel Rukeyser, Adrienne Rich, Anne Sexton, Denise Levertov, Diane Wakoski, Sandra Hochman. If you want to concentrate on an *established* living author, I'd recommend Albee or Tennessee Williams. (Either will present plenty of challenges.) If you like critics, try collecting the first editions of Edmund Wilson. The field is wide open and in the end, it's fun to collect the authors you admire and enjoy reading. Your taste will prove your collecting judgment in the end. Unless you have an unlimited bank account—and even if you have—make a plan; don't collect at random. Don't look for bargains. If a book is truly rare the price you pay today will probably look like a bargain five years from now. A signed copy of James Joyce's *Ulysses* will not get cheaper; nor will Marianne Moore's first book, *Poems;* nor Sylvia Plath's *Bell Jar* which she published under the pseudonym of Victoria Lucas in London, in 1963; nor Hemingway's *Three Stories and Ten Poems.* And then, there is in our midst a man who is as close to genius as one can come, Edward Gorey, writer and artist, whose little books are being bought up like the proverbial hot cakes. He may provide one of the most delightful single categories for a collector who wants to concentrate on one subject. He is immensely gifted and also prolific, and each of his books is a jewel. Some of them are very modestly priced, i.e., under $10.

Wherever possible, get an author to sign or inscribe your book for you—providing he's an author of importance and the book is a first edition. If the author is willing to make notations or corrections in the text of the book, great—its value increases. An autographed copy can often double the value of a book, or certainly enhance its value since it becomes, *ipso facto,* a unique, one-of-a-kind copy, a personal or possibly, an "association" copy. Don't write in your book (unless you are famous yourself) or underscore lines.

As an example of the importance of a famous author's inscription, Dylan Thomas' first book, *18 Poems* (London, 1914), in dust jacket and inscribed by Thomas, would fetch about $1,000; a copy without a jacket, not inscribed, about $400.

Keep your books away from windows or sunlight. Damp stains are to be avoided. A collection of value should be kept in a temperature-controlled room. Fragile books or booklets might be housed in slipcases or acetate envelopes.

Reputable dealers will always guarantee their wares; they will also guide and advise you. Each has a good reference library for ready consultation. There are many reference works and collector's guides to study; and auction records are important. Here are a few reference books to consider: *A Primer of Book Collecting* by Winterich and Randall; *The Book Collector's Handbook of Values* by Van Allen Bradley; *American Book-Prices Current,* published annually; *Gold in Your Attic* and *More Gold in Your Attic* by Van Allen Bradley.

When a dealer knows you are serious about collecting, he will help you if you level with him and don't use him for comparative-price-shopping-around purposes. A dealer is your best bet for buying at auction. A beginner should avoid competing with the experts in the auction room. There is a lot of specialized knowledge to acquire. A careful study of dealer and auction catalogs is one good way to begin learning about books and values. A special brand of savvy is required—a savvy not comparable to stock market investing. Taste and a special kind of instinctive response and literary judgment are called for. Plus a willingness to stick your neck out—for a *new* Ezra Pound or T. S. Eliot or Faulkner; new ones are always coming along.

Who are the hottest authors, including those living, to bet on for the present and future in terms of lasting worth and dollar appreciation?

Here's my personal lineup, and don't ask for logic or literary evaluation. These authors appear frequently in rare-book catalogs and at the auction sales, and their key books are climbing in price each season, especially their *first books*. They are virtually all foolproof and, in opening the list with Samuel Beckett, I indicate my high regard for the Big Irish Writers, who, through season after season, prove to be the most favored of all:

My "top ten" are:

SAMUEL BECKETT	(*En Attendant Godot*)
JAMES JOYCE	(*Ulysses*)
WILLIAM FAULKNER	(*The Marble Faun*)
WILLIAM BUTLER YEATS	(*Mosada*)
EZRA POUND	(*A Lume Spento*)
GERTRUDE STEIN	(*Three Lives*)
ERNEST HEMINGWAY	(*Three Stories and Ten Poems*)
T. S. ELIOT	(*Prufrock and Other Observations*)
TENNESSEE WILLIAMS	(*Battle of Angels*)
DYLAN THOMAS	(*18 Poems*)

I would follow the above "top ten" with twenty superstar authors to consider next, if you are able to accommodate a broad range of authors:

ROBERT FROST	(*A Boy's Will*)
EDWARD ALBEE	(*The Zoo Story; The Death of Bessie Smith; The Sandbox: Three Plays*)
WILLIAM CARLOS WILLIAMS	(*The Tempers*)
STEPHEN SPENDER	(*Nine Experiments by S. H. S.*)
D. H. LAWRENCE	(*The White Peacock*)
W. H. AUDEN	(*Poems*, 1930)
WALLACE STEVENS	(*Harmonium*)
JOHN STEINBECK	(*Cup of Gold*)

GWENDOLYN BROOKS	(*A Street in Bronzeville*)
EUGENE O'NEILL	(*Thirst*)
HENRY MILLER	(*The Tropic of Cancer*)
HART CRANE	(*The Bridge*)
F. SCOTT FITZGERALD	(*This Side of Paradise*)
EDWARD GOREY	(*The Unstrung Harp*)
JAMES BALDWIN	(*Go Tell It on the Mountain*)
ROBERT LOWELL	(*The Land of Unlikeness*)
SYLVIA PLATH	(*The Colossus and Other Poems*)
VLADIMIR NABOKOV	(*Lolita*)
VIRGINIA WOOLF	(*The Voyage Out*)
MARIANNE MOORE	(*Poems*, London, 1921)
KATHERINE MANSFIELD	(*In a German Pension*)

(*Caution*   After each of the above author's name I've put a book title in parenthesis; the book is one of the author's key books, a landmark-highspot title; in its first edition each is scarce to *very* rare. It's unlikely that you'll find many of these books in New York bookshops at this time. So please don't harass booksellers by phoning and asking for *A Lume Spento* or the signed limited edition on vellum of Hart Crane's *The Bridge;* nor is it likely that you can find a first edition of Gertrude Stein's first book, *Three Lives,* by making a few phone calls. Some of these books are priced as low as $35 and others run into the thousands of dollars.)

The following additional list of modern authors from England, France, and America is also recommended to all collectors. While this is our tertiary list we don't mean to imply that any of them are of lesser importance in literary terms; they are all highly esteemed in the market place and among readers. And there are others, not included, who merit inclusion; but lack of space, in addition to a subjective selective system employed by this writer, determined the present group for present purposes.

JAMES AGEE	PAUL BOWLES	JAMES DICKEY
CONRAD AIKEN	RAY BRADBURY	JOAN DIDION
GUILLAUME	ALBERT CAMUS	J. P. DONLEAVY
APOLLINAIRE	TRUMAN CAPOTE	H. D. (HILDA
JOHN ASHBERY	WILLA CATHER	DOOLITTLE)
DJUNA BARNES	LOUIS-FERDINAND	JOHN DOS PASSOS
DONALD BARTHELME	CÉLINE	NORMAN DOUGLAS
SIMONE DE BEAUVOIR	RAYMOND CHANDLER	LAWRENCE DURRELL
SAUL BELLOW	GREGORY CORSO	RICHARD EBERHART
JOHN BERRYMAN	BARON CORVO	RALPH ELLISON
ELIZABETH BISHOP	E. E. CUMMINGS	E. M. FORSTER
LOUISE BOGAN	EDWARD DAHLBERG	JOHN GARDNER

HERBERT GOLD

EDWARD GOREY

ROBERT GRAVES

GRAHAM GREENE

DASHIELL HAMMETT

JOHN HAWKES

JOSEPH HELLER

LILLIAN HELLMAN

CHESTER HIMES

CHRISTOPHER
  ISHERWOOD

RANDALL JARRELL

ERICA JONG

CAROLYN KIZER

MARY MCCARTHY

CARSON MCCULLERS

CLAUDE MCKAY

SOMERSET MAUGHAM

ARTHUR MILLER

A. A. MILNE

ANAÏS NIN

CHARLES OLSON

GEORGE ORWELL

ST.-JOHN PERSE

JAMES PURDY

MARIO PUZO

THOMAS PYNCHON

ADRIENNE RICH

LAURA RIDING

THEODORE ROETHKE

PHILIP ROTH

MURIEL RUKEYSER

ANTOINE DE SAINT-
  EXUPÉRY

J. D. SALINGER

CARL SANDBURG

WILLIAM SAROYAN

JEAN-PAUL SARTRE

SIEGFRIED SASSOON

ANNE SEXTON

GEORGE BERNARD SHAW

EDITH SITWELL

GARY SNYDER

JAMES STEPHENS

WILLIAM STYRON

J. M. SYNGE

ALLEN TATE

KURT VONNEGUT, JR.

DIANE WAKOSKI

MARY WEBB

EUDORA WELTY

NATHANAEL WEST

THORNTON WILDER

EDMUND WILSON

THOMAS WOLFE

TOM WOLFE

Note   The author cannot, will not, engage in correspondence relating to the buying or selling of rare books. Please consult a bookseller.

━━━━━━━

Death of a Bookshop

When Scribner's on Fifth Avenue in New York decided to give up its rare-book department, it was a sad piece of news for me and, I'm sure, for other collectors. A lot of history was made in that store. Harold Graves, the last manager of the shop and successor to the famous David Randall, had the lugubrious job of liquidating the stock and closing the department in 1973.

David A. Randall (until his death in 1975 with the Lilly Library at Indiana University) joined the Scribner rare-book department in 1935 and ran the show until 1956. John Carter, bibliophile *sui generis* (I published his *Books and Book-Collectors* at World in 1957), assisted him from England. Between them the New York rare-book business hummed. Its reverberations were felt around the world. The shop handled *two* Gutenberg Bibles in its heyday. Randall reviewed and clobbered (and rightly so) one of my very early books, a rare-book manual; but I respected his judgment and superior knowledge too much to hold it against him. I liked him too. Get a copy of Randall's book, *Dukedom Large Enough*. It's full of good book-collecting lore and vignettes of bookmen.

I don't know why Charles Scribner decided to give up the rare-book end of his very successful bookshop, "the cathedral of book-shops." Presumably it wasn't making enough money; I never asked him, since it is not my business to inquire. But I miss that part of his great store. I bought some of the best books and autographs I own from it, including my first edition of Coleridge's *Kubla Khan* (with *Christabel* and *The Pains of Sleep* [1816]). I also acquired some remarkable Thomas Wolfe letters from Scribner's. It was always a pleasure to step into its rare-bookshop door, to visit and browse. A shop like this should not have been allowed to die.

From the Journal: "A Thing of Beauty"

The acquisition of a first edition of Keats' *Endymion* (from Scribner's in November of 1971) enlivens my week. It begins: "A thing of beauty is a joy forever." When a line like that hits a poet, what can he do for an encore? Can I convey to my readers the excitement of reading that opening line from the first edition of this book of poetry? I'm sure most will not understand how one can work oneself up into a quiet state of hysteria over such an experience. Okay. But does it—could it—*mean anything* to you? Explore the notion.

The book has given me a sense of happiness, which is, I suppose, comparable to a sultan's having added a great beauty to his harem. Possessiveness is an evil, agreed—and the root of this evil is collecting. Why deny it—unless one has a plan to make the books and autographs available to the public, to students, to poets. Time will decide this. Meanwhile, I hold the book in my hand and wonder how many persons on this planet would share my feelings about the physical possession of this book by Keats. I hesitate to guess; the figure would probably depress me.

Keats was in his early twenties when he published this allegory dealing with ideal beauty. It was attacked viciously, and there are theories that the criticism helped to hasten his death. True or not, he died at twenty-six.

Another treasure acquired from Scribner's (on June 11, 1971) was a first edition (first issue) copy of Walt Whitman's *Leaves of Grass*, published in Brooklyn in 1855. "Published" is not an accurate word—"printed" would be more to the point. It was received with indifference or scorn, except by Emerson, one of the few civilized Americans of the time. He *greeted* Whitman "at the beginning of a great career." Emerson knew.

The Whitman is one of my most treasured books, and though the price seemed a fortune at the time, it is, thanks to time, one of the great bargains in my collection. Every time I remove the tall, green slender book from its slipcase, to read a page or two, I have the feeling that I am touching the poet. It is said that he set some of the type, and he may have handled the very binding I am holding.

John Carter

I've mentioned John Carter elsewhere in this book, but an additional comment is not without purpose. I knew him from the time I had the pleasure of publishing one of his books, and a bit of his expertise rubbed off on me. At least so I like to think.

Carter, who died at sixty-nine on March 28, 1975, has a historic place in book-collecting history for having exposed Thomas J. Wise, the famous book forger. Together with Graham Pollard, Carter unmasked this heretofore eminently respected British bibliophile in a book entitled, *An Inquiry into the Nature of Certain Nineteenth-Century Pamphlets*. Published in 1934, the book was virtually a David-vs.-Goliath encounter. (My inscribed copy seems to be missing from my library, but I do have a letter from Wise written shortly before he died in disgrace.)

Carter had many distinctions; one not generally known is that he was an expert in the field of musical manuscripts. He unearthed many forgotten or "lost" scores, including the original score of Mozart's *Haffner Symphony*. He also loved and collected detective fiction.

Any student of book collecting, searching for a thesis or bio-graphical subject, will find it in the life and works of John Wayn-flete Carter. He was an ornament to society, to literature, to the fraternity of bookmen.

Lawyers and Literature

One of the noblemen of the legal profession in New York is Melville Henry Cane, a poet of talent and sensibility, who continues, in his nineties (he was born in Plattsburg, New York, on April 15, 1879), to write excellent poetry—and to practice law. He represented the interests of Sinclair Lewis, Thomas Wolfe, and other men of letters. O Rare Melville Cane.

But unique among New York lawyers—and, alas, a man I never met—was John Quinn. He died in 1924 at the age of fifty-five. When I say unique, I mean just that. He was a self-made man, a lawyer who lived only from his earnings as a lawyer. This is not in itself unique. But the man was gifted with a special sight and artistic sense seldom found in a layman or a lawyer. His taste for art and literature was intense and he spent all his spare time and money cultivating (the word is used in its best sense) writers, poets, painters—especially men of genius who had not quite arrived at universal recognition.

For example, he recognized T. S. Eliot, Synge, Lady Gregory, Ezra Pound, Joyce, and Yeats, as well as Picasso, Gauguin, Matisse, Brancusi, Roualt, Duchamp, and Rousseau when they were barely known in America—or elsewhere. He provided legal aid to James Joyce when Joyce ran into trouble with the serialization of *Ulysses;* eventually, Quinn owned the manuscript. (Rosenbach acquired it later at auction: a long and complicated saga.)

Quinn bought works by the great unknown artists, and holo-graph manuscripts by writers who were yet to be recognized. He would give or lend money to artists in need, and kept up a heavy correspondence with them. He was the ubiquitous patron, "the bravest and most serviceable patron of modernism of his time, and probably the greatest collector of modern art." Aline Saarinen called him "the twentieth century's most important patron of living litera-

ture and art." He favored, above all, the living Irish writers; Yeats'
father called him "an angel."

A detailed biography of John Quinn, *The Man from New York,*
was written by B. L. Reid. What is significant in this story is the fact
that Quinn, whose livelihood depended solely on his daily appearance in his office or in the courtroom, had the time, the genius, the
will, to partake of the best around him and to befriend men and
women of genius through gifts, friendship, and old-fashioned patron-
age. In the process, he amassed an incredible private art and literary
collection. Collecting is obviously an art, and the results depend on
the passion, devotion, and seriousness of one's dedication to the
pursuit.

Though Quinn remained a bachelor throughout his lifetime—
and one might surmise that he had no time for romance or family—
his biography reveals some curious documentation relating to his
romantic affiliations. He was definitely not asexual. In this respect
he reminds me of A. S. R. Rosenbach, who also never married, but
who loved women only next to books. I suspect that if the choice
had been put to him, Rosenbach would have preferred a copy of
The Bay Psalm Book to the company of a beautiful woman. Possibly
I underestimate him.

9 *The Bookish Thing*

"But tho' Industrialism has now won an almost complete victory,
the handicrafts are not killed, & they cannot be quite killed, because they meet an inherent, indestructible, permanent need in
human nature. Even if a man's whole day be spent as a servant
of an industrial concern, in his spare time he will make something,
if only a window box flower garden."

—ERIC GILL

Quality Will Out

What is this bookish thing, this process of bookmaking?
It can be a creative act, performed with type, paper, cloth,
machines—and certain sensibilities. It consists of the conjoining of
psychic, mystic, and physical forces; the dynamics are similar to
those operating in the making of a play, a building, an opera; it is a
collaborative enterprise. At all times, the intent of the author
(creator) must be sensed, respected. There must also be a fine concern for the aesthetic elements; there are some moral forces involved, too.

Does the foregoing apply to all books? Certainly not.

Many books are manufactured like sausages, planned for a
sausage-consuming public. They are often made with cynicism; sometimes with a yawning, company-wide indifference. Most books of
fiction are in that category. I've seen publishers' typographers push
through a book's overall design in an hour's time; and I've seen copy-
editors grinding their teeth while applying their pencils to a manuscript. One can sense the copy-editorial venom content of the
physical book. The design and materials employed appear to result
from boredom, all with a sense of deliberate disharmony, to show
how little anyone cared. The result is deep-down mediocrity.

Some books, most of them, are ineptly made because there's no

385

decent emotional involvement whatsoever. There are certain kinds of books that have a plastic quality; packages that echo the products of toy manufacturers—Disneylike objects, lollipops, and bubble gum come to mind. They seem programmed for some mythical middle-American consumer, not for a reader. Only the Mickey Mouse watch is missing. These book things are produced as though by robots, at high-speed robot machines, with gummy plates and a watered-down piss-ink.

The above outburst is in no way an indictment of the industry as a whole; there are some excellent book manufacturers in the country. It just happens that there's a case to be made against many of the large, low-quality manufacturers because their output appears to be gaining acceptance as the standard.

Making books irrespective of profit is stupid. But on occasion a few pennies more can be justified to give a touch of quality to a book—say, for an extra impression of ink on the binding. Occasionally, too, a book must be made out of love of books, to give the publisher the feeling that he's earned his franchise.

During the thirties and forties I produced some books on my own, each in a limited edition, and mostly for pleasure. (Although I did have a faint hope of some profit.) In most of my conscious young adulthood (beginning at about fifteen) I wanted to *make a book;* bind a book; print a book. Actually, I was secretly rebinding, most crudely, some of my second-hand purchases—books that I'd bought for ten and twenty-five cents—in paisley silk, crushed velvet, and other exotic materials. One, a Baudelaire, I rebound in red silk brocade and doused with dime-store perfume.

But one of the first books that I issued as a private publisher, under my previously mentioned Black Archer Press imprint, was a story by John Cowper Powys, an early enthusiasm of mine. I had gone mad over his *Wolf Solent* and wanted to do a book of his on almost anything. The one I did do, in 1930, was a tale set in Patchin Place in New York City's Greenwich Village, and it bore the odd title (which the author adamantly refused to change) of *The Owl. The Duck. And—Miss Rowe! Miss Rowe!* (Incidentally, in the book Powys spoke of the "howls of prisoners from behind the bars of the Old Market Prison," referring to a place which, fortunately, was torn down in the early seventies.)

I found a small printer-binder with decent facilities who gave me some credit, and lo! I was a publisher. (Printers have faults, but they can be supportive, friendly, human.) The book was produced in an edition of 250 copies, each signed by the author. It was set in a sans serif type and bound in Inamachi vellum over boards. I designed it throughout. I still own one copy, but I've never seen it listed in any antiquarian catalog and wonder where the other 249 went.

Another early book I published was *Ivory Tower and Other Radio Plays* by Arch Oboler, at that time a popular radio playwright and director in Chicago. His book was issued in 1940 in a limited edition of 1,000 copies, and again, each was signed by the author. I was proud of the black and gold binding, the yellow and black title page, and the overall typography—which had proved a tough job for an amateur such as myself, since it involved the intricate arrangement of dramatic dialogue.

Oboler specialized in horror plays with Grand Guignol effects, and for the broadcasts, which originated in Chicago, he hired top-notch performers. Bette Davis and Alla Nazimova had roles in two of the plays that were printed in my book. Most of Oboler's works produced delicious shudders. Each opened with the admonition to turn out the lights; then doors creaked and wind seemed to moan in dark corridors. It was all Gothic skin-tingling stuff. I loved these plays, as did most listeners in the early forties, and some of the stories had high purpose as well as scary effects. Oboler, a vocal anti-Fascist, was not shy, and his plays often made statements that were daring for that period.

I loved every moment of publishing Oboler's book. I designed the jacket and prepared the modest ads. My selling resources, however, were limited and I doubt that I sold more than a third of the edition; I vaguely recall making a deal with Bob Simon, partner in Crown Publishers' remainder division, for selling the surplus at about twenty-five cents a copy. As I look at my dusty but beloved file copy now, with Oboler's inscription, "To William Targ—God, what a brave guy!" I confess immodestly that he was right. I had no organization or money for such an enterprise, just a burning in my gut to make some good books.

I've no regrets over the financial losses of my Black Archer Press. Most of my editorial judgments were good. In addition to the grati-fication I derived from publishing Oboler and Powys and other good writers, I took pride in having my name on a book. I was a *Publisher;* I had committed a creative act. It was like making a baby. I gave of my meager talents, my loving care; and I remember, with a blush, how I drove the printer and binder mad, demanding top quality and unrealistic delivery dates. I miss those days, when "art" came first. I was a bookseller-publisher in the tradition of the old English *stationers*. This was long before subsidiary rights became the First Law in publishing. It was before I had begun to learn something of a Balance Sheet, of Bookmaking, and Business Practice. Yet I survived for some twelve years, selling books, making books.

I'm glad to see that the tradition of the small press, the private, independent publisher, still prevails and, in fact, flourishes throughout America. (The Plantin Press and The Black Sparrow Press come to mind at once; elsewhere I speak about an American in Japan who is performing miracles on his own.) These vigorous adherents to the old traditions give secondary consideration to such matters as mass distribution, corporate image. They do give a damn about the craft: witness some of their books chosen each year by the American Institute of Graphic Arts. I hope none of them end up as members of conglomerates or appendages of broadcasting networks.

Small digression: I mentioned The Black Sparrow Press above, and wish to elaborate slightly. It thrives in Santa Barbara, California. In a period of about five years this press, devoted exclusively to works of poetry, issued 100 volumes. Some of the authors are Charles Bukowski, Ron Loewinsohn, Robert Duncan, Robert Kelly, James Purdy, Larry Eigner, Louis Zukofsky, Denise Levertov, Robert Creeley, Paul Bowles, Diane Wakoski, John Ashbery, James Tate, and Edward Dorn. The books are handsomely printed, often utilizing two colors. The paper-bound copies are priced modestly, although the signed limited copies run to $15 and $25; nevertheless, they are well worth the price. The point I want to emphasize here is made in the booklet they issued to celebrate the publication of their hundredth book: "Interesting to note that the whole press has been supported exclusively by the sale of the books. No foundations, no government grants to cloud the issues, no heiresses. It is commerce, & it has a cogency of its own."

Do you get the message? And they publish only poetry.

As an editor in a large trade publishing house I have the good fortune to participate in many areas of bookmaking; I'm privileged to speak at times for the kind of type design I think suited to a particular book; the binding materials and stamping dies; and I do have a voice in the jacket design. But in all truth, it isn't quite the same as doing it all yourself: you and just one small printer-binder. Not quite. At the same time, I must admit that I was gratified to be allowed to determine the physical character of most of my books at Putnam's. Wendel Roos and Ben Aiello were always warmly cooperative. Whatever one may think of these books, physically, I was involved in their conception—a real consideration for any editor who cares.

What I'm trying to say here is that every editor should somehow get his foot into the printshop door; he should smell the ink and hear the throb of the press; observe the bookbinding process if he can. He should, if possible, see how paper is made; a junket to a paper mill is something to remember. He should get a *tactile* acquaintance with the book by feeling the paper, the cloth, and the stamping, and examine the presswork, study the book's *personality*. I think Robert Frost should have written a poem called "Making a Book." (I wish I could.)

The quotation by Eric Gill at the head of this piece poses a sort of analogy; it has a profound meaning and I couldn't resist bringing it to your attention. If you can locate a copy of his book from which it is taken, *An Essay on Typography*, of which 500 copies were printed in London in 1931, get it. Read it. Also, read Robert Speaight's biography of Gill. It tells the full story of a liberated man, a type designer ("Perpetua"), and artist, engraver, sculptor, stone carver, and a polemicist of classic proportions. Gill was also a lovable eccentric of which there are too few these days. But most important, he knew how to make a book, as evidenced by his Golden Cockerill Press books, each one of which is a masterpiece.

C–S (1840–1922), Binder–Printer

Thomas James Cobden-Sanderson is another great Englishman who can't be found in my *Encyclopaedia Britannica*. He may be an odd and unfamiliar name to most of my readers. Nevertheless, he's an immortal, one of those odd ones who emerges from obscurity, makes his mark, achieves his destiny by fanatical dedication—and is gone. But his works remain a monument to an ideal: beauty in the book. His life story, too, is inspiring. He proved that a man can alter the course of his life in mid-stream, start from scratch in an entirely new area of activity, and succeed.

In brief, C-S was a master bookbinder and a master printer. But he was more; as a human being he was a real *rara avis*. In 1900, he founded The Doves Press (with Emery Walker) in Hammersmith, London. But let's start at the beginning . . .

Sanderson (his original surname) was the son of a civil servant, and his youth was spent in "mental anguish" and sickness. He tried for Holy Orders at Cambridge, but gave up on that. Later he tried law, and was admitted to the bar in 1871. He left law in disgust and sickness, went abroad to think, to recuperate, to sort out his life and future. During this time he met Annie Cobden (one of the lucky encounters of his life); they were married and he took her name as part of his own.

At a loss for a profession and direction, not to mention a means of livelihood, he decided, at his wife's and William Morris' urging, to learn hand bookbinding. He began an apprenticeship with de Coverly, a famous English binder. It soon became apparent that the student was to outdistance the teacher; in fact, in an extremely short time, Cobden-Sanderson showed signs of extraordinary competence, then greatness, in this highly specialized craft. His work became very much in demand.

He said bookbinding "gave me the means to live simply and in independence, and at the same time achieve something beautiful, and, as far as human things may be, permanent."

Putting it simply, he became the greatest hand-bookbinder of the nineteenth century, a supreme artist in an honored and ancient art. His tooling and handling of fine leathers and gold leaf showed C-S to be uniquely endowed with a taste and a precision seldom matched. The initials C-S, plus a date at the bottom of the inside back cover of a fine binding, means that T. J. Cobden-Sanderson personally bound the book—provided the date is *before* 1893. Work after that date bearing the name of The Doves Bindery, and his name, were done by his assistants.

C-S's bindery was officially set up in 1894. Today, any of his personally produced bindings would bring a huge sum, but I doubt that there's an opportunity to buy a single example of his work anymore; most or all of them are in great libraries and major private collections. Some of the white, blind-stamped, pigskin-bound copies of *The Kelmscott Chaucer* came from his bindery; the design was C-S's.

Inspired by the printing activity of his friend William Morris, C-S stopped his bookbinding activities and proceeded to establish a small printing press. His aesthetic standards were totally unlike those of Morris. C-S was fanatically pure in his taste. He entered the world of printing saying that bookbinding alone "was not enough to satisfy his search for 'man's ultimate and infinite idea.'" (It was as though Horowitz should give up the piano for the violin.)

With Emery Walker, C-S created a type based on Nicholas Jenson's fifteenth-century Roman, and by 1900 he was ready to carry out his plans. He hired a compositor and proceeded to make his first Doves Press book, *Agricola*, in 1901.

C-S's books, set in his Doves type, were mostly devoid of ornament or illustration. He did, however, respect calligraphic ornament and used it on occasion, sometimes breathtakingly well. He said that his books "depended for their beauty almost entirely upon clarity of the type, the excellence of the layout, and the perfection of the presswork," and they were in fact the ruthlessly simple application of C-S's dictum that "the whole duty of typography . . . is to communicate, without loss by the way, the thought or image intended to be communicated by the author."

His masterpiece was a five-volume Bible, produced in 1905; but there are a number of other books from his press that will also endure as examples of printing perfection; *Hamlet* is one; *Emerson's Essays* is another. The calligraphy occasionally employed in his books, with boldness yet great restraint (as in his Bible), is one of the ornamental wonders of his art.

After producing about twenty titles, C-S had a breakdown. His press closed down in 1916, and he chose (perversely, everyone will agree) not to allow anyone to use the type for any purpose. Quietly, he packed up his type, matrices, and punches, and, from the Hammersmith Bridge, dropped them all into the Thames. His *Journals: 1879–1922* relates the whole story. It is an extraordinary document and most moving. His destruction of the Doves type was a dramatic and lunatic act, obviously. But it isn't easy to account for the behavior of men of genius under certain conditions and emotional pressures.

C-S had achieved what he set out to do: he became a printer of fine books—one of the best of all time.

The foregoing is the merest sketch; his *Journals* and other writings, and in particular his beautifully written *The Ideal Book,* will fill you in on his views and life. He was visionary, mystical, determined. He communed with the stars.

His story, his inner struggles and his triumph as an artist, is one of the human sagas that should be known to all makers of books and all collectors of beautiful books.

The foregoing reminds me that for some years I tried to persuade a friend of mine to write a biography of C-S. He was my fellow New Yorker, Norman H. Strouse, one-time chairman of the board of J. Walter Thompson. Despite Norman's eminence as an advertising wizard (he handled Ford Motors, among other accounts) his real distinction for me was his deep-down bibliomania. He had a unique library in his triplex on Beekman Place; the top floor was devoted to books and to his mini-printing press on which he'd turn out small booklets and broadsides. He had a superb Doves Press/Cobden-Sanderson collection comprised of drawings, letters, and key books and bindings. His varied interests embraced fifteenth-century books and early printing, Ruskin, R. L. Stevenson, Macaulay—and Thomas Bird Mosher.

Strouse wrote and published a handsome book called *The Passionate Pirate,* which is all about Mosher, the printer-publisher from Portland, Maine. I think Strouse owned every book Mosher printed, some 450 titles.

What was so special about Mosher was not only that he had an exquisite taste in literature and bookmaking, but that he *pirated* his books; he didn't believe in paying royalties. Since some of the authors he published were George Bernard Shaw, William Butler Yeats, and Bertrand Russell—to name just a few of the major figures on his list—you can see the extent of his audacity. A lovable pirate we called him, although copyrighted authors may have called him something else. He died in 1923, leaving the world poorer. I read and owned many of Mosher's books in my youth. Just as a good part of my education derived from reading E. Haldeman Julius' five-cent Little Blue Books, I'm indebted to the Mosher books for my first encounter with many great writers.

Getting back to Cobden-Sanderson: If by some chance Strouse, who is now retired and luxuriating among the vine leaves of Napa Valley in California, has already written and published that book on Cobden-Sanderson without telling me, I'll never forgive him— unless he sends me a copy, bound in morocco by his hand-book-binding partner in crime, Charlotte Strouse.

By the way, Norman also published a charming little book called *How to Build a Poor Man's Morgan Library;* it is now out of print and has become a collector's item which probably only the Morgan Library can afford!

Typography: A Dialogue

Abe Lerner, my old friend: my authority on art, music, stereo equipment, cosmic forces, but mainly typography and book-making, paid me a visit recently. He gave me a present, too—a new book entitled *Frasconi: Against the Grain,* which Abe designed. (Anyone who knows anything about graphics and, in particular, the art of the woodcut, will be an admirer and collector of Antonio Frasconi.)

I asked Abe if he was in the mood to talk with me about book-making and the problems of producing decent books today, and about the *new* typesetting and printing methods.

Following is some of the dialogue I recaptured from a few hours' conversation supported by a tape recorder and a few beers.

TARG   Why is it that most book editors today know nothing about type and bookmaking? I spoke with a *wunderkind* editor the other day about the design of one of his books, and discovered he was oblivious to the design or materials of his book—that he wouldn't know Carolingian from cunnilingus. He was totally blank about type, paper, design—couldn't care less. A copy of one of his new books had just reached his desk. He never even glanced at the binding and failed to remove the jacket. These editors aren't con-scious of the binding design, dies, materials used, aren't interested.

I also know some publishers like that; some who don't know what Times Roman is. But does it matter, as long as the production people know? What's more to the point, why am I bothered by the schlocky quality of so many trade and paperback books I see these days. Are standards really on the skids? Are they really that bad? Are you listening?

LERNER   I'm listening. I'll get equal time. Getting to the point you're making, the answer is yes, it's true to a large extent. Book design has fallen under the baleful influence of advertising layout. In place of clarity and dignity on the reading page, with the type mass carefully controlled by margins and leading, there's the too-frequent pressure for "saving space" by using type too small, lines too long, and inadequate space between the lines.

TARG   And what about the ugly gimmicks?

LERNER   Yes, instead of well-formed typefaces for chapter openings and other display, we are treated to punch, socko, gimmicks. Constant novelty and punch are valid for advertising layout. But freshness in book design is very different.

TARG   So you blame Madison Avenue values for the lowered quality of book design, the repudiation of tradition?

LERNER   That's right. The straining for striking effects takes precedence. Running heads and page numbers, for example, are no longer considered mainly guides to the reader as he proceeds through a book, to be treated quietly in terms of decoration. They're made to dance and cavort on every page, to display the "originality" and "inventiveness" of the designer. The result is visual and psychological pollution that interrupts steady flow in the reading.

TARG   I can cite a perfect example of that—a recent book by Italo Calvino.* The book is shriekingly dominated by typographic gimmicks. But I want to get down to a more important matter— the composition itself, the new typesetting processes. The new technology is beyond me, frankly.

LERNER   Well, like the electronic calculator which does arithmetic very fast, computer composition can set books very fast. This is useful, of course, for long books, complicated books. It will take a good deal of experience to learn when to use it in cases where its benefits are obvious, and when not to use it where it is

*Invisible Cities.

not advantageous. But an immediate corruption in book design has been introduced by computer (and some other film) composition because of insensitive copying of metal-type design onto film.

TARG Well, why do some of the great typefaces look so lousy when produced by the computer?

LERNER Good point. The film-composition machine manufacturers have merely copied the currently popular good faces such as Janson, Baskerville, Times Roman, et cetera. But they've done this so ineptly that most of our books set on film are deprived of the efficiency and elegance of letter-forms as they were developed over the centuries. The fitting of the type pieces, the proportions of each letter, the independent yet related shapes of the italics, the feeling for the mass on the composed page—these and other essentials of a workmanlike craft are neglected.

TARG So how do we correct this? What can we do about it?

LERNER One thing publishers and their production managers can do is demand better type design from the manufacturers. Also, we must constantly apply pressure—tactfully—to printers and binders for better-made books. They'll produce a higher grade of work, without necessarily charging more, if they know that we, their customers, insist on it. To get their willing cooperation, we must deal with them decently, treating them as human beings and partners. We mustn't order them around or insult them. We can arouse their pride in workmanship; it's always latent in them and can be dug out by thoughtful discussion.

TARG I agree, but sometimes I get the feeling there's a cold war on and that the publisher isn't guilty; all he wants to get from them is quality and some decent service, to be treated like a valued client.

LERNER Well, you know how much guff the book manufacturer's service man has to take from a similarly harried publisher's production man. That's another matter. To get back to bookmaking, we must persistently hold up to printers the duties and pleasures of producing a quality job. Under the pressure of daily problems, most of us will tend to say, "Aw, the hell with it," allowing faults to go by and standards gradually to be lowered. So it isn't unreasonable or quixotic for the head of a publishing house, or his production man, to caution and criticize manufacturers against this tendency, whether they make paper or plates, or do printing and binding, or jackets. Always, someone has to keep his eye on the ball and make sure all the contributors to the final result don't go off the track. Plainly and simply, this means that a book must look good, must be a pleasure to hold in the hand, must be a felicitous aid to the author in reaching the reader. I know from experience that this can be done—I've been doing it, as you know, for some forty-five years.

TARG I want to get back to the business of the type, the oddities we see on the printed page these days—poor inking and such; and oy! the poor word-spacing per line, when straight prose lines look like poetry with wide spaces between words—*spaced out* is what I call some of that composition.

LERNER It's become worse since the computer came into use. It surprises me that typesetters allow such bad work to go out of their plants. But let's talk about something else that bothers me— the contemporary title page.

TARG Great! I have strong feelings about that subject; in fact I wrote a long historical essay on it, but my publisher thinks it's a bit too long and, I suspect, too dull, too pedantic, for inclusion in this book. Want to read it?

LERNER I'll take a look at it later. But I'd like to say that the art of designing a title page is diminishing, too. Relating the typefaces used on the title page to those in the text is often forgotten. Here again the desire for punch and socko dictate the choice and arrangement of type and ornament. Restraint and subtlety are in rare supply. Thus the opportunity for creating beautiful and meaningful layouts is wasted.

TARG Exactly. I say some things on that score. Remember Ben Franklin's title page for *Cato?* He was a printer with balls and taste. What we need today are more designers like P. J. Conkwright of Princeton University Press, or an American equivalent of Giovanni Mardersteig; his title pages are models of typographical purity. For that matter, we could use an American Officina Bodoni in New York. Right? Good title pages should be "house policy," examined like everyone examines jacket art—or am I getting carried away?

LERNER Not really; I'm with you. There's a particularly revolting new practice: the current vogue for introducing into period books (say, one about the twenties) all the available vulgarities of that period. To *suggest* the feeling of a period isn't enough for some contemporary designers; they must make sure you know they are hip, and they self-consciously bang every typographic and decorative drum they can lay their hands on. Camp and kitsch are embraced, replacing any feeling for beauty or standards of typographic taste.

TARG   One of my biggest gripes is with the mass-market paperback publishers. Their title pages are usually as alike as peas in a pod. They seem to have been produced by rubber-stamp makers, nondesigned by untrained people, and printed from watered-down ink. They are uniformly bad to uninteresting to pure *schrecklich*. A great many of them are simply laughable.

LERNER   And who's to blame? The house typographer and art director. Their thought and effort only go into covers. The publisher should be ashamed of such inept design and should require more from his staff. In other words, standards for the mass-paperback title page and the rest of the book's design should be set higher by the head of the house, as the late Allen Lane of Penguin Books did.

TARG   And the margins! I don't know where to put my thumbs when I read a paperback; there's literally no room to hold the bloody books. But *that's* a battle no one's going to enter—holding down the number of pages in paperbacks is important; costs are getting out of hand. So the type will be getting smaller, the margins narrower, and, oh yes, the title pages—but I doubt that anyone's going to care. In fact, as I hinted earlier—I meant to, anyway —except for a handful, most publishers don't care about design. The editors, by and large, don't know about printing design, don't know fine printing from doodly squat, if you get my meaning.

LERNER   I do, I do. How about a beer?

I Do Not Love Thee, Doctor Fell . . .

My diary for 1951 reminds me that I visited Oxford that fall as a guest of the printer of the university, the extraordinary Charles Batey. No more hospitable, vivacious—and informed—man could have welcomed me, and I felt honored as I sat in his office, surrounded by the biblioartifacts of Oxford's University Press, with copies of their books dating back to the sixteenth century. Batey took me over completely, and gave me not only a tour of the town, but a slow and hushed lecture within the ancient walls of the Bodleian Library, with its chain-bound tomes in old leather and parchment, dating from the thirteenth and fourteenth centuries. We also visited Blackwell's great bookshop, a scholar's paradise.

We talked and ate and drank in a pub; and then he took me to the University Press.

In comparatively freezing temperature I saw men at work, printing the Bible. The famous Oxford India paper was floating out of the press' rollers, and holding one of the sheets in both my arms I marvelled at the beautiful wet, black ink impressed like a lover's kiss on the snowy paper, so featherlight. I don't think there's a commercial printer in the world able to achieve what the University printers can; and though many years have passed since my visit, I suspect they're still at it, working without central heating and still unequalled for quality in printing, not to mention good typographical taste. (Batey did give me a "chemical" explanation when I asked him why the ink didn't freeze on the rollers. Apparently they were able to "doctor" the ink to accommodate it to the weather.)

One of the thrills of the visit for me was a gift copy of a small souvenir book, *The Fell Types* by Stanley Morison. And as a superbonus, Charles Batey opened a vault, pulled out several drawers, and let me see and *handle* some of the *original* Fell types—punches and type flowers more precious to a typophile than the Crown Jewels. The Fell types are among the most beautiful in the world; they're attributed in part to the hand of the sixteenth-century French printer-bookseller, Robert Granjon of Paris, and to others, probably Dutch printers, as yet still unknown. They are the oldest types, matrices, and punches in England, and were the gift of the English divine, John Fell, who acquired them at great expense and trouble, and presented to the university for use by its press.

If you are curious as to the quality of the Fell types, examine some of the books bearing the Oxford imprint; you'll see what felicity of type means.

One day, while making a bus trip to Stratford (now a kind of Shakespearean Disneyland except for its marvelous theatre), a charming English woman who was acting as guide on the tour, recited the following verse with a twinkle in her eye, as we rode through Oxford:

I do not love thee, Doctor Fell,
The reason why I cannot tell;
But this alone I know full well,
I do not love thee, Doctor Fell.

She chuckled as she recited the poem and I wondered, but did not ask, why its author (Tom Brown) chose not to love this great benefactor. To this day I'm not quite sure. All I know is that countless books issued at the University Press owe their beauty to the Fell typefaces and ornaments employed. In the typographical hall of immortals, there must be another version of the above poem, for Dr. Fell does deserve a new tribute. Not being a poet, I can't help. But Stanley Morison's great folio volume on John Fell, published in 1966, is the laurel wreath marking Fell's place in Oxford's history.

Mr. Typophile (1897–1966)

Paul Bennett was a man totally consumed by typography.

I was privileged to be among the speakers at Bennett's memorial services, the sort of chore I don't usually relish. In this case, though, it was an honor. I also wanted his widow Madge to know how I felt about her man, in a way I had failed to do heretofore.

Paul and I had many good visits—over an Algonquin luncheon table, at my apartment on Lower Fifth Avenue, in his Jackson Heights house, or in my office at World. We shared many bookish enthusiasms, and I learned much from him about printing, bookmaking, and the craftsmen involved. I also learned that there was a time when one should call a spade a spade, and if something was "crap," to say so.

In 1951 we published Bennett's *Books and Printing: A Treasury for Typophiles*. The idea was mine, the planning was Paul's, and Joe Trautwein designed the book. It is an outstanding, perhaps classic, example of the Useful Book, as well as a beautiful one. It illustrates by its own format and design the great traditions that influenced the appearance of books since the invention of movable type. The book was set in *twenty different typefaces*.

Paul Bennett was a force, an altogether human figure in the world of type and printing. He was, to paraphrase the Spinozan phrase, "a type-intoxicated man." He was tough, sentimental, exasperating, a perfectionist, an expert, an enthusiast. He was also a remarkable *doer*. Someone said of him, "He loved many things more than books and printing—and they were people." That sums Paul up; but not quite. He was the "onlie begetter" and publisher of one of the most extraordinary collections of books ever produced in America, The Typophile Chapbooks. These precious volumes add up to his real monument. And to quote Paul, "That's no crap." Every lover of books should own at least a few of these exquisite books (Duschnes and Chiswick are two booksellers who usually have an assortment of them on hand), and anyone planning to start a private press should examine some. They are jewels—and each was produced without corporate or serious financial support.

Give the Eye a Break!

Many books are made without regard for the eye's convenience, and I hold that anything less than 10-point on 12— except in the case of reference books and newspapers—is ruinous to the eyes in the long run. Reading for pleasure calls for decent, legible typefaces and ample white space. When in doubt, use Times Roman.

Reading for pleasure is, in the end, what books are all about. What I marvel at is the fact that countless millions of paperbacks are being read by men and women, and adolescents too, without the aid of a magnifying glass.

This book was set in 11 x 13 Caledonia.

"Perfect," Did You say?

By some ironic twist, linguistically speaking, the word "perfect" has come to be employed in the worst sense. To anyone aware of bookbinding, it is, in most cases, pejorative. A perfect-bound book is a book that is not sewn; rather, it is a book whose *four* edges have been trimmed. Its back side is glued onto an adhesive strip, which is the way most paperbacks and telephone books are bound. In ordinary, novel-size books, the saving, by avoiding the sewing process, is about fifteen cents. The life-span of a paperback book (perfect-bound) is limited to a few years; when the adhesive dries out, as it must, the pages will begin to come away from the spine as the book is opened flat. More and more clothbound books are bound in this fashion, and to open them for normal reading is an odd experience. There's a sleazy feel to the perfect-bound cloth book. The exception is in the large-size art or pictorial book. These special, high-priced books, when perfect-bound, rarely break up as do the paperbacks.

———

B. R. (1870–1957)

The above initials are familiar to most typographers, book collectors, and students of fine printing. They are those of Indiana-born Bruce Rogers, our foremost "arranger of type" and book designer. No American has been responsible for producing so large a number of beautiful books, and his genius and industry are unmatched in American book-production history.

B. R.'s books, each and every one of them, was created *con amore*. Everything he did bears his mark, the mark of imagination and exquisite taste. And in case one fails to sense his handiwork, his "signature," his famous thistle will be found somewhere in the book, usually in the colophon.

B. R. designed the beautiful Montaigne and Centaur types. He produced hundreds of books. In many of them his singular gift for employing printer's ornaments, punctuation marks, and flowers was displayed. He could take a handful of dull bits of metal and arrange them into designs of beauty, as witness some of the title pages in his books. He also wrote exceedingly well, and I had the pleasure of acting as editor on his book *Pi: A Hodge-Podge of Letters, Papers, Addresses, Written During a Period of 60 Years*, which he also designed. We published it at World in 1953. It's out of print now and I wish someone would reissue it, possibly The American Printing History Association?

Whether the young trade editors or the production men of today are interested in the designs and book work of B. R. is an interesting question to investigate. I doubt that many commercial publishers care—or even know about—the tradition of B. R. Alfred A. Knopf utilized his talents on occasion; Houghton Mifflin, in 1892, gave him great latitude early in his career, and he designed many fine books at the Riverside Press; later, he worked briefly for Cambridge University Press in England. He has been called the "typographic playboy," because of his amusing type designs and his urbane and entertaining speeches and writings. There is no one like him anywhere in the world of printing today, and one wonders why. One wonders too, why we have no successors to such masters of printing as Dwiggins, Gill, Updike, Cleland, Goudy, Rushmore, Morison. They were, by the way, all contemporaries of B. R. And all are now deceased.

As a one-time collector of printing and press books, I owned many of B. R.'s books, including his *Montaigne, Rime of the Ancient Mariner, The Odyssey, The Pierrot of the Minute, Gulliver, Utopia,* the 39-volume *Shakespeare,* and others.

At World, when Ben Zevin decided to produce a folio Bible, he assigned the job to B. R., who had already designed the great Oxford Lectern Bible in 1935. But now, Zevin wanted one of his own, and B. R. responded to the proposal, making the first American folio Bible.

B. R. began working on the World Bible in 1949, and it was completed in October of 1953. He died four years later at the age of eighty-seven.

As the work on the Bruce Rogers World Bible progressed, several of us—notably our art and production director, Abe Lerner, Ben Zevin, and I—had uneasy feelings about what we thought was excessive decorative treatment of the typographic framework. B. R. had chosen a sparkling typeface for the text, Goudy Newstyle, revising some of the letters and renaming the face Goudy Bible—all with the approval of Fred Goudy. Decorative three-line initials dotted every page at chapter openings, and immense floriated letters and borders opened and closed each of the books.

We had been nurtured on the total purity and freedom from decoration of the magnificent Rogers-designed Oxford Lectern

Bible; thus it seemed to us that the strong decoration weighed heavily on the World Bible, giving it too fussy and noisy an air.

Other voices in the book trade also privately expressed reservations to us on this score. Abe was allowed, finally, to take pen in hand. He screwed up his courage and wrote B. R. a tactful letter which was read and approved beforehand by Ben Zevin and me. In it Abe asked B. R. to look at his plan again and see if he didn't think that perhaps there was too much decoration. Rogers responded politely, but firmly held to his position; he was confident the decorative scheme was proper. His reply left us a little unhappy; there was nothing we could do but accept his judgment in the matter.

Looking through the World Bible now, after all these years, turning over the leaves slowly and thoughtfully, Abe and I have come to wonder what our fears were based on. B. R. was right and we were wrong. The decorative treatment is eminently successful, held in perfect control by B. R.'s genius, supremely beautiful in this monumental achievement.

We were there, in Abe Colish's printshop, when the first forms of the World Bible began to come off the press. And a landmark day it was. (Fred Melcher of *Publishers Weekly* was there, too.) I wrote a monograph covering the enterprise. Entitled *The Making of the Bruce Rogers Bible*, it was issued in a limited edition which B. R. designed, and it is now a collector's item. All the technical details of the production are recorded in this book—for the record.

Bruce Rogers and I had lunch occasionally at the Barbizon Plaza, and I enjoyed visiting him at his home in Danbury, Connecticut. His birthday parties—many publishers and printers joined the festivities—were always a special event for me. His wryness, dignity, and modesty were evident at all times, even when he was working on a major project. He was intolerant of second-rateness, but kept a "low profile" and his own counsel. I suppose the word "gentleman" could be applied to his person and manner—gentle man. But he was no pushover! No genuine artist is.

Beatrice Warde

To know her was to adore her, as the cliché goes. And true. She was a mighty potent and articulate force, "one of the boys" who possessed a touch of Bella Abzug, another woman I admire. I know of no woman who contributed so much, or had so much influence, on printing and on the typographical welfare of her times.

She began by writing, under the name of Paul Beaujon, scholarly articles on esoteric subjects such as the origin of Garamond type and the work of Fournier, which appeared in *Fleuron* and elsewhere, and she also produced learned articles on the typographers Jean Jannon and Charles Nicholas Cochin. She wrote like a passionate poet; she acted like an aproned craftsman at the stone. She was concerned with "how the little black marks got there on the page . . ."

Beatrice was the wife of Frederic Warde, the typographer; her mother was the beloved and irreplaceable May Lamberton Becker, children's book editor of the now-defunct *New York Herald-Tribune*. (May was world-renowned for caring and knowing all about children's books. She corresponded with thousands of writers, readers, and schoolchildren all her life. I persuaded her to become our "consulting" children's book editor at World, and she edited our Rainbow Classic series. She and I had glorious arguments concerning the suitability of titles in the series; she usually won. Only once did I stand firm: she felt that *Pilgrim's Progress* should go into the series, and I opposed the choice. Perhaps I was wrong, but I can't imagine many children of our time reading this book. The book has many merits, particularly the quality of its language, but kids will find it boring.)

But to get back to B. W.—

We published her *Crystal Goblet* at World in 1956. It sold out and went out of print, as do so many good books about books. I think it earned its keep, modestly. There is only a handful of books about printing, and I'm proud to have brought this one to the American reader and student. It's one of the books that helps me believe that I've paid my dues under the franchise of editor-publisher. In *The Crystal Goblet*, Beatrice Warde's historic essay propounding the notion that printing should be invisible was presented. Here's the opening paragraph:

> Imagine that you have before you a flagon of wine. You may choose your own favorite vintage for this imaginary demonstration, so that it be a deep shimmering crimson in colour. You have two goblets before you. One is of solid gold, wrought in the most exquisite patterns. The other is of crystal-clear glass, thin as a bubble, and as transparent. Pour and drink; and according to your choice of goblet, I shall know whether or not you are a connoisseur of wine. For if you have no feelings about wine one way or the other, you will want the sensation of drinking the stuff out of a vessel that may have cost thousands of pounds; but if you are a member of that vanishing tribe, the amateurs of fine vintages, you will choose the crystal, because everything about it is calculated to *reveal* rather than hide the beautiful thing which it was meant to contain.

Everyone in bookmaking misses Beatrice Warde—everyone, that is, who knew her, worked with her, heard her speak, or read her inspired writings. I'm sure that her co-workers at the Monotype Corporation in England miss her most of all.

(Feminist note: There are more women designing books in our industry than ever before.)

Bookmanship

Without belaboring the matter, I want to underscore one point: bookmanship is what publishing is all about. It involves many elements. To begin with, the tactile-visual aspects are important to understand. Binding, paper, type arrangement, dust jacket—these elements are not accidents in the making of a book. Each calls for expertise and taste.

How does the book feel in the hand, with and without the dust jacket? Do you remove the jacket when you first encounter the book, to see what the binding is like? I must know how the book feels in the hand, how it rests on the shelf, in the company of other books. Does it hold up in a window display—or does it fade into obscurity? Will the jacket reproduce well in advertisements? In the publisher's catalog? On the television screen? Does it have a real life of its own, a character and personality, making it unlike any other book? Ah! is it a book one can love and cherish? And will the author be pleased with it?

Some publishers will respond to the above with a shrug. Does the binding help sell one single extra copy? Who really cares about the typographic aesthetics? Well, someone should, and that someone should be the editor and the chief executive officer.

10 *Egress*

Book Reviews: The Agony and the Ecstasy

Colleagues, friends, and apprehensive acquaintances have asked me what, if anything, I'd say about the *TBR (The New York Times Book Review)* in my book. Some hinted that it would be tantamount to dropping the proverbial leaf in the Grand Canyon or wrestling with a greased bear, or sticking out one's tongue at the CIA or the American flag. The topic is rife in publishing (as I've indicated earlier) and comes up repeatedly throughout America, wherever book people gather. I've been asked if I'd utter the usual cranky complaints or be evasive; or would I be bold, as was Big-and-Brave Dwight Macdonald.

Frankly, it's a simple matter for simple discussion. No big issues are involved; merely justice. I'll present a few of my thoughts, and I assure you the sun will continue to rise and set at the appointed hours. (A few of these comments were printed in *Publishers Weekly* in an interview with Tom Weyr some time ago. Everything I said then I still hold to be true, and everything I think relevant will be stated here, and soberly.)

The *TBR* is remiss on a number of counts, and is guilty of a disservice to the *majority* of the readers, writers, publishers, and booksellers. As a *newspaper* it fails to function in accordance with its franchise—which is to present book *news*. Each year there are at least a few hundred worthy, newsworthy books that fail to get noticed by the *TBR*. Some may not be milestones in literature, but they are books in which the public would be interested.

The excessive and wanton waste of space (graphics, photos, and such) is apparent in every issue. At least six more books could be reviewed in each issue by cutting down on the "art."

The space wasted on specialized or "closed circuit" books is scandalous; this is also true of Letters to the Editor, which are of interest to only a small percentage of readers.

The most frequent indulgence is the overlong review of a book of limited interest. Example: a $35 two-volume history, *The Mediterranean*, by Fernand Brunel, was given a review in the May 18, 1975 issue. It occupied a total of some *twenty full columns*. This estimable work could have been handled in one third the space, but some power on high determined that this study of the Mediterranean world in the age of Philip II was newsworthy and of monumental interest to all *Times* readers. We don't question the importance and scholarship of Mr. Brunel and have no quarrel with the work, but how many other good books were sacrificed to accommodate it? This review is but one of many examples of editorial imbalance; and so many of these essay-reviews are written in the usual fruity prose of Academe, whereas the general reader simply wants the essentials.

The *TBR* has become tribal, with strong in-group concerns and an elitism complex. The editor's hand is heavy throughout.

The *TBR*'s concern with the general public's interest in entertainment and popular subjects is diminishing, and in this respect is unique in the whole *New York Times* complex, which is, unquestionably, the world's most complete *news*paper, always excelling in complete coverage and objectivity. The *TBR* is a maverick and sober scrutiny and analysis from within is long overdue.

Another example of excess and editorial astigmatism: the two full pages devoted to a biography of Shelley by Richard Holmes in the June 22, 1975 issue. As though a half dozen first rate biographies didn't already exist. Beginning on page one of the *TBR*, Mr. Morris Dickstein tells us a great deal about Shelley—almost as much as he does about the book he is reviewing. These two full pages could have been condensed to three columns and provided space for two other worthy books. Can you imagine the average reader of the Sunday *Times* plunging into this review with gusto, and then phoning his bookseller to send the $22.50 volume to him posthaste?

Just as the level of critical excellence is acceptable in the daily *New York Times*, so is the level of performance in the *TBR* generally the reverse. So many reviews are written out of personal pique. Depending on the particular neurosis of the reviewer, so goes the review.

Too many competent reviewers are ignored by the *TBR;* instead prejudiced, academic oddballs; defeated writers; boring dilettantes; and teachers of a low order get assignments. Very few books are reviewed by professional critics or qualified reviewers—or by reviewers without axes to grind.

The *TBR* rarely treats a book as news; usually, the reviewer revs up to display his personal medals, his erudition; then, after several hundred words or more, he gets down, unwillingly, to the book at hand. When a serious book, *The Conquest of Poverty* by Henry Hazlitt, gets 17½ lines in the same issue in which Barbara Howar's *Laughing All the Way* gets three full columns, including a good-sized photo of the author, one wonders about the editorial values guiding the *TBR*. When the excellent critic, Helen Vendler, gives six full columns to Calvin Bedient's book, *Eight Contemporary Poets;* when Shelby Foote's rehashing of the Civil War gets five columns; a biography of Hugh Hefner, a half-page review; a book of short stories by John Gardner, the front cover, plus three full columns; and when the inside back cover is devoted to a pastiche more suited to *The New Yorker*, dozens of fine books must obviously go begging—and I'm referring to a December 15 pre-Christmas issue!

The *TBR* indulges in too many bizarre, marginal exercises on books not even of remote interest to the general reader and the book profession. The publication suffers from an identity crisis. It often seems to veer toward the editorial direction of the *New York Review of Books*, the *Sewanee Review*, the *American Scholar*. It is no longer an identifiable creature. It's a zoological hybrid, an oddity, yet to be named and classified. It certainly is not the *Times Literary Supplement*.

The *TBR* runs boring essays of interminable length with tempest-in-a-teapot issues; sometimes they occupy space equivalent to at least four or five normal reviews. It often throws books of high quality into the mini-review columns, and at the same time, wastes full pages on trivia or self-indulgent essays by one of the editors. An author labors years on a book and gets knocked in the teeth with a stick of type.

By and large, the *tone* of the *TBR* is boring. Publishers rarely take its feature pieces seriously, and general readers with whom I've discussed this matter from time to time (and I have given this particular subject more than usual attention) do not, in general, even notice these articles, though oddly, they seem to read the *Sunday Times Magazine*. To prove my point, I asked more than twenty friends if they had read Allen Ginsberg's poem, "Mugging," on the inside back cover of the January 5, 1975 *Times Magazine*—and *every one* had indeed read it and commented on it.

The *TBR* is contemptuous and guilty of gross snobbery concerning the commercial book, as though only masterpieces were worthy of their attention and all else was to be treated as dirt. It usually puts down books simply because their authors are commercial successes or famous as high-schlock novelists.

There is more eccentric bias in any given issue of the *TBR* than any innocent reader might suspect. If you want information on an author's latest book—what it is all about, what it has to say, how well or poorly it is written—don't be too hopeful. As a rule, a kind of soggy rhetoric and literary posturing precedes the so-called review. Because impatience has a way of settling in quickly in the *TBR* reader, it will sometimes turn the reader off—or it may turn his stomach.

Oddities beyond counting occur in the *TBR*. Here's one that touched me personally. There was a review, three columns long, by someone named Mavis Gallant, of Simone de Beauvoir's book, *All Said and Done*. The review was totally destructive and lacking in one solitary favorable comment about the author or her 500-page book. What is interesting and ironic is that in the same week, in the *New York Review of Books,* the same book was reviewed (in a full page) and lauded by one of the world's foremost literary critics, V. S. Prichett, who is the literary editor of *The New Statesman* and *The Nation*. Is it possible that the same book is at once utterly worthless and also excellent?

What is of interest and not without cause for wonderment is the fact that while the *TBR* review made mincemeat of de Beauvoir, in their big pre-Christmas roundup, they decided to recommend this very book as one of the best books of the year. (By alphabetical accident, it led off the entire recommended list.)

I'm told that it is foolhardy to "attack" the *TBR* because retribution will follow. I don't believe this for a moment. It is possible that the present book may be ignored or shredded or thrown to the sharks. The truth is, if my publisher can withstand any of these eventualities, so can I. (He will probably spend money advertising this book in the *TBR* anyway.)

I must now contradict what is inherent in the foregoing—namely, that it is important, in fact vital, to the life of a book to be reviewed in the *TBR*. Not so. I could cite numerous books that succeeded though they never were reviewed by the *TBR*. I know of a famous author's work that sold around 60,000 copies in 1974, and was not reviewed in the *TBR*, nor in the daily *Times*. Elsewhere, it received almost unanimously fine notices. Other books made the *TBR* review *long after* they were high on the best-seller lists; in short, long after the news of the books was widespread, the *TBR* reported on them condescendingly.

What would I propose to remedy my allegations of misconduct, disservice, and so on? Well, here are a few proposals:

1. The *TBR* should give more hard thought to the general interest of a book before giving it more than a column of space. How large an audience will care? While I am the first to cheer the *TBR* for giving poetry, and especially new poets, good space in the sun, I think they get far too much space per title. Also, in most cases, the *reviewers* are unreadable (Helen Vendler excepted); the average *TBR* reader does not have the patience to follow the tortuous syntax and fancy verbiage of the reviewer.

2. The *TBR* should devote its inside back page ("The Guest Word") to a full treatment of book news and trade gossip. It treats this category of news inadequately in a compressed 6-point type calling for a magnifying glass.

3. The *TBR* should, at least once a month, run a column or two on rare books and happenings in the London and New York auction galleries. A great many *TBR* readers collect rare books.

4. It should cut the illustrations by half and give the space gained to more reviews.

5. Each week, the *TBR* should list "books published recently"—a simple listing of at least a hundred or so titles that will not be reviewed. These books, presumably legitimate works of general interest, certainly deserve a one- or two-line announcement. I think this feature would be followed avidly. It would have news value as well.

6. With one exception—Wilfrid Sheed—I'd eliminate all the confessionals, essays, and oddball causeries that appear in the *TBR*, taking up valuable space. Mr. Sheed, admittedly an asset to any publication, is one writer who should be retained—assuming the *TBR* feels the need of editorial relief.

7. I'd double-check to make certain no book is assigned for a review to an author's enemy or competitor in a given field. For example, I don't think Irving Wallace should be asked to review Harold Robbins (they happen to be close friends). Nor would John Simon be entirely suitable as a reviewer of a book by Clive Barnes. Yet it is a familiar gambit of the *TBR* to give a book *to the one absolutely wrong reviewer*. Every publisher can cite a few instances of this kind of quixotic (perverse) assigning of books and I'll give a recent example: Dan Kurzman's book, *The Race for Rome,* was published by Doubleday and reviewed in the *TBR* in February 1975. The reviewer chosen was Martin Blumenson, an acknowledged "General Clark man," who is Mark Clark Professor at the Citadel in Charleston, South Carolina. In my opinion, Blumenson couldn't possibly be objective about Kurzman's book—just look into his record and his published books. Kurzman, a responsible journalist and historian, expressed honest outrage at certain "rush for glory" tactics of the military; Dr. Blumenson seems to have misinterpreted Kurzman's position and hence clobbered the book. I noted that almost every other review of Kurzman's book around the country was favorable to exuberant.

As Harry Golden would say, "Enough already."

Finally . . .

William Faulkner wanted to put everything into a single sentence, "not only the present but the whole past on which it depends and which keeps overtaking the present." I too would like to sum up in one sentence what is most important to me and what I think might be a guideline for others. I'd commit myself to the following: *Try not to miss anything worth experiencing.*

If there is one other message I feel able and privileged to hand on to my reader, relating to living the sane and fruitful life, it is this: Our greatest enemy, during our sleeping and waking hours, is *fear.* With few exceptions, our dreams are shaped by fear; our lives are haunted by insecurity-and-loss spectres. We worry about losing loved ones, jobs, health, savings, status, public respect. We fear a multitude of unseen and nonexistent enemies. To paraphrase Shakespeare, we should arise each morning from sleep and declare Fear *the enemy* and say, "Avaunt thee, Fear—fuck off!" I think you will agree that most of the dreaded events in our minds never come to pass. So, as each and every fear element enters your consciousness, cope with it with the Italian gesture—the thumbnail salute.

One of our philosophers, Gertrude Stein, once said, "There is no use in telling more than you know; no, not even if you do not know it." This sentiment has guided me in the writing of this book. If I seem to have shortchanged you, this is the reason.

Envoi

The question was asked: What of my personal future?

My answer is obvious: to continue working and doing what I do best—as long as my eyes and vertebrae hold out. Didn't Voltaire say it is the only way to make life endurable?

Not working is unthinkable, is synonymous with sickness. Retirement is an obscene word in my lexicon; it is one step away from euthanasia. Not being involved in the book-publishing process is for me like not breathing. Sharing the joys and anguish and hopes with authors is my purpose, my need.

There's a notion lodged in one of the lobes of my brain—that a great manuscript/book, a world masterpiece, is awaiting me around the corner. As an editor, it's my fantasy that we'll meet up, that book and I, before I call it quits.

Recommended Reading

BAILEY, JR., HERBERT S. *The Art and Science of Book Publishing.* 1970.
BENÉT, WILLIAM ROSE. *The Reader's Encyclopedia.* Second Edition. 1965.
BENNETT, PAUL A. *Books and Printing.* 1951.
BLAND, DAVID. *A History of Book Illustration.* 1958.
BURLINGAME, ROGER. *Endless Frontiers: The Story of McGraw-Hill.* 1959.
———. *Of Making Many Books.* 1971.
CARTER, JOHN. *ABC for Book-Collectors.* 1952.
———. *Books and Book-Collectors.* 1957.
CHAPPELL, WARREN. *A Short History of the Printed Word.* 1970.
COBDEN-SANDERSON, T. J. *Cosmic Vision.* 1922.
CONNOLLY, CYRIL. *The Modern Movement.* 1966.
CROSBY, CARESSE. *The Passionate Years.* 1953.
DAY, KENNETH, ed. *Book Typography.* 1924.
DIEHL, EDITH. *Bookbinding: Its Background and Technique.* 1940.
DIRINGER, DAVID. *The Hand-Produced Book.* 1953.
———. *The Illuminated Book.* 1958.
DORAN, GEORGE H. *Chronicles of Barabbas.* 1952.
DOUBLEDAY, F. N. *A Few Indiscreet Recollections.* 1928.
DUTTON. *Seventy-Five Years.* 1927.
EXMAN, EUGENE. *The Brothers Harper.* 1965.
FABER, GEOFFREY. *A Publisher Speaking.* 1934.
GLAISTER, GEOFFREY ASHALL. *An Encyclopedia of the Book.* 1960.
GOUDY, FREDERIC W. *The Alphabet and Elements of Lettering.* 1942.
GROSS, GERALD, ed. *Publishers on Publishing.* 1961.
HACKETT, ALICE P. *Sixty Years of Best Sellers.* 1956.
HAYCRAFT, HOWARD. *The Art of the Mystery Story.* 1946.
HALDEMAN-JULIUS, E. *The First Hundred Million.* 1928.
HERSEY, JOHN, ed. *The Writer's Craft.* 1974.
HOBSON, ANTHONY. *Great Libraries.* 1970.
HOLT, HENRY. *Garrulities of an Octogenarian Editor.* 1923.
HOUGHTON MIFFLIN. *Fifty Years of Publishing.* 1930.
HOWARD, MICHAEL S. *Jonathan Cape, Publisher.* 1971.
HUNTER, DARD. *Papermaking.* 1947.
JACKSON, HOLBROOK. *The Anatomy of Bibliomania.* 1930.
JENNETT, SEAN. *The Making of Books.* 1951.
JOSEPH, MICHAEL. *The Adventure of Publishing.* 1949.

KERR, CHESTER. *A Report on American University Presses*. 1950.

KNOPF, ALFRED A. *Some Random Recollections*. 1948.

LATHAM, HAROLD. *My Life in Publishing*. 1965.

LEE, CHARLES. *The Hidden Public: The Story of the Book-of-the-Month Club*. 1958.

LEGMAN, G. *The Horn Book*. 1964.

LEHMANN-HAUPT, HELLMUT; WROTH, L. C.; and SILVER, R. G. *The Book in America*. 1952.

LEWIS, S. L. *One Man's Education*. 1967.

LIDDERDALE, J. and NICHOLSON, M. *Dear Miss Weaver*. 1970.

LITTLE, BROWN. *One Hundred and Twenty-Five Years of Publishing, 1837–1962*. 1962.

MADISON, CHARLES A. *Book Publishing in America*. 1966.

——. *The Owl Among Colophons*. 1966.

MEYNELL, FRANCIS. *Typography*. 1924.

MORISON, STANLEY. *Modern Fine Printing*. 1925.

——. *On Type Designs, Past & Present*. 1962.

MOTT, F. L. *Golden Multitudes*. 1947.

MUMBY, FRANK. *Publishing and Bookselling*. 1954.

MUNBY, A. N. L. *Portrait of an Obsession*. 1967.

NEWTON, A. EDWARD. *The Amenities of Book Collecting*. 1918.

OGG, OSCAR. *The 26 Letters*. 1962.

ORCUTT, WILLIAM DANA. *The Kingdom of Books*. 1927.

OSWALD, JOHN CLYDE. *Printing in the Americas*. 1937.

PAGE, W. H. *A Publisher's Confession*. 1905.

PARTINGTON, WILFRED. *Forging Ahead*. 1946.

Penguin Books: A Retrospect. 1951.

POWELL, LAWRENCE CLARK. *The Alchemy of Books*. 1954.

——. *Bookman's Progress*. 1965.

——. *California Classics*. 1971.

PUTNAM, G. P. *A Memoir of George Palmer Putnam*. 1903.

——. *Memories of a Publisher: 1865–1915*. 1916.

RANDALL, DAVID A. *Dukedom Large Enough*. 1969.

REID, B. L. *The Man from New York: John Quinn and His Friends*. 1968.

ROGERS, BRUCE. *Pi: A Hodge-Podge of Letters, Etc*. 1953.

SADLEIR, MICHAEL. *Nineteenth Century Fiction*. 1951.

SAWYER, C. J., and DARTON, F. J. H. *English Books, 1475–1900*. 1927.

SHEEHAN, D. H. *This Was Publishing*. 1969.

SHENKER, ISRAEL. *Words and Their Masters*. 1974.

SIMON, OLIVER. *Introduction to Typography*. n. d.

——. *Printer and Playground*. 1961.

SPEAIGHT, ROBERT S. *The Life of Eric Gill*. 1966.

STEVENS, GEORGE. *Lincoln's Doctor's Dog*. 1938.

STRAUS, RALPH. *The Unspeakable Curll*. 1927.

TARG, WILLIAM. *Bibliophile in the Nursery*. 1957.

——. *Bouillabaisse for Bibliophiles*. 1955.

——. *Carrousel for Bibliophiles*. 1947.

THOMAS, ALAN G. *Great Books and Book Collectors.* 1975.

TOWNER, WESLEY. *The Elegant Auctioneers.* 1970.

TYRON, W. S. *Parnassus Corner: A Life of James T. Fields.* 1963.

UHLAN, EDWARD. *The Rogue of Publishers Row.* 1956.

UNWIN, SIR STANLEY. *The Truth About Publishing.* 1960.

UPDIKE, D. B. *Printing Types.* 1922.

WARDE, BEATRICE. *The Crystal Goblet.* 1956.

WAUGH, ARTHUR. *A Century of Publishing.* 1930.

WELSH, CHARLES. *A Bookseller of the Last Century.* 1885.

WHEELOCK, JOHN HALL, ed. *Editor to Author: The Letters of Maxwell E. Perkins.* 1950.

WINTERICH, J. T. *Books and Man.* 1930.

WOLF, EDWIN II and FLEMING, JOHN F. *Rosenbach: A Biography.* 1960.

Index

Abrams, Harry, 163
Abramson, Ben, 38–39, 40, 45, 288
Abzug, Bella, 146, 333
Adams, Barbara, 145
Adams, Katherine, 40
Adams, Mary, 89, 308
Adams, Richard, 338
Addams, Charles, 133
Aiello, Ben, 389
Alcott, Louisa May, 201
Algren, Nelson, 8, 25, 117, 275, 359
Alinsky, Saul, 9
Amado, Jorge, 134, 135
Ambler, Eric, 63, 64
American Mercury, 34
American News, 242
Amory, Thomas, 56
Anchor Books, 227, 228
Anderson, Emily, 322
Anderson, Margaret, 159
Anderson, Sherwood, 93
Angelou, Maya, 321
Angoff, Allan, 332
Antioch Review, 71
Argus Bookshop, 288
Asquith, Margot, 161
Atheneum, 181, 259
Auden, W. H., 95–97, 273, 352, 373
Auder, Michel, 125, 130, 355
Austen, Jane, 354

Bacall, Lauren, 187
Baker & Taylor, 242
Baldwin, James, 128–29
Ball, Gordon, 111
Ballantine Books, 228, 326
Balzac, Honoré de, 238–39

Banker, Bob, 170
Bankhead, Tallulah, 58
Bantam Books, 106, 166, 172, 227
Barker, Nicolas, 369
Barondess, Dr., 133
Barrett, Oliver R., 368–69
Bartillat, Christian de, 102
Basler, Roy, 67, 68
Batey, Charles, 397–98
Bay, André, 102
Bay, Marie-Pierre, 102
Beach, Sylvia, 158–59, 160–61
Beardsley, Aubrey, 30
Beauvoir, Simone de, 10, 82, 85, 103–104, 115–16, 117–18, 156, 233, 275, 318, 359, 410
Becker, Mary Lamberton, 404
Beckett, Samuel, 25, 51, 91, 113, 114–16, 161, 162, 186, 373, 374
Behan, Brendan, 91
Bellow, Saul, 8, 25, 41–45, 293, 299, 357
Benjamin, Mary, 119, 120
Bennett, Arnold, 350
Bennett, Madge, 399
Bennett, Paul, 399–400
Bennett, Whitman, 45, 192
Benson, Deborah, 38
Berger, Yves, 102
Berkley, 228
Berle, Milton, 46, 345
Bernstein, Aline, 263–64
Bernstein, Leonard, 96
Bessie, Simon M., 181
Betjeman, Sir John, 95, 97
Biancolli, Louis, 199, 322–23
Bing, Rudolf, 47

Birstein, Anne, 133
Bixler, Paul, 71
Black Archer Press, The, 36–37, 59, 60, 223–24, 299, 386–88
Black Cat Press, 59
Black Sparrow Press, The, 388
Black Sun Books, 309
Black Sun Press, 215
Blacker, Irwin, 268
Blanck, Jacob, 258
Block, Bela von, 314
Blond, Anthony, 130, 208
Blumenson, Martin, 412
Blumenthal, Joe, 67
Bodenheim, Maxwell, 36, 54–55
Bogart, Humphrey, 187
Bonanza Books, 213
Bookazine, 242
Book Collector's Journal, The, 37
Book-of-the-Month Club, 163, 164
Bormann, Martin, 106
Boucher, Anthony, 64, 68
Bourne, Dr. Geoffrey H., 260, 261
Bourne, Nina, 184
Boswell, James, 79
Bowles, Paul, 108
Bradley, Jenny, 314
Braun-Munk, Eugene, 11, 104, 314
Brautigan, Richard, 361
Breinin, Patricia, 145
Breit, Harvey, 71, 76, 96, 196
Brent, Stuart, 43
Brentano's, 242, 302
Brett, George Edward, 211
Brett, George P., Jr., 211
Brett, George P., Sr., 210–11
Brice, Fanny, 264
Broad, Nina, 3
Bronowski, Jacob, 353
Brooks, Gwendolyn, 321
Brophy, Brigid, 82, 274–76, 321, 322, 342
Brown, Andreas, 110, 190, 191, 192
Browne, Francis, 236
Brunel, Fernand, 408
Bryher, 283

Buchwald, Art, 35–36, 44, 82, 85, 111, 156, 233
Burgess, Anthony, 261, 273
Burne-Jones, Edward, 70
Burns, George, 314
Burns, Robert, 368
Burton, Sybil, 312
Buttons, Red, 46, 345

Cain, James M., 63, 64
Caldwell, Taylor, 341
Calvino, Chichita, 240
Calvino, Italo, 240
Calvocoressi, Peter, 226
Cane, Melville Henry, 383
Calmann-Levy, 128
Cambridge University Press, 402
Canfield, Cass, 108–109
Capone, Al, 15, 16
Capote, Truman, 337
Capron, Marion, 74
Carroll, Lewis, 56
Carson, Johnny, 327
Carter, John Waynflete, 196, 380, 382–83
Carybe, 135
Cassell, 107
Cates, Curtis, 130, 317
Cather, Willa, 223, 224
Catton, Bruce, 68
Cendrars, 104
Ceppos, Arthur, 333
Cerf, Bennett, 68, 160, 193, 199, 214, 286–87, 302, 304–306
Chandler, Raymond, 63, 64
Chase, Ilka, 279
Chaucer, 69
Chiswick, 400
Chute, Joy (B.J.), 320
Chute, Marchette, 82, 254–55, 319–20
City Lights, 110
Clark, Lord Kenneth, 353
Clark, Shirley, 355
Cobden-Sanderson, Thomas James, 70, 389–93
Cohen, Arthur A., 82
Cohen, Barry Lee, 216

Cohen, Elliott, 285–86
Cole, William (Bill), 72
Colish, Abe, 403
Collier, John, 103, 261–62
Collier, Shirley, 262
Collins, Sir William (Billy), 84, 99
Combescot, Pierre, 102
Comden, Betty, 133
Commins, Saxe, 73, 305
Conkwright, P. J., 396
Connolly, Cyril, 99, 103, 296–98, 342
Constable, 105, 368
Coppola, Francis Ford, 113
Corwin, Norman, 82, 125, 276
Coryate, 29
Cosmopolitan, 177
Costa, Nicolas, 102
Costain, Thomas, 251
Coverly, de, 390
Covici, Pat, 208, 298–99
Coward, McCann & Geoghegan, 143
Cozzens, James Gould, 171
Crane, Hart, 372
Crane, Stephen, 223
Crawford, Joan, 187
Cromie, Bob, 16–17
Crosby, Caresse, 215
Crosby, Harry, 215
Crown Publishers, 213, 214, 387
Crowther, Bosley, 133, 284, 285
Crowther, Florence, 133, 284
Cuddy, Page, 113, 145
Cummings, E. E., 362–63
Cunard, Emerald, 161
Cunard, Nancy, 161–62
Curll, Edmund, 56–57

Daigh, Ralph, 111, 171, 172
Dale, Chester, 25
Dale, Mrs. Chester, 25
Dannay, Frederic, 64, 68
Darrow, Whitney, 214
Dawson, 121, 374
Day, John, 262
Day, Patricia, 146
Dayan, Moshe, 293, 328
De Felitta, Frank, 268

Dell, 228, 236
Derleth, August, 25
Dessauer, John P., 151
Deutcke, Franz, 207
Dewhurst, Colleen, 334
Diamond, Paula, 145
Diehl, Digby, 127
Diehl, Edith, 40
Dillinger, John, 16, 55
Dimondstein, 242
Dodd, Mead, 362
Doolittle, Hilda (H.D.), 283, 290
Doran, George H., 208
Doubleday, 143, 157, 170, 187, 227, 233
Doubleday, F. N., vi, 208
Doubleday Book Shops, 242
Doves Bindery, The, 390–91
Doves Press, The, 69, 70, 390, 391
Dreiser, Helen, 72–73
Dreiser, Theodore, 72, 73, 74, 82, 359
Droemer, Willy, 102
Dubinsky, David, 153
Duncan, Robert, 22
Dunninger, 61
Duschnes, Fanny, 70
Duschnes, Philip C., 69, 70, 294, 400
Dutton, E. P., & Co., 214, 255, 260
Dwoskin, Charles, 101–102
Dystel, Oscar, 172

Egoist, The, 215
Egoist Press, The, 159, 215, 283
Ehrlich, Arnold, 180
Elbert, Joyce, 103
Eliot, T. S., 91, 206, 215, 282, 373
Ellman, Richard, 159, 160
Emerson, Ralph Waldo, 7, 372, 382
Engstrand, Stuart, 25
Enoch, Kurt, 11
Epstein, Bill, 242
Epstein, Jason, 227
Epstein, Ted, 242
Evans, Joni, 145
Evans, Matthew, 95, 115

Faber, Sir Geoffrey, 208, 234

Faber & Faber, 95, 115, 139, 234
Farago, Ladislas, 106
Farrar, John C., 300–302
Farrar, Marguerite, 302
Farrell, James T., 25, 52, 63, 68, 71, 91
Faulkner, William, 71, 223, 305, 351, 354, 373, 412
Fawcett, 112, 171, 172, 228
Fayard, 104, 131
Feibleman, Peter S., 82, 259
Feldman, Lew D., 309
Fell, Dr. John, 398–99
Fellini, Federico, 334
Ferber, Edna, 279
Fielding, Henry, 79
Finberg, Chuck, 231
Firbank, Ronald, 342
Fischer, Bobby, 48, 199–201
Fisher, M. F. K., 277
Fitzgerald, F. Scott, 35, 70, 77, 91, 300, 359
Flammarion, 131
Flanner, Janet, 160–61, 318
Fleischer, Gerd, 102
Fleming, John F., 194, 195, 309, 372
Fonda, Jane, 334
Ford, Harry, 181
Forgue, Norman, 59
Forster, E. M., 14
Forum Books, 62, 65
Foster, David, 139
Fournier-Aubry, Fernand, 289
Frank, Gerold, 133
Frankfurt Book Fair, 101–102
Frasconi, Antonio, 393
Freedgood, Anne, 227
Fremont-Smith, Eliot, 151
Friede, Donald, 208, 298
Friede, Eleanor Kask, 146, 280
Friedman, Lillian, 243

Galbraith, John Kenneth, 316
Gallant, Mavis, 410
Gallimard, 118, 131, 291
Gandhi, Indira, 109, 110
Gans, Lex, 102

Gans, Mary, 102
Garcia Lorca, Federico, 95
Gardner, W. H., 119
Garrett, Eileen J., 61, 332–33
Gartenberg, Max, 216–17
Gautier, Théophile, 239
Gaver, Mary V., 139–40, 147
Gedin, Per, 102
Geiger, Elaine, 106, 148
Genet, Jean, 103, 131
Geracimos, Ann, 140
Gertz, Elmer, 330–31
Gibbs, Wolcott, 34
Gielgud, Sir John, 95
Gilbert, Stuart, 317
Gill, Brendan, 228, 229
Gill, Eric, 384, 389, 402
Gilliatt, Penelope, 133
Ginsberg, Allen, 22, 109, 110–11, 373, 374, 410
Giroud, Françoise, 104
Gish, Lillian, 34, 284, 285
Gitlin, Paul, 216
Glazebrook, Ben, 105, 368
Godowsky, Dagmar, 333
Gogarty, Oliver St. John, 91
Gold, Herbert, 124–25
Gold, Melissa, 124
Goldblatt, Louis, 10, 21–22, 58
Goldblatt, Roberta Pernecky, 10, 58
Golden, Harry, 58, 59, 82, 85, 142, 156, 233, 277–82
Golden Cockerill Press, 389
Golden Eagle Press, 362–63
Goldstein, Al, 351–52
Gollancz, Victor, 165, 292
Gongora, Elaine, 111
Goodman, Jack, 213
Gordon, Elizabeth, 140
Gorey, Edward, 5, 18, 133, 191
Gotham Book Mart, 189, 190, 191, 192, 194, 309, 313, 340
Gottlieb, Bob, 213
Goudy, Fred, 402
Goulden, Jane, 105
Goulden, Mark, 105, 106
Graham, Kay, 294

Grall, Alex, 104
Grant, Julia Dent (Mrs. Ulysses S. Grant), 68
Grant, Ulysses S., 68–69
Graves, Harold, 380
Green, Abel, 111, 286–87
Green, Grace, 286
Greenfield, Louis, 288
Griffin, Merv, 327
Grijalbo, Juan, 102
Gross, Gerald (Jerry), 106, 224–25
Grosset, 187, 224
Groth, John, 60–61, 75
Grove, Lee E., 195
Grove Press, 13, 318
Guild, Hazel, 102
Guinzberg, Harold K., 214
Gunther, Charles, 368–69
Guralnik, David A., 29
Guthrie, A. B., Jr., 80
Guy, Rosa, 321

Haag, Ernest Van Den, 31
Hackett, Alice Payne, 209
Hagel, Raymond C., 2, 267
Hailey, Arthur, 130, 177
Haldeman-Julius, E., 227
Hall, Manley, 61
Hammett, Dashiell, 63, 64, 65
Harcourt, 157
Harcourt, Alfred, 212
Harper, 260
Harper & Row, 140, 157
Harper's Bazaar, 177
Harris, Jed, 267
Hawkes, John, 133, 373
Hayden, Julie, 34
Haydn, Hiram, 199
Haynes, LeRoy, 291
Hearn, Lafcadio, 23, 24, 38, 39, 44–45
Hecht, Ernest, 130, 137
Heifetz, Jascha, 18
Heldman, Irma, 145
Heller, Joseph, 157, 323–24
Hellman, Lillian, 206, 318, 327
Hemingway, Doris, 76

Hemingway, Ernest, 61, 71, 75, 76, 77, 162
Hemingway, Leicester, 75–77
Hemingway, Mary, 75, 76
Henman, Rainer, 102, 317
Henning, Doug, 334
Hersey, John, 336, 358
Higham, David, 221
Highet, Gilbert, 353
Himes, Chester, 198, 290–92, 308
Himes, Lesley, 291, 308
Hirschfeld, Al, 312–13
Hirshorn, Clive, 106
Hitler, Adolf, 162
Hochman, Sandra, 13, 376
Hollander, Xaviera, 235–36
Holt, 214
Holt, Henry, 207
Hood, Allen, 242
Hopkins, Gerard Manley, 119, 120, 121
Horblit, Harrison, 196
Horch Associates, 88
Horos, Carol, 256
Houghton, 33
Houghton, Arthur A., Jr., 196
Houghton Mifflin, 234, 402
Hoyt, Larry, 243
Huebsch, Ben W., 35, 211–12
Hughes, Langston, 19, 161
Humphrey, Hubert, 308
Huneker, James, 196–97
Hunter, Ross, 125
Hurston, Zora Neale, 321
Hyde, Donald, 196
Hyman, Stanley Edgar, 71–72, 82

Iardella, Sabina, 145
Irish, William, 64
Irving, Washington, 208
Isherwood, Christopher, 125, 127

Jacobs, Sam, 362–63
Jaffe, Marc, 172
James, Louise, 40
James, William, 314–15
Janeway, Elizabeth, 133, 320

Jarrell, Randall, 181
Jeeves, Heather, 106
Jeffers, Robinson, 35, 127–28, 224, 305
Jessel, George, 236–37
Johnson, Lyndon B., 308
Johnson, Dr. Samuel, 79
Jones, James, 171
Jong, Erica, 13, 107, 126, 240
Joseph, Michael, 184, 207
Joyce, James, 9, 35, 91, 92, 114, 137, 159, 160, 161, 215, 305, 317, 372, 383
Joyce, Nora, 159

Kael, Pauline, 113, 133
Kandel, Leonore, 318
Kaplan, Jeremiah, 106–107
Karpf, Lila, 145
Kaufman, Bel, 133
Kaufman, Sue, 133
Kazin, Alfred, 70, 71, 72, 133
Keats, John, 381–82
Kelly, Gene, 106
Kelly, Pat, 125
Kenyon Review, 71
Kesim, Nurcihan, 102, 308
Keyes, Frances Parkinson, 341
Klepper, Lou, 242
Kling, Mary, 102
Klopfer, Donald, 304
Knaus, Albrecht, 102
Knopf, 33, 63, 65, 135, 157, 179, 184, 206, 207, 212–13, 227, 260
Knopf, Alfred A., 63, 165, 181, 206, 212, 213, 249, 402
Knopf, Alfred, Jr., 181
Knopf, Blanche, 63, 181, 188, 212
Kobler, Evelyn, 111, 133
Kobler, John, 111, 115, 133, 254, 289
Kogan, Herman, 16, 17
Kordel, Lelord, 158
Kosmos, 135
Kozinski, Jerzy, 319
Kreymborg, Alfred, 15, 161
Kroch, Adolph, 243
Kroch, Carl, 43, 58–59, 243

Kroch-Brentano, 243
Kronenberger, Louis, 71, 206
Kropotkin, Igor, 243, 279
Kupcinet, Irv, 17
Kurzman, Dan, 412

La Bruyère, Jean de, 203
Laffont, 3, 131
Laffont, Isabelle, 289
Laffont, Robert, 102, 288–90
Lamson, Philippe, 102
Lane, Sir Allen, 225–26, 227, 397
Lang, H. Jack, 42–43
Lanning, George, 71
Lantz, Robert, 220
Larrocha, Alicia de, 123
Latham, Harold, 26
Laub, Trudy, 243
Laufer, Doris, 243
Laughlin, James, 205–206
Lavin, Mary, 91, 92
Lawrence, Jerome, 122, 123, 125, 126
Leary, Timothy, 110
Lederer, Joseph H., 79
Lee, Gypsy Rose, 64
Lee, Robert E., 122, 125
Leek, Sybil, 61
Legman, G., 355
Leopold, Nathan, 16, 19, 331
Lerner, Abe, 67, 69, 393–97, 402, 403
Lesser, Joseph, 63
Levant, Oscar, 264–66
Levin, Martin, 249
Levin, Meyer, 25
Levine, Anne, 294
Levine, Bob, 294
Lewis, Lloyd, 25
Lewis, Sinclair, 383
Liberace, 328
Limited Editions Club, 13, 61
Lin Yutang, 82, 85, 156, 262
Lincoln, Abraham, 57, 96
Linden, Bella, 216
Linder, Erich, 102
Lindsay, Vachel, 26
Lippincott, 206
Lippmann, Walter, 35

Lipton, Lawrence (Larry), 25, 55
Little, Brown, 212
Little Review, 159, 160, 192
Liveright, Horace, 206, 208, 304–305
Living Library, The, 64, 68
Loliée, M. Bernard, 131, 309
London Times, The, 95
Long, E. G. (Pete), 69
Loo, Beverly, 145
Loren, Sophia, 334
Los Angeles Times, The, 83
Lovelace, Linda, 350
Lowell, Robert, 373
Lunt, Storer, 17–18
Lustig, Elaine, 82
Lynley, Carol, 345

McAlmon, Robert, 283
MacCampbell, Donald, 219
McCarthy, Bill, 243
McCarthy, Senator Joseph, 331
McCarthy, Mary, 128, 318, 354
McClure, Michael, 116
McConville, Maureen, 326
McCormick, Ken, 233
McCullers, Carson, 314
Macdonald, Dwight, 407
McDowell, David, 213
McFee, William, 63
McGinnis, Mae, 22
MacGowran, Gloria, 133
MacGowran, Jack, 25, 114, 115, 133
McGraw-Hill, 111, 144
MacGregor, Bob, 206
Machado, Alfredo, 104, 133, 134, 136, 137
Machado, Gloria, 134, 136, 137
McIntyre, Alfred, 212
MacLaine, Shirley, 334
Macmillan Company, The, 15, 26, 27, 28, 29, 30, 31, 32–33, 106, 143, 157, 210, 211, 237
Macmillan & Co., Ltd., London, 207
McNab, Allen, 25
McNamara, Robert S., 308, 327
Macrae, Elliott B., 214, 255
Macrae, John, 260

Madison, Charles A., 209
Maeterlinck, Count Maurice, 362
Maggs Brothers, 365–66
Mailer, Norman, 171, 293, 329–30, 334, 357, 374
Malamud, Bernard, 357
Maltz, Albert, 125
Mannes, Marya, 320
Mansfield, Katherine, 93
Manutius, Aldus, 7, 204
Marboro Bookshops, 272
Mardersteig, Giovanni, 396
Margolies, Joe, 302
Marks, Lillian, 276
Marks, Saul, 276
Marmur, Milly, 145, 170
Marx, Groucho, 264
Marx, Sam, 88, 313
Matson, Harold, 262
Maugham, W. Somerset, 63, 79
Meir, Golda, 293
Meissner, Otto, 207
Melcher, Frederic G. (Fred), 81–82, 225
Meller, Michael, 99, 102
Melville, Herman, 359, 360
Mencken, H. L., 33, 35
Menuhin, Yehudi, 314
Meridian Books, 82
Metzger, Judson, 23, 24
Meyer, Helen, 146
Michaux, Lewis H., 197, 198
Michener, James A., 24, 172, 177, 178, 179, 336
Milland, Ray, 187
Millay, Edna St. Vincent, 35, 74
Miller, Arthur, 298
Miller, Henry, 10, 13–14, 37, 125–27, 331, 342
Millett, Kate, 93–94, 153
Milne, A. A., 260
Minton, Walter J., 1, 31, 85, 90, 113, 116, 118, 208, 265, 369
Mitford, Nancy, 96
Modern Library, 68, 304–305
Molden, Fritz, 102, 133
Mollenhoff, Clark R., 327

Monroe, Harriet, 15, 290
Montagu, Ashley, 82, 85, 123, 156, 233
Moore, Marianne, 96, 160, 215, 282–285, 299, 373
Mori, Tom, 24
Morison, Stanley, 226, 398, 399, 402
Morley, Christopher, 287–88
Morris, May, 40
Morris, William (printer), 70, 390, 391
Morris, William (literary agent), 112, 254, 326
Moseley, Hardwick, 314
Moses, Robert, 334
Mosher, Thomas Bird, 392–93
Moss, David, 192, 193
Mozart, 199, 321–23
Mumford, Lewis, 360
Muni, Paul, 122
Murray, George, 16
Murray, John, 207

Nabokov, Vladimir, 172, 354
Nannini, Norma, 287
Nasatir, Marcia, 125
Nathan, George Jean, 33–34, 35, 82
Nathan, Robert, 125
Nathan, Ruth, 125
National Memorial African Book Store, 197–98
Nedwick's, 33
Neilson, Barbara, 145
Nevler, Leona, 146, 171, 172
New American Library, 83, 84, 172, 227
New Directions, 205–206
Newman, Ralph, 16, 67, 68
New York, 370
New York Review of Books, The, 409, 410
New York Times Book Review, The, 4, 65, 82, 94, 118, 190, 196, 228–229, 324, 407–12
New Yorker, 69, 92, 113, 228
Nice Book Fair, 128
Niemeyr, Oscar, 136

Nin, Anaïs, 13
Nixon, Richard M., 68, 148
Nordstrom, Ursula, 146
Norton, 17
Nureyev, Rudolf, 95, 341

Oboler, Arch, 387
O'Casey, Sean, 34, 91, 92, 114
O'Connor, Flannery, 234
O'Connor, Frank, 82, 91, 92, 93
O'Connor, Harriet, 92
O'Donovan, Michael. See O'Connor, Frank
O'Hara, John, 63, 341
O'Malley, Charles D., 69
O'Neill, Eugene, 35, 91, 305
Orlovsky, Peter, 110
Ornstein, Oscar, 136
Osborne, John, 342
Oulman, Alain, 102, 128
Oxford University Press, 397–99

Pacheco, Alvaro, 136
Pan, 106
Pantheon, 157
Paramount, 187, 188
Paris Review, The, 186
Parker, Dorothy, 35, 74–75, 91
Partington, Wilfred, 56
Partridge, D. C., 56
Partridge, Eric, 28, 29
Partridge, H. M., 56
Pattison, Alice, 40
Pavese, Cesare, 138
Pavlova, Anna, 18
Peebles, Melvin van, 108
Pelton, Robert, 136
Penguin Books, 63, 172, 225–28, 397
Penthouse, 177
Percival, John, 95
Perkins, Maxwell, 70, 149, 299–300
Perkins, Michael, 346
Perse, St. John, 104, 131
Phoenix Bookshop, 283, 309
Philipps, Thomas, 298, 369
Pilpel, Harriet, 216
Plantin Press, The, 388

Playboy, 76

Plimpton, George, 186

Pocket Books, 228

Poe, Edgar Allan, 56, 65, 208, 223

Pollard, Graham, 382

Popular Library, 228

Porter, Katherine Anne, 318

Pound, Ezra, 3, 35, 111, 126, 161, 234, 363, 373

Powell, Fay, 295

Powell, Lawrence Clark, 294–96, 321, 369

Powner's Antiquarian Bookshop, 33, 78

Powys, John Cowper, 386

Prashker, Betty, 143

Prideaux, Sarah T., 40

Pritchett, V. S., 410

Publishers Weekly, 81, 139, 140, 143, 151, 180, 211, 403, 407

Publix Book Mart, 294

Putnam, George Haven, 208

Putnam's, 1, 16, 20, 31, 56, 61, 68, 85–86, 88, 90, 92, 98, 101, 103, 106, 112, 116, 117, 125, 138–39, 141, 157, 166, 172, 188, 191, 208, 230, 233, 244, 259, 262, 275, 277, 291, 293, 313, 315, 326, 332, 345, 369, 389

Puzo, Erika, 122, 125

Puzo, Mario, 3, 111–12, 113, 122, 125, 133, 267, 314, 341

Queen, Ellery, 63, 64, 65

Quinn, John, 159–60, 383–84

Rainbird, George, 100

Rand, Sally, 46–47

Randall, David A., 380

Random House, 157, 160, 193, 199, 304–305

Ransom, John Crowe, 71

Raucher, Herman, 111, 262

Rawson, Eleanor, 146

Read, Piers Paul, 341

Redgrave, Vanessa, 334

Reid, B. L., 159, 384

Reincourt, Amaury de, 148

Remarque, Erich Maria, 90

Rey, Pierre, 116, 289, 350

Righter, Carroll, 61, 87–88

Rinzler, Alan, 125

Riverside Press, 402

Robbins, Harold, 52, 116, 147, 175, 177, 179, 216, 341

Robbins, Kathy, 145

Robinson, Edward Arlington, 223

Rodgers, Richard, 278–79

Rogers, Bruce, 82, 83, 401–403

Rolling Stone, 125

Roos, Wendel, 389

Roosevelt, Eleanor, 81

Rose, Carl, 229, 236

Rosenbach, A. S. W., 194, 195, 196, 383, 384

Rosenthal, Jean, 3, 102, 145, 289

Ross, Harold, 229

Ross, Ishbel, 19

Rosset, Barney, 320

Rota's, 309

Roth, Henry, 359

Roth, Philip, 340–41, 357

Rowohlt, Jane, 102, 308

Rowohlt, Ledig, 102, 308

Rudd, Hughes, 186

Rudolf, Max, 47

Ryan, Regina, 143

Saarinen, Aline, 383

Sackheim, Max, 163

Sadleir, Michael, 208, 351

Sand, George, 42–43

Sandburg, Carl, 25, 57–59, 67, 368

Saroyan, William, 360–61

Sartre, Jean-Paul, 103–104, 131, 240, 359

Sassoon, Beverly, 312

Sassoon, Vidal, 312

Saunders, J. B. de C. M., 69

Sautoy, Peter du, 95

Sayre, Connie, 145

Schaffner, John, 290

Schaffner, Perdita, 290

Scherman, Harry, 163–64

Scherz, Rudi, 102
Schulberg, Budd, 194
Schuster, M. Lincoln, 213, 230, 268
Screw, 346, 351–52
Scribner, Charles, 149, 381
Scribner's, 33, 157, 175, 208, 214
Scribner's Bookstore, 242, 243, 279, 380–81, 382
Seale, Patrick, 326
Segal, Eric, 111
Seldes, Timothy, 268
Shaffer, Peter, 338
Shagan, Steve, 187, 339
Shakespeare, 93, 141, 254–55
Shanks, Anne, 273, 324
Shanks, Bob, 324
Shawn, William, 229, 334
Sheed, Wilfrid, 324, 411
Shenker, Israel, 324
Shirer, William, 172
Signet, 171
Silberman, Ben, 33
Silver, Louis H., 196
Simenon, Georges, 363–64
Simmons, Jeffrey, 106
Simon, Bob, 213, 387
Simon, John, 319
Simon, John Y., 68
Simon, Kate, 82, 277
Simon & Schuster, 64, 157, 213, 244
Singer, Isaac Bashevis, 8, 133, 324
Sissman, L. E., 323, 324
Sizer, Nelson, 263
Skolsky, Sidney, 125
Sloane, Bill, 214
Smart Set, The, 34, 35
Smith, C. U. M., 138–39
Smith, Patti, 367–68
Smith, Susy, 61, 315
Smith, T. R., 206
Soliman, Patricia, 143
Souvenir Press, 130
Speaight, Robert, 389
Spectorsky, 76–77
Spender, Stephen, 95, 96, 97, 128, 129, 373
Spinner, Julie, 242

Starrett, Vincent, 25
Stein, Gertrude, 413
Stein, Shelley, 243
Steinbeck, John, 299
Steinberg, Saul, 133
Steloff, Frances, 159, 189–90
Stern, Madeleine B., 263
Sterne, Laurence, 354
Stevenson, John, 308
Stock, 11, 131
Stone, Irving, 178
Stowe, Harriet Beecher, 1
Straus, Ralph, 56
Streisand, Barbra, 333
Stroth, Rolf, 102
Strouse, Charlotte, 393
Strouse, Norman H., 392, 393
Strunk, William, Jr., 335–36
Susann, Jacqueline, 175, 176, 178, 179
Susskind, David, 324–25
Swift, Jonathan, 91, 92

Talese, Gay, 133
Tandy, Jessica, 115
Tankersley, 15
Targ, Alexander (Sandy), 124, 128
Targ, Anne Jesselson, 23, 46, 47, 48–49, 54, 69
Targ, Elisabeth, 128
Targ, Joan Fischer, 48, 128
Targ, Nicholas (Nicky), 124, 128
Targ, Roslyn, 3, 5, 10, 11, 58, 75, 87–89, 93, 102, 104, 109, 111, 112, 113, 115, 119, 121, 122, 123, 125–126, 128, 129, 130, 131, 136, 137, 146, 191, 198, 200, 266, 284, 285, 287, 291, 294, 308, 322, 324, 325, 355, 360, 372
Targ, Russell, 10, 23, 24, 47, 48, 49–54, 65, 89, 122, 124, 128
Targ (Torgownik) family, 2, 9–10, 17, 27, 239
Taylor, Clyde, 112, 113
Terkel, Studs, 8, 25
Times Mirror Co., 83, 84
Tolstoy, Count Leo, 41, 52, 329

Torre, Lillian de la, 64
Tower Books, 62–63, 65, 187
Trautwein, Joe, 399
Trollope, Anthony, 105, 350–51
Tunis, Edwin, 81, 82
Tunis, Lib, 81
Tuttle, Charles E., 24
Twain, Mark, 56
Tynan, Kenneth, 116, 133

Ullman, Charlotte, 40
Untermeyer, Louis, 274
Updike, John, 260, 341–42
Uris, Leon, 199

Vance, Vivian, 334
Vanderbilt, Gloria, 313
Van Steenwyk, E. A., 224
Van Steenwyk, Marion, 224
Variety, 102, 286, 287
Varner, Velma, 78, 142
Vaughn, Robert, 326–27
Vendler, Helen, 411
Vidal, Gore, 108, 327, 354
Viking Press, 212, 214, 244, 299
Vintage Books, 227, 228
Viva, 125, 130–31, 354–55
Viva, 177
Vogue, 177
Von Daniken, Erich, 61, 129–30, 156, 166
Vonnegut, Kurt, 334, 361

Wagoner, David, 55
Wain, John, 338
Wakoski, Diane, 121, 133
Walden Book Company, 242, 243
Walker, Emery, 70, 390, 391
Wallace, David, 282
Wallace, Irving, 176, 177, 179, 216, 341
Waller, Leslie, 111
Walsh, Richard, 262
Walter, Florence, 40
Warde, Beatrice, 404–405
Warde, Frederic, 404

Warhol, Andy, 355
Wartels, Nat, 213, 214
Wasserman, Jakob, 240
Weaver, Harriet Shaw, 159, 215
Wedick, Harry E., 31
Weidenfeld, Sir George, 292–94
Weil, Simone, 153
Weissberger, Arnold, 284
Welty, Eudora, 318, 335
Wertmuller, Lina, 334
West, Anthony, 133
West, Jessamyn, 318
West, Nathanael, 192–94
Weybright, Victor, 11
Weyr, Tom, 407
W. H. Allen, 106
Wheeler, Monroe, 283
Wherry, Toby, 243–47
White, E. B., 335–36
Whitman, Walt, 109, 111, 223, 374, 382
William Morris Agency, 254, 326
William Morris Press, 70
Williams, Liza, 130
Williams, William Carlos, vi, 373–74
Williams, Sir William Emrys, 226
Willingham, Calder, 66
Wilson, Bob, 283
Wilson, Colin, 139
Wilson, Earl, 345
Wilson, Edmund, 69, 296
Wilson, Woodrow, 19
Windsor, the Duchess of, 333
Winick, Eugene, 216
Winterich, John T., 70
Wise, Thomas James, 56, 382
Wittenberg, Philip, 15
Wolf, Edwin, II, 195
Wolfe, Thomas, 89, 263, 300, 374, 383
Wolff, Helen, 146
Women's National Book Association, 139
Wood, John, 327
Wood, Robert T., 250
World Publishing Company, 16, 25, 29, 33, 46, 58, 61, 62–64, 65, 66,

World Publishing Company (*cont'd*) 67–73, 75, 76–77, 78, 81, 82–85, 93, 122, 124, 142, 187, 195, 199, 208, 214, 224, 242, 259, 262, 276, 280, 288, 291, 292, 305, 315, 359, 362, 380, 403, 404

Wouk, Herman, 177, 245

Wright, Ellen, 66, 67, 103, 116, 118

Wright, Julie, 66

Wright, Lee, 64

Wright, Richard, 25, 66–67, 68, 82, 198

Yeats, William Butler, 60, 91, 92, 114

Young, Robert, 282

Youngman, Henny, 345

Yu, Charles, 59

Yutang, Lin. *See* Lin Yutang

Zara, Louis, 25

Zeitlin, Jake, 295

Zevin, Ben D., 62, 65, 66, 68, 70, 71, 75, 78, 83, 84, 195, 227, 278, 292, 402, 403

Zola, Emile, 239